CRUISE
of the
LANIKAI

KEMP TOLLEY
Rear Admiral, U.S. Navy (Retired)

CRUISE
of the
LANIKAI
Incitement to War

BLUEJACKET BOOKS

Naval Institute Press
Annapolis, Maryland

Naval Institute Press
291 Wood Road
Annapolis, MD 21402

First Bluejacket Books printing, 2002

Library of Congress Cataloging-in-Publication Data
Tolley, Kemp, 1908–
    Cruise of the Lanikai: incitement to war / Kemp Tolley.
    p. cm. — (Bluejacket books)
    Originally published: Annapolis : Naval Institute Press, 1973.
    Includes bibliographical references and index.
    ISBN 1-55750-406-7
    1. World War, 1939–1945—Naval operations, American.
2. Lanikai (Ship) 3. World War, 1939-1945—Personal narratives,
American. 4. Tolley, Kemp, 1908– I. Title. II. Series.
D774.L33+
940.54'5973—dc21

                                                    2002070348

Printed in the United States of America on acid-free paper ∞
09 08 07 06 05 04 03 02 9 8 7 6 5 4 3 2 1

To

*dear friend, superlative shipmate, and
acey-deucey player with promise, Charlie
Adair, whose timely intervention in the
release of* Lanikai *at Manila, then
Surabaya, and again at Tjilatjap, unquestionably saved from certain capture,
and probable death, all who sailed
in her*

and to

*those stalwart crewmen, Filipino and
American, whose determination, loyalty,
and know-how brought* Lanikai
through.

*You have caught Truth by the
tail; don't let go! And if I were a little
more pious than I am, I would be
tempted to observe that the Lord had
marvelously preserved you, and* Lanikai,
*unscathed through so many perils, in
order that you might bear witness to
the Truth.*

Excerpt from a letter written by
Justice Frederic R. Sanborn to the author.

Foreword

The United States Asiatic Fleet before World War II was essentially a political instrument designed to "show the flag." In no way a fighting fleet, it included the heavy cruiser *Houston,* the light cruiser *Marblehead,* a squadron of old destroyers, and another of submarines. It had no worthwhile antisubmarine capability, nor amphibious capability, although the Fourth Marine Regiment was assigned. Other than 25 patrol seaplanes, there was no air capability.

Fleet routine was described in the old song "We'll all go up to China in the Springtime!" Visits were made to Hongkong and various Chinese ports, including Shanghai, Tsingtao, Chefoo, Chinwangtao, and Tientsin. A handful of old gunboats made up the Yangtze and South China Patrols. Unfortunately, there were no visits to ports in Southeast Asia or Indonesia; a result of this policy was that when war came not one of our captains had experience in the treacherous waters south of the Philippines.

The Fleet had no experience in combined exercises with the British in Asian waters, although plans did exist for combined operations. After initial British Far East reverses their remaining naval forces were placed under the overall direction of the ABDA organization in Java, with Admiral Thomas C. Hart as the first commander of ABDA's naval elements.

A year before the outbreak of hostilities Admiral Hart had ordered the evacuation of all naval dependents from the Far East, and late in 1941 had sent the cruisers and most of the destroyers to Java. Left behind on Luzon were the submarines and a tender, the patrol planes, and most unfortunately, about 2,000 naval personnel. He also left the 67-ton auxiliary schooner *Lanikai,* which suddenly had become the subject of secret orders from Washington.

The skipper of *Lanikai* was Lieutenant Kemp Tolley who now, as a retired rear admiral, relates the *Cruise of the Lanikai.* The book is more than just another thrilling tale of war; it places the entire operation in the context of the times. Admiral Tolley has provided extensive documentation, including, for example, correspondence between Admiral Stark and Admiral Hart. I believe that some of this documentation has not previously been disclosed.

Too little has been written of these early days of conflict in the Pacific, when the Army and Navy were really fighting individual wars, and learned lessons that reshaped basic U.S. military philosophy. Those interested in the strategic direction of armed forces and in the command and control of these forces will find many examples here of "how not to do it."

I sincerely hope that the reader enjoys this book as much as I have.

Robert L. Dennison

Robert L. Dennison
Admiral, U.S. Navy (Retired)

Acknowledgments

Since first treading the deck of that remarkable little ship, USS *Lanikai*, I have been intrigued by her story and what lay behind that story. For 30 years, I have probed, questioned and read, compiling the material contained here.

Some, among them several eminent historians, are skeptical for one reason or another, of the thesis I have derived. None has been able to provide any worthwhile evidence to discredit it. Tantalizingly, the only four who came into possession of direct evidence have refrained from talking—in their memoirs, under direct questioning, or elsewhere: President Roosevelt, Mr. Harry Hopkins, Secretary of State Cordell Hull, and Chief of Naval Operations Admiral Harold R. Stark. Their silence is perhaps more eloquent than words.

A number of others support me fully. They include four-star and other admirals, members of Congress, and many well-known authors and historians. After their having read the evidence, we are happy to ask the readers to be the jury.

I am grateful for the help and advice derived from conversations or letters exchanged with the late Admirals William H. Standley, Thomas C. Hart, and Husband E. Kimmel; with Admirals Royal E. Ingersoll and Robert L. Dennison; with Vice Admirals Francis W. Rockwell, John L. McCrea, Edward N. Parker, Thomas H. Binford; with Rear Admirals Charles Adair, Welford C. Blinn, James R. Davis, Henry W. Goodall, Walter E. Linaweaver, Arthur H. McCollum, Redfield Mason, John L. Pratt, Harry B. Slocum; with Major General Charles A. Willoughby; with Captains Laurence F. Safford, Thomas K. Kimmel, and John D. Lamade; and with Commander E. George Pollak. Captains Northrup H. Castle and Fred K. Klebingat, the latter a living encyclopedia of Pacific schooner lore, have filled me in on South Sea Island traders and *Lanikai*'s earlier history, supplemented by Mr. Lester F. Stone, whose father built the ship. Many other kind and helpful individuals will be identified as their contributions appear in the text.

I am grateful to Colonel E. M. Grimm and that remarkable ex-guerrilla, Commander Charles Parsons, for information on *Lanikai*'s Manila days and her ultimate end.

Also very helpful have been Honolulu's Bishop Museum, Mrs. Matilda Dring of the San Francisco Maritime Museum, the British Ministry of Defense's Naval Historical Branch, the Australian War Memorial, Captain H. E. Rambonnet, R.N.N., Royal Netherlands Embassy, Washington, and especially, the U.S. Naval History Division's archives under Vice Admiral Edwin B. Hooper, ably seconded by Captain Paul B. Ryan and Dr. Dean C. Allard. The National Archives' obliging and expert staff, including Messrs. Mark G. Eckhoff, Garry D. Ryan, Francis J. Hepner, and Elmer O. Parker, produced many early *Lanikai* documents, and other pertinent material.

Messrs. Joseph W. Marshall and William J. Stewart, acting directors of the Franklin D. Roosevelt Library at Hyde Park, were helpful in research, as was Mr. Paul T. Heffron, of the Library of Congress.

The Baltimore County, Maryland, public library system, under the direction of Mr. Charles W. Robinson, has lent constant, valuable support in furnishing me with source material, and in obtaining items for me elsewhere which they did not have on their own shelves. Their reference personnel have been especially accommodating, knowledgeable and ingenious, and have saved me much leg work.

A particularly enthusiastic and helpful supplier of information and other sources was Captain Melvin E. Lepine, Chief, Harbors Division, State of Hawaii, who rounded up old port documents pertaining to *Lanikai*'s era, copied news accounts and gave every indication of being happy to sign on as an honorary crew member. Miss Agnes C. Conrad, Hawaii State Archivist, found me many old accounts and some rare old photographs.

Chief Archivist Arthur R. Abel, in San Francisco's Federal Records Center, and Chief Archivist Robert D. Jordan, in the Los Angeles Federal Records Center, combed their files for useful references to *Lanikai*'s fishing career.

The greatest single contributor of time and effort has been Lieutenant Commander Charles C. Hiles, USN (Retired), who has read the manuscript chapter by chapter, offering invaluable comments and corrections, especially on matters pertaining to cryptanalysis and the events leading up to Pearl Harbor, in which fields he is eminently at home.

In one brief period of *Lanikai*'s life, "before Pearl Harbor," she sailed in seas of glamour. That was when she played an active role in the motion picture spectacular "Hurricane," and her deck planks trembled in the presence of Dorothy Lamour. Regretfully, Miss Lamour's presence was notably absent during the long nights running south before the Japanese, nor did she, in later years, choose to add any of her own recollections to this account of the life of a long-forgotten schooner.

Some serious scholars might wonder why there are not more sources footnoted. In reassurance, let me say that much of this material is first-hand. In the parlance of an earlier war, "I vass dere, Sharlie." Or my informants were. With few exceptions, the manuscript passages covering events, engagements, or individual experiences have been reviewed for accuracy by those involved.

Some may look askance at revelations which might seem to cast aspersions. This is not a compilation of eulogies; that is the job for the biographer, most of whom take up the pen out of adoration for their subject. Nor is it a history adjusted downward to the least common denominator, offensive to none, glorifying to all. I have tried to set down history as it happened, with the hope that in some small degree it may contribute both to a knowledge of the way it really was—and to avoiding a repetition of mistakes which were detrimental to the best interests of the United States of America.

The final test, of course, is setting down all these items logically and understandably. In this area of prime importance, I am profoundly grateful for the friendly, expert advice and collaboration of those professionals par excellence, the U.S. Naval Institute's Managing Editor of Books, Mr. Glen B. Ruh, Senior Editor Lieutenant Commander Arnold S. Lott, USN (Retired), and Book Editor Mrs. Louise Gerretson.

Lani-Kai

*Town, Ko'olau-poko, Oahu. Literally,
marine heaven [a new name, probably
a transposition of Kai-lani, royal sea].
(From* Place Names of Hawaii,
by Pukui & Elbert.)

Chapter 1

In the sparkling December sky, one could look from Manila across the bay to the distant horizon where the Cavite Navy Yard still smoldered after the devastating Japanese air raid of 10 December 1941. In what recently had been one of the busiest harbors in the Far East not a ship rode at anchor. The seven great piers were empty, with the exception of a few lighters, tugs, the ancient submarine tender USS *Canopus*, and a few small craft. One of the latter, a white, 83-foot, two-masted schooner flying a U.S. Navy commission pennant, caught Flag Lieutenant Charles Adair's sharp eye. She was the USS *Lanikai*, outloading office equipment from the precipitously evacuating headquarters of Adair's boss, Admiral Thomas C. Hart, Commander in Chief, Asiatic Fleet, on a hectic Christmas Eve,* 1941.

That evening in the code room, as the Admiral was poring over messages describing the generally disastrous events of the day, Adair suggested that he, with some other officers, radiomen and radio equipment, sail the *Lanikai* to Java where the Admiral was going in a day or so to establish a new headquarters. Ramrod straight and Napoleon-sized, Hart was noncommittal on the proposal. "Let me think about it overnight," he said. "See me tomorrow."

Each forenoon, Hart's liaison man with General MacArthur, Commander Robert L. Dennison, a tactful, brilliant officer one day to become Supreme Allied Commander Atlantic,† visited Army headquarters to be briefed. On that fateful 24 December he had received shocking news. MacArthur, with somewhat uncharacteristic matter-of-factness, made an announcement that was a blockbuster: "Gentlemen," he sonorously intoned, "I intend to proclaim Manila an open city as of midnight tonight!"

*Subtract one day from all Philippine and *Lanikai* cruise dates to arrive at Pearl Harbor dates.
† 1960–63.

3

There had been no coordination with the Navy, nor advance warning. The Navy was prepared to hold out and had taken steps to support essential submarine operations. *Canopus* was lying alongside a Manila pier covered with camouflage netting, with only a few feet of water under her keel. If holed, she could settle comfortably to the bottom and carry on business as usual, servicing submarines from such of her shops as remained dry. Spare parts and torpedo warhead exploders had been distributed over a wide area ashore in Manila. A Navy hospital was being set up in the old Jai Alai auditorium. The Asiatic Fleet staff and its communication facilities were established on the Manila waterfront. Making Manila an open city would mean that all military and naval establishments would have to evacuate on a few hours' notice.

Immediately after this jarring announcement, Dennison asked to be excused. Hurrying to Navy headquarters, he repeated MacArthur's words to Hart. To say that Hart was startled is to put it mildly. He sprang from his chair. *"What?"* he almost shouted. "Sit down there and write that down—exactly what you just told me!" Hart studied it carefully and still found the thing incredible. The note he immediately wrote MacArthur minced no words. Starting off by saying that his liaison officer had just brought him news of the decision to declare Manila an open city as of the twenty-fifth, and that he had received only a 24-hour previous *hint* of any such action,* he continued:

> While, as you have been repeatedly informed, it has been our intention to carry on the war here from submarines as long as possible, this denial of the use of the facilities within the metropolitan area very much shortens the period during which these operations can be carried out from here.

That same forenoon I had gone ashore to headquarters for some sort of guidance out of the limbo into which *Lanikai,* my command of less than three weeks, had fallen. My arrival coincided precisely with that of nine Japanese bombers that swooped low over the Marsman Building. It trembled and swayed from the effects of a straddle. Glass splattered the offices. Admiral Hart, tin hat at a jaunty angle, had abandoned his traditional high-necked, stiff-starched white uniform and was in a comfortable open-collared, short-sleeved white shirt, the sort worn by "Yangtze River Rats." We shared a step of the basement stairway, the local substitute for a proper bomb shelter.

My trip served to remind headquarters that *Lanikai* still existed. It also made clear that in spite of the glowingly optimistic daily communiques, the situation was next to falling apart. Gone were all the wishful thinking and myths about the Japanese or about our own capabilities. What remained looked bleak and hopeless. The "open city"

* A 23 December U.S. Armed Forces Far East (USAFFE) message predicting the early retirement of all Army forces to Bataan and Corregidor.

announcement suddenly implied that we were not stopping the enemy and could not. Everyone had to reorient his priorities.

Back aboard ship, another air raid accompanied my al fresco lunch atop the after deckhouse. According to *Lanikai*'s journal, which served in lieu of a log:

> At 1320 air alarm sounded. Explosions heard to eastward.
> At 1530 got underway, on verbal orders of CinCAF and stood over to pier 7 . . . Taking aboard equipment from CinCAF headquarters, which appears to be evacuating to Corregidor and Mariveles. USS *Tanager* presented us with a 50-caliber machine gun.
> At 1740 air alarm sounded. Saw 15 or 16 planes flying low in port area . . . Got underway and stood out.

The real highlight of the day had been the magnificent addition to our low-level armament—*Tanager*'s gift. It very soon was mounted on a pedestal that had been purloined from the ammunition depot wall two weeks earlier. "*Now* let those slant-eyed bastards come in low," said a grim-faced "Guns" Picking, the chief gunner's mate. He clearly was disappointed that by nightfall the enemy hadn't obliged. Tomorrow Manila would be an open city, with no shooting back permissible.

Twilight comes early in the tropics. During the long night there was plenty of time to think. This Christmas Eve was very unlike one I had spent just a decade ago as a young ensign. I had got on good conversational terms with a very pretty girl who worked in a shop on Manila's Escolta, the main business street that meandered crooked as a cow path through the center of the old city. Matters progressed to the point of Nina's agreeing to take an after-work ride in my green roadster. We rolled down magnificent, tree-lined Dewey Boulevard, at the edge of the bay, where the elite lived. People were promenading, enjoying the brilliant sunset and the cool evening breeze.

"Please put up the top," Nina said in a very small voice. "I really shouldn't be seen alone with you in the car." She was so ill at ease that we made the ride a short one.

Nina lived in a large, old-fashioned Spanish style house on Calle José Rizal, a good part of town. We climbed the long stone staircase to the living quarters on the second floor and sat in a spacious, high-ceilinged room furnished with heavy Mediterranean colonial pieces. The curtains cut out most of what twilight still remained. Conversation came slowly. It was not overly warm, but Nina was perspiring so freely that her light dress showed large dark spots at the armpits.

What next? I thought. As if by telepathic command, the main act got under way. In a sort of single file pass-in-review, what must have been the entire family floated through the room; brothers, sisters, and several unidentified elderly ladies of the type which inhabited so many households in tales of the Victorian Age. Mama, her hair piled high on her head and dressed to the nines, was the rear guard. For each, there was a grave introduction, a handshake, a few syllables in Spanish, and then a discreet departure.

A servant brought cool, sweet drinks, without ice. We made a few more feeble attempts at light conversation. Then Nina stood up and thanked me for the ride and the visit. She hoped I would come again. Her hand as I took it in farewell was trembling and very moist. Small beads of perspiration stood out on her forehead.

In something of a daze, I drove the several blocks to the Army and Navy Club. Grouped at a huge, round table in the center of the bar room, a dozen submariners were having a final whisky-and-splash before going back aboard ship to climb into "bum freezers"—evening dress mess jackets—for the Christmas Eve parties ashore. Dice boxes passed around the table, ivory cubes clattering on the dark mahogany in final reckoning on which unlucky fellow picked up the pile of chits for the afternoon's libations. They listened to my tale with interest. "Brother, you have had a close call!" said an old-timer, as I picked up my drink with a shaky hand.

That escape of a decade earlier was not a patch on the one sparked by *Lanikai*'s lying alongside dock the busy afternoon of 24 December 1941. As per Hart's instructions, Adair sought him out early Christmas morning. With Adair was Lieutenant Commander Harry Keith, who had been skipper of the destroyer *Peary* and on her bridge when she took a bomb in her crow's nest on the tenth at Cavite. Tiny splinters had perforated Keith so painfully that he had been detached to Hart's staff.

Hart had slept on Adair's proposal. It was OK with him, he said. He would like to go with them, but he was in too much of a hurry. He was about to turn over local command to Rear Admiral F. W. Rockwell, Commandant, 16th Naval District, who, as *Lanikai*'s new boss, would be the one to give the green light.

It was a long haul from Taiwan for the Japanese planes, which guaranteed a bomb-free early forenoon. *Lanikai* was to finish loading and get clear before the first bomb break. Like a shark, the most delicate part of her anatomy was her snout. With all that cat's cradle of jib boom, martingale, and associated braces and spars bristling from her bow, an approach to the dock had to be made almost parallel to avoid smashing this delicate stuff. Her rudder was too small to give good control at slow speed. The critical moment came when it was time to back down to kill the ship's remaining way and come alongside. Her Union diesel was a magnificent engine, but 15 years is no longer young for *any* piece of internal combustion machinery. To back down, one didn't simply push in the clutch and snap the reverse lever, like a Chris Craft runabout. There *was* no reverse gear. The procedure was: stop the engine, shift the timing gear, then restart the engine in the reverse direction of rotation. Or more accurately, *hope* it would start. Sometimes it coughed, spat a time or two and died, as it had done that Christmas morning.

I was up forward inspecting the mild damage when Adair and Keith hopped the gap between ship and dock and hunted me out. There was urgency in their manner and no time for small talk or coffee.

"Skipper, we've got a proposition. How would you like to take a crack at breaking the blockade and running for Java? The boss is about to fly out. No room for much staff. He says as far as he is concerned, we can take the *Lanikai* south, but she belongs to Admiral Rockwell and we must ask him first. It's a long chance and your command. What do you say?"

My immediate, "When do we start?" was all Adair needed to send him scooting for minesweeper *Tanager*, also loading out staff gear and about to shove off for Corregidor, where Admiral Rockwell was waiting. Keith would ride in *Lanikai*, in case *Tanager* took a bomb on the way out.

At 9:10 A.M., crates of office gear and 25-odd "refugees" aboard, *Lanikai* stood out for Mariveles. Captain Kenneth E. Lowman, fleet medical officer, was on board, his projected hospital in the Jai Alai Palace a dead dream. The Navy Shore Patrol officer for Manila was there, too. Those happy days of ten-centavos-a-dance girls and the cabarets—huge Santa Ana, racy Paranaque, and all the others—were only a memory. There would be no more liberty hounds to round up after *ginebra,* the cheap, local firewater, had got the best of them.

A passenger priest held a short Christmas service for "refugees" (about half of them Army people) and the crewmen, possibly the only Yule military service in that whole beleaguered area, with the distant rumble of bombs as orchestral accompaniment.

Sitting on suitcases, munching sandwiches and awaiting a turn for a thick pottery coffee cup, the passengers gazed back—for many of them the last time—at Manila framed in smoke.

MacArthur's decision to open Manila made its huge oil stocks unavailable to the Navy. With the situation deteriorating at alarming speed, they must be destroyed. Lieutenant Malcolm McGregor Champlin, Admiral Rockwell's flag lieutenant, was seeing to it that the oil was also unavailable to the Japanese. At the Marsman Building, "Champ" had found only Commander Dennison and the flag secretary, Lieutenant Commander A. S. McDill, taking care of the last of the files and preparing to smash the radio equipment. If any oil was to be burned, he had to do it.

7

At the University Club, he found Lucian L. Rock, Philippines manager for Standard-Vacuum Oil Company, who promptly pledged his aid and advice. His company held the bulk of Manila's oil and gasoline, and Rock agreed at once to destroy it, but he was doubtful about the attitude of the British and French. The British could not be reached; they were in the suburbs playing tennis. However, Rock's persuasive powers prevailed on the others.

"There are enough petroleum products in the Pandacan area of Manila to operate the Asiatic Fleet for two years," said Rock. "What the Japs want is 'alkylate,' an additive to gasoline that transforms it into high octane stuff. It takes only a little, and there are thousands of gallons available." He knew also that the Japanese were in dire need of lubricating oil.

In short order, Rock set up the necessary instructions by telephone. City authorities loyally promised to send eight fire engines and a hundred police for security and to prevent any spread of the flames. By then, the manager of the British oil properties showed up. A lengthy argument ensued. The boss was in Singapore; there was no authority to act independently. "Would you rather see this oil in Japanese hands than violate your instructions as agents for the British owners?" Champ asked. "I am sorry, but we cannot violate our instructions, and that is *final!*" replied the manager.

Champ nodded to Mr. Rock, who picked up the telephone and called his foreman. "Go ahead as planned," he ordered. The "planned" included touching a match to the British oil along with the French and American. "I bought these gentlemen a drink," Champ later recorded, "and as they finished it, I assured them that their oil was in flames."[1]

Having arrived at Corregidor in *Tanager,* Adair's desire to head south was reinforced by what he found. He scribbled down in his pocket diary:

> 1300 moved to tunnel "Q" between air raids. Tunnel dark, dusty and poor facilities. Prefer to swim, if necessary. 1715 Keith came up to tunnel. Both of us began work on Admiral Rockwell. He said no chance get through Japs. We said we were willing to try and had Admiral Hart's OK, so he said all right. (Believe he was glad to get rid of us.) Grabbed my gear and ran for *Lanikai.*

Lanikai pulled alongside the pier at Mariveles at 2:10 P.M., with instructions to dump the Manila contingent and hurry back for any last-ditchers who might be stranded in Manila or Cavite. But in a sort of military musical chairs, several dozen Army officers anxious to shake Bataan and get out to Corregidor were taken aboard. At 5:30 P.M., we tied up at "the Rock," where Keith immediately took off to join Adair in assailing Admiral Rockwell for permission to sail south. Forty minutes later, out of breath, they were back at the pier, permission granted! Along with their good news they had brought four recruits, whose doubts on the wisdom of volunteering for *Lanikai* were clearly apparent as soon as they jumped down to the ship and made a lightning assessment.

One of them, a tall, slim lieutenant in shorts, knee-length white hose, short-sleeved white shirt and crowned cap device, could have been British. His English was impeccably Dartmouth. But the stripes on his shoulder boards were a trifle too narrow and the curl on the inner one too large. He was Lieutenant Paul Nygh, Royal Netherlands Navy, whose boss was planning to leave with Hart that night. The others were U.S. Navy—Radio Electrician C. A. Walruff and two assistants, veteran chief radiomen C. T. McVey and J. W. LeCompte. Things had reached the desperate point where *Lanikai* seemed the most reliable means of transporting a one-ton "portable" radio transmitter badly needed for the new headquarters in Java. These three were its chaperones.

Hart had retained two PBYs—Catalina seaplanes—for evacuation of VIPs. The first prepared to take off on the night of the twenty-fourth, loaded with passengers, including Major General L. H. Brereton, MacArthur's air commander, a 1911 Naval Academy graduate. The big, clumsy flying boat was plowing along at 40 knots, struggling to become airborne, when a *banca* loomed dead ahead in the murk. Pilot Harmon T. Utter kicked the rudder over hard to miss the boat. The plane heeled sharply and broke off a wing float. There was nothing left to do but shift the passengers to the remaining plane and hope to patch up the floatless one the next day for Hart.

The crippled plane, sitting camouflaged near the shore the following morning, was being repaired while pilots Utter and Pollock were enjoying a bath in a nearby hot spring. Their soak was cut short by sharp-eyed Japanese bombers who left nothing to repair. For Admiral Hart, the only way out now was the submarine *Shark*.

On the twenty-fifth, Hart turned over to Admiral Rockwell all Navy forces remaining within the Philippine coastal frontier—the submarines until they too pulled out, Destroyer Division "P" (the two cripples that had been under repair at Cavite, *Pillsbury* and *Peary*), Motor Torpedo Boat Squadron 3 and its six wicked, superfast little craft, and the miscellaneous collection of odds and ends of the Inshore Patrol. Hart included in his turnover letter to Rockwell the advice that he felt the time had passed for any remaining surface ships to escape to the south. The crack 4th Marine regiment, 1,600 strong, went under Army command.

At about 9:00 P.M., Christmas, Admiral Hart boarded *Shark*, and at 2:00 A.M. the next morning was en route to Java for a seven-day trip that Warrant Officer A. B. Ward, who rode with him, described as "hot and smelly and submerged except during darkness." Commander Den-

9

nison saw Hart off, and received instruction to report to Rockwell as acting chief of staff, since he could pass on Hart's plans and intentions, about which Rockwell had so far been in the dark.

There were no final handshakes with MacArthur. "Don't call *me;* I'll call *you,*" could be a thumbnail summary of something less than a warm association. Hart's last words to Dennison were, "Tell Rockwell the gates to the south are closed," words that we in the *Lanikai* did not hear.

Hart's local problems were over. MacArthur's were just beginning. His immediate task was to pull back the American forces in an orderly manner. Those in the north, in the great plain between Lingayen Bay and Manila, were to hold long enough for the smaller forces in the southeastern hook of Luzon, fighting a retrograde action, to get up to and around Manila before being cut off.

On that fateful day, the twenty-fifth, the northern U.S. forces were stretched thin across the strong defensive line of the Agno River. Behind that were three more "stand and fight" lines, each to be held two days. Only the fifth, just north of 3,867-foot Mt. Arayat, was organized for a protracted defense, so that the southern force could slip through to San Fernando. These latter had just begun their withdrawal from a defense at the enemy beachheads in the mountainous area east of 7,177 Mt. Banahao. They had close to 120 miles of hard going to make it safely through the gate. A tenacious, numerically smaller, but much better trained enemy yapped closely at their heels.

The twenty-fifth had been a rough day everywhere for the Far East Allies. But for *Lanikai* and her people it brought a Christmas gift provided by Admiral Rockwell that substituted a crack at freedom for certain capture and likely death.

Gladly quitting that magnet for Japanese bombs, Corregidor, *Lanikai* lay to off the Inshore Patrol station ship while goodbyes and the reason therefor were shouted across in the deepening twilight. Next stop was the Mariveles quarantine pier. Thousands of tons of assorted military supplies hastily brought out from Manila the past week lay dumped helter-skelter along a mile of open beach. Take what you wanted! No requisitions. No accounting. In fact, no storekeepers. Anything you could stagger off with was yours, no questions asked. In several hours ashore among the blacked-out scramble of boxes, the conundrum arose: which were beans and which were bullets? Or blankets. Or hard tack. Or coat hangers.

Provisioning for a cruise to where, we knew not, meant astute choosing best done in daylight. The issue was settled by the 11:20 P.M. alarm that sent the ship scurrying out to an anchorage less attractive to night intruders.

Filipino crewmen scrub down the decks on Lanikai. Behind the sailor (center) may be seen projecting vertically the "one machine gun" which President Roosevelt felt would add to Lanikai's legitimacy as a man-of-war. Chief Engineer Wilcoxen, inside doorway, makes coffee in the galley.

Before the first Filipino fighting cock had sounded off next morning, *Lanikai* was back alongside a temporary ramp, awaiting the first light to shine on the box labels. Between almost hourly air alarms, we filled up with tools, rope, canvas, flour, salmon, rice, toilet paper, lumber. The major problem was what *not* to take.

Harry Keith came staggering back with a five-gallon drum of green paint and the word that there was plenty more—perfect for covering *Lanikai*'s high visibility white hide. "Get some swabs, too!" called Bosun Kinsey. "We ain't got time fer paint brushes." For a man whose jaw had dropped so low on first seeing the ship, "Boats" had rapidly learned the ropes of a windjammer, literally and figuratively.

The bottle of compressed gas was less of a success. It merely corroborated our lack of knowledge of Navy gas bottle identification markings and confirmed that carbon dioxide does not burn, the latter established by hooking it up to the little propane stove in the galley.

Chief Radiomen McVey and LeCompte meanwhile had located the "portable" radio we were supposed to take to whatever our destination might be. Thirty years later, McVey reported on *Lanikai*'s radio installation. "I don't recall the type transmitter, but it was some ancient 'pooperdyne' that defied all treatment." Then he continued:

> That "semi-portable" was the world's greatest misnomer. I have distinct recollections that one crate was stamped "270 pounds," another was "240 pounds," and the transformer was even heavier. When we were loading at Mariveles, you may remember that the air raid warning was sounded and you ordered us to get underway. Frenchy LeCompte and I had to choose—we could stay on the dock with the equipment, or get it loaded and bring it with us. Would you believe that he and I, with one foot on the dock and one on the gun'l, lifted all that equipment on board by the time that engine was started and the lines cast off. I don't know why we didn't come up with double hernias.

A great pillar of flame and smoke arose from a French freighter anchored in Mariveles Bay, hit by Japanese bombers en route to Corregidor. We picked up one of the drums of gasoline she had jettisoned.

Tied up close under the Mariveles cliffs, the old submarine tender *Canopus,* too slow to run for it, had lumbered out from Manila on Christmas Day, in conformity with MacArthur's open city pronouncement. She was to be left behind to service submarines coming in with antiaircraft ammunition and medicines and taking out key personnel. In spare time, her artificers made gun mounts for the forces ashore on Bataan, repaired small boats and automotive equipment, and provided hot baths for sweat-soaked, dirt-caked Army nurses in from the field.

During daylight air alarms, any crewmen momentarily unemployed scurried ashore to take shelter in the deep caves that had been carved and blasted out of the adjacent cliff. If bombs came close, smudge pots aboard were lighted and the ship's tanks trimmed to give a heavy list. Perhaps the Japanese would accept the deception and believe her out of action.

With our scrounging ashore successfully concluded, we awaited darkness for *Lanikai* to transit the minefields and take departure southward. One last stop was made alongside *Canopus* to top off diesel tanks. Lying under the big ship's overhanging stern, *Lanikai* was not much larger than several motor launches that swung at the boat booms.

An interested group of *Canopus* bluejackets lounged over the taffrail and looked down at *Lanikai*. "Go to sea in *that* thing? You guys must be nuts!" The jibing was good-natured. "You gotta outboard motor?" inquired one. "They don't need no oil hose. Just hand 'em down a coupla quarts in a can." There were suggestions the Japs might use the ship for fish bait; it was about the right size. "Better blow up yer water wings before ya start." The general concensus was that it would be more sensible to stick around under the protection of *Canopus,* where it would be safe.

The journal entry for 26 December unfortunately fails to describe the doings or the feelings of the little group about to launch themselves on a tremendous adventure. There had not been much spare time to devote to setting thoughts down on paper. Indeed, if the journal had been brought out, it probably would have wound up being painted green, as was everything else. Swabs are not dainty paint applicators, nor are gun tubs neat palettes. But by the time darkness fell, *Lanikai* no longer glowed a ghostly white in the light of the half moon already well up in the sky as she commenced picking her way down the swept channel.

About halfway out, a blinding light illuminated the ship and the water around her. It was impossible to see to pick out channel buoys or do more than bend over the small magnetic compass on the roof of the after deckhouse, and steer the course, hoping to God the tidal current was weak. For some reason beyond the explanation of any rational man, that Corregidor searchlight held *Lanikai* in its powerful beam for three agonizing minutes, like a bug skewered on the point of a pin. For any Japanese picket submarine outside, we must have made a magnificent silhouette.

Although the journal was devoid of the day's details, it did commence with an open-ended statement that would set the standard for the next three months:

> In accordance with the verbal authority of the CinC U.S. Asiatic Fleet, this vessel got underway at 1940,* out of Mariveles Harbor, Luzon, destination unknown.

* 7:40 P.M.

Chapter 2

My own arrival in Manila, early in December of 1941, was almost as precipitous as my later departure, and for much the same reason—the Japanese were not much more than a five-inch gun shot astern. I had been assigned to the gunboat *Wake,* in the Yangtze Patrol, and as U.S. forces pulled out of China, the *Wake* had been left, with a few shipkeepers, at Shanghai. Two other river gunboats, the *Oahu* and *Luzon,* had literally sneaked out of Shanghai the night of 29 November in a desperate run for the so-called safety of the Philippines. I was aboard *Oahu.*

Since their launching at Shanghai in 1927 they had faced the hazards of the Yangtze's floods and roaring rapids and the capricious actions of bandit troops along the river's banks. For the last four years they had watched the ponderous Japanese military machine slug its way up the Yangtze in a bloody war euphemistically labeled by Tokyo as "the China Incident."

The two small gunboats ran through the Taiwan Straits on 2–3 December, beset by a typhoon that rolled them 50 degrees on a side and badgered by Japanese warcraft with guns trained ominously in their direction. Japanese planes zoomed overhead at almost masthead level when the weather allowed. From the Japanese flagship came a succession of international signals—peremptory demands that we enter a harbor in Taiwan, to all of which Rear Admiral William A. Glassford, Commander Yangtze Patrol, aboard *Luzon,* replied "not understood."

On our first forenoon in Manila—4 December 1941—the welcome change from Shanghai's bleak winter found us basking in the warm sunshine under a turquoise sky, digesting the first solid meal in days and repairing typhoon damage.

Yet it was a historic day. Admiral Glassford's two-star flag came down. "Yangtze Patrol disestablished this date," was the message the *Luzon* sent out. It was the official act which brought to an end an era which had seen four generations of American sailormen penetrate 1,700 miles into an alien country's heartland. They had started in clumsy paddlewheelers almost a century earlier and had wound up refugees in Manila Bay in their specialized craft designed for the Yangtze.

Aboard the *Oahu*, where typhoon-drenched blues were hung out to dry and we were adjusting to starched, high-necked whites, the message was hardly noticed. But the day did bring to the *Oahu* a message of considerably more interest for me than the one which ended the patrol where I had spent three years: "Lt. Tolley detached, proceed immediately to command USS *Lanikai*" was amplified by instructions to report to Fleet headquarters as soon as possible.

Any young naval officer finds his first command a thrilling challenge. But the USS *Lanikai* was a ship no one had ever heard of before. At Fleet Headquarters, where I met Commander Harry B. Slocum, the fleet operations officer, I found out why. The *Lanikai* had just joined the Navy, and she wasn't exactly a ship—she was a windjammer, a two-masted interisland schooner. The *Lanikai* was at the Cavite Navy Yard, Slocum explained, and her entire crew consisted of four or five assorted civilian Filipinos who had come in a package with the ship, which had been chartered for "one dollar a year for the duration." "Arm her with one cannon of some kind, one machine gun, provision her for a two-week cruise, get a crew aboard and be ready to sail in 24 hours," said Slocum.

Graduated from the U.S. Naval Academy twelve years earlier, I scarcely qualified as a veteran. But I had lived through enough navy yard overhauls to know that one confers, then plans, then requisitions, then inspects, until after much paper work, cajoling, changes, extended coffee breaks, weeks—perhaps months—later, the job is done. I respectfully pointed this out. "The rules do not apply in this case!" Slocum explained. "Cavite has been directed to give you the highest priority, on your verbal request, without paper work of any kind. Of this you can be absolutely assured; the President himself has personally ordered it."

If I was impressed by this lightning from Olympus, the authorities at Cavite were no less so. "Sign this receipt for 'one schooner' and tell me what you want!" said Lieutenant Commander R. T. Whitney, assistant captain of the yard. Telephone calls to Ordnance, Supply, Hospital, Communications and Personnel mobilized the Navy Yard's resources. A gun—an ancient three-pounder of Spanish-American War vintage with a bright brass pedestal—already was being bolted to the after deckhouse. That was the biggest "cannon" the yard felt could safely be fired without collapsing the 27-year-old ship's structure. And there would be *two* 30-caliber Lewis machine guns, left over from World War I, although the President had directed only one. Half a dozen Insular Force* Filipino

* A U.S. naval unit of 1,000 Filipino seamen, legally restricted to duty in the Philippines.

seamen were on the way, another Presidential "suggestion." Somebody had gone down to the ship and sworn in the Filipino crewmen already on board who, speaking no English, were wholly at a loss to understand what it was all about. But they amiably accepted the bags of white uniforms, then immediately dug out the little, round white sailor hats and proudly put them on.

The powder train thus set alight, and the best wishes of Commander Whitney accepted, I found my way down to Machina Wharf, where the *Lanikai* was moored. The results already were apparent. Monster cockroaches by the hundreds scuttled for safety as bags of rice and cases of salmon slammed down *Lanikai*'s hatches—bread and meat to the largely Filipino crew. Into a Coca Cola cooler on deck went canned hams for the Caucasian element. Beans, flour, catsup, canned milk, and boxes of condiment indicated the automatic reaction of Supply Corps veterans to the request for balanced rations for two weeks' cooking over the bottled gas stove in the tiny galley amidships.

The happy moratorium on paper work in outfitting extended to the internal workings of the ship itself. She was singularly innocent of the stacks of files that burdened the peacetime life of the ordinary naval officer. There were no personal or health records, inventories, mess accounts, powder magazine, or engineering forms. That the record might not be wholly blank, I planned to keep a journal, perhaps illuminated by photographs. The first entry suggested that there were other things to do:

> *5 December:* At 0900 this ship was commissioned a United States naval vessel, accepted from the Captain of the Yard, Cavite, by Lieut. Kemp Tolley, USN, commanding. The Navy Yard band played the national anthem, the commission pennant was hoisted, then "God Bless America" was played to wind up the ceremony. At 0915 commenced receiving stores, ammunition and equipment from the yard. A three-pounder boat gun has been mounted on the after deckhouse and two 30-caliber Lewis guns forward, thus completing our armament.*

By ones and twos the men arrived. Chief Gunner's Mate Merle L. Picking had been first and, other than myself, was the only American aboard at the ceremony. Being told off to hoist the commission pennant and having got it proudly in place, he turned with interest to view the many hundreds of yard workmen ashore who had stood by for the music. "That was nice!" he said. Then exhibiting the practicality we were to find henceforth in this excellent man, he added: "But it must have cost the Navy 50 man-hours of work while those fellows stood around at attention."

As Chief Boatswain's Mate "Charlie" Kinsey arrived on the dock,

* See appendix for crew list.

16

Admiral Thomas C. Hart, Commander in Chief, Asiatic Fleet.

Lanikai under way, her boxy superstructure cutting down her speed.

"Guns" Picking works on his "main battery," the 3-pounder Spanish-American War quick-firer, as Prudencio Tumbagahan mans the helm and "Doc" Cossette tends his fishing line.

his jaw dropped down and he stared at *Lanikai* and the ant-like activity aboard. He walked forward and squinted at the ship's nameplate, then called down to Picking, who already was checking out his "main battery." "I've got orders to the *Lanikai*," said Kinsey in a thick Georgia drawl, "but this *cain't* be *it!*"

"Have you ever been in sail before, Boats?" I inquired, after Kinsey had at last been convinced that this was indeed *it*. If "Boats" *had* been in sail before, his state of shock precluded any reply. I was left to comfort myself with the thought that more than a decade had passed since I had sailed anything, and that was merely a catboat on the Severn at Annapolis.

Although Commander Slocum had been skimpy on details, it was clear even to one far removed from top level planning that the mission was likely to be one way. If I managed to survive, it would be by swimming, in which event excess baggage would be no help. Nor did I want those devils gloating over my class ring and sword if I were captured. So my baggage was light: typewriter, camera, a few khaki shirts and slacks, "steaming" cap with grommet removed, sneakers, and one set of white shorts and shirt for old times sake. They all tucked easily into the small locker, smelling of mold and paint, that other than a bunk provided the only furniture in the six-by-six cabin. Class ring, sword, inspection blue uniform and new cap were entrusted to a friend who lived in quarters ashore. All the rest, the small treasures of a young bachelor who traveled light, were packed in a trunk and sent to the Navy Yard for storage and never seen again.

In spite of the desperate efforts of all concerned, the 24-hour time limit in which to be ready for sea could not be met. The sixth of December 1941 found the moss-encrusted old radio refusing to emit a single beep, although signals could be received.

The journal entry for that day was again short:

> Moored port side to starboard side of USS *Tanager,* Machina Wharf, Navy Yard, Cavite. Receiving electricity from yard. At 0800 mustered crew on station; no absentees. Received from the ammunition depot 400 rounds 30-caliber; 200 rounds 45-caliber; 50 rounds buck-shot shells, 12-gauge.

Ready or not, on 7 December (6 December Washington time) no further delay could be brooked. The President's message had said, "AS SOON AS POSSIBLE AND WITHIN TWO DAYS IF POSSIBLE . . ." I crossed Manila Bay for the last time for final instructions and to report on the condition of the ship, including the lack of means to transmit by radio. I had already dropped off my will and a last letter home the day before, entrusted to a good friend and classmate, Francis Jordan, executive officer of the *Luzon*. Aboard the little ferry *Dap-Dap,* in a wicker chair under the awning, a cool breeze blowing, the forty-minute crossing gave time for reflection. My thoughts were divided—the adventure on which I was imminently to be launched, and about which I had had only the sketchiest suggestions, and my past, with which this bay and city had been so intimately and pleasantly connected since I was born there.

As Manila's flat skyline drew closer, I could make out details aboard ungainly, homey old *Canopus*. People were leaning over the mahogany rail on her top deck, looking down on the several "pig boats" moored alongside for servicing, just as I had done so many times in the two happy years I had served in her a decade before. Forty or more merchantmen swung at anchor in the bay.

Along Dewey Boulevard, the fronds of those magnificent palms that bordered the street moved ever so slightly in the forenoon sea breeze. Children were romping along the edges of the Army and Navy Club pool, mothers in bathrobes perched on the benches by the fence, perhaps trading gossip on who danced with whom cheek-to-cheek at the club last evening. It was 1935, or '25 or '15 all over again.

My thoughts flashed back to the many moonlight evenings in the tiny outrigger *banca,* the native canoe I kept under the club porch. The air was so very soft, and the sea smooth as glass and iridescently glowing with each dip of the paddle. Marcia, and May, and Tina, and that tiny German blonde whose name had faded . . . and Maria, the *mestiza* I dared not take inside the club. All were so very pretty and gay, they must long since have married and flown. But the memories were sweet. . . .

"Here are your orders," said Commander Slocum, passing over a small envelope. "You will open this only when you are clear of Manila Bay. I can tell you that you are headed for the coast of Indo-China. If you are queried by a Japanese man-of-war, you are to explain you are looking for a downed U.S. Navy patrol plane."

I had two major concerns: the inoperative transmitter and fresh water. *Lanikai* had been designed for a crew of four or five, whose tastes ran more to beer. Now she carried nineteen. That presented no problem to Slocum. "You can work on the radio en route," he said cheerily. "You have a radioman first class assigned. As for water, you have a set of international signal flags, don't you? If you run short of water, simply ask a passing Jap for some."

The wide gap between two stripes and four stars made it logical enough that Commander Slocum, the operations officer, rather than Admiral Hart, should brief me, in spite of the apparent importance of the matter.

There was, in fact, an excellent reason why Hart was not available. About noon on the fifth, a flying boat had arrived from Singapore and disembarked a businesslike, quick-moving little man in a vice admiral's uniform of the Royal Navy—Tom Phillips, one inch shorter than Napoleon and just as determined. A battleship man who had some misgivings about the airplane's being here to stay, he had fallen at odds with Prime Minister Churchill, whose favorite uniform was that of a Royal Air Force commodore. But Churchill, as did many others, recognized the outstanding qualities of Phillips, which was why he had just arrived in the Far East to take command of His Majesty's naval forces in those parts, including the newly assigned World War I battle cruiser *Repulse* and the modern battleship *Prince of Wales*.

Air Chief Marshal Sir Robert Brooke-Popham, British commander in chief, Far East, had made several visits to Manila during 1941 for some fruitless conferences with Hart and MacArthur that had done more harm than good, through Brooke-Popham's noisy flamboyance around town that had widely advertised to the Japanese the probability of joint Anglo-American planning. There would be none of this foolishness with Admiral Phillips, who would be kept under wraps at Cavite, where the secret conference went on for two days.

Lanikai's journal for 7 December (6 December Pearl time) recorded the last day of peace. She still was moored alongside minesweeper *Tanager*. The last three crewmen reported aboard: Engineer Wilcoxen, Radioman Burt and, as we were to thank our lucky stars for later, "Doc" Cossette, a pharmacist's mate equally useful at curing small ills, hauling in big fish or ignoring the Geneva Convention by manning a machine gun. Ironically, their records and pay accounts were left at Cavite for "safe keeping."

> At 1410 Navy Yard tug came alongside and took ship in tow to clear mooring.
> At 1415 got underway in accordance with CinCAF confidential despatch orders.
> At 1420 hoisted jib staysail and forestaysail.

There was no need to hurry. *Lanikai* would have to lie at anchor overnight inside the bay's entrance. Ships were allowed to transit the minefield channel only in daylight. That the minefield was more bluff than reality hopefully was a high level secret. In a 7 October letter to Chief of Naval Operations Admiral Harold Stark, Hart had complained about defective mines: "One broke loose from its anchor and was recovered by fishermen. The antenna was found so covered with barnacles that *it* would not possibly have functioned. . . . *We simply have a mine that is no good. I can't see why these things don't get found out sooner* . . . too much letting our thoughts be governed by the damned Battle Fleet."

By 4:45, *Lanikai* had covered the fifteen miles to an anchorage near Corregidor, for our first supper "at sea." At about 3:30 A.M., a radioman nudged me awake with a message: "ORANGE* WAR PLAN IN EFFECT. RETURN TO CAVITE." There was no point in waking the crew before dawn. I went topside to collect my thoughts in the cool night air. The lights that had twinkled in profusion last evening on Corregidor had gone out and would not come on again for a long time.

* Identification as Japanese.

Chapter 3

The events leading to *Lanikai*'s mission had been building up over a period of international turmoil that began in the autumn of 1940, but in the chaos and confusion of early December 1941, there was neither the time nor the possibility to inquire into what eventually was a tangled web of circumstances. Only after thirty years has most of the story been uncovered, and it is now apparent that parts of it will never be fully explained.

While the crewmen of *Lanikai* were wondering how to fight a war with an antique cannon, it is necessary to flash back to the year before, when they had been assured this would not be necessary.

In Boston, in October of 1940, President Roosevelt had ringingly proclaimed, "I have said this before, but I shall say it again and again and again: Your boys are not going to be sent into any foreign wars." If Admiral Hart heard these words, he obviously was not impressed; nine months earlier he was importuning Stark to get cracking on allocating funds, the relatively piddling sum of $96,000, for Navy storage tunnels on Corregidor. "I am as positive as I have ever been of anything," he wrote, "that if we do not proceed to complete the underground work, and at once, the future is likely to show that we were much at fault . . . room for a fair supply of torpedoes, ammunition, spare parts, supplies . . ."

Hart was bucked up in November 1940 to receive a letter from the CinC, U.S. Fleet, Admiral J. O. Richardson, that he was preparing, for possible dispatch to the East Indies area, a detachment of four heavy cruisers, an aircraft carrier, nine destroyers, and four fast minelayers, all to report to the CinC, Asiatic, if and when they arrived. The news was confirmed by a letter from Stark to Hart, 12 November 1940: ". . . One thing (and this is for your ears only) you can depend upon is that we would support you, probably by sending a naval reinforcement to you at Soerabaja or Singapore, and," Stark cryptically added, "by other means."

Somewhere along the line, there was concern about the feeble state of Asiatic defenses. On 21 February 1941, Admiral Ingersoll sent a secret message to CinC Pacific, information to Admiral Hart, that, "Pressure is still being exerted to send reinforcements to the Asiatic Fleet. I am continuing to advise against such a step but may be overruled." There were only two people in a position to do this—Admiral Stark and Armed Forces CinC Roosevelt. Ingersoll concluded by directing Commander in Chief, Pacific Fleet (CinCPAC) Kimmel, who concurrently was Commander in Chief, U.S. Fleet (CinCUS) to have six 1,500-ton destroyers and four heavy cruisers prepared to depart on short notice. The last few words must have sent Hart up on his toes: "There still exists possibility of a carrier being sent." But this, too, like all the other reinforcement promises and plans, blew over.

On 28 November 1940, Admiral Richardson wrote Stark that he thought torpedo nets within Pearl Harbor were neither necessary nor practicable. "The area is too restricted . . . ships not within torpedo range of the entrance." Earlier that same month, British aerial torpedo attacks had sunk three Italian battleships in Taranto, a harbor about the depth of Pearl's. In April 1937, while entering Tokyo Bay in a merchant ship, I had seen Japanese planes drop parachute-supported torpedoes from a thousand feet or more. Chaser boats picked them up. In 1967 I asked a retired Japanese vice admiral what he knew of this. His reply suggests that perhaps my intelligence report could have been put to more use than apparently it was:

> During those period the strength and performance of aircraft torpedo was so low that they had to release it from a low altitude (below less than 40–50 meters). Therefore in order to heighten the level they have been experimenting with a parachute or special fin which makes torpedo path in the air smoothly. I believe this is what you have seen.
>
> The torpedoes used in the attack of Pearl Harbor were experimented and manufactured from March of 1941 and they were able to complete just in time for the Task Force to leave for Hawaii.

In October 1940, Admiral Richardson had had a set-to with the President over retaining the Fleet in the Hawaiian area, "a goddam mousetrap," as Richardson put it. Harry Hopkins had offered some gratuitous advice on the subject, at which Richardson suggested that perhaps his knowledge of naval affairs suffered from some shortcomings, or words to that effect. Richardson was in fast company when he got into a bucking game with Roosevelt, Hopkins and Hull, whose alter ego, Stanley Hornbeck, was one of the strongest proponents for keeping the Fleet at Pearl. On 6 January 1941, with no personal advance warning, Richardson was informed he was to be relieved of command. "You hurt the President's feelings," Stark told him.

Four days before that, Ambassador to Japan Joseph C. Grew

entered in his diary a sentence Richardson's successor, Admiral Husband Kimmel, might have read with more profit, had not acting Director of Naval Intelligence, Captain Jules James, made such a casual evaluation of it. "There is a lot of talk around town," wrote Grew, "to the effect that the Japanese, in case of a break with the United States, are planning to go all out in a surprise attack on Pearl Harbor. Of course I informed our government." By probably something more than coincidence, Admiral Yamamoto, top Japanese sea commander, wrote on 1 February 1941 to the chief of staff of the 11th Air Fleet, requesting his opinion on just such an attack. Yamamoto had discussed the subject with his own chief of staff the preceding year.

In the summer, action intensified. On 22 June 1941, Hitler electrified the world by Germany's "surprise" attack on the USSR, about which Stalin had been futilely warned by a number of sources, mostly wholly reliable.

In July 1941, Japanese bombers damaged the Yangtze River gunboat USS *Tutuila* $27,045.78 worth. Admiral Shimada, CinC of Japan's China Seas Fleet, said, "Very sorry!" Admiral Hart was so incensed he wrote Stark he had almost sent him a plain language message recommending that we send a squadron or two of our best fighters to Chungking to protect *Tutuila* and our embassy by attacking any Japanese planes that were found in the air anywhere near them.

On 7 July 1941, American troops landed in Iceland, a move which prompted Rear Admiral Richmond Kelly Turner, Navy War Plans director, to ask the President if this did not seem to conflict with his October and December speeches of the previous year guaranteeing that "no American boys will be sent abroad." The President, answering not a word, leaned his head back, his long cigarette holder elevated at a jaunty angle indicating mischievous amusement, and gave vent to a chuckle as his reply.

On 24 July 1941, Japanese troops landed in strength in French Indo-China, ending the phantasy of French sovereignty, which in fact had ceased to exist with the fall of France thirteen months earlier. The American reaction was quick and drastic: two days later a freezing of all Japanese assets in the United States.

Also in July, on the twenty-eighth, an event occurred which would have a momentous impact on American affairs in the Far East: the Field Marshal of the Philippine Army, Douglas MacArthur, was given the rank of lieutenant general, U.S. Army, and command of the newly constituted U.S. Army Forces Far East (USAFFE). Heretofore, Admiral Hart had been on the very best of terms with his U.S. Army opposite number commanding the Philippine Department; first, Major General Walter Grant, then Major General George Grunert. Hart and the U.S. Army rarely laid eyes on MacArthur, who kept largely to himself with his young wife and son atop the new wing of the Manila Hotel, in a penthouse originally built for Manuel Quezon before that powerful figure moved into Malakañang, the presidential palace. In March 1940, in one of his monthly informal, chatty letters to Admiral Harold Stark, Chief of Naval Operations, Hart gave an assessment of the Field Marshal: "He has accomplished a vast amount of work. I think that in General MacArthur, and his Staff,* the Filipinos have made about the wisest expenditure that has happened since they took charge of their own affairs."

It is an unfortunate fact that very often the professional historian is precluded by certain taboos from "telling it like it was," thus by lack of knowledge forcing the general public to abdicate its responsibility for avoiding a repetition of the past's mistakes. In this sense, the story of the 1941–42 collapse of the "white" empires in Asia would be incomplete without a clear understanding that they fell divided in planning, goals, and in ordinary common understanding. The fall we experienced divided might have been inevitable in any case, but it could have been less precipitous and less humiliating. It was indeed this very humiliation which opened the way for the exit of the West from those parts—not just for the transitory duration of Japanese occupation, but perhaps forever.

One of those divisions was within our *own* "empire." MacArthur had been a "boy prodigy" general officer in France in 1918 when Hart, relatively speaking, was in knee pants as a U.S. Navy commander. As Chief of Staff of the U.S. Army, MacArthur had worn four stars half a decade before Hart got *his* four as CinC Asiatic. Invited to train the Philippine Army in 1935 as a field marshal, it was the equivalent of *five* stars he had just unpinned to find himself one rank junior to Hart and three years younger. According to Rear Admiral F. W. Rockwell, then commandant 16th Naval District at Cavite, and who later rode a torpedo boat out of Luzon with MacArthur, the latter was "very proud, and profoundly resented any affront. His imagination and conception of things were evident in his sense of drama. He loved theatrical situations."[2]

The net result of all this was that the Hart-MacArthur relationship got off to a bad start, when it was only after several weeks delay that MacArthur, obviously ill at ease, finally brought himself to make the first call on Hart, which the latter pointedly returned at once.

The fur began to fly almost immediately. In a more or less routine administrative message, Hart radioed his subordinates at Shanghai and Hongkong that because of the special conditions familiar only to naval personnel on duty in Chinese ports touched by U.S. vessels carrying troops en route to or from the United States, the Navy would assume

* Which included Lieutenant Colonel Dwight D. Eisenhower.

authority over Army personnel granted shore leave in Shanghai or Hong-kong. A mailgram copy was passed to USAFFE. That did it! No collaboration! No mutual agreement! A *fait accompli*. Not bothering with Hart or his own chain of command, a furious MacArthur wrote a blistering letter to Hart's boss, Chief of Naval Operations Admiral Harold Stark. It bitterly complained about Hart's "arbitrary and illegal action," which "dictatorial procedure cannot fail to arouse the bitterest resentment throughout the ranks of this Army."

Under these inauspicious circumstances, the first face-to-face business meeting between Hart and MacArthur, on the former's request, was a two-and-a-half hour conference on 22 September 1941. On his part, Admiral Hart explained the Navy's deployment to the south and the reasons therefor. He recorded in his notes that, "At the end of a rather long recital, General MacArthur replied that 'the Navy had its plans, the Army had its plans and that we each had our own fields. The Army is glad to know of the Navy's plans but its own plans are virtually independent thereof and there seems no possibility of conflict between them.' He had no questions whatever, made no suggestions, and offered no objections. The impression was that the Commanding General thought that close cooperation was not vital."

On 24 September, four days before that somewhat less-than-cooperative meeting of minds, a slight, exceedingly clever 29-year-old Japanese ensign, Takeo Yoshikawa, attached *sub-rosa* to the Japanese consulate general in Honolulu, received a directive from his Tokyo boss. The message, Tokyo's #83, in a system designated by the U.S. Army as J-19, was deciphered by them on 9 October. It requested routine reports "with regard to warships . . . those at anchor . . . tied up at wharves, buoys and in docks . . . *make mention of where there are two or more vessels alongside the same wharf.*" [Italics supplied.]

Clearly, this was a clue of the first magnitude concerning Japanese interests and intentions. Tokyo's request to be informed when two Pearl Harbor ships were *one outboard of the other at the same dock* could point only to consideration of the use of torpedoes, obviously from the air, as it was not likely any major effort against the fleet while inside Pearl Harbor would conceivably be based on surreptitious entry of submarines—although one midget did manage to penetrate the harbor on 7 December, where it did no harm before being destroyed.

The real payoff in the message was the laying out of the harbor in grid coordinates, which strongly inferred setting up air targets. Some erroneously maintain that this was standard Japanese reporting procedure. General Sherman Miles, Assistant Chief of Staff, G-2 (Military Intelligence) at the time of Pearl Harbor, was questioned before the Joint Congressional Committee on this point: "Wasn't this message quite different from the others? . . . Have you found any others like it? . . ."

"I have not found any similar," replied Miles.

Colonel Charles Willoughby, MacArthur's intelligence officer, did not fail to grasp the significance when he read a copy surreptitiously supplied MacArthur's chief signal officer, Brigadier General Spencer Akin, by Washington friends. Of it, he wrote:

> We saw some of the intercepts in Manila, on a relay through special channels. . . . It was known that the Japanese Consul in Honolulu cabled Tokyo reports on general ship movements. . . .
> In October his instructions were "sharpened." Tokyo called for specific instead of general reports. In November, the daily reports were on a grid-system of the inner harbor with co-ordinate locations of American men of war; this was no longer a case of diplomatic curiosity; co-ordinate grid is the classical method of pin-point target designation; our battleships had become "targets."[3]

To fully assess the above, one must go back a couple of decades and examine the American cryptographic effort, about which much has been written—some with prejudice, some based on only partial knowledge, but all agreeing that fundamentally, it was the most important single weapon in the U.S. arsenal. Those involved in cryptanalysis have been required by oath to maintain secrecy on pain of $10,000 fine and a year in the pokey, so the researcher's task is a delicate one.

In 1929, Secretary of State Henry Stimson's pious dictum that, "Gentlemen do not read each others' mail," for the time being halted State Department crypto activity. But a broken Japanese code had given the United States a heavy advantage in the 1922 London Naval Conference, wherein the Japanese were accurately backed down to what the U.S. negotiators knew to be their maximum concession. This was the 5–5–3 ratio in capital ships, translated by the irked, face-conscious Japanese into Rolls-Royce–Rolls-Royce–Ford. This earlier coup, plus Stimson's unrealistic move, served to briskly stimulate the U.S. military and naval crypto effort. The tiny group of professional Navy intelligence officers had been made aware of U.S. Navy backwardness in crypto through observation of the French, British, and U.S. Army in World War I and the State Department's "Black Chamber" under the remarkable Herbert O. Yardley.

From about 1932 through 1938 the Army worked almost exclusively on diplomatic traffic. Then until 1940, the Navy handled all Japanese diplomatic traffic other than "Purple," the top diplomatic system, plus numerous Japanese Navy systems.

In August 1940, after 18 months of labor so gruelling it broke his health, Colonel William F. Friedman solved "Purple," the final breakthrough via a flash of intuitive genius on the part of an Army civilian,

Harry Larry Clark. Concurrently, the Navy code crackers, under the brilliant cryptanalyst Commander Lawrence Safford, later awarded $100,000 by Congress for his outstanding contributions, had broken a new Japanese fleet system designated JN-25, continuing the steady progress made since 1924. A Navy solution for the "Red" machine, predecessor of "Purple," contributed heavily to the Army's success with the latter.

By Pearl Harbor, the Navy had about 750 in the crypto business, including interceptor and direction finder personnel. Some 150 of these were college girls, later to become WAVES, who spent up to six hours a day in the courses developed by Safford, who headed the Communications Security Group, Office of Naval Communications.

Most of the Japanese messages were intercepted by various stations in the United States (see appendix). A few, naturally, were missed. Army's monitoring station MS-5, at Oahu's Fort Shafter, was so close to the commercial transmitters handling the Tokyo-Honolulu-Tokyo traffic that they could be copied solid. With the exception of "Purple," they were bundled up and sent to Washington via biweekly "Clipper" seaplane airmail, or ship, with a two-week delay or more for those missed by the continental stations. The "Purple" messages, in Japanese cipher, were reenciphered in an Army system and sent on via radio to SIS (Signal Intelligence Service) for processing.

In the United States, arrangements had been made with certain of the commercial radio companies to get photo copies of potential enemy traffic, but with many Nisei employed in the Honolulu radio offices, this was considered too dangerous a tactic. However, on 4 December 1941, Captain Irving Mayfield, naval district counter intelligence officer, approached RCA director David Sarnoff,* vacationing in Oahu, to wink at the law protecting customers' privacy and give him copies of the Japanese messages. He agreed. The first pickup on 4 December, of outgoing messages only, by Mayfield, went to Commander Joseph J. Rochefort, in charge of the complex of intercept and direction finder stations spread from Alaska to Samoa. All this was done without reference to Washington and without Captain Mayfield's knowledge that five miles away, the Army's intercept station MS-5 was getting solid copies of RCA transmissions, which handled the Japanese traffic on even months, and of Mackay Radio, which the Japanese used on odd months. In fact, Mayfield knew nothing of MS-5's activity. Nor did General Short, nor his intelligence officer, Colonel K. J. Fielder.

Thus, the Tokyo message to Ensign Yoshikawa on Pearl Harbor grid coordinates was intercepted on 24 September by MS-5, reached Washington by mail on 6 October, and by the ninth, copies deciphered by the Army's SIS were in the hands of the Washington high command.

---

* In 1944, made a brigadier general, A.U.S.

In the subsequent investigational storms which arose over this directive to Yoshikawa, it came to be known as the "bomb plot" message. For the moment, we shall push it to the back of the stove while looking into another fascinating and closely related *denouement,* the question of responsibility for dissemination of intelligence.

For years, the Office of Naval Intelligence (ONI) had "enjoyed" a reputation as something of a dead end for promotion. As late as 1929, it counted a sad little total of twenty officers, working with obsolete files in an obsolete fashion, with little money. Its organizational instructions directed ONI to "secure . . . information concerning foreign countries . . . strength, disposition, and probable intentions of foreign naval forces." Paragraph (2) said: "Evaluate the information collected and disseminate as advisable."

Admiral Hart's view is perhaps not atypical. It was his habit to write memos on matters which irked him, then never send them, the tension perhaps relieved by setting down his thoughts. He wrote such a one in July 1940 and filed it:

> CINCAF is supplied with such information as goes into ONI from China and (usually after some lapse of time), from Japan. The Commander in Chief gets nothing *from* ONI, which naturally has additional sources of information, and has come to feel that he is entirely on his own in this most important respect. Considering the magnitude of our ONI establishment, I submit that the effort may not be getting employed to the best advantage.

While Hart consigned his complaint to the files, Admiral Kimmel sent *his* 18 February 1941 letter to Admiral Stark. It read like Kimmel wondered who, if anybody, was in the front seat, driving. An officer fresh from Washington had told him ONI thought it was *Operations'* function to furnish the CinC with secret information. He had heard also that *War Plans* considered it was *ONI's* "pidgin."

"I don't know that we have missed anything," Kimmel said, "but if there is any doubt as to whose responsibility it is . . . will you kindly fix that responsibility."

Over a month later (22 March), with Delphic ambiguity, Stark left Kimmel still up in the air: "Kirk* informs me that ONI is fully aware of its responsibilities in keeping you informed concerning foreign nations, and disloyal elements within the United States." There was nothing about who, if anybody, would enlighten the CinC Pacific on what the *Americans* were doing or planning.

What Hart and Kimmel also never were told was that as of three weeks later, "Kirk" (Director of ONI) would be in no position to carry out his aforesaid "responsibilities." On 14 April 1941, War Plans director

---

* Captain Alan G. Kirk, Director of Naval Intelligence.

Rear Admiral Richmond Kelly Turner and Captain Kirk got together in Assistant Chief of Naval Operations Royal Ingersoll's office to thrash out the question of responsibilities, on which they had been unable to agree between the two of them.

A man with a very short fuse, Turner, as described to me by one of his former subordinates, got along well enough with what he considered to be first class naval officers, grudgingly tolerated second class officers, and utterly despised third class. As any organization inevitably harbors a sizable percentage of what Turner felt to be of the latter two categories, it is not surprising he had a lot of enemies. There are in fact some who went so far as to rate him the most hated man in the Navy, a point hotly contested by others who felt Admiral Ernest King merited this distinction. But all this should not sway any judgment of Turner's professional ability. What we are concerned with here is the arrogance and strong will that resulted in his dominance of his boss, affable, accommodating CNO "Betty" Stark, to a degree that was likely to act to the disadvantage of others on the same general command level —such as the Director of ONI and the Director of Naval Communications, Rear Admiral Leigh Noyes. The latter, as time went on, became a pet peeve of Turner's: "That Noyes and his damned *secrets!*"

With Ingersoll unable to umpire an agreement, the party moved to Stark's office. Turner took the position that War Plans should prepare the estimate of enemy intentions, interpret, evaluate and disseminate all information on possible enemy nations. He maintained that ONI was simply a collection agency. Stark, who held Turner in particular esteem,* decided in his favor, although nothing ever was provided Kirk in writing to change ONI's functional chart.

Kimmel did not let the subject die. On 26 May 1941, he wrote a lengthy memorandum to Stark, pointing out that CinCPAC felt himself "in a very difficult position . . . as a rule, not informed of policy, or change of policy . . . and . . . as a result . . . unable to evaluate the possible effect upon his own situation. He is not even sure of what force will be available to him." Further, he expressed the belief that the situation was "susceptible to marked improvement." . . . that "Full and authoritative knowledge of current policies and objectives . . . would enable the Commander in Chief, Pacific Fleet to modify, adapt, or even reorient his possible courses of action to conform to current concepts."

If the reader is beginning to wonder how all this policy ping-pong bears on the Asiatic Fleet in general, and *Lanikai* in particular, it must

---

* On 31 July 1941, Stark wrote to Captain C. M. Cooke, commanding the battleship *Pennsylvania:* "As you probably know from our despatches, and from my letters, we have felt that the Maritime Provinces are now definitely Japanese objectives. Turner thinks Japan will go up there in August. He may be right. He usually is. . . ." Cooke turned the letter over to Kimmel.

be recalled that it was on the readiness and availability of Admiral Kimmel's Pacific Fleet that our so-called "bastion of the Pacific," the Philippines—not to mention the Netherlands East Indies and Malaya—counted for vital support, either as a source of direct reinforcement or of powerful diversionary action.

In spite of Turner's coup, Kirk, in the absence of any written instructions to the contrary, continued to follow the dictates of his conscience and his ONI charter by sending about ten important Japanese intercept translations to Kimmel during July. Then General George Marshall, Army Chief of Staff, got into the act and through pressure on Stark, put a stop to it. This was a double deception of Kimmel, in that not only was the pipeline cut, but in view of the subsequent lack of messages, with no explanation why, he was laboring under the delusion that the reason was there had been nothing of importance to report.

Kirk had been naval attaché in London for two years before becoming Director of ONI, which assignment he had taken at the express request of Secretary of the Navy Frank Knox, who had heard him speak at a symposium and concluded Kirk knew more about the European war situation than any naval officer suitable for director. The understanding with Knox was that Kirk would very soon be released to sea duty in order to qualify for selection to flag rank. Kirk took over from Captain Jules James, who as assistant director under Rear Admiral Walter Anderson, had "fleeted up" to acting director on Anderson's 24 January departure for sea without relief. A year senior to Kirk, James obviously could not revert to assistant, so he opted to go to sea also, with its enhancing possibilities for advancement.

James had another good reason to be out of it, having had his crack at tangling with Terrible Turner. The latter had proposed, as he would more successfully later with Kirk, that War Plans take over enemy intentions estimates. James refused, pointing out that this was ONI's job, as clearly outlined in his organizational chart.

Now we may return to our gay young friend Yoshikawa, who while enjoying the delights of the geishas in Honolulu's many Japanese restaurants, was at the same time taking airplane flights over Pearl Harbor, swimming near its entrance, observing things from restaurant balconies which overlooked the anchorage, and sending voluminous radio messages back to Tokyo on what he had observed, as per the "bomb plot" message instructions.

Lieutenant Commander Alvin Kramer, crack ONI translator and evaluator, who had spent three years in Japan studying the language and people, felt the bomb plot message to be sufficiently important to merit a special "flag" pinned to it. Captain Kirk was equally impressed, but with his specific duties for evaluation and dissemination usurped by Stark's oral directive, he pressed Turner, who had assumed these responsibilities, to relay the message to Kimmel. Turner refused.

Within that week, matters came to a showdown, irreverently and clandestinely called "the *Oktobr Revolutsion*," and euphemistically described as, "Trouble on the Second Deck," by A. A. Hoehling.[4]

In the general shakeup and shift of personnel which followed, "ONI was capsized," as put by Captain H. F. Kingman, head of ONI's Domestic Intelligence Branch. Kirk thus found his opportunity to collect on Knox's promise of a short "cruise" in ONI; in six days he was on his way to sea.*

The chief of ONI's Intelligence Branch, Captain H. D. Bode, who had joined Kirk in pressing Turner to transmit the message, was relieved of his duties the same day, the ninth, and was detached for sea duty on the sixteenth, after a mere nine months in the assignment.†

As for Hart, it was fortunate that his intelligence officer, Commander Redfield ("Rosy") Mason, was superlatively good. He once was tested standing behind a screen with a Japanese. A second Japanese in front could not distinguish who was who. He could riffle through a deck of cards, then name their order, a type of memory useful in stowing away with computerlike accuracy the many thousands of ideographs which one must know in mastering the Japanese language. There is little wonder why the final instructions for the evacuation of Java were summarized in, "Burn the files, safeguard the codes and get Mason out."

Returning once more to the bomb plot message—if Kimmel was denied this highly valuable clue on Japanese intentions, then how the devil did Hart and MacArthur get it? Brigadier General Spencer Akin was one of the outstanding officers in the Army Signal Corps, so when MacArthur took over command of USAFFE, he requested Akin's services. In 1940 and until about May of 1941, Akin, as a colonel, had been head of SIS, under Chief of Army Communications Colonel Otis K. Sadtler, with whom he was on very friendly terms. When the bomb plot message

---

* Kirk was selected for rear admiral six weeks later. He commanded the U.S. naval task force at the Normandy invasion, retired as a four star admiral, then served as ambassador to Belgium, Luxemburg, the USSR, and Nationalist China.

† By an ironic coincidence, Bode commanded the cruiser *Chicago* at the 8 August 1942 Battle of Savo Island. *Chicago* survived, but one Australian and three American heavy cruisers, under the operational command of Rear Admiral Richmond Kelly Turner, were sunk with the loss of 1,023 lives and negligible damage to the Japanese. It was the greatest sea disaster in American history.

Turner survived physically and professionally to become a four star admiral commanding the Pacific Fleet Amphibious Force, highly regarded by many. Bode, "the melancholy Dane" as he was sometimes called, probably brooding over the American disgrace, committed suicide the following spring.

came in, Sadtler was probably acting Chief Signal officer, as the regularly assigned one, Brigadier General Joseph Mauborgne, had received his walking papers from Marshall the previous month and did not show up at his office until officially retired in October 1941.

A special cipher, used exclusively for intelligence purposes—forwarding raw intercepts—was held by the Army's Philippine intercept station MS-6, by Honolulu's MS-5, and SIS. The MS-6 station was, of course, available to Akin.

We can reconstruct with fair assurance of accuracy what took place: When Sadtler learned that General Gerow, chief of Army War Plans, and Marshall had refused to send a translation of the bomb plot message to MacArthur and Short, and that Turner and Stark had done the same for Admirals Hart and Kimmel, Sadtler took a calculated risk. He knew that Marshall had given strict orders that no *translations* of Japanese intercepts be sent out to the field. But Marshall had authorized the special MS-5, MS-6, SIS cipher for sending raw (undeciphered) intercepts *to* SIS. He had neglected to mention anything about sending raw intercepts *from* SIS. So Sadtler sent the raw intercept of the "bomb plot" to Akin, trusting to his imagination and initiative to pass it to the Navy's station "C," where there were facilities for deciphering it that MS-6 did not have. This clearly was the cunning mind of the veteran cryptanalist at work. Sadtler's mental telepathy paid off, as we see in Willoughby's reference to the "relay through special channels," we have mentioned earlier.

It is obvious that copies of MS-5 intercepts should have gone to Navy Station "H" (Honolulu) as routine; they could crack almost everything but "Purple." The bomb plot message, with its attendant delays, and its nontransmittal to Kimmel aroused Safford. He framed a message to Rochefort to make some such local arrangements with the Army, then took it to Rear Admiral Leigh Noyes, Director of Naval Communications, to release. "No! No! No! I am *not* going to send that message!" he told Safford. If Admiral Bloch* doesn't know what is going on out there, let him tell Rochefort to go to Colonel Powell† and make the necessary arrangements!"

Safford remonstrated: "But Admiral Bloch doesn't know what is going on out there and what is in those messages." Noyes was adamant. "I am not going to tell any district commandant how to run his job," he said.

Noyes had steadfastly refused to direct Station "H" to extend their activities to other than Japanese naval codes, surveillance over direction-finding units, and traffic analysis. Written orders of about November 1940 restricted them to those activities in that order.

* Rear Admiral Claude C. Bloch, 14th Naval District Commandant, responsible for Hawaiian naval defense.
† Colonel C. A. Powell, General Short's signal officer.

On 1 December the Tokyo–Honolulu circuit really started warming up with messages that had they been broken in time and correctly assessed and used, would most certainly have averted Pearl Harbor and greatly changed not only the course of the war, but American attitude toward it.

Starting on the first, the rising crescendo in SIS and its Navy equivalent, OP-20-G, was equalled by that in Station"H." There, Commander Rochefort's crew struggled with the 1 December unexpected change of Japanese naval call signs, usually made every six months, but this time after only one month. It was a portentious indication of imminent action *somewhere*. Even more alarming, the Japanese carriers had disappeared from the radio traffic pattern. Their suspicions could hardly have been more valid. The next day, Admiral Nagumo and his Pearl Harbor Attack Force received the message, "NIITAKA-YAMA NOBORE."*

That same day, the second, Consul Kita in Honolulu received instructions to burn all codes other than PA-K2 and LA. This put Rochefort in something of a bind. Without reference to Washington, he had begun working on some of the stuff handed over by RCA to Mayfield, it now being RCA's month to transmit Kita's traffic. But PA-K2 hadn't been in use for some time and it took awhile for Rochefort's people to make sense of it, although long since broken.

Meanwhile, again dated the second, a real whinger came in from Tokyo for Ensign Yoshikawa:

> IN VIEW OF THE PRESENT SITUATION, THE PRESENCE IN PORT OF WARSHIPS, AIRPLANE CARRIERS, AND CRUISERS IS OF UTMOST IMPORTANCE. HEREAFTER, TO THE UTMOST OF YOUR ABILITY, LET ME KNOW DAY BY DAY. WIRE ME IN EACH CASE WHETHER OR NOT THERE ARE ANY OBSERVATION BALLOONS ABOVE PEARL HARBOR OR IF THERE ARE ANY INDICATIONS THEY WILL BE SENT UP. ALSO ADVISE ME WHETHER OR NOT THE WARSHIPS ARE PROVIDED WITH ANTI-MINE NETS.

Alas! This vital message that not even War Plans Director Rear Admiral Kelly Turner† could have ignored, was not received in Washington until 23 December and was not broken until the thirtieth. It had come by mail, as George Marshall, with a king-sized fear of compromise, had forbidden the reincipherment of any but the most important Japanese intercepts and the immediate forwarding of them from the field, unbroken, to Washington by radio.

---

* "Climb Mount Niitaka," meaning, "Attack as planned on 8 December." Mt. Niitaka, on Taiwan, was the highest mountain in the Japanese Empire.

† On 6 December, Navy Secretary Knox inquired at the daily top level meeting: "Gentlemen, are they going to hit us?" Turner's reply was, "No, Mr. Secretary. They are going to hit the British. They are not ready for us yet."[5]

One of the first PA-K2 messages to go out from Kita/Yoshikawa subsequently raised a storm in the JCC investigation. It covered a set of signals developed by an Axis spy, Otto Kuhn, shipped out from Germany after an unfortunate contretemps over his daughter Ruth, who had become Goebbels' mistress at sixteen. By use of bonfires, or lights in certain houses, or pennants on small boats, or fake want ads via a Honolulu radio station, an offshore submarine or radio-equipped fishing sampan could relay to Nagumo's Attack Force the number of battleships and carriers present. Ominously, the signaling schedule ended as of 6 December.

Intercepted by the Army's station MS-7 at Ft. Hunt, Virginia, this message had been sufficiently clarified by noon on 6 December to fascinate a newly appointed Japanese translator in Navy's shop. Although there was no provision for overtime pay, she stayed on after lunch, trying to interest others in her hunch. Unfortunately, with the approaching weekend and preoccupation with a series of apparently highly important "purple" messages then coming in, the message lay unheeded until Monday morning, 8 December.

A 6 December Honolulu to Tokyo message was another clincher. It covered in detail the barrage balloon situation and wound up with,

```
    I IMAGINE THAT IN ALL PROBABILITY THERE IS CON-
SIDERABLE OPPORTUNITY LEFT TO TAKE ADVANTAGE OF A
SURPRISE ATTACK AGAINST THESE PLACES [PEARL HARBOR
AND AIRFIELDS IN VICINITY]. IN MY OPINION THE BATTLE-
SHIPS DO NOT HAVE TORPEDO NETS....
```

It, too, was translated on Monday the eighth.

Thus ended "the week that was." The "how" and "why" of it will be developed in a later chapter.

In October 1941, Soviet agent Richard Sorge brought off one of the greatest espionage coups of all time. As a German "press correspondent" in Tokyo, he had made himself the intimate confidant of German ambassador Eugene Ott and of high Japanese government officials. Shortly before he was unmasked and liquidated, he was able to tell his Moscow masters by clandestine radio that the Japanese definitely had decided to strike southward and not at Siberia. The desperately pressed Soviets, with the Germans knocking on the gates of Moscow, were thus free to withdraw large forces from the Far East that turned the tide. Had this not been done, it is highly likely Moscow would have been taken, the USSR would have collapsed, and as Japan was counting on, the Siberian plum would have fallen into Nippon's yard with no effort on her part. The south's oil, rice, tin, rubber, quinine—over half the world's supply in some of these categories—loomed more fetchingly than the barren wastes of Siberia, which they would get automatically anyway. One man, Richard Sorge, thus possibly had sealed the fate of two empires—the Japanese and the Hitlerite.

On the seventeenth of October, Premier Prince Konoye, a moderate, vainly having tried to persuade Roosevelt to meet him in either Alaska or Hawaii, had to admit failure in achieving a *modus vivendi* with the United States and was replaced by hard-lining General Hideki Tojo. This marked the end of any real hope for détente and set the stage for inevitable war.

The shape of that war, as far as U.S. Far East forces were concerned, could have been plotted with fair certainty in that same October. On the twenty-third, Admiral Hart wrote a letter to General MacArthur on the subject of air operations and joint planning. In the case of Army aircraft operating over water, Admiral Hart suggested that for the sake of mutual safety and optimum results, the Army aircraft, while in the vicinity of Navy ships, should fall under Navy operational control. MacArthur's long reply was two weeks in gestation and lowered the boom with a thud. In part, it said:

Dear Admiral Hart,

I have carefully considered your letter . . . embodying the suggestion of Naval control of Army Air Forces operating against an enemy who is over the water. I find the proposal entirely objectionable. It is possible that under extraordinary conditions elements of an Army Air Force in support of a Fleet might advantageously operate under temporary Naval direction, but in this sense, the term "Fleet" cannot be applied to the two cruisers and the division [*sic*] of destroyers that comprise the combat surface elements of your command. This is especially striking when judged in comparison either with the potential enemy naval forces in the Western Pacific or with the Air Force of this Command which is rapidly being built up to an initial strength of 170 heavy bombers and 86 light bombers, with pursuit in proportion. It would be manifestly illogical to assign for control or tactical command such a powerful Army air striking force to an element of such combat inferiority as your command. . . .

If bombing operations should be undertaken by the Army against objectives situated over-sea, you would of course be informed and consulted if available, but if you intend to convey the thought that such a mission could not be undertaken without your concurrence, the point is untenable.

/s/ Douglas MacArthur

The friendship, thus delicately nurtured, was not warmed by Hart's needling of the Commanding General over his wearing a World War I wound stripe. He had qualified for the honor through suffering burns on some tender parts of his anatomy, achieved by sitting in a puddle of mustard gas. The issue had been a sensitive one at the time and even more so later. But "Doug" managed to get in his licks, too. Hart lived in the Manila Hotel, under MacArthur's magnificent penthouse. On one occasion, MacArthur had received a message telling of forthcoming substantial air reinforcements, with instructions to pass the word to the Navy. Having had Mrs. MacArthur telephone first to insure Hart's presence, Douglas trotted down in his bathrobe, his first appearance in Hart's modest digs. "When you get yourself something like *this*, Tommy," smiled Doug, as Hart digested the message, "you might manage to qualify for the big league."

Thus did one sharpen one's teeth on one's friend, the better, presumably, to cope with the enemy.

Aboard the *Lanikai*, of course, it was an entirely different ball game. The state of affairs on 8 December 1941 found us poorly equipped to cope with anything.

Chapter 4

The USS *Lanikai,* a month before Pearl Harbor, did not exist as such. No one had ever heard of her. Yet the events which were to send her off on a unique adventure were the subjects of headlines—or top secret documents—in high places half around the world. While her scratch crew still stowed rice and cans of green paint in preparation for the voyage "south," it is well to examine the events which brought the ship into being.

5 November Unknown, of course, to the Americans, a Japanese Combined Fleet operation order directed war preparations to be completed by early December.

A memorandum from Marshall and Stark warned the President the U.S. Pacific Fleet was inferior to Japan's fleet and could not take the offensive.

7 November Stark wrote to Hart that although the Navy was already at war in the Atlantic, the country didn't seem to realize it and was apathetic.

10 November Churchill assured Roosevelt that in case of war between Japan and the United States, a British declaration would follow "within the hour."

17 November Ambassador Grew, in Tokyo, warned Washington "to guard against the probability of Japanese exploiting every possible tactical advantage such as surprise."

18 November Maxwell D. Hamilton, chief of the State Department's Far Eastern Division, and known to some as "Slapsy Maxie," came up with the novel idea of giving Japan the funds to buy all or part of New Guinea, in exchange for Japanese merchant or warships.[6]

19 November The State Department warned United States citizens in the Far East to get out.

21 November Things looked black to Secretary of State Cordell Hull, but the day brightened somewhat by Kurusu's telling him Japan would not necessarily be bound by the terms of the Tripartite Pact with Italy and Germany.

The Pearl Harbor Attack Force assembled in Hitokappu Bay, Kurile Islands.

22 November Roosevelt suggested a *modus vivendi** to last six months, having already been sounded out by Ambassador Nomura on the subject on the tenth.

The Chinese were bitterly opposed to *any* appeasement of or agreement with the Japanese, seconded by the British and Australians. The Dutch were in favor of *détente*. Actually, these countries were deeply disturbed over what the United States as senior partner might have been maneuvering them into. They had been told very little of what was going on and felt they might well find themselves far out on the end of a shaky limb, ready for a bone-shattering drop to earth.

An intercepted message to the Japanese ambassadors Kurusu and Nomura revealed that the previous deadline of the twenty-fifth had been extended to midnight the twenty-ninth, after which there was absolutely no possibility of an extension and "things are automatically going to happen."

24 November United States forces occupied Dutch Guiana.

All top U.S. military commands were alerted that the chances of a favorable turn in negotiations were very doubtful and that a "surprise aggressive movement in any direction including attack on the Philippines and Guam is a possibility."

25 November The War Council, Roosevelt, Hull, Stimson, Knox, Marshall and Stark, met for a long discussion. Stimson, the meticulous diarist, noted that Roosevelt felt the attack might come as soon as 1 December, "for the Japanese are notorious for making an attack without warning, and the question is what we should do. *The question was how we should maneuver them into firing the first shot without too much danger to ourselves.*" [Italics supplied.] The *modus vivendi*'s final terms were smoothed out. The whole show left Stark up the air. Somewhat distractedly, he wrote Kimmel:

> I won't go into the pros and cons of what the United States may do. I will be damned if I know. I wish I did. The only thing I know is that we may do most anything and that's the only thing I'm prepared for; or we may do nothing—I think it is more likely to be "anything."

---

* Roosevelt's 17 November memo to Hull:
1. United States to resume economic relations. Some oil and rice now, more later.
2. Japan to send no more troops to Indo-China, Manchuria, or any place to the south, such as Malaya, Thailand or the Netherlands Indies.
3. Japan to agree not to invoke the Tripartite Pact, even if the United States gets into the European war.
4. The United States to *introduce* Japanese to Chinese, to talk things over, but United States to take no part in the conversations.

It was a sorry position in which the Commander in Chief of the United States armed forces had left his senior naval subordinate.

A very large Japanese expedition was spotted at sea below Taiwan, moving south.

26 November This was the day of decision on both sides of the Pacific.

An intercept from Hanoi to Tokyo, dated the twenty-fifth, ominously warned that, "No doubt the Cabinet will make a decision between peace and war within the next day."

There was a parade of worried diplomats in and out of the State Department and White House. The Chinese ambassador, along with Chiang Kai-shek's influential, rich, trouble-shooter T.V. Soong (Mme. Chiang's brother), called on Roosevelt, bitterly protesting the proposed *modus vivendi* and threatening that it would wreck Chinese will to continue resistance. Ignoring all normal protocol and lines of diplomatic communication, the Chinese had been contacting senators, bankers, and other private citizens in their campaign to promote support of Chiang.

A concerned Roosevelt next conferred with Hull.

Secretary Stimson somehow had missed personal participation in this three-ring circus, but it was he who tossed the bombshell that made the day a milestone in history. Telephoning Roosevelt the news of the Japanese force headed south, he came very nearly being blasted loose from his handset. The President "fairly blew up—jumped into the air," Stimson records. "Utter lack of good faith. It changes the whole situation!" the President angrily shouted. To hell with any *modus vivendi!* It was out the window.

Hull had called in his Far Eastern experts for a complete reappraisal before inviting Kurusu and Nomura over at tea time. The latter two no doubt happily anticipated good news on the *modus vivendi*. But the tea was bitter. Hull handed them what variously has been called a peace proposal, an offer for further negotiations, or a *modified modus vivendi*. The utterly dumbfounded Japanese called it what it was: an insulting ultimatum. There was a heated two-hour discussion, during which the Japanese said it would be useless to send such a thing to Tokyo. In their message doing just that, the American purple machine operators at once were able to read that the two envoys felt negotiations were a closed issue and that the United States could be expected to occupy forthwith the Netherlands East Indies, as they recently had Iceland and Dutch Guiana.

Stimson had got wind that something big was going on and telephoned Hull in the morning of the twenty-seventh to find out what it was. "I have washed my hands of it!" said Hull. "It is now in the hands of you and Knox—the Army and the Navy." Breathlessly telephoning the President, Stimson had the terrific news confirmed.

That same morning, the war warnings that have been a matter of so much dispute went out to the major field commanders.* The Army message contained a phrase missing from the Navy warning: "If hostilities cannot, repeat cannot, be avoided, the United States desires that Japan commit the first overt act." This was inserted on direct order to Stimson by the President, whose sensitive political nerve ends reminded him that even after the recent German attacks on the destroyers *Greer* and *Kearney* and the sinking of the *Reuben James* with heavy loss of life, the American public was stone cold to any idea of going to war with *anybody*. It would take something really horrendous on Japan's part to give FDR the slightest hope of getting a declaration of war out of Congress. *And a declaration of war he must have!*

On 3 August 1941, the President left New London, Connecticut, in his yacht, *Potomac*, pains being taken to give the appearance of a fishing holiday. Transferred secretly at sea to the cruiser *Augusta*, he arrived in Argentia, Newfoundland, for his first face-to-face meeting with Winston Churchill, also on a fishing expedition and a desperately urgent one. Britain was broke. Lone ally Russia was reeling backward. It was 1917 all over again.

What Roosevelt promised Churchill in private over the nuts and wine probably never will be known precisely. Of this meeting, Churchill spoke in the House of Commons in January 1942: "The probability since the Atlantic Conference, at which I discussed these matters with President Roosevelt, that the United States, even if not herself attacked, would come into the war in the Far East and thus make the final victory assured, seemed to allay some of these anxieties, and that expectation has not been falsified by events."

Senator Arthur Vandenberg, senior member of the Senate Foreign Relations Committee, first heard of his government's secret commitments to Britain via the above ponderous Churchillian rhetoric, weeks after the commitment had been executed. What Vandenberg *ex post facto* learned was that if Japan attacked the British or Dutch in the Far East, the United States was slated for war with Japan *whether* or *not* Japan attacked the United States. But of this, the Congress, the general public and the U.S. Navy's fleet commanders never had been given an inkling. Admiral Kimmel, whose fleet was intimately committed through War Plan 46, found out about it well after Pearl Harbor. Admiral Hart, Commander in Chief Asiatic, whose ships were committed in direct and instant support of the British at Singapore, first discovered Roosevelt's secret promise accidentally, verbally and informally from Vice Admiral Tom Phillips on 5 December. On the sixth, Hart received startling con-

* See Appendix.

firmation from Captain J. M. Creighton, U.S. Naval Observer at Singapore. It was almost verbatim with London's instructions to Air Chief Marshal Brooke-Popham, CinC Malaya, and read in part: "We have now received assurance of American armed support in cases as follows: (A) We are obliged execute our plans to forestall Japs landing Isthmus of Kra or take action in reply to Nips invasion of any part of Siam. (B) If Dutch Indies are attacked and we go to their defense. (C) If Japs attack us [British]. Therefore, without reference to London put plan in action (first) if you have good information Jap expedition advancing with the apparent intention of landing in Kra; (second) if the Nips violate any part of Thailand. . . ."

We see from part (C) that the United States was committed to enter the war in the Far East *even though the British fired the first shot!*

The President's dilemma now becomes clearly apparent: The Japanese were about to attack the British and Dutch, which was known in Washington from intercepts of Japanese messages. Or perhaps the British would attack the Japanese, as their London instructions allowed. Washington also knew that Japan included the United States as a *possible* but not *sure* combatant. But even though the Japanese might not immediately attack the United States—"fire the first shot"—Roosevelt had obligated the United States to go to immediate British and Dutch assistance, regardless of *who* started it. This promise was of course made without benefit of constitutional legitimacy. Had Congress or the general public got wind of it, there would have been hell to pay. It is clearly evident then, why it was *absolutely necessary* to "maneuver Japan into firing the first shot without too much danger to ourselves," get Roosevelt off the hook, and raise an outburst of popular enthusiasm in the best tradition of *Remember the Maine!* at best, or at very least, legally justify immediate armed aid to Britain in the Far East.

Returning to the chronological sequence, we find that on the twenty-seventh, Washington's die having been cast for war, all hands were commencing to have second, more sober thoughts. The British, toward whose property the Japanese were advancing, the Australians, and the Dutch were all deeply disturbed at the turn of events. But Hull and undersecretary Welles tartly let them know that it was their shilly-shallying in not offering advice and coordinated support sooner that had led to the United States taking some definitive action. As long as they hadn't *put* up, then *shut* up and get busy battening down hatches.

One dissident, Dr. Stanley K. Hornbeck, a top wheel in State's Far East Division, was willing to place bets: 5 to 1 against war before 15 December; 3 to 1 by 15 January, and even money only by 1 March. One hopes the good doctor's luck with the ponies was better than in prognosticating D-day for the war he had done a good bit to bring on.

U.S. Army

*General Douglas MacArthur, commander of all forces in the
Philippine Islands, stops to talk with Major General Jonathan
Wainwright, commander of the Philippine Division, 10 October 1941*

The National Archives

*Well might Winston Churchill look smug at Argentia, New-
foundland, August 1941. President Roosevelt, left, had just promised
him American aid in the Far East in the event of a Japanese attack
on the British and a continuance of anti-Axis incidents in the
Atlantic. Under Secretary of State Sumner Welles stands in the
background. Commander in Chief, Atlantic Fleet, Ernest King and
Chief of Staff George Marshall are at right.*

28 November   Having been handed the baton by Hull the day before, Stimson was itching to crack somebody over the head with it. "Let's start right now!" he recommended to the President, suggesting MacArthur bomb the Japanese task forces at sea near the Philippines. Stimson had never forgiven the Japanese for humiliating him in 1931, when as Hoover's secretary of state he had tried unsuccessfully to reverse the Japanese occupation of Manchuria without the force to turn the trick. His efforts to rally international support, which had caused Japan to leave the League of Nations, had earned him the soubriquet, "Wrong Horse Harry."

28 November momentously continued.   The War Cabinet met at noon and discussed a situation which imposed a mammoth dilemma: a major Japanese expedition was headed for territory not only *not* American, but geographically exceedingly remote from the United States and all her interests. Stimson, as usual, recorded the gist of the proceedings: How could FDR "insure the support of the American people for a decision to fight Japan? Would the American people be willing to fight for Singapore and Bandoeng? It was the concensus that the present move completely changed the situation. . . . It was now the opinion of everyone that *if this expedition was allowed to get around the southern point of Indo-China and to go off and land in the Gulf of Siam . . . it would be a terrific blow . . . It was the concensus of everybody that this must not be allowed . . .* [emphasis supplied] . . . that if the Japanese got into the Isthmus of Kra, the British would fight. It was also agreed that if the British fought, we would have to fight." There was considerable discussion about the President's sending a personal message to Hirohito, and some chat about the USS *Panay* incident.*

General Short, Army commander in Hawaii, drew Admiral Kimmel's attention to that part of the Army war warning (not included in the Navy one) desiring "that Japan commit the first overt act." Notwithstanding, Kimmel sent off Task Force 8, under Vice Admiral William Halsey, to Wake Island with a load of aircraft. His orders were to shoot down anything obstructing him.

A Tokyo intercept told Ambassador Kurusu to keep talking, even though the American note was a "humiliating proposal."

Lord Halifax, British ambassador, anxiously inquired of Welles if the negotiations had really broken off. His government was "greatly excited," as was the Australian, which offered a try at mediation. But Hull brushed off their Minister Casey with the news that "the diplomatic stage is over."

The President's agonizing dilemma was compounded by the translation of a 19 November message transmitting the "Winds Code" to

---

* Yangtze River gunboat sunk on 12 December 1937, which caused worldwide furor at Japanese aggressiveness and disregard of rights of foreigners in China.

Japanese embassies. The key phrase would be sent out in plain Japanese at the beginning and end of news broadcasts after the definite decision was made on who would be the enemy:

United States: *higashi no kaze, ame*—east wind, rain
USSR: *kita no kaze, kumori*—north wind, cloudy
U.K., N.E.I.: *nishi no kaze, hare*—west wind, clear

This clearly indicated options. Admiral Richmond Kelly Turner, Navy War Plans director, who had usurped ONI's prerogatives in making intelligence estimates, thought until almost the very last the wind would be northerly.*

On 16 October, Admiral Ingersoll released CNO despatch 162203 to the CinC's Atlantic, Pacific and Asiatic Fleets. There is no doubt that Turner originated it. His initial is at the side and his telephone extension at the top. In the 1972 recollection of Admiral Royal Ingersoll, who in 1941 was assistant CNO, he feels it logical and probable that Turner originated it. Either CNO Stark or Ingersoll are the only possible ones who could have made the pencil changes toning down the original draft. They are indicated below:

THE RESIGNATION OF THE JAPANESE CABINET HAS CREATED
A GRAVE SITUATION X IF A NEW CABINET IS FORMED IT
WILL PROBABLY BE STRONGLY NATIONALISTIC AND ANTI
AMERICAN X IF THE KONOYE CABINET REMAINS THE EFFECT
WILL BE THAT IT WILL OPERATE UNDER A NEW MANDATE
WHICH WILL NOT INCLUDE RAPPROCHEMENT WITH THE US X
IN EITHER CASE HOSTILITIES BETWEEN JAPAN AND RUSSIA
        a strong possibility
ARE ~~EXPECTED SOON~~ X SINCE THE US AND BRITAIN ARE HELD
RESPONSIBLE BY JAPAN FOR HER PRESENT DESPERATE SITUA-
        also
TION THERE IS / A DISTINCT POSSIBILITY THAT JAPAN MAY
ATTACK THESE TWO POWERS OR ~~MAY SEIZE BORNEO OIL~~
~~FIELDS~~ X IN VIEW OF THESE POSSIBILITIES YOU WILL TAKE
DUE PRECAUTIONS INCLUDING SUCH PREPARATORY DEPLOY-
MENTS AS WILL NOT DISCLOSE STRATEGIC INTENTION NOR
CONSTITUTE PROVOCATIVE ACTIONS AGAINST JAPAN . . .

The "grave situation" was brought about by Washington's failure to support Konoye by Roosevelt's refusal to meet him in Hawaii or Alaska for a "cooling off" meeting. Thus, Konoye was replaced by Tojo, who far from being the fire-eater Turner suggests, was chosen as the only man it was felt could restrain the rambunctious Japanese Army.

It should be remembered that it was in October that the magnificent Soviet spy Richard Sorge had been arrested in Tokyo just after

* In 1936, commanding the cruiser *Astoria*, Turner had taken the ashes of Japanese ambassador Saito from Annapolis to Tokyo. There the grateful Japanese tendered him their thanks, high honors and a litter of Japanese poodles. The whole thing had inspired Turner to look into matters Japanese more fully, so that by 1941, he considered himself an authority on the country and its intentions.

advising the Fourth Bureau at Moscow that the Japanese would move southward, thus affording Stalin his God-given chance of moving masses of his cold weather Siberian troops to the west to save Moscow. There is no record of Stalin's having passed this word to the Americans.

Instead of the hard-boiled posture expected of Tojo, he continued to press for a solution at the admonition of the Emperor, and it was Tojo who proffered the *modus vivendi* which was rejected by Roosevelt and Hull, who countered with what the Japanese considered an insulting ultimatum. It must be remembered that the Pearl Harbor Attack Force was subject to recall up until almost the last minute before launching the planes, had any *real modus vivendi* been arrived at.

Returning to the "winds" again, suppose they should be westerly and clear only? Then America's potential allies would be knocked off in detail, while the United States sat on its ditty box, to be taken care of later at the Axis' leisure.

To momentarily escape the pressure, the President left for a short holiday at Warm Springs, Georgia.

29 November An intercept from the Japanese ambassador in Bangkok to Tokyo suggested a neat way to lure the *British* into firing that first shot: force them to attack the Thai near Singora as a counter move to a Japanese landing at Kota Bharu. The Thai would then request Japanese aid. *Some* slant eye must have been reading the British mind. Or mail. This sequence is precisely what the British had considered, and as a result of our secret commitments under Rainbow 5, would have morally but unconstitutionally dragged the United States in. As for the Americans, their diplomatic codes were known to be so wholly insecure that until State had been furnished machine ciphers, FDR used Navy crypto systems to communicate with his London, Moscow, and Paris ambassadors.*

---

* By August 1941, the Germans had broken several top U.S. State Department codes. In the same month, the Italians clandestinely got a copy of the Black Code, a relatively new U.S. military attaché system that allowed the Axis to read the American messages from Moscow, and even more vitally, the very long dispatches of our military attaché in Egypt. These described in detail the logistics and planned operations of British forces in North Africa which in effect provided Desert Fox Erwin Rommel a seat at the British High command conference table.

During 1942, long messages from FDR to Stalin via the U.S. naval attaché sometimes contained garbles that took all night to solve. In a day or two, the reply would be back from the Kremlin for encipherment and transmission to Washington. This not only saved the Soviets heavy cable tolls, but gave them the plain language of both incoming and outgoing messages to match the cipher messages in the telegraph office. This provided the Soviet "cryppies" a great opportunity denied us. The one-way street covered not only the Kremlin-FDR traffic, but the frequent and flowery messages of congratulations and good wishes on various national holidays, victories and birthdays.

Also on the twenty-ninth, a sick and worried old Hull made a long telephone call to the President in Georgia, urging his immediate return. Something *must* be done immediately about that Jap force headed west.

30 November Panicky British, Dutch and Australians urged Washington to try to delay hostilities.

1 December The Japanese cabinet secretly decided on war.

A 30 November intercept from Tokyo to Berlin and Rome asked them to declare war on the United States as soon as the conflict began.

An intercepted Tokyo message instructed their diplomats in London, Hongkong, Singapore, and Manila to destroy their code machines.

The Japanese envoys, in the dark over Tokyo's plans, made one more appeal to an unreceptive Hull for an understanding—perhaps a second level meeting at Hawaii—Henry Wallace or Harry Hopkins versus Prince Konoye or Viscount Ishii.

At approximately 11:45 A.M. Roosevelt arrived at the White House. Hull was already there. Stark arrived at 12:50. Admiral Leahy, the President's chief of staff, undoubtedly would have been on hand, too, but he was on a trip to Europe. Stark, leaving at 1:25, overstayed the President's lunchtime by 25 minutes. As he was leaving, presidential special assistant and alter ego, chronic invalid Harry Hopkins, drove in from the old downtown Naval Hospital for a belated lunch and a post mortem on the conference. Whatever went on obviously was far too hot for a telephone conversation, so Hopkins must be dragged from his hospital bed. There is no record of the proceedings. "It was the President's policy not to have a transcript made at such a conference," the Roosevelt Hyde Park Library director wrote me. Hull's and Stark's files are equally bare.

Following events chronologically again, the blow-off point seemed close.

2 December A Tokyo intercept directed their Washington embassy to destroy all secret documents and all copies of all codes except one copy of each of two specified codes.

The fatal day was set in Tokyo in an Imperial order, extremely closely held. Washington, of course, was ignorant of it:

THE HOSTILE ACTIONS AGAINST THE UNITED STATES SHALL
BE COMMENCED ON 8 DECEMBER

3 December Both Lieutenant Commander Arthur McCollum, head of ONI's Far Eastern Branch, and Commander Lawrence Safford, cryptographic and code security chief, could see from the intercepts that war was so imminent that Admiral Kimmel *must* be given a definite warning.

McCollum had worked up what later was proved to be a highly accurate, two-and-a-half page, single-spaced memorandum covering the entire Japanese situation over the preceding two months. On 1 December, he recited it before Admiral Stark and most of his assembled principal staff officers. McCollum then boiled his estimate down to a dispatch summary and was directed by his boss, Admiral Wilkinson, to take it to Admiral Turner for his coordination and release. The latter, in McCollum's words, "so amended the dispatch as to make it worthless,"[7] saying that if he still wanted to send it, that was the way it would go. At the same time, he showed McCollum the 27 November war warning that Kimmel's defenders later felt so inadequate and misleading. It was the first McCollum knew of its existence. McCollum took his emasculated message back to Wilkinson and there is no record of its ever having gone out.

Failing here, McCollum got Wilkinson to release a more innocuous message which might still turn the trick:

```
TO:  CINCAF, CINCPAC, COMMANDANT 14TH AND 16TH NAVAL
     DISTRICTS.

    031850 [1:30 P.M., 3 DECEMBER WASHINGTON TIME]
HIGHLY RELIABLE INFORMATION HAS BEEN RECEIVED THAT

CATEGORIC AND URGENT INSTRUCTIONS WERE SENT YESTERDAY
TO JAPANESE DIPLOMATIC AND CONSULAR POSTS AT HONGKONG

X SINGAPORE X BATAVIA X MANILA X WASHINGTON AND LON-
DON TO DESTROY MOST OF THEIR CODES AND CIPHERS AT

ONCE AND TO BURN ALL OTHER IMPORTANT CONFIDENTIAL AND
SECRET DOCUMENTS
```

Safford, with views and motivations identical with McCollum's, induced Commander Joseph Redman, Assistant Director of Naval Communications, to release one to the same addressees as McCollum's, as a tipoff to Kimmel and Hart:

```
    031855...TOKYO ONE DECEMBER ORDERED LONDON X HONG-
KONG X SINGAPORE AND MANILA TO DESTROY PURPLE MA-

CHINE XX BATAVIA MACHINE ALREADY SENT TO TOKYO XX
DECEMBER SECOND WASHINGTON ALSO DIRECTED DESTROY

PURPLE X ALL BUT ONE COPY OF OTHER SYSTEMS X AND ALL
SECRET DOCUMENTS XX BRITISH ADMIRALTY LONDON TODAY

REPORTS EMBASSY LONDON HAS COMPLIED*
```

The two messages had one immediate result: a chewing out of Wilkinson and Redman by Turner and Noyes, respectively, for releasing them. The second, Safford's, caused Admiral Kimmel to inquire, *What is 'Purple'*?

4 December This was the date the controversial "winds execute" was received. To those outside the secret, it must have seemed the Japanese weatherman really must be hitting the saké jug; it was to be simultaneously rainy and clear, with east and west winds.

---

* Safford's use of the word "PURPLE" was *not* inadvertent; he was trying to alert Kimmel to sources.

In anticipation of this receipt, confirming who would be the enemy, communications director Admiral Noyes had Lieutenant Commander Kramer prepare a set of 3 x 5-inch cards carrying the three code phrases and their meanings, for distribution to all MAGIC recipients. This was so Noyes, who loved to be able to produce ":scoops" at the various high level conferences, could personally telephone the "good news" (the top brass still seemed to hold out hopes that Japan would knuckle under to Hull's 26 November 10-point ultimatum), or the "bad news," as the case might be.

As soon as Noyes saw the teletype sheet bearing the clue that Britain, the N.E.I., and the U.S.A. were the targets, he began telephoning around. Lieutenant Colonel R. F. Bratton, head of the Far East Section of MID, was not satisfied with the version he got from his boss, Colonel O. K. Sadtler, acting chief signal officer, so Sadtler called Noyes back. The latter cut him short, saying he could not find his "card," but that it meant "England." Noyes was excited and late for a conference in the CNO's office, a prime flap over the Rainbow 5 war plans leak that had appeared that morning in the *Chicago Tribune* and the *Washington Times-Herald*. An Isolationist plan to bring out the Administration's secret moves toward war, it greatly embarrassed official Washington by revealing the illegal commitments to the Dutch and British that apparently had been made. It also provided potential enemies with valuable information. The burning question was, who leaked?

In the upper echelons, the newspaper revelations overshadowed even the "winds execute." But not with Safford. He drafted several messages pertaining to communications security, the last one being taken for release to the top—Ingersoll, who let it go with Turner's "OK." It directed Guam to destroy all classified documents except one strip system and the direction-finder code. As far as Safford was concerned, "winds execute" meant "war with the U.S." and soon. He was getting his house in order. As far as Kimmel was concerned, the three messages of the third and fourth meant that the flow of information from intercepts was once more loosed, and that he would be getting *everything*. In this, he was to be sadly mistaken.

For the Army's part, Sadtler drafted a message to General Short, warning him of the imminence of war and cautioning him not to get caught like the Russians at Port Arthur. Chief of Army War Plans, General Gerow, refused to release it. General George Marshall was a loyal subordinate of FDR's. Marshall had Gerow in his pocket, and Stark (an equally loyal man) as well, and through Stark, Turner, who needed little encouragement to sit on subordinates.

Some argue that the "winds execute" was not vital; that the universal burning of codes in Japanese embassies and consulates on potential enemy soil was a solid guarantee of intended Japanese attack on *all* the "Allies."

Actually, this was not wholly sound reasoning. If the Japanese *had* intended to delay their attack on the United States—or the Philippines —which FDR desperately feared, they had no assurances the United States would not attack *them,* in which case their secrets would have been compromised had they not been burned in advance.

The acknowledgement of completed code burning by the various Japanese missions abroad was a single word: "HARUNA." Possibly one or more Japanese establishments in British-controlled territory failed to HARUNA, because on 7 December, along with a joyful, boastful announcement of a "death-defying raid" at Pearl, Japan's station JZI added: "Allow me to make a weather broadcast at this time: west wind clear."

To Admiral Hart, war's outbreak was merely a confirmation of the war warning of 27 November, his "Purple" machine gleanings and his own good sense. Shortly put, stand by for a ram!*

5 December Admiral Phillips arrived at Manila. Admiral Hart discovered he had a *de facto* ally by virtue of FDR's August secret diplomacy, recently reconfirmed to Ambassador Lord Halifax in Washington —Hart privy to neither.

Phillips dominated the two-day conference. He spoke in detail of British plans and available forces. Their basic policy was protection of sea routes and convoys—dispersal of forces, with which Hart disagreed. There had been some progress in joint planning with the Dutch but the Aussies and New Zealanders were playing it close.

Phillips urgently requested the loan of eight of Hart's thirteen old four-pipe World War I destroyers. Considering Hart had only just informally been made aware of his new brotherly status vis-a-vis the British, he understandably refused.

General MacArthur was on hand to present the U.S. military picture, which he painted in rather more rosy colors than the facts justified. In selling their British guest, MacArthur's optimism was exceeded only by his imagination: "Admiral Hart and I operate in closest coordination. We are the oldest and dearest of friends. There is nothing that will not instantly respond to the combined, coordinated efforts of we two. Isn't that so, Tommy?" With a sharp recollection of MacArthur's recent letter of assessment of friend "Tommy's" fleet, it is understandable that Hart sat mute.

MacArthur's closing passage indicated not only a somewhat unjustified optimism, but a rare lack of appreciation of the role and capabilities of air power as already demonstrated in Poland and over the Channel:

---

* In his testimony before the JCC, Admiral Hart said: "The Asiatic Fleet had to await attack. It could not attack. So, manifestly the measure was to so dispose ourselves that when the attack came it would inflict as little damage as possible; and under the circumstances that obtained out there the only way to do so was following the principle of dispersion and concealment. That is what we did."

"We intend to fight to destruction on the shore line! The inability of an enemy to launch his air attack on these islands is our greatest security. Even with the improvized forces I now have, because of the inability of the enemy to bring not only air but mechanized and motorized elements, leaves me with a sense of complete security!"*

On the way out with Admiral Glassford, who was slightly deaf, normally somewhat aloof Hart took his arm and incredulously inquired: "Did *you* hear what he *said*, Glassford?"

"Climb Mount Niitaka"† was sent to the Pearl Harbor Attack Force.

6 December U.S. ambassador Winant in London was so excited he somewhat redundantly headed a message "triple priority and most urgent," warning Washington that: "British Admiralty reports two parties seen off Cambodia Point (*Pointe de Camau*) at 3:00 A.M. London time this morning, sailing westward toward Kra 14 hours distant in time. First party 25 transports, 6 cruisers, 10 destroyers. Second party 10 transports, 2 cruisers, 10 destroyers." This was 11:00 A.M. Manila time. When Tom Phillips got the news there at tea hour, Hart suggested that if he wanted to beat the Japanese to Malaya he had better get cracking, so shortly after 6:00 P.M he jumped in his seaplane and headed for Singapore. Hart had found Phillips his kind of man, to the point of saying he would be entirely content to serve under him if the contingency arose and hoped his considerable seniority would not stand in the way. But in their cosigned message to London and Washington‡ the gist was merely that they agreed agreement was necessary. It reflected nothing more than a joint readiness to counter such moves as the Japanese might make. As to *how*, jointly, there was not a clue. The message reached Washington at 11:00 P.M. the sixth, but War Plans director Admiral Turner didn't see it until too late the next day to rectify the policy vacuum in which Hart was forced to work.

The ABDA (America-British-Dutch-Australia) team was a paper lineup with never a single practice scrimmage, no signals (literally and figuratively), no planned plays and only sandlot gear. On the opposite bench glowered the best-equipped, best-coordinated outfit of the century, honed to a peak of perfection and readiness by years of rigorous training and discipline that only a Japanese would have sustained.

Mystification over Phillips' claim to U.S. support, corroborated by Captain Creighton's Singapore message, prompted Hart to try to pry out of Washington where he stood: "070645 LEARN FROM SINGA-

---

* On 8 December, 108 twin-engined bombers and 84 Zero fighters all but wiped out MacArthur's air force on the ground. By 23 December, Japanese tanks and motorized artillery were rumbling down the paved road from Lingayen Gulf toward Manila.
† "Carry out the planned attack on Pearl."
‡ See Appendix.

PORE WE HAVE ASSURED BRITAIN ARMED SUPPORT UNDER THREE OR FOUR EVENTUALITIES. HAVE RECEIVED NO CORRESPONDING INSTRUCTIONS FROM YOU." "Uncle Tommy" might just as well have saved his electricity; no reply ever was forthcoming.

The buzzards were coming home to roost. In early 1941, Admiral Stark had told his aide, Commander John McCrea, that "The British and Dutch should get together, making their plans and leaving us out of it. They are the main parties at interest and should shape their plans accordingly, remembering that we might not get in the war." Stark had twice tried to get the fleet brought back to the mainland from Hawaii, but the State Department objected. Hart was pulled this way and that by such conflicting views. Only a month previously Stark had instructed special messenger McCrea that, "This is extremely confidential. Tell Admiral Hart there will be no backing down. The President, the Secretary of State, Mr. Welles, and Secretary Knox do not desire war with Orange [Japan]. However, there will be no weakening in policy—nor appeasing. Pinpricks are to be avoided."

The handicaps of such an ambiguous policy were compounded by what Hart found on the scene to be an absence of any real *gung ho** spirit in his most probable allies, as revealed by his keen analyses. The Dutch and Anzacs, he wrote Stark in March 1941, were all for using their ships in guarding their own trade routes, but not going after the enemy's trade routes. "The N.E.I. Navy is no stronger than we thought," he told Stark. The Dutch Air Force was all white, but not so the Navy. Even the submarine crews were part Malay, a shocker to old submariner Hart, who had some fairly strong views on the benefits of *apartheid*. As for the Netherlands East Indies Army, he felt the Japanese could walk right through it. Nine-tenths of the men were native. Even a great many of the high officers were either Malay or Eurasian.

The British view of the Dutch was no less comforting: "Do you know how far I would trust those Dutch?" a top British officer asked Hart's chief of staff, Captain Purnell. "Just as far as I could throw a bull by his bollix." It is hardly necessary to add that the sentiments were wholly reciprocated.

Topping off this wobbly pyramid was Air Chief Marshal Brooke-Popham (known locally as "Brookham"), who looked like a "politico" to Hart, "adequate in Air subjects but is very little of an Army officer. When one tries to get him thinking of, say, a brigade in an important area, his mind runs off on moving some small squadron of obsolescent planes. He seems rather muddleheaded . . . clearly shows his years, 62–63, dozes off when he should not." (The British mentioned "Brookham" had contracted sleeping sickness in Africa.)

* Chinese: "work together"

At one point between dozes, the Air Marshal had come up with the bizarre observation that the Japanese were not air-minded and that his Brewster Buffaloes were better than anything the Japanese could field.

Vice Admiral Sir Geoffrey ("Windy") Layton, CinC China Station, was different. Hart liked him: "Good man . . . frank, direct, forceful." He was soon to be relieved by Vice Admiral Tom Phillips under the new title, CinC British Naval Forces Far East. If Layton had to go, thought Hart, thank God it was Phillips who took over!

Perhaps MacArthur had something in his humiliating reference to Tommy's "fleet." When Hart looked out the third story window of his Marsman Building headquarters on Manila's waterfront, naval might in sight was something less than impressive. Spotted around the bay were the seaplane tenders *Langley* and *Childs,* submarine tenders *Canopus* and *Holland* and the destroyer *John D. Ford.* With the exception of 15-year-old *Holland,* the others were prime vintage—at least 20, and *Langley,* 30. Looking through his binoculars at Cavite, nine miles across an arm of the Bay, Hart would not be much further bucked up by what he saw there: the 80-year-old destroyers *Pillsbury* and *Peary* under repair after a collision, two overhauling submarines and the submarine tender *Otus.* *

Also in the Bay were World War I minesweepers *Lark, Quail, Tanager, Finch, Whippoorwill, Bittern,* and *Pigeon,* the latter configured as a submarine rescue vessel, and the 20-year-old tankers *Pecos* and *Trinity.* Patrolling off the harbor entrance were World War I coastal gunboats *Tulsa* and *Asheville.* The only "modern" ships, if one may be so charitable as to thus classify them, were the 1928-built keelless little soup plates, the Yangtze River gunboats *Luzon* and *Oahu.* Properly speaking, none of the nineteen were effective warships in the offensive sense, although essential adjuncts to a rounded fleet. Only six of them would survive the next five months.

Also at Cavite was feeble featherweight *Lanikai,* feverishly trying to meet the President's deadline. Miraculously, she would be among the few survivors.

What did gladden professional submariner Hart's soul was the thought of those 29 fat "pig boats," two of them patrolling at sea, the others alongside one or another of the three tenders or anchored out. Only two were for the moment unavailable—under repair at Cavite.

* Commissioned 19 March and far from completion by 8 December, *Otus* was being converted from the merchantman SS *Fred Morris.* Hart had complained bitterly to Stark that she had come out loaded with 7,000 tons of the finest lubricants, destination Japan, in very special drums, over twice the usual size, costing five times the usual price.

Six of the 29 were ancient, uncomfortable World War I types, badly deteriorated and prone to breakdowns. But the others were so spanking new that final alterations and additions still were being made. It would be many months before the horrifying truth had been brought to light —not a single torpedo in that potentially powerful force was worth, in plain sailor's language, "one good goddam."* In the field of military armament, the supposedly technically superior Americans had been left far behind by the supposedly "imitative monkeys" of Japan. Radar and proximity fuses were still around the corner to help even the score.

The original war plans called for an early withdrawal of naval forces to Dutch and British bases, but MacArthur's optimism about holding indefinitely had rubbed off on Hart in spite of himself. Against the advice of that half of his staff that took a dim view of the effectiveness of the Far East Army Air Forces, Hart recommended to Washington on 27 October that he remain based at Manila and fight the inevitable war from there. With the foot-dragging that Hart wrote Stark was so characteristic of the Navy Department's business with the Far East, they dallied until 20 November in saying "NO!" By then, it was too late to carry out alternate plans and shift thousands of tons of spares, fuel, and torpedoes south.

Following the new guidelines, war's outbreak found the old light cruiser *Marblehead* well south, at Tarakan, Borneo, along with five destroyers. Destroyer tender *Black Hawk* was at Balikpapan, Borneo, with four destroyers. New light cruiser *Boise* was off Cebu, and heavy cruiser *Houston* at Iloilo, Panay, where newly appointed Commander Task Force 5, Rear Admiral William Glassford, joined her at teatime on D-Day, the eighth. By the twelfth, he was leading a motley force south as fast as the slowest ship (*Trinity*) would go—ten knots: *Boise, Holland, Otus, Isabel, Gold Star, Trinity, Pecos, Langley, Barker, John D. Ford, Pope, Paul Jones, Parrott,* and *Stewart*. Independently headed for Makassar were *Tulsa, Asheville, Lark, Whippoorwill,* and *Seadragon*. Nobody had troubled to inform the Dutch at Makassar, so they can be excused if they were a little exercised over rumors that the better part of the Japanese navy was headed their way.

Vice Admiral Tom Phillips, at Singapore, was on even leaner rations than Hart. He had his two heavy ships, *Repulse* and *Prince of Wales,* but only six destroyers. The brand new aircraft carrier HMS *Indomitable* had run aground on Jamaica en route. He optimistically

---

* One old submariner from among the top scorers felt so aggrieved 30 years later that he gave me an assessment which would probably receive a hearty, "Hear! Hear!" from many of his contemporaries: "A monopolistic torpedo station, controlled by grossly inefficient Civil Service bureaucrats, nominally commanded by weak-kneed naval officers, had provided the U.S. Navy with next to worthless torpedoes at the start of a major war for national survival."

hoped for two more battleships by 20 December, two more in six weeks, then one more later. Four heavy and 13 light cruisers had been promised him as well. The total of seven battleships was only a little fewer than a British Admiralty agenda of 22 November 1940 had recommended as a sensible spotting of the 15 Yankee battlewagons: Singapore 10, Atlantic 5, Hawaii 0. A British request for four American heavy cruisers for Singapore was turned down as too much of a loss to the Pacific Fleet and not enough to really help Singapore much.

It is interesting to speculate on what would have been the outcome had all these allocations been made and if Malaya had received the more than six hundred aircraft and three hundred tanks that Britain sent to the Soviet Union in the summer of 1941. Indeed, it is the opinion of such experts as Liddell Hart that the loss of Singapore, and with it most of the Far East, could be laid at the door of German Field Marshal Rommel and Churchill. The latter was obsessed with clearing North Africa, where all British resources went that might have gone to the Far East in those four months of grace during the summer of 1941.

The weekend of 6–7 December 1941 would bring some relief from the crisis atmosphere for a group of Asiatic Fleet staff officers. They were going over to Bataan to hunt wild boar. "Be back before Sunday night!" warned Hart. "The bubble will burst any time after that."

About 3:30 A.M. Monday, 8 December 1941, a radioman rushed in to the staff duty officer, Lieutenant Colonel William T. Clement, USMC. The message he brought was short and to the point: "AIR RAID ON PEARL HARBOR." The operator had recognized in the distinctive keying of the hand-sent message the radio "fist" of an old friend at Pearl Harbor. It was a solid guarantee that the rest of the transmission, "THIS IS NOT A DRILL," was authentic.

Chapter 5

Aboard the USS *Lanikai,* the first day of World War II was very much like the last day of peace that preceded it. At least, we had survived so far, as the journal for 8 December 1941 indicated:

> At 0615 got underway in accordance with orders to return to Manila, feeling very glad to be alive. A delay of several days [in war's outbreak] would have meant the sure loss of the ship. Notified the crew a state of war existed with Japan. Hoisted foresail, jib staysail, and jib. Tested machine gun battery.

The opening attacks of the war came as surprises, but not the war itself. For weeks there had been a partial blackout, dimmed street lights and doused neon signs. Everybody "knew" there were Japanese spies and saboteurs about. Strange planes had droned at high altitude over coastal northern and western Luzon for the past week. Vigilantes patrolled the streets in a country where private firearms were used in the Latin way—loosely, exuberantly, and very often fatally. It was not wise to roam around darkened streets at late hours.

Individual reactions were varied, but in many minds that one question, "When will it start?" had been given a definite answer by the Japanese. Now we knew.

Ensign George Pollak, a fellow passenger to the Far East with me in the SS *President Harrison* in August 1941, was bunking near the Cavite Navy Yard, his new station. He had hit the sack early Sunday night, vaguely aware of people clattering in from time to time after a big night across the bay in Manila. Then there was some real commotion. Aviators who shared George's digs were "suiting up." Fixed firmly in George's mind are the words: "Pearl Harbor has been bombed. The squadron is going out." There was a small, informal ritual at the office that morning; neckties were removed and ceremoniously dropped into the wastebasket. Most of the officers present would not wear ties again for a long time;* in Japanese prison camps neckties were not *de rigueur*.

Father Clifford E. Barry Nobes, in charge at All Saints Mission, Bontoc, was at Sagada Mission, twenty miles from home. It was a special occasion, the annual baseball game between two traditional rivals.

A breathless messenger came running from the home of an American staff member. "Pearl Harbor has been bombed by the Japanese!"

"Pearl Harbor? That's in Hawaii, isn't it? Come on! we have lots of time to finish the game!"

A few minutes later another boy rushed down to the field. "Japanese planes have been seen over Baguio!"

That was only a hundred miles away. It altered the picture.

"The Director of Public Safety in Manila had ordered all public gatherings to disperse! Trucks are soon to be requisitioned by the Army!" Announcements came like drumbeats, each more penetrating than the last. This was serious. If there was to be a war, the Saints wanted to be in their own home town, a long hike from Sagada.

So Sagada agreed to forfeit. All Saints jumped into their truck and set out over the winding mountain road for Bontoc, a little place so remote and rural that its name has entered the language as the ultimate in farawayness: "the boondocks."

That night, all of Bontoc's six trucks rumbled out carrying reservists to their eventual deaths on the beaches at Lingayen or the prison camps of Cabanatuan.

The seaplane tender USS *Childs* was tied up to the fuel dock at Sangley Point, near the Naval Air Station, topping off aviation gasoline tanks. The ship had been on a war alert for a week. With one 4-inch gun and four 50-caliber machine guns, she still represented a large fraction of Admiral Hart's operational sea power close at hand. Her skipper, Commander J. L. Pratt, was awakened from a sound slumber by duty officer McCarthy. He lifted himself on one elbow and tried to sweep away the cobwebs to assimilate Admiral Hart's totally in-character, terse alert: "JAPAN STARTED HOSTILITIES GOVERN YOURSELVES ACCORDINGLY."

"Captain, are you awake?" said McCarthy, as Pratt stared at the message. "Yes, Mac, I'm very much awake," he answered. It didn't take Pratt long to climb into his khakis and hurry over to headquarters, where Captain Frank D. Wagner, the "Commodore," Commander Patrol Wing 10, and several staff officers were buttoning up long-laid plans. The situation still was too vague to set up strikes against the enemy.

Admiral Husband Kimmel was not the only one in his family who didn't get a timely warning. Son Thomas Kimmel aboard the old submarine S-40, at Manila, like others there, was generally aware through

---

* Admiral William Halsey's first official act after assuming command in the Southwest Pacific was to dispense with neckties. It was strictly enforced.

the newspapers that things were deteriorating. Several submarine patrols had been established, generally north of Manila, but there were no special stand-by-for-war instructions.

With no air conditioning and scarcely more than bunk space for each, it was out of the question, health and morale-wise, for the officers to live aboard the "S" boats in port. Twenty-one additional submarines arrived on station in 1941, with tender *Otus* still under conversion at Cavite. Living space aboard tenders thus was more than tight. So in early November 1941, the "S"-boaters were set up in an apartment across the street from the Army and Navy Club, on breezy, posh Dewey Boulevard.

On the morning of Pearl Harbor, young Kimmel arose routinely, unalerted and unalarmed. On his walk to the boat landing through the club lobby, he saw a screaming headline on the bulletin board that the Japanese had bombed Pearl. Not really believing it, he proceeded down to the float to catch transportation out to his ship. Other officers on the landing shared his doubts, which were not shaken until he arrived on board and read the message that Admiral Hart had fired off five hours earlier.

In light of that 27 November Washington message, "THIS IS TO BE CONSIDERED A WAR WARNING . . . EXECUTE AN APPRO-PRIATE DEFENSIVE DEPLOYMENT . . ." the question, naturally enough, has been asked why all but two* Asiatic fleet submarines were lying doggo in Manila Bay instead of having been hurried out days before to sit in ambush along the routes of advance of the Japanese invasion forces then known to be at sea, and where. Perhaps the question has been muted because the subs, unlike the Pearl Harbor ships, were not lost in surprise attack. Actually, had they been on offensive stations at sea, their effectiveness would have been minimal through faulty torpedoes. But nobody knew that then.

The stern admonishments over weeks to commit no overt act or give the Japanese any opportunity to claim aggressive American moves undoubtedly bore some weight in Hart's decisions. Certainly he had no doubts about his chief offensive weapon. Walking *Houston*'s deck with a visiting officer one January 1941 night at Olongapo, he stopped to gaze over the rail at several submarines lying at anchor. "Isn't that a fine sight—those fine ships?" he said enthusiastically. "They will make their presence felt when the war comes!"

In the Navy, it is not only tradition—it is dogmatic doctrine—to tell a subordinate *what* to do, but not *how* to do it. In the war warning, the inclusion of that insidious word, "DEFENSIVE" infringed on both Kimmel's and Hart's independence of action in preparing themselves to meet an attack. In the business of war, "defensive" is too often a

---

* S-36 was off Lingayen; S-39 at Sorsogon Bay, Luzon.

Grasping the rail of a U.S. warship, Secretary of State Cordell Hull chats with the sailor president, Franklin D. Roosevelt. "What we have got to do, Henry," Hull had told Treasury Secretary Morgenthau on 10 December 1940, "is to get five hundred American planes to start from the Aleutian Islands and fly over Japan just once. . . . If we could only find a way to drop some bombs on Tokyo."

Secretary of the Navy Frank Knox and Admiral William A. Glassford, Jr., who was Commander Yangtze Patrol until early December 1941, then Commander Task Force 5 under Commander in Chief Asiatic Fleet, Admiral Thomas C. Hart. Glassford relieved Hart in mid-February 1942, assuming the title of Commander Naval Forces Southwest Pacific.

euphemism for "defeatist." We can only hope that in thus running against naval tradition, Admiral Turner as originator and Admiral Stark as ultimate OK'ing authority were furnishing this stultifying admonition solely as a result of Roosevelt's repeated insistence that the Japanese "fire the first shot," and get him that *casus belli* he needed so badly he could taste it.

As far as any Pacific Fleet deployment was concerned, Kimmel's only options were to remain under Oahu's protective air umbrella, such as it was, or scatter to sea; his own available two carriers had been sent off by Washington's implied orders on resupply missions to Wake and Midway, leaving his fleet naked except for his own antiaircraft guns.

When the radioman handed staff duty officer Lieutenant Colonel William T. Clement Pearl's message of the attack, Clement immediately called Admiral Hart to alert him he was coming over with a highly important communication. Hart needed no further hint as to its content. He inquired if MacArthur knew, and was assured he had been informed. On a scrap of scratch paper, Hart jotted down a brief message (see page 62) and handed it to Clement, who hot-footed the three hundred-odd yards back to naval headquarters in the Marsman Building.

That Hart's original draft in his saw-tooth squiggle was preserved for posterity is due to the remarkable performance of Marine Sergeant Joseph J. Reardon. As the situation at Manila had become more tense, and sporadic shots pinged out more frequently on the darkened streets, Reardon had been assigned to a reluctant Hart as personal bodyguard. In civilian clothes, two big pistols bulging under his jacket, the sergeant had become Hart's shadow.

About 4:00 A.M., after Hart had eaten a hasty breakfast, he joined the excited group at headquarters. Chief of Staff Captain Purnell charged off to Army Headquarters to give MacArthur's chief of staff, Sutherland, news of the attack. Reardon continued to shadow Hart until the latter departed for Java on 26 December.

On 27 September 1945, back from Japanese prison camp, Reardon wrote in part to his old charge:

> As it became apparent that the "Rock" would fall I personally destroyed the files, but in so doing there were two pieces of paper that I thought would be a nice souvenir so I placed them in my wallet. At the time of the invasion (in the interim I had been promoted to warrant officer) I commanded one of the platoons that took part in the engagement, was wounded by being shot through the abdomen by a rifle bullet and was in the hospital at the time of the surrender. The Nips stripped us of course but somehow missed my wallet and in the ensuing three years of captivity I managed to keep it concealed.

Then, after Hart had replied, expressing much interest, Reardon wrote again on 7 October, enclosing the two papers:

> . . . I held on to them prinicipally because, after being captured, I heard so many arguments, pro and con, principally among Army officers as to the time they were officially notified that the war had commenced, why they lost their planes on the ground, etc., and the arguments finally ended, as a rule, with all hands agreeing that 'they didn't get the word'. . . . [Colonel Clement] called me at about 0400, 8 December and told me to report with all the Marines available so I personally know that [the message] was written a good while before then. . . . The fact that the Admiral would like to have [the messages] more than repays me for the trouble I had to go through to hold onto them.

This little incident is just one more added to the illustrious history of the Corps that suggests why in the United States the word *Marine* is spelled with a capital *M*.

All these people at the end of the line, little and big, took war's outbreak almost casually, as a foregone conclusion. But not the man in the White House. He had sweated out that last week in an agony of apprehension that the Japanese would bypass the Americans for the time being, even though the 4 December execution of the "winds" code revealed the United States as a prospective victim.

During this trying period there occurred an intriguing *denouoment* sometimes termed the "Merle-Smith episode." Whether the message involved was delayed en route or was deceptively or accidentally "lost" for two days in Washington is not a vital matter. But the uncovering of the background of the message's inception is a key bit of evidence that two days before Pearl Harbor Roosevelt knew that the Far East war had started, through invocation of the terms of Rainbow 5 by the Dutch and Australians.

Rainbow 5 was a war plan which had grown out of staff conferences between the British, American and Canadian military-naval authorities in Washington between 29 January and 27 March 1941. In highest secrecy, the conferees had arrived at the "ABC" agreements on joint anti-Axis action. These agreements were then expanded to include the Dutch, in the Netherlands East Indies, in the "ADB" agreement. Then these two were combined as the "ABCD" agreement, from which was developed Rainbow 5, another name for United States master operating plan WPL-46. Admiral Richmond Kelly Turner's explanation of it before the Joint Congressional Committee Investigating Pearl Harbor (JCC) was that, "It was a worldwide agreement, covering all areas, land, sea and air. . . ." In writing the guidance memorandum for the Ameri-

Asiatic Fleet, Priority
Japan started hostilities
govern your selves
accordingly.

Awakened about 3:00 A.M., 8 December 1941 (2:00 P.M. Washington, D.C., time; 8:30 A.M. Pearl Harbor time, both 7 December), Admiral Thomas C. Hart scribbled this message to alert his fleet.

can conferees, Admiral Stark and General Marshall laid down the U.S. position in detail, ending up with what would have deeply interested the rank and file of the Asiatic Fleet had they known of it:

> 5 (d)　Should Japan enter the war, United States operations in the mid-Pacific and the Far East would be conducted in such a manner as to facilitate the exertion of its principal military effort in the Atlantic or navally in the Mediterranean.

The massive stickler in the resulting concrete-hard agreement, ABC-1, was that the United States Congress, which then still jealously guarded its treaty and war-making prerogatives, had no inkling of the plan's content or vast scope, or indeed of its very existence.

What in effect ABC-1 did, half a year before Pearl Harbor, was to write off United States' obligations to defend its own Far Eastern territories in favor of British interests in the Atlantic and Mediterranean, and to commit the United States to massive military and political action on her entrance into the war.

In a sense, formal entrance would simply have been acknowledgement of a status quo in the Atlantic. With the passage of the Lend-Lease Act on 11 March 1941, the United States had *de facto* entered the war against Germany. On 8 October 1941, the war entered the shooting stage when the President authorized U.S. Navy ships and aircraft to fire on

German war craft under any condition of meeting in "Hemisphere Defense Zones," so designated by executive order and embracing roughly the western half of the Atlantic.

Hitler cagily refused to take the bait by declaring war as a result of the aggressive American acts which followed, such as the USS *Kearney*'s attack on a German submarine. But of far greater importance was the fact that the American public and Congress failed to react to these incidents and steadfastly maintained a cool disinterest in entering *any* war. Clearly anticipating this state of affairs, Admiral Stark on 15 February 1941 sent Admiral Hart a message of instructions on the forthcoming Anglo-Dutch-American staff conversations at Singapore,* an extension of the Washington staff conferences that would eventually hammer out Rainbow 5. In part Stark said:

> Due to the fact that doubt exists as to whether the Congress would declare war in case of Jap aggression against any other country but the United States, your representative will express my view that any strategic arrangement of the British and Dutch which depend for their efficacy upon intervention by us would not be sound.

Reduced to plain English, Roosevelt summed this up nine months later: "We must somehow maneuver them into firing the first shot."

The JCC proceedings brought out that although the Commander in Chief of the armed forces had informally OK'd Rainbow 5, the war plan eventually thrashed out of the "ABCD" conference, he had refused to formalize it by appending his signature. This was squeezed out of Admiral Stark by Senator Ferguson, the Admiral's testimony making clear his discomfiture at putting his chief in an artful light:

> I do know the President, except officially, approved of it, although it shows he was not willing to do so officially until we got into the war. Nonetheless, I sent that plan out on April 3. . . . I told Kimmel and told Tommy—Admiral Hart—that I had read to the President my official letter of April 3 and that the President had approved it and knew I was sending it out. Therefore, I think it safe to say that the President certainly approved of it. He approved of my sending it out, although he had not officially approved it.

Thus, in the 27 November "war warning," Stark had included in his instructions to Kimmel at Pearl:

```
...EXECUTE AN APPROPRIATE DEFENSIVE DEPLOYMENT
PREPARATORY TO CARRY OUT THE TASKS ASSIGNED IN WPL-
46....
```

* Hart rushed the results of this conference to San Francisco by special air messenger. There, some nitwit put it aboard the USS *Nitro*, headed east via the Panama Canal. On hearing of this gaffe, Hart wrote Stark: "I fear that our preparations for national defense are suffering unduly from the ministrations of fools, a lot of whom are on shore."

WPL-46, Rainbow 5, had no official sanction, not even the Commander in Chief's signature. *That* would be withheld "until we got into the war," by which time Congress would be sufficiently enraged to support the necessary declaration to make Rainbow 5 legal, although they would have no idea what it contained. But Kimmel and Hart were being told to stand by to execute it. Which would come first? The execution or the legitimization? The President prayed it would be the latter. *The Japanese must fire that first shot!*

To return to Colonel van S. Merle-Smith, U.S. Military Attache in Australia—at 5:00 P.M. 4 December (3:00 A.M. 4 December Washington time), he and his assistant, First Lieutenant R. H. O'Dell, were called to the office of Air Chief Marshal Sir Charles Burnett, Chief of Staff of the Royal Australian Air Force, to hear some startling news from Commander Saom, the Dutch liaison officer: As a result of the advance of the several Japanese task forces, the Dutch government at Batavia had implemented section A-2 Rainbow 5, thus involving *all* its signatories. Australia had cooperated; joint air operations had been set in motion.

This was a matter of such grave importance that it would be the subject of an urgent meeting of the Australian War Council that evening. Merle-Smith wanted to send off an immediate message to Washington and the Pacific areas, but Burnett requested he wait. Thus, it was 11:00 A.M., 5 December Australian time, 9:00 P.M., 4 December Washington time, when Merle-Smith finally got off two messages after a delay of 17 hours. One went to MacArthur, and one to General Short at Hawaii, with a request it be re-transmitted to Washington. Records of messages received in the Philippines were of course lost. The re-transmitted copy to Washington also was "lost" until it finally surfaced officially at 7:58 P.M., 7 December, two days overdue according to a research on the time it should have taken.

It is not so important that this message, revealing that war had begun and Rainbow 5 invoked, arrived after Pearl. The *vital* aspect is that it would be naïve to assume that by 5 December this information was not in the hands of the Australian, British, and Dutch embassies in Washington, the British Foreign Office and probably the Dutch government-in-exile at London. It is certain to have been discussed at the highest level in Washington.

Thus, we see the unprecedented 5 December evening call by Lord Halifax, British ambassador, at the private residence of Secretary of State Hull. A memorandum recording the meeting makes it crystal clear that Halifax had the shattering news from Australia and was desperately seeking reassurance that the United States would stand by its Rainbow 5 commitments:

> The Ambassador called at my apartment at his request. He said
> he had a message from Eden, head of the British Foreign Office,

setting forth the British view that the time has now come for immediate cooperation with the Dutch East Indies by mutual understanding. This of course relates to the matter of defense against Japan. I expressed my appreciation.

(Initialed "C.H.")

What else did you express, good, grey, Secretary Hull? Whatever it was, it apparently was sufficient to warrant Halifax's flashing the promise to London, then to Singapore, where it dovetails with Phillips' and Captain Creighton's disclosures to an astonished Hart that he and the British were now allies in fact. Hart's incredulity resulted in his message to Stark, asking confirmation of this highly informal execution of Rainbow 5. (The plan had been sent to Hart in April by special messenger.) Hart's message was never answered. Events had caught up with it.

Roosevelt, by his personal diplomacy with Churchill and the staff agreements resulting in Rainbow 5, had put us technically at war with Japan through the action of countries over which we had no control, but "allied" countries—and with the near certain assurance that Congress would *not*, nor would the American people, support a declaration of war under any such circumstances. Oh! Those baseless, tricky Japanese! Why won't they get off that first shot?

But at last they did, and Mme. Frances Perkins, Secretary of Labor and intimate Roosevelt friend, tells us the result:

> A great change had come over the President since we had seen him on Friday.* Then he had been tense, worried, trying to be as optimistic as usual, but it was evident that he was carrying an awful burden of decision. The Navy on Friday had thought it likely it would be Singapore and the English ports if the Japanese meant business. What should the United States do in that case? I don't know whether he had decided in his own mind; he never told us; he didn't need to. But one was conscious that night of 7 December, 1941, that in spite of the terrible blow to his pride, to his faith in the Navy and its ships and to his confidence in the American Intelligence Service, and in spite of the horror that war had actually been brought to us, he had, nevertheless, a much calmer air. *His terrible moral problem had been resolved by the event.* [Emphasis supplied.][8]

You leave us with a tantalizing conundrum, "Ma" Perkins. *What* moral problem? The narrow escape from the petard on which so many rulers have been hoist in history when they have disdained to act "by and with the consent" of constitutional guidance? What else?

Yes, Pearl had solved the problem. As to what degree the body and soul of the United States had been mortgaged in Rainbow 5, the public

---

* The "bad news" from Australia should have been available in Washington on the fifth, or possibly even the fourth.

and Congress neither knew nor cared. They were too angry. The gamble of the Administration had paid off, by a combination of fair management, great good luck, and incredible Japanese stupidity in attacking Pearl.

Roosevelt's problem was not the only one solved by Japanese bombs. So was Hart's problem with MacArthur over control of the latter's airplanes when operating over water jointly occupied by U.S. warships. For all practical purposes, after lunchtime on the first day of war, MacArthur had no more airplanes to control.

How could such a thing happen?

A mixed bag of circumstances contributed to this heavy blow: underestimation of the enemy, poor planning, inadequately trained flight and ground crews, short range antiaircraft guns shooting superannuated ammunition, pure chance, and just plain flap.

Few written records survive to nail down without question who did what and when. The views put forward by the principals—MacArthur, Brigadier General Sutherland, air force commander Major General L. H. Brereton, and bomber commander Lieutenant Colonel E. L. Eubank and others, not only varied widely from one another, but in many cases later radically changed from the original versions. There was at least one person whose views were not clouded with equivocation or double talk: Major General Henry ("Hap") Arnold, chief of the U.S. Army Air Corps. Having telephoned Brereton immediately after Pearl Harbor to warn him about getting caught on the ground, he naturally enough was not living up to his nickname when he called a second time after hearing of the very disaster he had just cautioned against. "How in hell," a furious Arnold shouted over the static background of the transpacific telephone, "could an experienced airman like yourself get caught with your planes down?"

A few indisputable facts stand out of the confusion. At about 5:00 A.M., General Brereton tried to see General MacArthur to get his permission to bomb Formosa as soon as the planes could be readied. He managed to penetrate only as far as the chief of staff, Sutherland, who told him to prepare for the attack but to await MacArthur's approval before heading north.

Meanwhile, the Japanese on Formosa had been delayed in *their* takeoff by ground fog, and were suffering a first class case of jitters in expectation of American bombs raining down on *them* before they could shout *"Banzai!"* and head south.

A small, early morning enemy raid over north Luzon had alerted U.S. fields and all planes took off, the bombers without bombs, in observance of Arnold's injunction not to be caught napping on the ground. By 11:30 A.M., the "all clear" having been sounded, the bombers landed in order to arm for the raid on Formosa tentatively scheduled for late afternoon, so that withdrawal could be made under cover of darkness.

Skipper Tolley pores over the atlas, the only source of chart material.

Looking aft on the port side, from the area of the forward deckhouse.

Antiaircraft and plane crews were enjoying a routine lunch, when shortly after noon, completely without any local warning, high explosives came shrieking down from 108 twin-engined bombers, escorted by 84 Zero fighters. At Clark Field, all but one of the B-17's were lined up on the runways. The fighters were just readying for takeoff. At Iba Field, American fighters, low on gas, were circling to land.

For two hours the Japanese bombed and strafed. Obsolete 3-inch guns, shooting ammunition made as far back as 1932, lobbed shells thousands of feet short. Many of the fuses were duds. It was a sorry show. In one day of war, the U.S. Far East Air Force had been eliminated as an effective weapon, its bases smashed and over half its planes destroyed on the ground without ever having struck a blow.

Chapter 6

Japan's overwhelming success in creating an "incident" at Pearl Harbor had completely eliminated any need for the *Lanikai* to set sail for a possible meeting with hostile ships in the South China Sea. Her prime mission no longer existed. What else could she be used for?

There was some talk of fitting her with asdic gear so that she could listen for submarines. Cruising off the harbor entrance under sail, she would be noiseless except for the "ping" of her transducer. Even if she were detected, no submarine skipper in his right mind would waste a torpedo on such a piddling target. Meanwhile, she was added to the miscellaneous collection of craft in the Inshore Patrol under Captain Kenneth Hoeffel, and lay at anchor off Cavite Navy Yard awaiting developments.

A peaceful day swinging around the hook gave an opportunity to examine our surroundings with a little more care than had been possible during the madhouse period of preparation for sea. Awnings were rigged over the after deckhouse and well deck, running rigging was neatly racked up on the belaying pins, and everything made shipshape about the decks.

The steel men-of-war at the docks were busy "clearing ship"— getting rid of unnecessary combustibles. A *Lanikai* salvage party discovered half a dozen handsomely upholstered wicker chairs sitting unchaperoned on the pier. They fitted admirably atop the after deckhouse. The *Lanikai* and practically everything aboard her except engine, anchor, and chain was highly combustible anyway. Why worry about a few more sticks of tinder?

We got to know each others' names and had a start at building a ship's company from what had been a dozen and a half widely disparate people hurried aboard under heavy stress at short notice. Of the four Filipinos who had come with the ship, only the engineer, Crispin Tipay, a moon-faced, cheerful little whiz at machinery, spoke any useful

English. The old boatswain, Magtulis, rated as a coxwain in the Insular Force, and his equally venerable assistant, Belarmino, seaman first, made up for their lack of English by an uncanny ability to divine what was wanted. The "bosun" could make a picture-perfect rope splice, smell out shoal water, and predict the weather with accuracy. Belarmino soon became "Chips," through his skill at carpentry with a very few of the simplest hand-forged tools. He could give an acceptable haircut. He could start with a scrap of bacon rind and soon parlay it up through several sizes of bait fish to a whopper that would feed half the crew. When a complicated maneuver came up, such as going alongside dock— no easy trick with a twenty-foot bowsprit and associated braces sticking out like giant cat's whiskers—Belarmino took the helm, without a word from anyone.

Old Velarmino, ship's cook, face deeply seamed and hair graying, had been brought back from retirement and had forgotten most of whatever English he might have known. But not his magic with the pots and pans. When the bottled gas for the range in the tiny galley ran out, he built a wood stove from a ten-gallon oil drum and set it in a box of sand on deck. This was more like home. He served up in many forms those Philippine staples, rice and fish, or chicken when he could get it. Wrapped around a stick, like a caduceus, his bread strips gave the Americans a break from three-times-a-day rice.

The seamen were a devoted, good-natured lot. Any or all could have disappeared into the bush during the lean, hard days that were to follow, but none did. I might personally take a hand on deck, perhaps hauling in the mainsheet to come a little closer to the wind. "No, no, Keptin! *I* do eet!" an observant sailor would protest.

The three and a half bottles of whiskey found on board were contributed to "Doc" Cossette's medical locker. We had no ship's store for slop chest items a sailor needs—mending gear, matches, film, toothpaste, cigarettes and such. But with the same informality that blessed the ship in all things connected with paper work, I bought half a dozen cases of Coca Cola ashore to feed into the small cooler in the after cabin. A drinker made his check beside his name, the total to be paid back "sometime." That the next payday would be Java, two months hence, was not a matter of immediate thought or consequence. The outline for our future was very indistinct from where we stood.

The *Lanikai*'s former owner Northrup Castle, a veteran Pacific sailorman, was wholly correct in his assessment of her characteristics; she was not a lively lady. With the bluff expanse of those clumsy boxes, the forward and after deckhouses, how could she be? Schooners with sleek, fine, unencumbered hulls, such as the famous *America,* or her North Atlantic working sisters, with no topside protrusion other than a small hatch, could sail rings around *Lanikai*. But there were good reasons for her matronly shape, as I learned many years later from a veteran of half a century in sail and steam, Captain Fred K. Klebingat. In the humid, hot South Seas, who wanted to suffocate below decks? Even more importantly, there must be a "trade room," a sort of general store where natives could come aboard and view with bug-eyed wonder the piles of gaily colored cloth, machetes, fish hooks in many sizes, combs, needles, ribbons, pots and trinkets to delight the heart of the simple.

Navigation must have been "by guess and by God," as the saying goes. One old schooner skipper asked Klebingat if he had a spare *Nautical Almanac*. "Now I'll come fifteen or twenty miles closer to my destination," he happily told Klebingat on receiving the precious book. As for the natives in their big outrigger canoes, east or west was guesswork. But latitude was more exact. Their "sextant" was half a coconut bored with a ring of holes the right distance below the rim. One sighted through a hole, across the far rim at a fixed star. The instrument was leveled by half filling it with water and keeping its surface aligned with a line circling the inside of the shell.

I did not know all these things then, that first night of war, lying under the stars on a mattress inside a life raft atop the after deckhouse. I knew only that being skipper and sole officer of such a ship was an experience so exciting that sleep was slow in coming.

That day we had spent in sailing the bay, checking sails and engine. The lure of walking familiar old paths brought us to anchor not far from the Army and Navy Club. It had been ten years, almost to the day, that I had first enjoyed the magnificent winter sunset across Manila Bay from the Club lawn. The sky seemed to be on fire, in a variety of shades of rose, purple and lemon orange. For a young man basically from the temperate latitude of Maryland, it was hard to adjust to the fact that this was almost midwinter. The memories came flooding back. There had been people in summer things—men in bobtailed white mess jackets and ladies in filmy, sleeveless dresses. Swimmers splashed and shouted in the big outdoor pool. Filipino "boys," some with graying hair, hurried around, anticipating the wishes of young Navy wives fresh from Prohibition days in America. Back home, they had never tasted anything better than the foul juices concocted in Norfolk or San Pedro, variously and usually obscenely named after something to do with panthers. Now, they were imperiously demanding this or that particular brand of whisky, without the *e*. Whisky, of course, was the euphemism for scotch; "bourbon" at the Army and Navy Club in 1931 Manila was just a word in the dictionary.

Also just a word for future dictionaries was *apartheid,* but nonetheless, true to the colonial code of the British, who set the Far East social pace, no Filipino graced the Club's roster. And woe betide the ignorant young officer who bumbled in with a glowing Filipina girl on his arm, no matter how gorgeous she might be. If the freezing glances of the wives failed to get the message through, one could count on the skipper's far more direct approach over his desk next morning. Democracy in the cabarets and rooms above was one thing; in the Club, quite another.

The events of early December 1941 had wrought a great change. The club was close to deserted. The pool was empty of people. There was no waiting line in the barber shop. In the bar that could have seated a hundred people, I drank my mug of San Miguel beer alone. For those two items, beer and haircut, I still am in debt to the club, the chits long since ashes in the ruins of the original building, wrecked in 1945 in the city's recapture.

Back aboard ship, my thoughts were crowded with memories of the past, the day's happenings and concerns about the future. If I had been ready for sleep, the Japanese did not give me long to try. About 9:30 P.M., in the universal gloom ashore, flares popped out to mark the location of Nichols Field, a fighter strip near Manila. The vigilantes who had warned against agents and provocateurs were being justified. Japanese planes came roaring in overhead. The field burst into columns of flame and skyrocketing fragments, as more of MacArthur's few remaining defensive planes burned and exploded on the ground.

Cavite was not large as navy yards go, but it was essential to the functioning of the Asiatic Fleet's superannuated ships. Rear Admiral Francis W. Rockwell, commandant, 16th Naval District, and concurrently commandant of the yard, arrived on 4 November 1941. Two predecessors had been invalided out after short tours. Wives and children went home in 1940, so full attention of all hands could be concentrated on catching up with years of penny-pinching neglect which had been accentuated by the prospect of an independent Philippines in 1946. The Washington budget builders saw no sense in spending money on property about to be given away.

Lieutenant Richard K. Anderson, USN, arrived in September 1940, and had time to learn of some of the things that needed "catching up."[9] The rainy season was tapering off, allowing sunny afternoons for golf, tennis, or swimming. Yard hours were from 7:30 to 3:30 to beat the heat and spare the body. Across an arm of the bay, 45 minutes in the soft breeze, aboard the old steam mini-ferryboat *Dap-Dap*, was the gayest, cheapest, poshest gathering place for the U.S. armed services anywhere in the world, the Army and Navy Club. Farther up magnificent, palm-lined Dewey Boulevard was the Polo Club. Destroyer squadron 5 officers had organized a polo team some years before, but while the fleet was up north in China for the summer, the feed bill had mounted to the point where it was exchanged for the ponies. And that was the end of a short-lived "DesRon" mounted unit.

The Polo Club was favored by the older officers, who sometimes found the Army and Navy Club a trifle boisterous. There also gathered the gay Manila aristocracy, of new money or ancient blood. Some were considered too dark to have been acceptable at the Army and Navy Club, in the unlikely event the black-eyed senoritas would have consented to subject themselves to the less than discreet stares of young lieutenants charged with more whisky than was good for them.

Farther along, at Nichols Field fighter strip, the Carabao Club offered horseback riding on fullsize steeds imported from the United States.

It all was quite in contrast to Dick's recent four years at the Philadelphia Navy Yard. There he had helped build the battleship *Washington*, working seven days a week, from 8 A.M. until, sometimes, midnight.

Filipino labor cost 40 cents an hour. But even at that, the $4,000 allowed for a destroyer machinery overhaul didn't do much to a ship built contemporaneously with the Model T Ford. "In many instances, I kicked a hole right through the ship's side where the old plating had deteriorated," Dick recalled.

There were no permanent air lines on the repair piers for running rivet guns, chipping hammers, or drills. The Japanese had made it clear they considered any such improvements would be contrary to mutual agreement that the U.S. not strengthen Guam and the Philippines and they would refrain from the same in the mandated islands.

The only crane capable of heavy lifting was a very old coal-burning steam affair mounted on a barge that had to be towed from job to job. The crew was an able and wily lot. They had to be. Aside from the idiosyncracies of their clumsy charge, they had learned to cope with those of a former commandant's wife who complained that the smoke was spoiling her window curtains. So lifts had had to be scheduled while "la Senora Almirante," as the workmen called her after the Spanish fashion, was off to the Baguio mountains or doing the Manila shops.

The old drydock *Dewey* had been towed out via the Suez Canal shortly after American acquisition of the Philippines. She was not able to cope with the increased work load, so the only alternative was the Spanish-built marine railway nearby. Its hauling-out motor was one that General Electric probably would have prized for its museum—serial #39. The railway's incline was so steep that a destroyer had 40 feet of its keel exposed before the stern came to rest on its blocks. Old small boatman Anderson likened this to a canoe with its bow hauled up on the bank, the stern still afloat, presenting a perilous stability situation well known to any Midshipman who has taken his girl boating on the Severn at Annapolis.

No one ever dreamed of mistreating an elderly destroyer this roughly. There were no stability diagrams or calculations of bending stresses for such a problem. The first trip up was a harrowing experience for Anderson, who had made the calculations, and for the destroyer skipper. Both felt that the fragile old ship's ascent without rolling over or breaking in half justified their immediately repairing to the station club for a restorative.

Finally, carriage and ship creaked slowly back into the water. The first coat of plastic antifouling paint to be applied in the Far East shone on her underbody, increasing her speed over that with the old style coating. God knows, she needed it. The Japanese destroyers still were knots faster.

Admiral Rockwell's "home defense" forces were the odds and ends, some too small to go to sea, others too feeble to be used as real warships. Principally, they were the old coastal gunboats *Asheville* and *Tulsa,* the CinC's yacht *Isabel,* the six minesweepers, *Lark, Bittern, Quail, Whippoorwill, Finch,* and *Tanager.* China river gunboats *Oahu* and *Luzon* were added on 5 December and *Mindanao* on the tenth. Tug *Napa* and *Fisheries II,* a Philippine government yacht, brought up the rear.

On 6 December, Lieutenant J. R. Davis, a young Civil Engineer Corps officer, without authorization and on his own initiative, had slit trenches dug. But there was not nearly enough room for all hands. There simply wasn't sufficient acreage on the cramped little peninsula. Equally foresighted Admiral Hart had doggedly pushed the tunnel projects on Corregidor, including the soon-to-be vital communications space. The torpedo and spare parts tunnels on Mariveles were too late to perform their intended functions, but did serve as admirable air raid shelters.

The 28 big seaplanes of Hart's "air force," Patrol Wing 10, were not bunched wingtip to wingtip like those on Oahu, but were dispersed to Davao in the southern islands, or concealed in high grass on Laguna de Bay, a huge estuary behind Manila, or at Olongapo on the west coast, or at Sangley Point. Their tenders, *Childs, William B. Preston,* and *Heron,* were widely scattered, too. Aircraft crews had been brought to a high state of readiness and ability to identify vessels by months of flying neutrality patrol to insure that the belligerents were not using Philippine waters.

On 2 December, Hart set up a fleet organization with himself commanding Task Force 1, based on Manila Bay. In it were the 29 submarines, plus tenders *Otus, Canopus,* and *Holland,* with rescue vessel *Pigeon;* Patrol Wing 10; the six motor torpedo boats, five destroyers and the two tankers, *Pecos* and *Trinity.*

Task Force 5, under Rear Admiral William Glassford, to be based on a British or Dutch port, included cruisers *Houston* and *Marblehead,* eight destroyers and their tender, *Blackhawk.* At war's outbreak, Glassford's Task Force 5 was already steaming south. The new six-inch-gun cruiser *Boise,* eventually to be known as "the Reluctant Dragon," after her propensity for missing action, had arrived at Manila on 5 December with an Army convoy and was added to Task Force 5, as some people accused, "snatched" by Hart.

Largely blind except for *Boise's* primitive radar and lacking information or positive instructions, Glassford herded his heterogeneous little force southward. Set down in his notes is the well-justified complaint that, "Not once during the ensuing days were our feeble efforts at sea, either on the offensive or defensive, supported in the air. While lacking many things . . . we felt the lack of air support more than anything else. Granted that even though the planes had been at hand, such was the lack of mutual understanding and joint plans between the Navy and various air forces, including the U.S. Army Air Force, it is probable the sea forces would have suffered just the same."

Glassford's scanty instructions were to act at discretion and maintain radio touch with the British. His proposal to divide into three task groups—one to operate in the western area to be available to support the British at Singapore or the Dutch—was disapproved by Admiral Hart, who still was not wholly sold on surrendering control of any of his few ships to the British.

Lack of liaison seems to have been a failing not just between sea and air forces. As Task Force 5 crawled south at the speed of the slowest ship, the 10-knot *Trinity,* rumors had reached Makassar, the gorgeous, movie-set capital of the Celebes, that a large, unidentified force was headed their way. Was it Japanese, or *what?* The lone Dutch naval officer present, Commander Albert de Bats, climbed into the only aircraft available, an open two-seater. He adjusted his goggles and waved to the ground crew. "If I don't come back, they are Japanese," he shouted, over the warm-up roar of the single motor.

For years, assignment to duty at Cavite had been looked on by line officers as being sent to the steamy, dirty "Devil's Island" of the Asiatic Station. But when *der tag* came on 10 December, able, energetic Admiral Rockwell had built on the efforts of predecessor Admiral Smeallie to make Cavite as ready as such a flimsy, long-neglected, ill-defended facility could be.

Of the hundred-odd officers at Cavite, a very few were evacuated aboard plane or submarine, and so escaped capture by the Japanese. Of those captured, approximately 16 survived prison camp. Those who had not been promoted while "missing in action" were raised a grade on release, plus another promotion in January 1946 which evened them with their "outside" contemporaries.

Commissions were back-dated, but the pay was not retroactive. "Greetings!" said the Internal Revenue Service, "and welcome back. You are in arrears for the 1943 and 1944 income taxes. You are exempt for 1942, as you are classified as being in the Philippines that year. But the others you spent in Japan, which does not come under the special military exemption." A few years later, Congress passed an act removing this inequity for tax purposes, but back pay was not included.

Bachelor officers were a notch lower. Quarters and subsistence allowances comprise a sizeable chunk of a shore-based young officer's pay. It was adjudicated that after the transfer of 16th Naval District forces to Army command on 30 January 1942, the Army was furnishing the quarters and rations (in a tunnel or pup-tent, two scanty meals a day), so that no allowances were to be paid shore-based, unmarried officers. After capture, the Japanese kindly made arrangements for food and shelter, so the no-allowances feature continued under the new management.

If the Far Eastern war had not been decided that first day by the loss of the American Army Air Force, it most assuredly was through the Royal Navy's loss of two major warships two days later, and the destruction of the Cavite Navy Yard, near Manila.

Chapter 7

On 2 December 1941, while the old Yangtze Patrol gunboats *Oahu* and *Luzon* were refugeeing their way from Shanghai to Manila, one of the Royal Navy's newest and biggest battleships, the *Prince of Wales,* had arrived at Singapore to beef up the defense of that vital British outpost in the Far East. She joined the World War I battle cruiser HMS *Repulse,* both ships under the command of Vice Admiral Tom Phillips, a peppery, aggressive little man who was not the only naval officer in the world who took a dim view of the efficacy of aircraft versus battleships.

On 8 December, while the *Lanikai* and friends in Cavite waited for the war to arrive in the Philippines, the *Prince of Wales* and *Repulse,* with four destroyers, sailed from Singapore to take the war to the Japanese off Malaya. There had been intelligence that Japanese landings were in progress near Kota Bharu, about 350 airline miles to the north. Phillips was expecting to meet at least one battleship, three or four cruisers, escorting destroyers, and hopefully, many troop-laden transports —the most important target.

With no air cover at all, and only limited air reconnaissance, the task force soon was spotted and tailed by the Japanese, its vital element of surprise lost. Shortly after noon on the tenth, the ships were attacked by 34 high level and 51 torpedo bombers, which sent both battleships to the bottom in less than an hour with the loss of over eight hundred officers and men, including Admiral Phillips.

The traditional antitorpedo tactic of laying down a barrage of big gun splashes ahead of the approaching planes did no good. The aircraft were faster than anything the British had ever seen, and some of the torpedoes were dropped from a height unheard of in the West—up to four hundred feet.

Without Japanese interference, 2,000 of the 2,800 aboard were picked up by the British and American destroyers. Next day, a sentimental Japanese aviator dropped a wreath in the sea at the spot of the sinking. With these acts, Japanese chivalry ceased. Thenceforth, they accepted no quarter and gave it only grudgingly and cruelly.

Tom Phillips, who had gone down with his flagship, could ill be spared. With him went earlier frail hopes of welding Allied ships into a task force formidable enough to give the enemy pause.

The outbreak of war had softened Admiral Hart on Phillips' Manila request for destroyers. He assigned a division of four, fueling at Balikpapan, Borneo, with their tender, USS *Blackhawk*. But they had to delay departure until daylight opening of the antisubmarine booms. Perhaps this was their salvation. Antiaircraft armament in each consisted of one short-barreled, iron-sighted 3-inch gun, making them close to defenseless against aircraft.

Richard Corry, a crewman in USS *Whipple*, wrote me that

> We hightailed it for Singapore, refueled and put to sea immediately to look for survivors of the *Prince of Wales* and *Repulse*. As we withdrew southward, with the slopeheads visible on the horizon at times, I always looked to the east, believing that our own Pacific Fleet certainly would appear to relieve the situation. Little did I know until I got to Pearl Harbor what had happened. Later, south of Java, we picked up 236 survivors from the USS *Langley* and *Pecos*, and headed for Fremantle.

What those in *Whipple* and many others in far higher places failed to realize is that even if half the fleet had not been disabled at Pearl, the maximum possible effort would have been a raid on the relatively nearby Mandated Islands. To have supported the fleet on any Far Eastern relief expedition would have required 75 tankers, 24 of them fitted for fueling at sea. Of the latter there were exactly four.

All ships were far from full war complement. The shorthanded crews would have been exhausted after three days of wartime watch standing. Japanese carriers outnumbered American in the Pacific ten to three. Their fleet had a one- or two-knot speed advantage, allowing them the choice of avoiding or forcing action. Their wakeless, 49-knot "long lance" torpedo could break ships' backs with a 1,000-pound warhead. Approximately 500-pound U.S. Navy warheads, mounted on torpedoes that ran one-fifth the Japanese distance at lower speed, left a telltale wake of bubbles. One type ran four feet deeper than it was thought to; another, ten feet, thus likely to go harmlessly under the target. Defective exploders more often than not failed to detonate the warhead, even when the torpedo was heard to thunk into the enemy's side plating. Peacetime parsimony was costing dearly.

Had the two fleets met in December 1941 before the American

The schooner Hermes *at San Francisco early in her career.*

Hermes *at Honolulu before her name changed to* Lanikai.

losses at Pearl, it is the opinion of both Admirals Nimitz and King that the result would have been an American disaster.

The tenth was solid catastrophe not only off Malaya. *Lanikai* lay at anchor near the Cavite Navy Yard while I lunched aboard a minesweeper alongside dock. At 12:30, a popular newscaster, "Don" Bell, came on the air. "Our troops are doing well," he said as an opener. This was a euphemism by then well understood to mean that the retreat continued. His broadcast went unfinished; sirens wailed ashore and the general alarm aboard ship sent people to action stations. The wardroom stewards commenced dogging down steel battle ports. I left my unfinished coffee and hurried ashore, headed for the other end of the yard and the pier from where I could signal for *Lanikai*'s little motor dory.

Anyone directly under the bombs is inclined to lose objectivity. One man slightly less exposed as the curtain went up tells the story as he saw it from the deck of a merchantman in the harbor.

Navy Electrician's Mate First Class Joseph Vargo was deviously en route via the only passage available from Vladivostok to San Francisco, aboard a Swedish freighter. He was headed home after two years of using his little black box to sniff for hidden microphones in the USA's Moscow embassy plaster.

Vargo's only venture ashore in Manila's wartime confusion was to visit the Army's communication center to send three radiograms—to the President, Secretary of State, and Secretary of the Navy. The addressees of the telegrams, coupled with a set of casually shown orders from the U.S. ambassador, directing "Joseph Vargo, Esq" to "proceed to the United States as soon as possible, using your own discretion as to means," had quickly got him passed on from corporal to major to colonel. The subject of the messages, essentially, was to put pressure on the Soviets to let Vargo's pregnant Soviet wife out of the USSR. The one to FDR suggested using as a club the withholding of soon-to-arrive USSR Ambassador Litvinov's credentials.

The colonel was deeply impressed. "You executive branch people certainly have it when it comes to clever codes!" he said admiringly, ordering the messages to be sent top precedence.

Pleased with himself at his success and glad to get back to the calm safety of his seagoing home, Vargo joined the skipper on the cool, breezy topside for some pre-lunch herring and schnapps.

"I saw a vee formation of planes flying toward Cavite," Vargo recalled. "I said, 'Well, Captain, by golly, there are the Americans. The Japs will never come around *here*.' And then I saw *another* vee. I counted them; twenty-seven planes—thirteen and thirteen and a leader. Then, *all* of a *sudden*, BANGO! BOOM! Right on Cavite!

"With our binoculars we saw a destroyer moving, shooting. Bang!

Booom! Boom! There was a big plane trying to take off, a giant Navy flying boat. Then I saw nine more planes approaching. So I told the Captain, 'Boy! There's nine Americans going to tangle with those two squadrons of Japs.' But instead, these nine planes picked out the ships in the harbor, where *we* were."

Now it was Vargo's turn to sweat. The Swedish freighter was a diesel ship, under way as soon as the anchor chain could be cranked in. But it was time wasted; the high flying nine missed everything in the harbor but one merchantman, and passed on to add their remaining bombs to already blazing Cavite.

Since the start of the "China Incident" in 1937, I had been a front row witness to at least two hundred air raids of varying intensity in Canton, Hankow, and Chungking. It had developed in me unconsciously a psychology that air raids were dangerous only to other people. True, once or twice we had been near missed, but other than the loss of the Yangtze gunboat *Panay*, these things were looked on as rare accidents. From the presumably safe sanctuary of our gunboat, we used to watch the Japanese raids with interest. It always was a good show—the "whooooceecc" of the falling bombs, rising to a shrill pitch ending in a thunderous "whoomp!" which sometimes jarred the ship. From the city came a great, sustained roar, like the sound of distant surf, the mingled shouts of frantic Chinese scurrying for someplace other than where they were. Gracefully arching tracer trails, like flower stems, followed anti-aircraft shells aloft. Then a little puff at the end of the stalk appeared, like an instantaneously blooming, smoky purple chrysanthemum. At night, with red tracers streaming down from the planes toward the probing searchlights, the raids were even more spectacular.

Now, at Cavite, the two groups of Japanese bombers, 24 and 27 planes at 20,000 feet, approached lazily, it seemed no faster than a drifting cloud. I was halfway to the pier. The planes had made a practice run and were circling back. Perhaps it would be wise to find some shelter. The heavy work benches in a nearby shop looked like solid splinter protection. I crawled under one. Filipino workmen looked on with interest and some amusement. Wearing hard hats, they were well drilled in avoiding overhead hazards. Many of them, unable to read and grown up close to the jungle, clearly understood the symbol of a monkey holding a coconut aloft. Such pictures hung above shop areas where overhead dangers threatened. The workmen had heard overflying aircraft for years. Nothing had fallen, not even a coconut.

Firing commenced from the yard's and ships' guns about 12:45 P.M., the bursts well below target. It was not until 1:04 P.M., after a leisurely initial practice run, that the first stick fell, a tight pattern into Bacoor Bay. It missed a U.S. Army plane which had just made a forced landing in the water, probably the only victim of the American artillery. The small yard tug *Santa Rita* simply disappeared under columns of muddy water. At 1:13 P.M., another big cluster straddled submarine tender *Otus*, opening seams and punching holes in her upper works. One bomb made a bull's eye hit down submarine *Sealion*'s hatch, sinking her. The *Seadragon*, alongside, took some damage. Bombs in the same salvo wiped out the receiving station ashore and hit destroyer *Pillsbury*. The destroyer *Peary* had a direct hit in the crow's nest atop the mast over the bridge. A cone of tiny splinters slashed down, painfully peppering skipper Lieutenant Commander Harry Keith and killing nine officers and men, almost all those on the bridge.

Another salvo crashed down at 1:36 P.M., farther up the yard, erasing the Commandancia from the map. By this time, *Otus*, unable to heave in her anchor chain, cut it with a torch. Without the formality of taking in her mooring lines, some of which had been cut with axes, she charged out of those parts as fast as cold engines would take her.

Submarine rescue vessel *Pigeon*, an ex-mine sweeper, was rudderless at the moment, a small matter for that extraordinary man, Lieutenant Richard Hawes, her skipper, who got a Navy Cross for his day's work. Having rigged a jury rudder while the bombs were falling, Hawes first towed out powerless minesweeper *Bittern*, then went back for submarine *Seadragon*, all the ships smoking from the intense heat of the shoreside fires. Little blazes were breaking out everywhere aboard from the heavy shower of firebrands rocketed aloft by exploding torpedo air flasks in the workshops close by.

The rattling thunder of the first bomb salvo suggested to me that protection more substantial than a workbench was indicated. The second string was closer, and the third closer yet, by which time I was on the beach under the pier which had been my original goal. An elderly lieutenant, one of several companions "down under," had wholly lost his cool and was chest deep in the water, shouting close to unintelligible obscenities at his tormentors high overhead, slobbering and shaking his fists.

"Get out, you fool!" somebody shouted. "Haven't you heard of dynamiting fish? If a close one hits in the water, you'll be crushed!"

There would be no motor boat piloted by a grinning Belarmino; *Lanikai* was presenting a rapidly diminishing stern, headed for the open bay at an all-out six knots.

The planes left as lazily as they had come, behind them a scene of utter disaster. Huge fires burned throughout the yard. From time to time heavy detonations suggested that perhaps delayed action bombs had been dropped, but actually it was exploding torpedo air flasks, nearly two hundred of them, in the shops for overhaul. They were mostly destroyer types, and would be sadly missed in the lean days to come.

Again the defense had been a sorry one. Three-inch shells, from the biggest guns in the area, fell far short. In an even more ridiculous performance, 30- and 50-caliber machine guns had chattered away in complete futility, the effect wholly confined to improving the gunners' morale by doing *something,* even though it might be akin to throwing the anchor overside with no chain attached.

But at least the ancient Spaniards had built well. The three-hundred-year-old powder magazines, holding enough explosives to have blown the whole area sky high, were not penetrated.

Nearby stood a beautifully shiny, very large red fire engine, driven up while we were under the pier and abandoned by its crew. "Take me and use me!" it almost seemed to say. Half a dozen sailors had appeared, dazed and smoke-blackened. We managed to start the engine and drove it to the seawall within water-reaching distance of its suction pipe. The sailors laid out hose toward some motor cars whose tires had burst into flame from the blistering heat of nearby burning buildings. But try as we might we could not work out the combination to make that damned *pump* operate. What bitter frustration! But what a futile attempt it would have been. The whole world seemed to be on fire around us.

By ones and twos wounded and burned men drifted down to the pier, some carrying stretchers laden with those more badly hurt than themselves. A 50-foot motor launch drew alongside and started loading the stretcher cases for transfer to Manila. There was a small water cooler in a shack on the pier from which we filled little paper cups and carried them to the mutilated, uncomplaining, blood-covered men in the boat. Many were unable to speak, but their eyes said thanks, as the midday tropic sun beat down on their unprotected faces.

With the American air umbrella blown inside out on the first day of war, Admiral Hart had grave doubts that he could use his surface forces in north Luzon waters. After the destruction of Cavite on the tenth, with no opposition whatever by American aircraft, any remaining hope vanished. He had one option left: get out. But where to? With the British *Prince of Wales* and *Repulse* gone there was no nucleus for any meaningful Allied offensive fleet, and no plans to form one from the scattered naval forces remaining. Admiral Hart's pets, the submarines, now numbered only 27 American and 12 Dutch altogether. They should have played havoc with the Japanese invasion fleets. But the American torpedoes were close to worthless. The Dutch submarines did well at first, but in Admiral Hart's words, "did not keep the sea long enough." Thus, those early landings were allowed to slip through the Allied fingers to set up bases and air fields on Allied territory that in three months would decide the fate of Singapore and Luzon, and with them the Far East war for the time being.

The Japanese air successes really should not have been a surprise to anybody. Crews had been brought up to a high state of efficiency in three years of actual warfare in China. Devoted little Japanese girl-sans lovingly polished each Zero rivet head smooth and flush, adding a knot or more to an already very fast airplane. General Claire Lee Chennault, Chinese Airforce, commanding the American mercenary unit popularly called the "Flying Tigers," had made a report in 1940 on the superb Zero and his tactics in downing it with the inferior American P-40. But Chennault was an *enfant terrible* who had been considered good riddance when he retired as a deaf, disgruntled U.S. Army captain in 1937. So his report was "filed," as just some more of "that crackpot's" bombast.*

MacArthur had told Hart on 22 September 1941 that the state of his air force was not good—that the ninety to one hundred Filipino pilots were superior to the average U.S. pilot. The Army Air Corps was an insubordinate outfit, he added. Even more revealing, Hart discovered MacArthur was unfamiliar with the capabilities of radar. If that was not enough to rock Hart's equanimity, Chief of Staff Sutherland did *his* best. He showed Hart a chart of "warning services" which depended on observers around the periphery of the islands. Hart said that a comparatively few people with radar would get much better results and their observations would not be confined to high visibility conditions. (Sutherland's fine network didn't help much at Clark Field. There were rumors that Japanese agents had cut the wires.)

Shortly after the Sutherland and MacArthur revelations, Stark wrote Hart of the fine new radar installation on the Galapagos Islands, off the Chilean coast. With his typical wry humor, Hart replied that it made him very happy to learn that those famous Galapagos turtles were now in a position to get reliable advance warning. He was sorry he couldn't say the same for himself.

* An example of what Chennault considered the dinosaur mentality of his superiors was the reaction of General Charles Summerall, U.S. Army Chief of Staff, when in 1928 he was asked to witness one of Chennault's new ideas: mass parachute jumping by airborne troops. Before it was over Summerall disgustedly walked off, saying something to the effect, "What won't that crackpot Chennault think up next?" Within a week, Soviet representatives had offered Chennault a long-term contract with the rank of colonel, at $1,000 a month, to train parachutists.

Chapter 8

With the destruction of the Cavite Navy Yard on 10 December, there was no more talk of fitting *Lanikai* with asdic. Any such equipment in the yard was ashes, along with everything else. Even Admiral Rockwell, the morning after the raid, owned nothing more than the sweat-soaked dirty clothes he was wearing.

Many years later, the Admiral described the Japanese air raid:

> As I was about to sit down to lunch in the commandancia, the air alert sounded and I "took cover" in an open ditch we had dug across the front lawn. A few hours later the entire Navy Yard was a heap of blazing rubble and we had lost all our personal belongings except the clothes on our backs. We spent that night in an open school yard nearby and for the next two weeks were like so many rabbits—running from one hole to another dodging bombs that fell almost every day.

Another Cavite officer whose life style abruptly changed was Lieutenant Knut Engeset, USNR, who had come out East in July 1941. In the feverish two days we had spent getting *Lanikai* ready "as soon as possible after receipt of this despatch" Engeset had been an interested visitor aboard. I soon found out why; he had skippered the ship out from California in August 1939. In a lilting Swedish accent he told me about the trip. Light winds on the ten-day passage to Honolulu forced them to use the engine most of the way, burning up 1,500 gallons of diesel oil. Her seven-man crew got only a fleeting look at the "Paradise of the Pacific"; the day after arrival they were off for Manila, on a course South of Yap and around Mindanao to avoid the typhoon belt. In preparation for *Lanikai*'s starring role in "Hurricane," the topside condenser for the big freeze room had been taken off for cosmetic reasons. Nobody since had bothered to break it out of the hold, screw up the four bolts that secured it, and reactivate the plant. In any case, a 40-ton freeze room would have been a little outsize to cool rations for a seven-man crew and make ice cubes for the skipper's whisky-and-splash. So after a fashion as old as history, the ship's company was augumented by one large pig and 26 chickens. Penny, a four-month-old terrier pup, soon lost her playmates; the pig became pork and the chickens ended up in the skillet during the 30 days to Manila.

Born 50 years earlier in Sweden, Engeset was a big, bluff, red-faced man who looked like he had stepped out of a Robert Louis Stevenson tale of the South Seas. More practically, from my point of view, he looked like a prime choice to have along for companionship and advice. He had been a naval reservist since 1916, with 25 of the intervening years in sail.

"There are two good reasons against *that,*" and Commander Slocum. "First, he is senior to you. Second, the President said that *one* officer would suffice."

Fate is a strange master. The expendables, myself and *Lanikai,* escaped and survived. Engeset was captured on Corregidor, spent the war in prison camp, and on 3 May 1946 died as a result of the rigors of captivity.

Improvisation was the order of the day. Admiral Rockwell, who lost his collar insignia during the Cavite raid, had new ones pounded out of Philippine silver pesos. *Lanikai* was "armor plated." The latter was suggested by the evidence of Japanese use of instantaneous fuses in thin-walled bombs that scattered many small splinters. The schooner had strong metal awning stanchions on each outboard side of the after deck-house. A substantial ridgepole ran amidships just under the main boom. A heavy plank platform was laid across this framework. On the deck under it, the roof of the deckhouse, went a layer of sandbags. In theory, the wood platform would detonate the bomb and the sandbags would stop the resultant splinters or strafers' bullets. This made the mainsail unusable, but gave a small citadel to protect crew members not manning the guns or the wheel. Thus "armored," *Lanikai* joined the Inshore Patrol.

With MacArthur's Air Force smashed on the eighth, the British battleships sunk off Malaya and Cavite destroyed on the tenth, the eleventh was the first day of a new order of things in the Far Eastern war. From then on, the Asiatic Fleet was doomed, though few of the lower echelon people realized it. A later estimate of forces calculated as a minimum to relieve the Far East situation listed 7 to 9 capital ships, 5 to 7 aircraft carriers, 50 destroyers, 60 submarines and, a little more precisely, 1,464 aircraft.

In Admiral Hart's post-relief notes, he mentioned that, except for meager direct observation by reconnaissance planes, he had gotten very little information about the enemy other than from the C/I (Communication Intelligence) unit at Corregidor, euphemistically labeled "Fleet

Radio Unit C," or FRU for short. "It continued to be of the utmost value" Hart wrote, "and without its services ABDAFLOAT* would have had to carry on very much in the dark." Following their evacuation from Corregidor, FRU set up shop at Lembang, Java, where it grew to a total of over twenty officers and men.

The Dutch themselves were no slouches in this area of endeavor. During the dark period of Japan's centuries of self-imposed isolation, the Dutch had been almost the only Europeans allowed in the country. Their pool of Japanese language experts as a result of this tradition was large and competent, greatly benefitting their cryptanalytic effort.

The day following Cavite's destruction, the Naval District communicators—ten officers and a hundred men, moved out to Corregidor to share facilities with FRU, which operated nominally under the Chief of Naval Operations. "They didn't want to let us in," one of Cavite's radio gang later wrote me. "They even kept Admiral Rockwell cooling his heels for nearly two hours before they decided to admit him."

The FRU boys were well justified in being spooky; they held one of the war's most valuable and most secret weapons, in a country where "secrecy" was not a respected word. The loose American rank-and-file concept of security was exemplified by the widespread practice of ships' coding boards breaking down every intercepted U.S. naval message for which they held the key, whether addressed to their unit or not. All too frequently the information so gained was passed on to their news-starved comrades in the wardroom, whence scraps inevitably leaked to the mess deck, then to the next port's pubs.

The FRU "C" operators of the Asiatic Fleet's "Purple" machine, a replica of those in Washington and London, held only the Asian keys. It could crack the Tokyo, Bangkok, Saigon, and Singapore Japanese diplomatic chat, but not the agonized conversational ping-pong between Tokyo and Japanese ambassadors Nomura and Kurusu in Washington.

Unlike the close restrictions on Hawaii's FRU "H," Cavite's FRU "C" had a free hand both to process and to intercept Japanese traffic, aided in the latter by an Army C/I unit which had no facilities for decrypting. MacArthur shared the results, sometimes grumbling that they were holding out on him. Compared to this cosy set-up, Kimmel and Short in Hawaii were far out in left field.

As *Lanikai* worked her way seaward, the harbor and bay that only a few days before had been crowded with 200,000 tons of merchant shipping, plus a good many miscellaneous warships, was almost empty for the submarines. Of these, only the periscopes were visible as they sat on the bottom awaiting the end of the morning alert. Admiral Hart had sent Task Force 5 on its way south before war broke. The merchant

* The Australian–British–Dutch–American combined naval command set up in January 1942.

ships followed his urging and headed off independently toward Australia during the first few days of war. Only one was lost, a Frenchman loaded with 6,000 tons of rice and flour. Her cargo would be urgently needed in the last ditch defense of Bataan, so she was anchored near Mariveles. There Japanese bombers set her afire on Christmas day.

One of the biggest of the merchant ships was the French MV *Mareschal Joffre,* a valuable potential troop carrier. But she lay in effect on dead center, her crew divided as only Frenchmen could be, between Vichyites and Free French. The minesweeper *Bittern,* overhauling at Cavite, had lost so many of her essential parts in the holocaust that she was written off. So her skipper, Lieutenant Thomas Warfield, was available. He was sent with a boarding party to the *Joffre* where he sorted out the crew, Vichy to port, Free French to starboard. The Vichy group was promptly set ashore. About a hundred naval air ground crewmen and several aviators with zero sea experience were rounded up and put aboard, some to stand watch, some for the ride, and others to casually hang around with a ready weapon to keep an eye peeled for any possible Vichy saboteurs in Free French clothing. That same evening, *Joffre* was under way, and as Admiral Hart set down in his notes, "They got to Australia without incident, quite an accomplishment for a young lieutenant." The ship went on to the United States, where she was commissioned as the USS *Rochambeau* (AP-63).

In December 1966, Admiral Hart wrote me one of his "safety valve" memos, suggesting how it happened that the Asiatic Fleet was prepared for the blow:

> It is now 25 years since the surprise attack on Pearl Harbor. Marking an anniversary of it, there is being a regular spate of publishing. All the weeklies are coming out with special numbers. The title of one of them is, "The Mystery of Pearl Harbor." Mind you— *"mystery"!!*
>
> What an astounding lot of words have been used on the subject over the last 25 years. During six months of the war years, I spent all my time on the subject; taking sworn testimony of Naval Officers; as counsel before the Navy Court of Inquiry; a long day as witness before the Joint Congressional Investigation; and so forth. I became over-saturated with it.
>
> And now, this month, more and more rehashing of all those words. It can be held that it all began with the loquacity of Japanese officials *before* Pearl Harbor in their diplomatic code. Japanese minor officials over the world kept the air full of their dispatches. Translating it was easy enough but very laborious because of its mass. There were kernels of grain but it was mixed with a tremendous amount of chaff.

That same characteristic has carried over into most of the writing on the subject of Pearl Harbor by many in this country. That is—a small amount of grain mingled with tons of chaff.

It can all become a very simple matter by confining one's self to just one Navy Department dispatch which was sent on 27 November 1941. It came to be known as the War Warning dispatch and it was addressed to the Commanders-in-Chief U.S. and Asiatic Fleets. . . .

The War Warning dispatch was in itself rather wordy—some chaff in it. While it was usual for the coders to put in extra words to confuse code breakers, the message did contain information which was really redundant. But there was real GRAIN in it:

It was in just ten words divided into two sentences. The first was—

THIS IS A WAR WARNING

That is definite, cogent and as strong as words can be. The addressees were, in the last analysis, told the situation.

The second sentence was—

EFFECT AN APPROPRIATE DEFENSIVE DEPLOYMENT

That was a direct and definite order for all those addressed. They were told what to do but without any attempt to specify just how they were to accomplish it. And that is correct command performance; tell the commanders in the field what they are to do and leave it to their discretion, after considering their respective situations, just how the order is to be carried out.

I venture to interject my own opinion that I do not know, in all Naval history, a better command performance than was contained in the War Warning.

In weighing Admiral Hart's reaction to the "war warning," one must remember that he had access to vital information that Kimmel did not: the contents of intercepted Asian "purple" radio traffic, translations of Japanese lower level traffic through his Cavite Station "C," plus information passed clandestinely to MacArthur from Washington that Hart was privy to. Admiral Kimmel, in command of the Pacific Fleet in Hawaii, got nothing from the comparable Navy Station "H" on Oahu. He did not know the "Purple" code existed and was told by letter by Admiral Stark, the Chief of Naval Operations, at almost the last minute, that he hadn't the foggiest notion what would happen.

The war warning made sense to Hart because it directed a "defensive deployment" which in his case, meant withdrawal to the south, as long envisaged in the event of imminent war against Japan. In Kimmel's case, "defensive deployment" meant nothing. Where was he to "deploy"? Go hide with his fleet in some remote, supposedly safe spot in the broad Pacific, emptying his fuel tanks while his planes patrolled overhead, expending aircraft, pilots and gasoline in futile attrition?

Kimmel had been directed by this same war warning to be prepared to carry out the provisions of WPL-46, the first act thereof being an attack on the Japanese Mandated Islands to relieve pressure on the Far East. To be ready instantly to do this, Kimmel had to be fully "gassed up," for an operation that would stretch his resources to the utmost, including urgent requirement for patrol seaplanes for long range scouting. Even though they were in short supply, Kimmel has been criticized for not using these planes in routine searches which might have revealed the Japanese approach, but which in any such process would have lowered unacceptably their potential for carrying out their primary war plan functions. Kimmel's assigned first mission was to hit the Marshalls. Had he not been prepared to do so, he would have been culpable. The fleet does not exist to protect the base; entirely the contrary. In this, the Army and Naval District forces failed miserably—having been kept no better informed than Kimmel and having shared only a pittance under the "Europe first" allocation of war supplies. (See Appendix for Admiral Bloch's complaint.)

This was by no means the first serious war warning. If indeed the 27 November warning had been unequivocally intended, as the Washington group held in the Joint Congressional Committee (JCC) investigation, the normal concomitant from the point of view of anyone who heretofore had been held as much in the dark as Kimmel, would have been *an immediate order for general mobilization.*

Thus this situation of widely different interpretations is not as anomalous as on first hand it may appear. In their own minds, Kimmel and Hart were both right, and on the basis of circumstances which uphold the honesty of each.

Why were the Pearl Harbor and Manila situations so strikingly dissimilar? A realistic survey of the Hawaiian reconnaissance platforms—planes and ships—clearly shows there were not enough to provide coverage of all possible enemy approaches over the year during which alarms had gone out. The newly installed radars were execrably handled, a result not to be unexpected in the military profession, where striking innovations have all too frequently been received with suspicion-tinged contempt by tradition-bound older officers.

Admiral Nimitz has written that our greatest stroke of good fortune was that the Japanese did not find the U.S. Fleet at sea. The faster Japanese force, he said, with a carrier advantage of six to two, could have chosen battle on its own terms. In all probability, Admiral Nimitz continued, our ships would have been sunk in two thousand fathoms with a loss of all hands, instead of settling a mere forty feet to the soft mud bottom of Pearl Harbor, which saved thousands of trained men vital to the manning of our great wartime fleet yet to come.

An interesting commentary is offered by Lieutenant Commander C. C. Hiles, (SC) USN (Retired), probably the most knowledgeable individual on the Pearl Harbor attack alive today. He points out that both of Admiral Kimmel's carriers were absent on reinforcement missions to Wake and Midway. Therefore, he had no adequate air cover and would never have risked a pitched battle, *if* he could have avoided one, in view of superior Japanese speed. In Hiles' view, Kimmel probably would have dispersed the fleet for security until he was certain of the tactical situation and his two carriers had returned. This appraisal Hiles bases on the assumption that Kimmel would have been unaware of the composition of the Japanese attack force, and on extensive correspondence with Kimmel.

Commander Hiles concludes by suggesting that the Nimitz appraisal is subject to some imponderable factors, not the least of which is the unlikelihood that the Japanese attacking force under Nagumo, on finding the U.S. Fleet gone from Pearl Harbor, would have lingered long enough for U.S. forces to have located it and given battle. It is a certainty that the Japanese would not have gone after the U.S. Fleet: their attack was purely a hit-and-run proposition. Such were their orders.

Prewar, Admiral Kelly Turner, chief of Navy War Plans, had predicted the Japanese would first occupy Guam. The main striking force then would return to home bases, with a smaller striking force at Halmahera. Next move would be to knock out U.S. air bases in the Philippines, then assault Luzon. At the same time, there might be an attempt to reduce the Netherlands East Indies and Borneo. Alas! Japanese daring and superior staff work allowed them to strike simultaneously at Pearl, Guam, Malaya, Hongkong, and the Philippines. The American reaction was predictable: it swung violently the other way—stand by to set up a line of defense in the Rocky Mountains. CNO's 091812 of December 1941 was a long (335 word) secret priority composed during the forenoon of 9 December by Marshall, Stark, Turner, and Gerow, the latter the Army chief war planner. Quoted in part, it makes clear the state of confusion in which the U.S. high command found itself two days after Pearl:

```
...BECAUSE OF THE GREAT SUCCESS OF THE JAPANESE
RAID ON THE SEVENTH IT IS EXPECTED TO BE PROMPTLY FOL-
LOWED UP BY ADDITIONAL ATTACKS IN ORDER RENDER HAWAII
UNTENABLE AS NAVAL AND AIR BASE IN WHICH EVENTUALITY
IT IS BELIEVED JAPANESE HAVE FORCES SUITABLE FOR
INITIAL OCCUPATION OF ISLANDS OTHER THAN OAHU INCLUD-
ING MIDWAY MAUI AND HAWAII. UNDER PRESENT CIRCUM-
STANCES IT SEEMS QUESTIONABLE THAT MIDWAY CAN BE RE-
TAINED BUT IT IS HOPED THAT JOHNSON PALMYRA AND
SAMOA MAY BE. IN EXPECTATION OF FURTHER AIR RAIDS AND
INADEQUACY OF DEFENSES OAHU CNO CONSIDERS IT ESSEN-
TIAL THAT WOUNDED VESSELS ABLE TO PROCEED UNDER OWN
POWER SHOULD BE SENT TO WEST COAST AS SOON AS POSSI-
BLE WITH DUE REGARD TO SAFETY FROM CURRENT RAIDING
FORCES AND VERY GREAT IMPORTANCE OF EFFECTIVE COUNTER
ATTACKS ON THESE RAIDERS BY YOU. UNTIL DEFENSES ARE
INCREASED IT IS DOUBTFUL IF PEARL SHOULD BE USED AS A
BASE FOR ANY EXCEPT PATROL CRAFT NAVAL AIRCRAFT SUB-
MARINES OR FOR SHORT PERIODS WHEN IT IS REASONABLY
CERTAIN JAPANESE ATTACKS WILL NOT BE MADE....
```

This astounding message was addressed for action to the Commander in Chief, U.S. Pacific Fleet, Admiral Kimmel, and for information to the three west coast naval district commandants. The Commander in Chief, Asiatic Fleet, was left in the dark as to this dire state of affairs, as was the Joint Congressional Committee three years later, where the message framers testified that the defenses of Hawaii *had* been adequate, thus adding a few more spikes to Admiral Kimmel's hide, already pretty securely nailed to the barn door.

All this was a little late for Kimmel, who wryly commented that, "Assuming for the first time on December 5th, I had all the important information then available in the Navy Department, I would have gone to sea with the fleet including the carrier *Lexington* and arranged a rendezvous with Halsey's carrier task force built around carrier *Enterprise* and been in a good position to intercept the Japanese attack."[10] He could hardly have done otherwise without appearing pusillanimous. But it would have been sheer disaster. The U.S. Army aircraft on Oahu would have been no help; the fighters were limited to a range of fifteen miles from land, and it later was repeatedly demonstrated that the heavy horizontal bombers, the B-17's, were unable to hit moving targets. But the B-17 question was largely academic anyway; there were only six of them operational on Oahu on 7 December.

Chapter 9

Early on the morning of 12 December, the *Lanikai* picked her way carefully through the buoyed minefield channel supposedly guarding Corregidor and was soon rolling gently on the open sea, barely making steerage way under three jibs and a foresail. The engine was secured; the idle propeller churned in the wake and held us back. But there was no need for haste. We were operating under confidential orders handed me earlier that morning by the senior officer on patrol duty:*

> Your mission primarily is to search for and report to Station Cast all approaching vessels and aircraft. Patrol Stations Affirm and Baker plus gap under sail.

Thanks to the Japanese, the events of the previous two days had been anything but well ordered. When the air raid hit Cavite on 10 December, the crew of my new command, without waiting for either orders or captain got under way and headed for the safety of the bay where they spent part of the night. Where I spent that night, I have no recollection; some friend picked me up off the blood-soaked San Felipe ferry and took me to his ship.

Later, my crew brought *Lanikai* in, and next morning, as I climbed over the bulwarks, I was greeted with "My God! It's the old man. He's alive." From the bay, the night before, they had watched the holocaust at Cavite and decided that for me it had been an outsize funeral pyre, courtesy of the Japanese.

We were no more than settled down on patrol when the Japanese were back again. At 9:35 A.M., enemy planes appeared over Corregidor, seven or eight miles way. Like a movie with the sound track out of phase, the detonations reached us many seconds after we had seen the flash and

* Lieutenant Commander D. L. Smith, skipper of the *Oahu* on the Shanghai-to-Manila run earlier in December. *Oahu* was sunk by gunfire on 4 May. Smith was taken prisoner 6 May and died in captivity.

flying debris of the explosions. More alarms sounded throughout the day. The Japanese were taking full and leisurely advantage of their newly won total air supremacy.

The thirteenth was a repeat of the previous day—patrol, then lunchtime visit of nine Japanese planes over Corregidor, where, according to *Lanikai*'s journal, "they received a hot reception." How hot, the fascinated gallery aboard *Lanikai* could accurately assess; five minutes later, only *eight* silver-grey enemy planes, now down to about 3,000 feet, passed directly over the ship, strafing as they went, the bullets making pretty splashes close aboard.

On the fourteenth, we discovered *Lanikai*'s talents did not include heavy towing. Having picked up a drifting waterlogged lighter loaded with soggy flour from the French merchantman anchored in Mariveles, we found there was no place far enough forward of the rudder to secure a towline. *Lanikai* and her clumsy charge simply went in tight circles until relieved by an Army tug.

The fifteenth was more eventful:

At 8:10 A.M. hoisted foresail and three jibs.
At 3:00 P.M. chased and overtook fishing schooner which proved to be Filipino.
At 3:10 P.M. fired seven blind loaded and one service round from 3-pounder to test gun, ammunition, mount, and ship's structure. Test satisfactory and found gun very accurate at 500 yards.

Oh, how desperately we wished that schooner would be loaded with Japanese infiltrators! Ammunition had been laid out ready. The disappointment of not being able to use it on an enemy had been partially compensated for by the test, wherein to everybody's real astonishment, nothing fell apart. Cavite's conscientious engineers and workmen had set a steel stanchion from gun base clear through to ship's keel. The only disgruntled participants were the cockroaches, jostled from their roosts at each blast. If there were any rats aboard, they kept their secret. Or perhaps there had been, but with traditional seagoing rats' wisdom, they had divined the intent of the President's message and left for safer duty earlier in the game.

In the beginning, with Corregidor's ammunition still in fair supply, the Japanese bombers were wary of the only modern installation in the Philippines. Even at 20,000 feet an occasional enemy plane came cartwheeling to earth in flames, the crew presumably riding it down, as no parachutes blossomed out.

Following the usual high level attack on the "Rock," the enemy planes would clear the Corregidor danger area and drop down to lower level to strafe whatever lay afloat. Sailing slowly back and forth off the harbor entrance, we were occasional beneficiaries of these bursts of bullets that sent the unemployed scurrying for the "citadel," while our two 30-caliber Lewis beat a tattoo in counter action. *Lanikai* received no hits, nor was there ever any evidence that the enemy suffered from our feeble efforts.

The three pounder designed well before the birth of the airplane, her long, slender bright steel barrel as delicately balanced as a jeweler's scale, unfortunately was not a "sky" gun, as it could be elevated only about twenty degrees. The gunner set his shoulder against a crotchlike stock and grasped a pistol grip with trigger enclosed, trying to keep the crosshairs of his sighting telescope on the target. A second man cranked in range and deflection on the sight bar. A third slung two-foot-long cartridges into the open breech, the plug then closing automatically. With trigger held down, the shell went on its screaming way as soon as the breech block closed behind it. Then instantly the chamber opened automatically and spat out the empty case. With a good crew, such a gun could fire thirty high explosive shells a minute, until the barrel turned red.

At night we lay at anchor inside the minefield. The nightly motion picture, standard in the smallest Navy ships, was not for *Lanikai*. Nor were there books, or newspapers, or magazines The only entertainment was watching Corregidor's powerful searchlights finger the sky, probing for the Japanese "bed check Charlies" that droned high overhead or came in for minor nuisance attacks that for small expenditure exhausted the garrison by denying it sleep. For those aboard *Lanikai,* the ship might as well have been a thousand miles at sea. Except for an occasional hail when passing close to another ship, or for the constant chatter on the short-range TBS radio, installed after war's outbreak, we were wholly divorced from the world's doings and contacts.

Although there had been a 25-plane raid on the fifteenth, there was none at all the next day. Perhaps it was weather trouble; the bigger planes still were flying from Taiwan fields, over five hundred miles away. The wind was so strong that everything *Lanikai* had in the air blew away—a signal halyard with the ship's call letters—WJDQ, the union jack, and a large anchor ball—all of which straightaway sank. There was one consolation; with the lovely wartime hiatus in paperwork, there would be no survey report in quintuplicate to explain the loss.

While we had been less sparing of fresh water than would have been the case had the Camranh Bay mission been carried out, qualms on that score were justified. In the ten days since leaving the dock, the 2,000-gallon tanks were near empty. There was no necessity here to follow Commander Slocum's earlier suggestion—"signal the first passing Jap man-of-war and ask for some." Instead, the quarantine pier at Mariveles, in the little bay facing Corregidor, furnished 1,800 gallons of mountain spring water and 100 pounds of ice.

In thus deviating from a daily offshore patrol routine because of the dull demands of logistics, we missed the stellar performance of the day, frightful proof of the efficacy of at least one of those mines Admiral Hart had so unflatteringly commented on in his letter to Admiral Stark a few months earlier.

The SS *Corregidor* was not much of a ship for size, but she was a giant in historical background and in the affections of the many who had ridden her. A slim, speedy little interisland craft of 1,900 tons and 316 feet long, she could crank up 22 knots. In World War I, she had been among the very earliest of a breed which would metamorphose into a type destined to dominate the next war on the sea: she had been a seaplane carrier, His Britannic Majesty's Ship *Engadine*. She had flown flight reconnaissance for Admiral David Beatty in the North Sea and for the first time in history had spotted the enemy before they had appeared over the horizon to those aboard ship. She had towed the battle-damaged cruiser HMS *Warrior*, then taken off her 705 officers and men before the fatally damaged vessel sank. Now, on 17 December 1941, a quarter of a century later, her brass plaque on the bridge attesting to her gallant past, she was loaded to the marks with another seven hundred —Manila "refugees" frantically fighting to keep one jump ahead of the invaders. In her hold were several batteries of 75 mm. field pieces and mortars to beef up General Sharpe's Mindanao defense forces.

Lieutenant Commander George E. Pollak* describes the scene:

> The channel through the minefield was a simple dogleg affair. . . . The patrol boat captain took the outbound skipper to the turn in the channel, gave him the new course and distance for clearing the minefield . . . The *Corregidor* made her turn and began picking up speed. Then for some reason which shall never be known, she veered strongly off course and headed into the field. A few moments later she struck a mine. Within a few minutes only debris floating on the swift and deep-running currents of the channel remained as indication of the short-lived tragedy. The small boats that ventured into the area managed to pick up some survivors. . . .[11]

By this stage, even the most sanguine Inshore Patroller must have realized that *Lanikai* was less a threat to the Imperial Japanese Navy than she was to herself by blundering through the minefield channel twice a day. So from the eighteenth through the twentieth, she was

---

* As a "fresh caught" reserve ensign, Pollak was one of those aboard the SS *President Harrison*, with me in August 1941. He was assigned to the Cavite Navy Yard, where during an introductory inspection by Admiral Rockwell shortly thereafter, Pollak stepped up to him and saluted. In a hoarse stage "aside" to his chief of staff, Rockwell said, "My God! Are *all* these junior officers *ashore?*" Later, he had been involved in designing and installing that stout stanchion that supported *Lanikai*'s "main battery."

allowed to ride at anchor between Mariveles and Corregidor, to watch as a routine matter the twice daily Japanese raids, which judging from their accurately predictable arrival times, must certainly have been scheduled by a former member of that meticulously time-conscious organization, the Japan State Railways.

This pragmatic new assessment of *Lanikai* resulted in a 21 December order to proceed to Cavite. It was about time. The larder was close to empty of all but rice and salmon. Before departure from the "war zone," the TBS radio was surrendered to *Oahu,* thus losing our last connecting link to the outside other than the human larynx. *Oahu,* together with *Luzon* and *Mindanao,* minesweepers *Quail, Finch,* and *Tanager,* and submarine rescue vessel *Pigeon* remained as the sole seagoing defenses of Manila Bay's entrance.

It was a foul day. The wind blew a gale. *Lanikai* was soaking inside and out. The midships hatch which led to the engineroom and stores was a wide-open sluice for the downpour to fall straight into the bilges. Its protective awning had to be unrigged to allow use of the foresail. Bread taken aboard ten days before had become green with mould, unfit even for fish bait. The Caucasian crew members fell back on the rice which in a few more weeks would become the staple starch. It might have been tropic debilitation, but those whose blood had been thinned by months of blistering heat found the change in weather to be a chilling one.

Before a driving gale, three jibs, foresail and engine shoved *Lanikai* along at eight knots to Sangley Point, near Cavite, where by courtesy of Japanese oversight, a drum of gasoline and ample fresh water still were available. The project was what sometimes is described in naval parlance as a "midnight requisition," in this case, one which prewar might have been a little tricky to justify officially in that *Lanikai* as yet had no 50-caliber gun:

> At 1855 moored port side to ammunition dock, Cavite. Took on board 3,000 rounds of 50-caliber machine gun ammunition and one 50-caliber machine gun mount from top of wall. A pitch black, squally night, and feeling the way with difficulty in the blackout. The Navy Yard still smouldering and sentinels rather with the wind up. Had some difficulty getting through safely. The sentinels were U.S. Marines, a breed not loosely trifled with.[12]

The surreptitious entry accomplished, we eased our way back to only slightly less explosive surroundings, the fuel pier. A gun to fit the night's plunder perhaps would come tomorrow—from good friend Adolph Roth,* skipper of the minesweeper *Tanager.*

Lanikai's umbilical cord had not yet been cut, but the scissors were

* Lieutenant Commander Egbert Adolph Roth died 24 October 1944 as a Japanese prisoner of war.

out and ready. In marking this point of close to no return—the word "celebrate" perhaps is inappropriate—a bottle of the choice bourbon which came with the ship was retrieved from Doc Cossette's medical stores and shared with the Caucasian members of the crew. (Filipinos are not hard liquor drinkers.) In the dimly lit, stark interior of the after cabin we lifted our glasses to each other in a sort of silent pact for survival. There was not much talk. Those exhausted professional sailor-men probably would not have understood the words *"sauve qui peut,"* but that was where we stood, and they all clearly sensed it.

Colonel James W. Keene, USMC, read the *Proceedings* excerpt quoted above and replied in the July 1963 issue of the magazine:

> Please assure Rear Admiral Tolley that while the U.S. Marine sentries stationed atop the Naval Ammunition Depot, Cavite, that memorable night in 1941 were "a breed not loosely trifled with," the second lieutenant who posted them there would have been only too happy to have provided the *Lanikai* with two 50 caliber machine guns with mounts. At that time I had more of those weapons than I could possibly man with the few Marines and Fleet Reserve Steward's Mates I had available. I could have even made available the services of an excellent armorer to assist the *Lanikai*'s crew in mounting them. I would be less than candid if I failed to admit our envy of those seagoing types who had the chance to escape and fight again, while we had to stay behind. We survivors of that weird, pitch black, and squally night salute the *Lanikai* and her gallant crew.

A burned child may dread the fire, but a bombed sailor is inclined to be spooky about *everything,* until the new, unfriendly order of things becomes more routine. Those two 50s would have been most welcome at Surabaya, months later, when Japanese strafers were close to rolling their wheels on the masthead. But on that black Cavite night, we felt on our own, without friends, quite alone.

Chapter 10

By the time the U.S. Navy had been at war with the Japanese for two weeks, the USS *Lanikai* had settled down to her life in the Navy probably as well as we had adjusted to life in *Lanikai*. What none of her crew knew then was that life in the Navy was nothing new for the ship; she had been in the U.S. Navy before some of them were born. It took a long while to uncover her full story, to learn that she had served in World War I; that she had once been known as USS *Hermes;* that she had narrowly escaped disaster once before at the hands of the Imperial Japanese Navy; that she had played an exciting role in a 1937 movie—the cinema spectacular "Hurricane"; and that on the very decks where we slogged around in sweat-stained khakis the sarong-clad figure of Hollywood's Dorothy Lamour had once supercharged the atmosphere for miles around.

Before World War I, the principal product of the South Sea Islands was copra. Jaluit Gesellschaft, a German company, owned a number of schooners in this trade—they carried copra to Honolulu in return for the simple necessities of life in the islands: cooking pots, knives, fish hooks, and, to obey the dictates of the ubiquitous missionaries, brightly colored cloth to cover full-breasted, innocent nakedness of those children of nature, the "natives."

Among Jaluit Gesellschaft's exotically named little windjammers—*Neptun, Triton, Aeolus, Mercur*—was *Hermes,* one day to become *Lanikai.* She was built in 1914 by W. F. Stone, who gathered a lifetime of honors as a boatbuilder on San Francisco Bay, as did his father and his son. The Stone family began by building wooden ships in San Francisco in 1853, when grandfather W. I. Stone arrived from Dartmouth, England, where he had been an apprentice boat builder. Forty years later, in 1893, his son W. F. took over, and in 1912 commenced to break in *his* son Lester F. Stone.

Hermes was built in their Oakland yard, at the foot of Diesel Street, for Williams-Dimond Company, agents for Jaluit Gesellschaft of Hamburg, Germany.

On 15 October 1914, the 600-ton German cruiser SMS *Geier* and her collier *Loksun* arrived off Honolulu. Normally, *Geier,* as a World War I belligerent, would have been allowed 24 hours for revictualling and minor repairs before being required to make herself scarce. But the blandishments of the Germans, abetted by the generally pro-German sentiments (really traditionally anti-British) of many Americans, prevailed on the Honolulu authorities to extend this to three weeks.

About 11:30 P.M. on 23 October, lookouts in the USRCS (U.S. Revenue Cutter Service Ship) *Thetis,* according to her log, ". . . sighted two naval steam launches without lights acting strangely. Hailed them but received no answer. Lowered boat and attempted to board without overhauling launches. Fired one round blank charge 3-pounder at one launch." Next morning's dawn cleared the mystery: a large, grim-looking warship was slowly steaming back and forth just outside the three-mile limit. She was the 14,000-ton Japanese battleship HIJMS *Hizen,* armed with four 12-inch, a dozen 6-inch, and a multitude of smaller guns. *Thetis'* crew and the curious bathers at Waikiki were looking at a sort of chameleon. *Hizen* had been built for Russia in the United States by William Cramp and named *Retvizan.* She had been damaged in 1904 by Japanese torpedo boats at Port Arthur, then repaired, then scuttled before surrender. The thrifty Japanese had raised and refitted her, so that now she was keeping a watchdog's eye on citizens of the country who originally had put her together.

This would be a busy day all around. After breakfast, *Thetis* eased out to *Hizen's* vicinity and found near her the 105-foot, 150-gross ton German schooner *Aeolus,* of Bremen, loaded with 65 tons of copra, seized at sea as a prize. Launches were going back and forth between the two ships and to the German collier *Loksun,* anchored safely inside the three-mile limit, to deliver to her *Aeolus'* crew. That night, the darkened Japanese launches again intruded into coastal waters, to within half a mile of Honolulu harbor entrance. Once again they were chased by *Thetis* and warned to stay outside the three-mile limit. The 25 October 1914 *Honolulu Sunday Advertiser* carried more details:

> *Aeolus,* returning from the Marshall Islands with a load of copra, came unsuspectingly over the horizon heading for the harbor entrance. A patrol boat from the Japanese ship *Hizen* intercepted and took over. *Aeolus* was brought alongside and the crew sent ashore to *Loksun.* A Japanese crew was put aboard who took her a few hundred yards off *Hizen.* About 8:10 P.M. the crew abandoned her,

searchlights came on and 14 shots were fired. Then out lights. Two hours later, fires started, probably by a Japanese party, since the ship had not sunk. She burned for several hours, probably due to the copra load.

On the twenty-sixth, the *Advertiser* carried the story of a more successful blockade runner, the race to safety in harbor of *Hermes*. She had left Jaluit on 15 September, dropped a government doctor off at Nauru and then headed for Hawaii. She arrived off Molokai the night of 24 October, while unbeknownst to her people $70,000 worth of ship and cargo were merrily blazing off Honolulu in the form of schooner *Aeolus* and her copra. Crossing Molokai channel next morning, *Hermes'* skipper H. A. Schmidt spotted *Hizen* and recognizing it for a foreign warship, hugged the coast of Oahu inside the three-mile limit.

No doubt still savoring *Aeolus'* blood, two fast launches with *Hizen* close astern tally-ho'd after the new quarry. In the heat of the chase the three-mile limit once more was violated. *Hizen* and bloodhounds charged across the line and boarded *Hermes*. The Japanese hauled down the German flag, but doughty skipper Schmidt, claiming asylum in territorial waters, hoisted it right back up again. Meanwhile, watchdog *Thetis* appeared in the offing, three-pounders unlimbered and warning signals whipping in the wind. Like a big, mean mastiff's recognizing the inviolate limits of a poodle's yard, *Hizen* turned and lumbered off, while *Geier's* and *Loksun's* crews cheered as *Hermes* came safely alongside dock.

The Japanese clearly were not extending themselves to be endearing. Over the horizon, adding to *Hizen's* close-in threat, lay the 10,000-ton armored cruiser *Asama*, four 8-inch and fourteen 6-inch guns. The nightly forays into territorial waters continued. On the twenty-sixth, two U.S. Navy launches under Ensigns Parker and Berry came out from Pearl Harbor to join *Thetis'* launches in organizing the nightly games of hare and hounds that continued until *Geier's* internment and *Hizen's* departure.

A request from *Hizen* to receive newspapers via the Japanese consul was curtly refused. "I shall stand by and wait for *Geier* to come out," *Hizen's* skipper said with exaggerated Japanese politeness in an interview on board. He added he would stick close to port day and night, but would take every precaution to avoid violating neutrality. What with the obviously deliberate nightly incursions by the darkened launches and encouragement of local Japanese fishing sampans to illegally contact *Hizen* in spite of repeated Revenue Service warnings, one might conclude that the Japanese skipper was something less than candid.

We must remember that this was a period of clearly manifested Japanese truculence toward the United States, born of the immigration crises, our Open Door policy in China, and what the Japanese people considered a short-changing in the American-arranged peace with Russia in 1904. The tension was sustained by action on the part of several western states to pass laws excluding Japanese from owning or even leasing land. Throughout this period and until the bombshell of Germany's infamous Zimmermann telegram catapulted the United States into the war, Germany had made all sorts of back door efforts to pry Japan loose from her British alliance and switch sides. Japanese and Germans were the same basic species—natural allies, Berlin said, sentiments capitalized on one war later. Germans swarmed in Mexico, most of them military reservists. Japanese fishermen swarmed off our and the Mexican coasts. A Japanese-Mexican alliance directed against the United States would divert American attention from Europe and weaken her material support of the Allies. That the pragmatic Japanese were careful to let these horrendous possibilities leak is not surprising; it would up the price the Allies and America could be blackmailed into paying to keep Japan on their bench, such as standing still (almost) for Japan's infamous Twenty-one Demands on China in 1915. The presence in April of that year of a division of Japanese cruisers, one of them, HIJMS *Asama,* conveniently aground in Turtle Bay, Southern California, did little to lessen American sensitivity.

By February 1917, U.S. relations with Germany having been broken, war was not a matter of "if" but "when." A survey was made of the eight assorted German interned ships at Honolulu under the guise of "sanitary inspection," but actually preparatory to an imminent takeover. Life aboard was grim. In *Hermes,* the inspectors found she had a water supply "in which mosquito larvae breed . . . decomposed fruit and vegetables, unsanitary toilet . . . filthy clothes." The Board of Health sharply ordered them to "clean up the mess!"

The Germans had no need to be clairvoyant to read the signs. John F. Stone, a Honolulu cub reporter in 1917, wrote years later that he vividly recalled on 5 February 1917, "watching the German crew hack down the foremast and the mainmast of *Hermes* and throw the navigation instruments into the harbor."[13] Perhaps Stone's memory had faded; subsequent owner Northrup Castle and veteran schooner man Captain Fred K. Klebingat remember something more typically and fiendishly Teutonic; they sawed the masts in two just above the keelson, cleverly concealing their handiwork so that any undue stress would bring them crashing down. But the diabolic plan failed and repair was easy. The masts simply were lowered those few inches and restepped.

Plans had been shaped up well in advance for the bigger interned merchant ships, four of them between 3,500 and 5,000 tons and three averaging about 1,500 tons each. With such names as *Staatssekretar Kraetke* and *Gouveneur Jaeschke,* the first order of business after the 6

April war declaration was to rechristen the ships with something pronounceable; second, repair the sabotage and get cracking hauling U.S. war material.

*Geier,** as a warship, and *Loksun,* as a naval auxiliary, were a different sort. The Navy took them over immediately and with much relief. The little "cruiser" had been a prickly nettle. First the officers had been removed. Then several of them had got permission to go aboard on some trifling errand, shortly after which, on 4 February 1917, fire broke out, obviously an attempt to destroy the ship. With full magazines, 10 torpedo war heads and 2,000 pounds of black powder on board, Honolulu's harbor waterfront could have suffered more than just a few broken windowpanes. After this, *all* the crew was removed except one lone sailor to hoist and lower the German colors. The German skipper, Grasshof, who in a sort of reverse royal prerogative, signed his numerous letters of complaint with his last name only, sent off a final scorcher to the Commandant. One man could not do proper honor to the Imperial German naval ensign, he wrote. Henceforth, without abasement of any of his internee rights, the flag formality would be dispensed with.

Since internment, the German sailors had been drinking their beer and yodeling their stein songs at the Criterion Saloon or the Encore, both favorite international sailors' hangouts. Old seadog Captain Fred K. Klebingat, then before the mast in a windjammer, wrote me of an encounter with some of *Geier's* crew over a few mugs of suds: "They called her the cruiser with the wooden armor. A non-com told me the Japanese were chasing the *Geier,* but they thought this old tub was going at the speed *Jane's Fighting Ships* listed. She could really do about eight knots. And whenever the *Geier* called, the pursuers had been there about two days before, then dashed on." Klebingat wondered if perhaps it was not a design to keep a Japanese cruiser busy, to give von Spee's crack armored cruisers *Scharnhorst* and *Gneisenau* a chance to make the Atlantic unmolested in their escape from the Far East. He thought that perhaps the Japanese were not looking too keenly for a fight anyway. They already had collected their loot, Germany's China concession, Kiaochow, plus the Marshalls and Carolines.

After 2 February, shore leave for the Germans was stopped; the populace had grown too hostile to risk it. *Loksun's* personnel was as fractious as *Geier's.* Told off to tame these lions was one who would see something more of at least *Hermes:* Captain Thomas C. Hart, commanding Pearl-based submarines. As Commander in Chief, Asiatic Fleet, 24 years later, he would send *Hermes,* renamed *Lanikai,* on her way, *one* way.

And what about little *Hermes?* She lay in limbo until midsummer,

---

* As the USS *Carl Schurz,* had an undistinguished 15-month career, winding up on the East Coast, still with her eight 4.5″ guns.

1917. It is perhaps something more than a coincidence that Secretary of the Navy Josephus Daniels then and Franklin Roosevelt in 1941 should have had such closely related ideas. That Roosevelt was at that earlier date Daniels' assistant may or may not have been another coincidence. At any rate, on 26 July 1917, Daniels wrote to the Shipping Board that he felt *Hermes* would be valuable for submarine work, "on account of the fact that she has all the appearance of a merchant vessel and can play the part of a 'mystery' ship very well."

Somebody in the daisy chain must have felt the "mystery" ship usage required some explanatory expansion; on 11 September 1917 the Shipping Board wrote back that the President (who certainly must have had more important things to think about) wanted to know whether *Hermes* was suitable as a submarine chaser. The Navy Department possibly harbored a romantic who savored the derring-do of the famous raider Count Felix von Luckner and his windjamming *Seeadler;* in a lightning-fast five days they came back with the answer that she was not suited to *chase* submarines, but would be used as a "mystery ship."

The mystery man must have lost his franchise; it was not until 10:00 A.M., 1 April 1918, that the commission pennant climbed *Hermes'* mast, and according to the log, "Ensign hoisted smartly to the peak." The monitor USS *Monterey* sent her honor guard and the Naval Station band tootled the national anthem. Lieutenant (jg) John T. Diggs, USNRF, the only officer, read his orders to a crew of twenty-five assorted ratings, mostly USN, a few NRF, all American except seamen Ah Sam, Ah Pong, and two Filipino stewards to tend the young skipper's wants.

Bulwarks bristled with two elderly Colt machine guns and a one-pounder cannon scrounged from the *Monterey*. Into the hold went ten tons of pig iron ballast to take the place of the trade goods out, copra in, that used to keep her stable.

The new warship's first battle assignment was something less than likely to rock the dirty Hun. On 29 August, she set out along the Hawaiian chain to farthest Ocean Island. Skipper Diggs held orders to report signs of any recent landings on those islands, or any form of wreckage. Watch out for the enemy bases or wireless installations. The last item was to report on bird life. The Biological Survey in Washington wanted to know if there were any poachers about, and if the rabbits had chewed up all the vegetation on Laysan.*

No evidence of enemy deviltry or sailors in distress turned up. Not even a message in a bottle. But skipper Diggs was a jewel of a naturalist in sailor's clothing. Returning to Pearl Harbor on 2 October after 2,600 miles, mostly under sail, he produced in loving detail a magnificent

---

* Again by a striking coincidence, 24 years later the scenario was identical; only the cast was different when, as *Lanikai*, the ship was sent in March 1942 to perform a similar search along the west Australian coast. Only the bird-beak and bunny-tail count would be omitted.

24-page report on island fauna that must have had the Washington Biological Survey cracking its heels together.[14]

Had our animosity toward Germans expanded to war on the birds, we would have been amply prepared intelligence-wise, but with all the birds and bunnies checked out, the Navy found itself hard put to find useful employment for *Hermes*. The father of Captain R. S. Balch (SC) USN found her something less than romantic. Son Balch wrote me that: "Not knowing what to do with her, the Commandant often required my father to sail in her on his inspections of the outer island communication facilities. This he hated to do above all else because *Hermes* often took a week to make an overnight trip and all on board were dreadfully seasick. But then, lieutenants junior grade, as now, had little to say in such matters."

Captain Balch added a paragraph that corroborates the generally high regard in which Stone-built ships were held: "Her hull was indeed sturdy; five inches of planking forward. On at least one occasion, she was dynamited off a coral head without serious damage." There was no comment on the degree of blasting to which the errant navigator was subjected.

On 26 November 1918, skipper Diggs was ordered to presumably better things, relieved by Ensign (Deck) Edward Hollin, USNRF. His cruise was short. On 23 January 1919, the Inspection Board arrived at 1:00 P.M. and with their departure an hour later the commission pennant and ensign fluttered down. There was no band, no guard, no speech. Only memories.

It is an interesting coincidence that Franklin D. Roosevelt twice signed what were in effect death warrants for *Hermes/Lanikai*, the two events separated by 22 years. The first case resulted from a problem facing the Hawaiian territorial government. Leprosy occasionally popped up here and there, for which a colony had been established on Molokai. But the only way to get patients to it was to hire a special craft at considerable expense. No regular passenger service would touch them. How about turning *Hermes* over to the Hawaiian government as a tender for the leper colony? In July 1919, Assistant Secretary of the Navy Roosevelt, acting for his absent boss, thought it was such a great idea that he wrote a letter to Governor McCarthy the same day he saw the request, turning *Hermes* over on a temporary basis until the President signed the necessary bound and printed executive order, a mere formality. To be sure nobody henceforth ever might get *Hermes* confused with any former *USS* connotation, Roosevelt sent explanatory directives to all Navy Department bureaus, all sixteen naval districts, the Judge Advocate General, Solicitor for the Navy, and the commanders in chief of the Atlantic,

Pacific, and Asiatic fleets. The paperwork probably cost more than the vessel was worth.

All this was in vain. With *Hermes* sitting in death row at Pearl Harbor, the island government by 20 April 1920 had made an agonizing reappraisal. They had insufficient funds to operate the ship, thus averting a shunned, dead-end life for her under the leper's cloak.

Laid up in "rotten row," *Hermes* might have been a little dowdy, but she was not altogether forgotten. As is sometimes the fate of unprotected ladies, she surreptitiously was being taken advantage of by the Pacific Air Detachment as a floating storehouse for spare parts, both material and human. Being handy to operations, some of the more adventurous, cockroach-immune, mosquito-proof aviators slept aboard her, including Commander John Rodgers, who in 1925 came within a few miles of completing the first mainland-Hawaii Navy flight.

By 1920, some of the brighter officers had begun to feel that the flying machine was practical after all. Emboldened by this favorable trend, the Air Detachment's commander wrote to the Chief of Naval Operations in May, asking him to make an honest woman of *Hermes* by legalizing her clandestine association with airmen. Extended flights were being held in abeyance, he pleaded, pending arrangements for a suitable base vessel. All she would need was a dynamo at $226, a radio at $350, and a set of $260 batteries. He could man her with his own troops, including three officers "with sufficient sea experience perfectly competent to take command for purpose of establishing a base on distant islands." The District Commandant stamped his approval and in an amazingly short span of two weeks, the CNO agreed. For the benefit of aspiring present-day yachtsmen, the cost of materiel upkeep was a mere $450 per month, exclusive of the 8 gallons of fuel per mile she swallowed.

By 15 December 1920, *Hermes'* glamorous new look had attracted other suitors. The Oahu Shipping Company, Ltd., wanted her for $20,000. "Just the thing for Hawaiian inter-island trading," they said. "Nothing doing!" said Commander Emrick, her new Air Detachment sponsor. The romance had prospered. He would consider the painful thought of cooling it only if the sale price were applied to constructing a building ashore to take her place. How this building would sail out to establish bases was not explained. Anyway, said Emrick, she was not worth $20,000 but $25,000. This was down from brand-new 1914 $60,000.

"Fly-fly" boys traditionally are longer on action than on paper work. If under AirDetPac *Hermes* ranged the Pacific, renewing friendships with the aviators' feathered colleagues, setting up bases, spying on what the Japanese were doing with their new war spoils, or simply catching weekend fish, one cannot say. The paper trail is cold. But if she was acting in character, it is safe to suspect she was doing a little of all these things.

By 1925 the battleship was still queen, but Air had come of age.

There were huge carriers, converted from battle cruiser hulls, the mighty *Saratoga* and *Lexington*, known in the fleet as *Sister Sarah* and *Lady Lex*. It was scarcely dignified that the flagship of the Naval Air Detachment, Pacific, should be a little bucket smelling faintly of fish, no longer than an F5L patrol seaplane.

But an aging lady cannot be too choosy. When in May 1925 an enterprising fellow in American Samoa beckoned, *Hermes* pricked up her topsails. She would be ideal in local Samoan commercial traffic, said the naval governor, with a free ride for government freight and minimum freight charges for the government's wards, the carefree natives. In much the same character as the ten-minute Chinese harangue being translated as, "He say NO!" the Judge Advocate delivered himself of a four-page "brief" which said nothing in the law made this deal possible. The bad news was communicated to Samoa by mid-September, the disapproval saying not a word about legality, but mysteriously excusing themselves ". . . in view of the other needs of the Service . . ."

By 8 January 1926, "the other needs of the Service," in the highly doubtful possibility there ever had been any, had melted away: The Chief of Naval Operations "desires *Hermes* be surveyed for sale," a desire seconded by Secretary Wilbur on 28 June, who appended her obituary, "Unfit for Naval Service." Stricken from the Navy list on 1 July and appraised at $5,000 a week later, she soon was launched on another career, once again "in trade," under the ownership of Mr. Paul Beyer.

This time she could be detected well to leeward by the fragrance of fish rather than the perfume of copra. Under Captain "Bill" Anderson, the little schooner, workhorse of the Lanikai Fish Company, combed the teeming fishing grounds along the Hawaiian chain west, and the Line Islands to the south, Palmyra, Kingman, Christmas and Fanning.

Beyer had renamed the ship *Lanikai*, after a small village on the east coast of Oahu, and of more practical importance, installed a new engine and a 40-ton capacity, ammonia-type freeze room.

The original three-cylinder Atlas had been built back in the days of tiller-steered automobiles and five-cent beer. It burned a cheap petroleum product called "distillate," using gasoline only for priming.

In place of spark plugs, the old Atlas had a make-and-break metal device called an "igniter." The more expert engineers knew how to delicately position the engine at "stop," so that when the "start" bell was rung, they could flick an igniter on the point of sparking and off she went. With an engine of such volatile temperament, it was wise to have the engineer always on ready call. His bunk was in the engineroom.

The 30,000-pound, eight-foot-high Union diesel installed by Beyer made 375 r.p.m. all out, and was the eighteenth the company had built. According to three outstanding experts who knew *Lanikai* well, no better engine ever went to sea.

As for the freeze room, it was a victim of man's susceptibility to suspicion of things new. Local fishermen, lacking the wherewithal to install such a plant as *Lanikai's*, started a whispering campaign against such a bizarre novelty as frozen fish in a place where even ice was a rarity. Who knew? Perhaps the fish had been dug out of an Antarctic icecap and were a hundred years old. Local tradition had it down through the generations that the only good fish was one still flapping.

In 1929, The Lanikai Fish Company sold out to Captain William G. Anderson and several friends, who formed the Hawaiian Sea Products Company. Their aim was to work pearl shell beds discovered by Anderson in the islands west and south of Hawaii. He was as at home in the pearl beds as a rabbit in a briar patch, having been born on Fanning Island of a native mother and come up to Honolulu for his schooling.

Anderson had installed a radio transmitter, an innovation which came none too soon. The 8 August 1931 Honolulu *Advertiser* carried a headline, "LANIKAI MAKES PORT UNDER OWN POWER, Staunch Little Schooner Made Adventurous 2,800-mile Cruise." There had been concern about the ship, out nearly 70 days. Her crew and passengers were described by the *Advertiser* as having undergone "more thrills than they would have had in a half-dozen ordinary voyages." She had broken her propeller shaft and lost her screw. The wrench had damaged the stern post and stuffing box and the spares were beyond installing properly by the ship's company. Things got progressively worse. With seven hundred miles to go, a radio for help brought the destroyer-minelayer USS *Gamble* on the run. In proper Navy fashion, "repairs were quickly made." *Lanikai*, heavily bearded crewmen, and 20 tons of choice fish were soon in port.

Lanikai was not to beep her new radio for long. First, for some unrecorded reason, the U.S. government forced the closing of the pearl beds. They continued to fish in the northwest chain of islands, but a combination of suspicion of frozen fish and tumbling prices in general brought operations to a halt. Depression had jerked the net from under the market. Tuna went for $2\frac{1}{2}$ cents a pound. The more exotic breeds, such as those the Japanese relished raw, brought a mere 12 cents. The catch was scarcely worth the cost to cool it.

As the commercial gloom deepened, Northrup Castle, whose missionary forebears had come out to the Islands in 1837 to bring *mumus* and morality, bought *Lanikai* in 1933 for $5,000. There was a saying that the missionaries had come out to do good and had done well, but in 1931 even a few thousand dollars were hard to come by. The ship had been laid up for two years and was much deteriorated. Sea Scouts in most unscoutsmanlike manner had whooped it up on board and done considerable damage. That jewel of a Union diesel engine needed a complete overhaul. A new suit of sails, four or five thousand square feet of board-stiff Nr. 2 canvas, was outfitted at a cost of $750, a price tag that in 1973 would scarcely cover the cost of a nylon flying jib.

"She was a sturdy, handy boat," old seadog Castle[15] said. He had pearled and fished the Pacific for years and had commanded four U.S. Navy ships in World War II. "*Lanikai* had enough beam to be comfortable," he added, "but unfortunately she wasn't a very good sailer."

Money was more than tight when Castle acquired *Lanikai*. In spite of his being a scion of the great Hawaiian firm of Castle and Cooke, *Lanikai*'s new owner and wife both had to drop out of school and start catching fish—aboard a *paying* yacht—hopefully, money *in* rather than fecklessly *out*, as is usually the case with yachts. Equally broke college chums joined up as super-cargo, mates and engineers, and as would happen again under the Navy, Filipinos ably manned the deck.

With navigational knowhow and modest equipment, Castle and his motley crew could go where most local fishermen could not—to the far-flung reaches of the Hawaiian archipelago, as far west as Midway and south to Palmyra and Kingman's reef, all unspoiled, unfished paradises.

In 1936, Captain Harry W. Crosby, of Seattle, Washington, bought *Lanikai* from Northrup Castle and came out to the islands to pick her up. Young Harry C. Bush had had a love affair with the ship ever since he first met her in his Sea Scout days, then later cajoled Castle into signing him on as a 16-year-old radio operator. So, maintaining the romance, Bush signed on in the same capacity under Crosby.

With the new skipper and his family aboard, they left Honolulu on 16 February 1936 and made a landfall off San Diego two weeks later. From there, they sailed to San Francisco, whence *Hermes/Lanikai* had sailed on her maiden voyage almost 22 years earlier. On arrival at Lake Union, Seattle, her sails were unbent and struck below. Bush and another crew member "ship-kept" until May, when the two went to Alaska for the salmon season. They came back in autumn and wintered over in her. She had no source of heat, and Lake Union partially froze over. But *Lanikai*'s cabin timbers were so thick that an electric heater carried them through.

In early 1937, Sam Goldwyn bought the vessel for use as a prop in the prospective spectacular "Hurricane," starring Jon Hall and Dorothy Lamour. Departing Seattle in May, she hit something underwater, sheared off the shaft and lost the propeller. A diver located the propeller and soon she was under way once more when a storm carried away some of the forward rigging.

Having survived these real-life vicissitudes, she was soon to undergo some startling real *looking* but actually marvelously contrived ones under the masterful hand of director John Ford. The huge fans that blew up the "hurricane," smashed the "island" (San Clemente), and battered Dotty and "native" friends were supposed to dismast the ship. To avoid spoiling what was believed to be a perfectly good mainmast, it was lifted out and a splintered telephone pole substituted. This was a rare piece of good luck for future serious sailors; the lower part of the mainmast was found to be a spongy mass of rot, surrounded by a thin skin of deceptively sound-appearing wood. Northrup Castle, hearing of it, thanked his Hawaiian luck piece that the rotten stick had held during violent blows when he was up in the crosstrees, conning her through the passage into a storm-swept coral atoll.

Following the movie making, *Lanikai* became a sort of Goldwyn pet, a rich man's yacht for him and Ford and a poor man's yacht for studio employees when the moguls were elsewhere. Gruff old Rear Admiral John Ford, USNR (Retired) and Dotty Lamour, her glamorous pareu-clad days enshrined in the memories of an older generation, are still in Hollywood. There were times during the long tropic nights of running before the Japanese that we dreamed charming little idylls of Dorothy's coming back to haunt the ship. But she never did.

According to a yellowing document found in *Lanikai*'s chartroom in 1942, "the motor yacht *Lanikai*" was sold on 6 April 1939 by Samuel Goldwyn, Inc., to George W. Simmie ". . . as the sole owner of the vessel called the *Lanikai*. . . ." Simmie was acting as agent for a remarkable individual named E. M. Grimm. An American resident of Manila with extensive holdings in the Philippines, Mr. Grimm was on his way home from a visit to the United States when the war broke out. His ship was diverted to Australia. As a Naval Reserve officer, he found no suitable unit there which he could join. Anxious to get into the scrap, he went with General MacArthur's newly created staff, making every landing along the route to MacArthur's final triumphant return to Leyte.

Grimm had intended to use *Lanikai* for an extended trip around the world. He had reconditioned and rearranged everything below decks. Unfortunately, the European "unpleasantness" grew to such alarming proportions that the world tour fell apart. Crispin Tipay wrote me in 1971 that,

> After six months of initial outfitting in a Manila dockyard, *Lanikai* set sail for our first fishing trip off the bay area, to nearby Corregidor and Mariveles. On board were Messrs. Simmie, the company's boss, Grimm, manager, and the quarantine doctor, plus another American. We went on much longer cruises later, with the same people aboard, to such far-away places as Mindoro, most of the larger ports in the Visayas and Mindanao, and to Palawan and Jolo off Borneo. As I understood it, this was both business and pleasure. On the last trip prior to the Navy's taking possession of the *Lanikai*, we left Manila on 1 October 1941 and returned December 3rd, only five days prior to Pearl Harbor.

Adair luxuriates in one of the wicker chairs salvaged from Cavite's docks when the warships stripped ship. The camp chair forward will be occupied through the night by McVey or LeCompte, chief radiomen, passengers and volunteer lookouts.

Moros near the Japanese-held island of Jolo in their graceful, narrow outrigger canoes take our empty Coca-Cola bottles with gratitude.

Tipay's recorded date of return to Manila would dispose of a red herring that might suggest an earlier covetous eye cast on *Lanikai* by Cavite—before the urgent, secret Washington directive to Hart that resulted in *Lanikai's* instant acquisition. To avoid overlooking any cranny, however, the aforementioned fishy business must be brought forth: On 29 November, the Commandant 16th Naval District at Cavite radioed priority to the Chief of Naval Operations that,

> PRESENT SITUATION INDICATES EXTENSIVE MINESWEEPING MANILA BAY MAY BE NECESSARY IN NEAR FUTURE X URGENTLY
>
> REQUEST AUTHORITY TO TIME CHARTER AVAILABLE CIVILIAN VESSELS AND ACCOMPLISH NECESSARY CONVERSION X CON-
>
> SIDER PRESENT NUMBER OF NAVY MINESWEEPING VESSELS TOTALLY INADEQUATE FOR JOB AND CIVILIAN SHIPS WILL
>
> NEED EXTENSIVE ALTERATIONS FOR PURPOSE X APPROVAL CINCAF THIS ACTION HAS BEEN RECEIVED (290542)

Neither this mysterious message nor any other sources reveal what was behind the "urgent request." CNO must have been not only equally mystified, but busier with other things, as he waited until 2 December (021607) with a "routine" precedence reply, one sufficiently cool to put the project on ice, as nothing more in its connection turned up:

> IMPRACTICABLE TO TIME CHARTER BOATS AND DO EXTENSIVE CONVERSION. PURCHASE CAN BE MADE IF SET PROCEDURE IS
>
> FOLLOWED. CAN RIVER GUNBOATS BE USED OR YAG 2, 3 AND 4 BE CONVERTED. ADVISE IN DETAIL REQUIREMENTS AND
>
> WHAT DOES EXTENSIVE MINESWEEPING COMPRISE.

It is thus possible that Com 16 already had his eye on *Lanikai* as a likely candidate for an auxiliary; there would not be too many even marginally appropriate craft available in Manila. But in any case, the next Washington secret priority swept aside any compunctions about "time charters" or anything else encumbering. The Navy wanted *Lanikai* for use as a patrol boat to guard the Corregidor minefields, Cavite now said. It was wood, and virtually nonmagnetic, they logically explained.

With Luzon Stevedoring Company's manager and *Lanikai's* owner Grimm still en route back from the U.S., the ship's turnover to the Navy was taken care of by the company's representative, Charles Parsons. The offer was to charter her for an indefinite period at one dollar a year, the ship to be returned in like condition on completion of service.

The Navy alibi was well devised. Nearly thirty years later, Grimm, the former owner, learned from me the real reason. His reaction was predictable. He had spent twenty years of his life as a Naval Reserve intelligence officer, then through the war in the U.S. Army, ending up a colonel. As a result, he was seldom surprised at *anything*, he guaranteed. But the telegram he had just read astounded him.

The "telegram" was a copy of one addressed to the Commander in Chief, Asiatic Fleet, Admiral Thomas C. Hart, from the Chief of Naval

Operations, Admiral H. S. Stark. It opened with the wholly arresting and probably unique line that: "THE PRESIDENT DIRECTS THE FOLLOWING BE DONE AS SOON AS POSSIBLE . . ." It was a message of the highest priority then in effect and the highest secrecy classification available, that in the years to come would stir researchers, authors, friends, and enemies of Roosevelt to resolve what lay behind the enigmatic words which followed. The court historians and the revisionists approach the question each with his built-in bias. None has heretofore laid out in one comprehensive study before the ultimate jury, the American public, all the circumstantial evidence. The *direct* evidence was locked in the brains of at most, four men, between noon and 1:30 P.M., 1 December 1941.

Chapter II

Aboard the *Lanikai,* cut off as we were from communications with the outside world, all we knew of the war was what we could see going on at Cavite and Corregidor. But the Japanese were driving hard and fast, everywhere, and as dispatch after dispatch reached Admiral Hart, their smashing successes astonished even that imperturbable gentleman and on 15 December, he radioed Admiral Glassford, easing his way southward with Task Force 5, that,

> THE RAPID DEVELOPMENTS OF THE PAST WEEK, WITH THE UNEXPECTED SUCCESSES OF THE JAPANESE AIR FORCE OVER LUZON, HAVE THROWN THIS FLEET INTO A GENERAL SITUATION WHICH WAS NOT EXPECTED TO DEVELOP FOR A CONSIDERABLE TIME, IF AT ALL. . . .

Minor landings had been made at Aparri and Vigan on the northern Luzon coast on the tenth and at Legaspi, on the east coast, on the eleventh, where the Japanese used small craft that made hopeless targets for submarines, even if they had had decent torpedoes. They proved equally elusive for the Filipine troops ashore, many of whom had never fired a single practice round from their artillery pieces.

With fighter air cover gone, Patrol Wing 10's seaplanes evacuated for the south on the fifteenth, leaving Hart without local air reconnaissance. On the seventeenth, the ten surviving B-17s of MacArthur's original 35 left for Java, thus wiping out the possibility of any air counterattack against the Japanese beachheads.

On the nineteenth, MacArthur wrote a sharp note to Hart concerning an "estimate of the situation" dated 10 December, which MacArthur took to be Hart's personal product:

> With the initiative in the hands of the enemy, consideration of his early successes, and preponderance of forces available to him, there is the contemplation of a long war, facing the loss of, and ultimate recapture of the Philippines.

Hart soon set MacArthur straight on Navy staff procedure in a 20 December reply:

> . . . Your letter opens with a quotation from an estimate. That paper appears to have been prepared by Admiral Purnell at the direct request of General Brereton and supposedly to be for his aid in handling Army Air Forces in the immediate future. . . . Any formal Navy estimate of the situation would naturally be signed by me or indicate that it was by my direction. . . . The most important despatches between the Navy Department and me contain information and opinions which may amount to a brief formal estimate. I believe I have kept you informed concerning the content of those despatches. It hardly seems necessary to say that I fully appreciate the strategic importance of Luzon.

Also on the nineteenth, Sangley Point, home of the high-powered radio station, naval hospital and fuel depot, was largely neutralized by unopposed Japanese attack, leaving nothing further in that area for Rockwell to command. Moving to Corregidor on the twenty-first, he found it a disappointing substitute even for wrecked Cavite. Power house, water works, fuel dumps, and most of the communications facilities were above ground. The emplacements for the powerful 14-inch fortress guns, planned before the air age, were wide open to the heavens. The only provision for modern war was the tunnels, four of which were Navy, thanks to Admiral Hart's unflagging efforts over the last two years. One housed radio equipment, two were for personnel, and the fourth for 16th Naval District and 4th Marine headquarters. Food, submarine spares, and torpedoes were tucked into any available space. There was a desk and bunk each for Admiral Rockwell, chief of staff H. J. Ray, and the yeoman. Far East charts were piled on top of stacked crates of canned tomatoes. A reduction to one typewriter probably was the prime contribution to efficiency.

Rockwell's world may have shrunk, but not so for that of Malcolm M. Champlin, his flag lieutenant. After his 1934 graduation from the Naval Academy, Champ left the service because of poor eyesight. He was an FBI agent on the Baltimore waterfront when recalled to active duty in 1941, in time for the SS *President Harrison*'s fateful last trip to the Far East.

The *Harrison*'s passengers were predominantely service people. But there was the inevitable group of missionaries, on their way back to China posts after six months' home leave refilling their spiritual gas tanks at "Stateside" conferences and revivals. Champ felt a certain nostalgia listening to their daily hymnals; as a missionary "padre," his father had taught at Tokyo University.

Leavening the brethren and the military was a handful of commercial types: a young salesman en route Rangoon, where 1,400 of his company's trucks awaited mechanics to ready them for the rugged trip up the Burma Road; an importer of orientalia on a buying mission to Shanghai lugubriously predicting it would be his last trip. Colonel R. M. Beecher, USMC, destined for prison camp, awarded the loving cup for the bridge tournament, first prize going to the senior missionary—"From one Christian soldier to another," as Champ later described it.

"You'll soon be back here," Admiral Glassford told him in Shanghai, when he learned of Champ's FBI background. "I can use you." Shanghai's reputation as a center of intrigue and espionage and double-double cross had been greatly enhanced by the war.

At Hongkong, Champ was hornswoggled into contracting for the traditional tourist bait, a summer suit from the equally traditional obsequious Indian tailor. "Ah! Meestah Offisah! You nevah hoff to worry about *thees* suit!" guaranteed the smiling, bowing tailor, after having insinuated several stiff scotches-and-splash into the neophyte customer. Naturally, the tailor's delicate conscience was eased by the knowledge that he was fracturing the truth only slightly. After the first washing, his promise would be valid; the suit's owner would pass it on to some Filipino three sizes smaller.

At Cavite, Champ immediately noted the paucity of defenses in this "bastion of the Pacific." Where were the AA guns? The fighter air strip for defending planes? Over the peanuts and San Miguel beer at Cavite's Nutshell Cafe, he listened to amusing anecdotes. There were rumors Hart and MacArthur could not sit at the same table due to unresolved protocol difficulties; an elderly retired Filipino steward's mate had showed up for active duty in a chauffeur-driven Cadillac; the old Scotsman living in the civilian enclave between Sangley Point and the Yard was a spy; all the Japanese running photo and barber shops were at least majors in the Japanese Army reserve, and so forth.

On 5 November 1941, the new commandant for the Sixteenth Naval District, Rear Admiral F. W. Rockwell, World War I Navy Cross holder, arrived from duty at the prestigious Naval War College. There was no more talk of Champlin's becoming a Shanghai sleuth. He stood by while the only local commander junior to Rockwell, Brigadier General Jonathan (Skinny) Wainwright, made his formal call. Rockwell hurried through calls on MacArthur, High Commissioner Francis B. Sayre, and Hart, then got down to business. Shipyard work speeded up. Hammers pounded, riveters rat-tatted away, sparks flew, flammables and excess explosives were hurried elsewhere. Everything went on 24 hours a day, seven days a week, including the steam crane, its smoke problem no longer a consideration.

And on 10 December, the bombs came raining down.

There were no more calls in white gloves and sword. Champ's first post-bombing assignment was to save the Yard's eight hundred gas masks from a merrily blazing warehouse. Collecting a party of volunteers, they braved the flames and secondary explosions rocking the area, stepping around the whole and dismembered dead in their path. "Will you speak for us?" asked one of the volunteers after the job was done. Champ was at a loss. Speak for what? "We are prisoners released from the brig," the man said. "Mebby somehow we could stay out."

Champ's next stop was the Marsman Building, across the arm of the bay, to tell Admiral Hart that with the exception of the ammunition and fuel depots, Cavite was gone.

On his return to Cavite, Champ found that old Scotsman's house empty of Scotsman and Japanese wife. There was a radio direction finder and a carrier pigeon coop, but the birds—human and feathered—had flown.

At Sunset Beach were a hundred new-design mines that must be disposed of, but could not be blown up in one gigantic bang without destroying Filipine homesteads for miles around. They must be sunk in the bay. Volunteers Champlin and Lieutenant (jg) Henry, the latter just two weeks in the service, rode from Corregidor to Sangley aboard barefoot "Dick" Hawes' *Pigeon*. En route an "automobile committee" was selected from the fifty-odd enlisted volunteers, many of them from those valiant men who had saved the gas masks, thanks to which their prisoner status had become "ex." They would have to find trucks and make them go.

Working their way through the rubble of Sangley Point, the group assembled at the gate, where they were joined by five Philippine Constabulary men bearing sawed-off shotguns, which Champ had issued some days before to cope with the hundreds of stray dogs, starving, hungrily sniffing cadavers, potentially dangerous animals after the death or speedy departure of their native owners.

An American civilian foreman found ashore solved the manpower problem. He had been wondering what to do with the hundred or so Filipino laborers who still faithfully showed up for nonexistent work every morning in the abandoned base. The only enemy so far to enter the area had been one Japanese tank, which had not ventured into the Navy Yard, probably suspecting it was mined.

Things began to happen. The party sledge-hammered a PBY and spare engines into uselessness at the Pan-American Airways base. They found a usable 4-ton mobile crane. But Sunset Beach was five miles from Sangley. Champ telephoned the Luzon Stevedoring Company, erstwhile owners of *Lanikai*. Lighters? Sure! One hundred and fifty of 'em, spread all over the bay. Meanwhile, the automobile committee had had good hunting. Several battered trucks had been coaxed into sputtering action. A third of the mines were trucked down shoreside the first night. At dawn, the weary men headed for Corregidor aboard *Pigeon* to wait out the day and its ubiquitous enemy aircraft.

By 4:00 A.M. the following night, all the mines were aboard a lighter. *Pigeon,* lighter in tow, headed for deep water. But even with large holes chopped in its bottom, the damned thing refused to sink. "Tow her sideways, with the hawser secured to its far edge!" suggested *Pigeon's* "Bosun" Taylor. At ten knots, in the bay's deepest water, over she went, the mines flipping out like so many marbles from an upturned cigar box.

In the melee, *Lanikai* was forgotten. The night of the twenty-second she anchored a mile west of Sangley Point, in a good position to move in any direction except straight up—Corregidor, Cavite, Manila, or the far reaches of the 30-mile-wide bay.

After breakfast, probably rice and fish, *Lanikai* got under way for Sangley Point, where my emergency cache of best blue uniform, raincoat, inspection cap, sword and class ring supposedly lay intact in a friend's quarters. There was no need to land to verify the awful fact: a direct hit had obliterated the house. My two trunksful of other effects had already fed the flames in a Cavite warehouse. I could neatly pack what remained of my worldly possessions in a couple of shoe boxes. But there were compensations; the lifting of responsibility for personal trinkets gave an almost exhilarating feeling of freedom from the shackling encumbrances of peacetime fuss and feathers. It admirably fitted the new nature of things—the transformation from peace to war.

A planned look-see in the ashes for some trace of class ring or sword soon was aborted:

> At 0810 discovered that Japanese planes were over Manila. Guns surrounding the bay went into action.
>
> At 0820 lay to off USS *Finch*. Skipper Davison sent over some fresh provisions, fruit and news.*
>
> At 0840 got underway for Manila.
>
> At 0930 anchored . . . off Yacht Club.

Very early that same morning, Japanese troops started coming ashore at Lingayen. This was the beginning of a flood of bandy-legged, humorless little sons of Dai Nippon that soon would swell to a force of

* The mortality among my 1929 classmates in the Far East was high. Commanding Asiatic Fleet ships were W. L. Kabler, Navy Cross, *Heron;* T. W. Davison, Navy Cross, *Finch;* J. B. Berkley, *Tulsa;* J. M. Bermingham, Navy Cross, *Peary;* J. W. Britt, *Asheville;* E. A. Roth, Navy Cross, *Tanager.* F. D. Jordan served as executive officer of *Luzon,* and H. C. Lang in the 4th Marines. The last five died in action or as prisoners of war. W. J. Galbraith, in *Houston,* survived as a prisoner of war. A. J. Miller made it safely in *Barker,* commanding her on the trip home, last Asiatic Fleet ship to reach the United States. Of our eleven, only six escaped death or capture.

50,000, other landings being largely in the nature of feints. The hastily thrown together, poorly officered Filipine reserve divisions were no match for the veterans of three years of China warfare.

Several weeks later, Commander Dennison, acting chief of staff for Admiral Rockwell, went up on top of the "Rock" to have a chat with General MacArthur. He had found almost everyone in the various tunnels, except MacArthur and Sutherland, who remained topside. Dennison wanted to know why the forces to the south of Manila, opposing the Legaspi landing, couldn't hold. MacArthur broke out some oil company road maps, which were all they had. He told Dennison the Filipinos were insufficiently trained and that if they ever engaged the enemy they probably never could disengage and would be completely destroyed. MacArthur then explained in great detail how the forces could withdraw from the north, south and east, converging on Bataan, and with remarkable prescience even predicted the date on which Bataan and Corregidor would surrender.

MacArthur's bold promises to "fight to destruction at the beaches" soon collapsed into a hasty but well-handled retreat of the regular U.S. Army and Philippine Scouts into Bataan peninsula, along with such of the Philippine Army and reserves as had not melted into the "boondocks." The withdrawal miraculously was unhampered by any Japanese air activity, which could have raised merry hell along the few good roads, clogged solid with moving guns, trucks, and tired men.

On the twenty-third, perhaps the Japanese air force was too busy mother-henning the landing at Lingayen; Manila lay quiet the whole day and night. On the twenty-fourth, however, it was business as usual not only in the local airspace, but in the Hart—MacArthur cockpit. Things had rocked along on the prewar pattern, as Hart's recording of a meeting with the Commanding General shortly after war's outbreak suggests:

> I knew the general was coming and had ready in my office the location chart showing where all submarines were. He barely glanced at the chart, and after I had gotten off two or three sentences, again launched forth into one of his characteristic "speeches" about his own side of the war. It was only by using some sharpness and repeatedly interrupting him in turn that I was able to tell him anything of the Navy situation at all. He asked no questions whatever, evinced no curiosity, and as has too often been the case, the interview was quite futile as far as furthering any meeting of minds between us.

MacArthur's 24 December surprise announcement of making Manila an open city was the climax of this uneasy relationship. A fortunate concomitant for *Lanikai* was that it opened the door for a flight to freedom.

On 26 December 1941, four U.S. Navy ships threaded their way through the Corregidor swept channel: *Lanikai, Peary,* and *Pillsbury*— the last surface warships to escape from Manila Bay other than motor torpedo boats—and submarine *Shark,* carrying Admiral Hart to Java. By April 1942, only the unlikeliest of them all—*Lanikai*—was still afloat. One of the first stories written about this hegira was entitled, "The Lucky *Lanikai*," by Charles A. Walruff, in the September 1943 issue of *Yachting.* It was a title both euphonious and appropriate.

About 9:00 P.M., *Lanikai* passed one of the Yangtze River gunboats, lying to, outside the minefield as station ship. We slid by in black or rather more accurately—dark green silence; the camouflage job was largely completed. No cheery blinker lights winked a goodbye signal. Thenceforth anything sighted afloat and probably any plane aloft could only be enemy. We were like a fledgling bird taking that first scary flight from the nest, hoping to remain unspotted by any predator by sailing well inshore to blend our low silhouette with the hilly coast.

Lanikai's response to the moderate seas was a symphony of creaks and groans from below and a slapping of blocks in the running rigging topside. Every noise seemed frighteningly magnified in an environment where there was no outside sound except the slap! slap! of waves against the ship and the muffled chug of the auxiliary engine.

It had been a grueling day, rounding up supplies and swabbing on green paint, but there was no lack of eager lookouts straining all senses to catch a whiff of smoke, spot a feather of bow wave, hear the clang of a slammed steel hatch, or a tool dropped on a patrolling enemy's deck plates. Sounds carry a long way on a still night at sea.

By 4:00 A.M. on the twenty-seventh, we were beyond Calavite Passage, a likely spot for blockading enemy ships. We had slipped through the noose, and were now in Indian country, where chance encounters were the major danger. Obviously there could be no safe movement at sea during daylight. We would sail at night, having pored over the chart to find a likely haven reachable by sunrise.

Things had not yet shaken down into routine by a long shot, in spite of the three weeks most of us had been aboard. Individually, we were still feeling each other out. To those professional sailormen who consider that ships have personalities, it would have been apparent that *Lanikai* herself was not sure of her new masters. For twenty-seven years, she had been the mistress of knowledgeable lovers. The old gal could be expected to show a certain wariness in the hands of callow iron ship sailors. In spite of her modest size, she was no Severn River catboat off for a Sunday afternoon's outing.

The new arrivals aboard had injected a wholly different element into the personnel structure, although the "recruits" were adaptable old-time sailormen and fell into place with no gear grinding or backfires. Two of the six passengers were senior to me, but with characters of such a sterling nature that no hint of conflict in this anomalous situation ever arose.

The Dutchman, Lieutenant Paul Nygh, was a six-foot, slim, impeccably turned-out fellow with a hawk face and small black moustache. He was wearing a naval uniform, but like a great many civilians all over the world who had been dragooned into military service, had been slightly miscast. As were numbers of other able-bodied Hollanders, he was a reservist—a cavalryman. But in the Netherlands Indies, where the war found him, cavalry was not the paramount answer. Real horses do not prosper there, either in the moist tropical heat, or on the available forage. The pint-sized Malay ponies, like the ones that trotted so briskly ahead of the Manila *caromatas,* would have left Nygh's long legs trailing on the ground. The only other local alternative, the caribao, has never made a very good cavalry mount. So Paul Nygh was transmuted into a naval officer, observer at Manila, with only the vaguest idea of which was fore and which was aft. Thus, Paul was off the *Lanikai*'s watch list, allowing him to sleep all night and stay awake all day with an eye peeled for trouble, while his night-watching shipmates took their fitful, fly-disturbed snooze as the ship lay concealed in some small coastal enclave.

Charles (Sparky) Walruff was a technician whose previous naval experience had been mostly out of sight of the passing ocean—down in some ship's innards, ministering to the wants of the communications equipment. Two years older than I, he was an aggressive, cocky little individual who had risen from enlisted radioman to warrant officer, an accomplishment that in pre-World War II days called for superior ability, dedication, and push. There were no qualms about putting Sparky on the underway deck watch list. What he didn't know, you could be sure he would soon make it his business to find out.

Charles Adair was of that genus described in wardroom language as "nature's nobleman." Well over six feet tall, imposing, and with a pleasant expression that reflected a marvelously good disposition, he had that rare combination, common sense and intelligence. He had stood near the top of his 1926 Naval Academy class, three years senior to me.

Charlie had arrived in the Philippines a few months earlier to serve as Admiral Hart's personal aide and flag lieutenant. But Hart was independent and self-reliant, as men of small stature often are. He wrote me in 1970:

> I had not had a real flag lieutenant for some months; had divided the job among two or three and was just too worried by my circumstances to make any changes.

Consequently, Charlie was largely cast on his own resources in finding a means of escape from the Philippine trap, which the staff, though not the rest of us, knew was very soon to snap shut. It was in this quest that he spotted *Lanikai* lying alongside dock below Navy headquarters that fateful Christmas. With his remarkable insight, he instantly translated this frail little craft into the best of a half dozen superficially more safe options. Hart was leaving next day by PBY or submarine, where space was precious. In *Lanikai* lay not only salvation* but a bonus—adventure.

It was a providential gift that the senior officer of the lot, Lieutenant Commander Harry "H" Keith, was such a universally sound shipmate. A 1923 Academy graduate, Harry was a good-humored extrovert with a booming voice that projected optimism under the gloomiest circumstances.

"Hey look! Here's some more!" he would gleefully shout, holding up a palm full of tiny shreds of shrapnel that had painfully worked out of his hide during the day's snooze. It was this peppering that had caused him to be detached from command of the destroyer *Peary*, after she had been hit in the 10 December Cavite holocaust. As an engineering specialist, he had been attached to the Fleet staff to recuperate. With Cavite destroyed and the repair ships gone south, there was not much "engineering" to be done. So Keith, like Adair, was left to his own devices in arranging an escape, and was a ready recruit to take a ride in *Lanikai*. He knew *Peary* was going out the same night, but the thought of that blood-spattered bridge and his butchered men had left him cold to any thought of returning to her.

As senior line officer aboard, Keith could have complicated my decision-making and made life difficult, as many a naval officer I have known would have done. There were daily discussions on our next move, where a wrong guess might well have meant the end of the line. But after the final summing up, there was no argument and no pressure. The attitude of Keith and Adair was unspoken but plain throughout those perilous months: "It's *your* ship, Skipper, and *your* decision." (God bless those two gallant gentlemen!)

Of the Filipino crew members who shared our adventure, a good example is Crispin Tipay, who came with the *Lanikai* as an original hand. He, along with his five shipmates, was given a white hat as badge of office and a paper to sign that would change his way of life completely thenceforth.

Born in 1912 in the boondocks, Batangas Province, Tipay was the eldest of three brothers and two sisters. When he was seven, the family moved to Manila for two years, then back to a farm near his mother's Bicol home. There, young Crispin, at nine, was a prime helper in the

---

* Admiral Hart was known for strictness and, at the same time, deep concern for his men. He has often expressed his anguish at having to leave so many of his Far East personnel to a clearly predictable dire fate. Of Adair, he wrote me in October 1970 that: "I abandoned him in Manila. I should have done much better and it is something which has long hung on my conscience."

fields. He had gone to school before and in Manila, but the farm was many miles away from the nearest institution of learning of any kind. In a September 1971 letter, he related what happened next:

> When I was 16 years old, mature enough to realize the hardship of work in the country with practically no improvement in life in sight, I decided to go back to Manila on my own, to start a new life —to look for a better job and to further my education.
>
> In Manila, I was fortunate. The Luzon Stevedoring Company was hiring quite a few seamen to work on their some ten bay and river tugboats. I was hired on the spot as an apprentice seaman/line handler. It was a good thing I got a job so soon. Not only was I able to send some money to my parents in the province, but had some money left to support myself by attending evening classes at the Harvadian Institute of Manila.
>
> After almost three years as a seaman, it was my good fortune to be chosen as an oiler, which gave me the basic training to become an engineer. Day and night, the copy of the Diesel Engine Manual was never very far from my side.
>
> By the time Mr. Simmie brought the *Lanikai* to Manila, I was already a licensed tugboat engineer, having passed the Civil Service exam. When the ship needed a chief engineer, I was lucky to be singled out.*

At 8:15 the morning of the twenty-seventh, with the sun uncomfortably high, *Lanikai*'s anchor splashed down in a small, semienclosed bay on Mindoro's west coast. From the journal's description it sounds more like a prime vacation spot than we looked on it that day: "Well protected from wind and sea, an admirable sand beach, and high escarpments surrounding three sides that make an effective place of concealment."

Whether the "place of concealment" was indeed "effective" or the five twin-motored bombers that roared over at 11:00 A.M. carried careless observers, or ones with bigger game in mind, the nervous watchers below could only guess. There was less doubt in the minds of those in the area we so fortunately had just left. Eighteen heavy bombers hit Corregidor at lunchtime, while 18 more hit Manila, an open, defenseless city. A few minutes later, 18 more heavies were at work pounding Mariveles. Ten others headed for Corregidor. Nine new arrivals went for Manila at 12:45. Forty minutes later 18 more pasted Corregidor.

The sorely beset Allies struck back twice on this action-packed day: Brooke-Popham was relieved at Singapore by Sir Henry Pownall, and American PBYs attacked shipping at Japanese-occupied Jolo, well to the south of where *Lanikai* then lay. It was a brave foray against great

---

* See appendix for other crew members.

odds. They flew in from the south like so many fat, laboring, migrating ducks, two waves of three each. Three planes crashed near Jolo and one elsewhere. The enemy picked up five survivors. Two were tortured, then executed in the most brutal manner—burned to death for refusal to divulge information. It was a magnificent exhibition of bravery that impressed the onlookers, those connoisseurs of courage, the Moslem Moros of Jolo.

The two chief radiomen, LeCompte and McVey, took one appraising look at *Lanikai*'s communications equipment and immediately resigned themselves to a prolonged holiday. It was beyond help.

Fleet Communications Officer, Lieutenant Commander W. E. ("Hap") Linaweaver, had done his best. In Manila he dug up a $25 "Echophone" receiver, a little grey metal box about the size of a gallon rum jug. It was our only link with civilization while at sea. Several times nightly, the sounds of London's Big Ben boomed out over short wave half a world away, followed by five minutes of news which by its omissions told more than the spoken words. During those suspense-packed interludes, all movement aboard stopped. No engine-room equipment turned over. Pumps, generator, the Coca-Cola cooler that acted as refrigerator—anything that might provide electrical interference was cut off. There must be no drowning out of the feeble whisper in clipped British accents that kept us in tenuous touch with the world. Or rather more accurately, the world around Britain. There was sparse news of the Far East or none at all. In late December there would have been nothing but disaster to report. Morale as it then was could not stand much of *that*.

In spite of Harry Keith's brave jokes, the gloom was deep. Crouched over the little Echophone the preceding night, we had heard of something that could not be covered up—the fall of Hongkong. It had been expected to hold out 90 days. Military wizard Brooke-Popham had recommended earlier that it be reinforced by several battalions, but even Churchill couldn't stand still for such an obviously futile gesture of Imperial gallantry. Eleven thousand prisoners fell into enemy hands. It was exactly one century since the British had first taken Hongkong from the Chinese.

Hart's ships were gathering at what was hoped might be the southern wall, Java. On Christmas Day, the harbor of Surabaya held the bulk of the surface fleet: cruisers *Boise* and *Marblehead*, tenders *Blackhawk, Langley, Holland, Childs, Preston,* and *Heron,* half a dozen destroyers, gunboats *Asheville* and *Tulsa,* yacht *Isabel,* minesweepers *Lark* and *Whippoorwill.* Heavy cruiser *Houston* was convoying *Otus, Pecos,* and *Gold Star* to Darwin, along with destroyers *Alden, Whipple,* and *John D. Edwards.*

The bomber scare over, *Lanikai* spent the rest of the twenty-seventh touching up the green paint. Some driftwood was collected ashore for Cooky's oil drum stove in a sandbox amidships. The galley propane was about gone. At a 6:00 P.M. sunset, we got under way, lookouts alert.

I've heard you can smell a Jap ship a mile downwind," someone said in a guarded voice, as though the Japanese themselves were eavesdropping.

"Yeah! Fish. They roll in it. Comes out through their hides. Then they wash their hands in carbolic. Nuts on disinfecting. Wear face masks when they've got a cold. If they're upwind our Filipino boys'll sniff 'em out. They can smell a wild boar in the jungle a hundred yards away."

This line of chatter reinforced the already strong tendency toward wide open eyes, cupped ears, and quivering nostrils. "I smell smoke!" said Keith. There was strained silence except for the sounds of anxious sniffing.

"Yeah! Wood smoke." But there were doubts. "How the hell could it be wood smoke? We're a mile from land. Any fire big enough to make smoke out here could be seen."

There was no question about it; a new tang floated on the mild breeze. It was not our own diesel smoke, either. The greenest neophyte aboard knew *that* difference. It was agreed that although the Japs had some old crocks, nobody ever heard of one of them that burned wood.

It wasn't pure wood smoke, either. "Not anything electrical," said Sparky Walruff, who could tune in on cooking insulation or hot phenolic resin like an old-time sailorman could scent a leaky barrel of rum.

Then someone climbed down the ladder from the deckhouse to the poop. "Christ! It's *us!*" he yelled. "We're on fire!" Smoke was billowing out of the after deckhouse door from a scuttle that led down to a lazarette under the poop and abaft the engine room. In the darkness after moonset, it had not been apparent from above. There was a rush to fire quarters. Tipay knew just what to do. The big gasoline bilge pump in the main hold amidships clanked over and spun into action with a roar like a PT boat. To hell with the Japanese! Let them hear it. Better consider the real menace that might soon have us lighted up like Times Square.

The unaccustomed motion had jarred loose an old mattress from a pile of badly stowed gear. It had fallen across the hot auxiliary exhaust pipe, where it lay charred and smoking, ready to burst into open flame. If the olfactory organs of the topside sniffers had been confused, they may be forgiven. They had been asked to identify the smoke from a mixture of damp horsehair, mattress ticking, and raw cotton, laced with a sprinkling of seagoing cockroaches.

This was not the first time that lazarette had been the cause of some heart palpitations, as I learned many years later from Harry C. Bush. He had been radio operator on board under Northrup Castle and

125

later, when she was owned by Captain Crosby, he wintered over in her at Seattle in 1936–37. One day while the ship was in drydock, Bush, poking around in the lazarette, turned up a couple of large, rusty canisters. On the orders of the representative of the new owner, Sam Goldwyn,* Bush tucked one of the canisters under his arm, shinnied precariously down a shaky ladder to the dock's bottom, then made his way to the nearby Coast Guard cutter for disposal advice. The welcome was not warm, as Bush records it in a 1971 letter to me:

> When I informed the officer of the deck what I had, what appeared to be black blasting powder, and he observed the deteriorated condition of can and contents, he almost had apoplexy. He ordered that I should immediately leave the ship, can and all, but with the greatest caution and delicacy.

Appealed to higher up the line, the Coast Guard took over the tricky stuff in traditional *Semper Paratus* fashion. Had *it* ever nudged the hot exhaust pipe, not just a little pungent smoke would have arisen; *Lanikai* would have been rendered spectacularly poopless.

We were safely over the first couple of jumps, and high ones at that, not the least of which had been simply permission to go. But with the combination of fat tropic moon and high visibility, there was no room for excessive optimism—*yet*. We were all very much on the *qui vive*. That dark spot off the bow, moving slowly our way—were we off course and headed for an unexpected islet? Was it a Jap on patrol? Or was it just the shadow of a small cloud drifting across the moon's face? Moonset at 2:00 A.M. brought heartfelt relief.

At a perfectly programmed 7:00 A.M., *Lanikai*'s hook splashed down into 80 feet of bottle green water. The steep shore rose so close we could have thrown a bone to the furtive, half-wild dogs that slunk down to look us over and lift long, hungry snouts to catch the tantalizing aroma of breakfast—sizzling fish and rice boiling in coconut milk salted with sea water. How long this cruise would last was anybody's guess. So was the location of the next revictualling port, if any were ever reached. We might find times ahead when nature was not so bountiful. There was no sense in squandering irreplaceable tinned provisions when the Filipino crewmen could parlay a strip of bacon rind into breakfast for eighteen in no more time than it took to tidy up the forecastle after anchoring. And the hold was well stocked with big bags of rice. The Filipinos had seen to *that* during the frantic twenty-sixth at Mariveles beach.

This was Manangas Bay, totally enclosed except for the narrow entrance. Its shores hiked steeply up to 800-foot peaklets, all luxuriantly

---

* Who in 1937 used *Lanikai* in making the cinema "Hurricane."

swathed in tall, junglelike vegetation in *Lanikai* green. We blended perfectly.

This was the first day since 8 December that any of us had felt even a modest degree of relaxation from tension. If we were not actually in Mother Earth's womb, we were, for the day at least, under her protective skirts.

The high-risk hours passed without sighting any enemy aircraft. Well protected from outside surface discovery, spirits up, we hoisted anchor at 3:00 P.M. and shifted to the south end of the small bay to see what we could see.

This was our first "scrounging" expedition ashore since departure, other than collecting a few sticks of driftwood for Cooky's oil drum stove. What would the natives be like? Most of the American crew members were old Far East hands, but they undoubtedly had followed prewar Asiatic Fleet tradition in staying where the families, clubs, and scotch whisky were. The families had left for "Stateside" a year earlier, but the ships still hung around Manila. Many Navy people never had been much beyond Manila's urban sprawl. The twenty miles of twisting, narrow, pot-holed asphalt between Cavite and Manila was about all the "countryside" the average officer ever saw. Bluejackets, carless in those days of $21-a-month seamen, saw even less. The Cavite road was a thread strung with beads—villages peopled with a tough lot, as urban fringes in any country are likely to be. Their children, pigs, dogs, and chickens that swarmed on and along the road were conditioned to avoiding horse-drawn *caromatas* with their tinkling harness bells, and the plodding carabao dragging heavy-wheeled carts. But their mental computers had not caught up with the motor car.

"If you hit a kid or an animal, *don't stop!*" the Navy Yard people warned new drivers. "Get the hell out and report it to the police station. Most of those country boys have a bolo strapped on their backs. They might stop after hacking up your tires. Then again, they might not."

The launch was hoisted out and our little party putt-putted in to the white, gently shelving strip of beach that would have looked at home on a Florida vacation advertisement. A few modest nipa houses high on stilts straggled off under the palms in a flat pocket between the hills. We pulled the boat part way up on the beach and walked across the narrow expanse of sand to what passed for the village street. Not a human was in sight.

Pigs, the universal Far East garbage dispose-all, lay under the huts, twitching their hides to shake off flies. Chickens clucked and scratched busily in the dirt. A few mangy, skinny dogs growled *pianissimo*, keeping well clear, too worm-ridden and hungry to put up any show of defiance.

Were we walking into an ambush? The Japanese already were well south of us. They had landed at Jolo on the twenty-fourth. Perhaps they were here too. Or perhaps the natives had read the tea leaves and switched sides. We had no way of knowing what the Filipino attitude had become as a result of the Manila "open city" declaration.

A lone figure appeared at the far end of the street. We approached each other warily, like unacquainted mastiffs, sniffing each other out. Several of us with Springfield rifles had already loaded the chamber, and were holding the pieces high, finger on trigger, like a man expecting to flush a covey of partridges. Those with Colt automatics had their hand on the grip and the holster flap open.

The brave little man was coming up step by slow step, his heart undoubtedly pounding no less than ours. In precise, carefully enunciated English, as though he were holding a class in pronunciation, he called out to us that he was the village schoolteacher, deputized to sound out the "invaders." Women and children had beat it for the hills, he explained later, when we had identified ourselves. The men had grabbed what few guns the village possessed—mostly ancient single-barreled fowling pieces—and were hiding in the jungle nearby, watching anxiously.

The only non-Filipinos generally to be found in such a remote village would be Chinese or Japanese. The Chinaman would have a little open-front *tienda,* displaying dusty jars of condiments, gaudy piece goods, cheap pots and dishes, fish hooks, and all those minor necessities that the wonderfully talented native craftsmen could not make from bamboo, rattan, or palm fiber, or beat out of scraps of old iron. Through centuries of Far East peace and war they had survived times of trouble by slamming tight the shutters and pulling themselves into the woodwork until the storm passed.

The Japanese would be in one tiny enterprise or another—barber, doctor, dentist, agent for copra or hardwood, or even photographer—eking out a scanty living by snapping a rare formal wedding ceremony, or portrait of some grave-faced little tyke uncomfortable in formal confirmation duds.

Was there anything to those old-timers' tales we used to hear in Cavite's Nutshell Cafe that all Japanese were spies? Perhaps. The Reverend Clifford E. Barry Nobes, whose prewar station was in the hills north of Manila, wrote me in 1971 that after war broke out, a local Japanese who had married a Filipina, and worked as a photographer for many years, turned out to be a lieutenant colonel in the Imperial Army. "This is not hearsay," said Father Nobes. "We knew him well. His children belonged to my congregation. When the Japanese moved into Bontoc, he proudly told me of his high rank in the Imperial forces."

The schoolteacher soon was reinforced by villagers, drifting up one by one. "Are there any Japanese here?" we inquired. Who the local

Japanese were or what Imperial finery they might have climbed into when their military arrived no one would ever find out. "They unfortunately were killed resisting arrest," explained a member of the Philippine Constabulary, who had come in from his foxhole and joined the rapidly expanding confab.

In those few short weeks of war, interisland trade had all but dried up. The villagers were already short of rice. They were glad to receive some in exchange for fresh meat—flapping, squawking chickens carried back aboard upside down by the legs to an eager Cooky.

All hands comfortably stuffed with rice, coconut, bananas, and fried chicken, we upped anchor at dusk, 6:30 P.M., and were soon outside, headed south, following the west coastline of Bushanga. If there had been any doubts as to on whose side the Philippines stood, that pleasant afternoon among those simple, friendly people dispelled them.

On that same day, in desperately beset Corregidor, MacArthur radioed Washington on a subject that soon would explode into a bitterly hot exchange:

```
I SUGGEST WASHINGTON EMPLOY COUNTER PROPAGANDA
ESPECIALLY WITH REFERENCE TO ACTIVITY OUR NAVY TO
OFFSET CRESCENDO OF ENEMY PROPAGANDA WHICH HAS AP-
PEARED IN ALL ELEMENTS OF SOCIETY, CLAIMING U.S. IN-
ACTIVITY IN SUPPORT OF FILIPINO EFFORT, WITH ESPECIAL
REFERENCE TO APPARENT INACTIVITY OF U.S. NAVAL
FORCES. THIS THEME IS NOW BEING USED WITH DEADLY
EFFECTIVENESS AND I AM NOT IN A POSITION HERE TO
COMBAT IT
```

This was a crucial point in the Filipino-American withdrawal to Bataan. On 29 December, the Japanese were hammering at the D-4 line, halfway to Manila. Beyond that, only the D-5 line remained, 15 miles south. Two Japanese tank regiments were making an end run to the east of the D-4 line, threatening to slash through the one Filipine division, the 91st, which was fighting a desperate retrograde action. The American and Filipine troops coming up from Legaspi had reached Los Banos on Laguna de Bay, halfway to Manila. The 91st must hold or the Legaspi outfit would be cut off from the Bataan redoubt.

If the Japanese had heard about the "open city" status of Manila, it hadn't impressed them. They kept right on bombing it. Then on the twenty-ninth, they concentrated on Corregidor. Squadron after squadron wheeled over the fortress at 20,000 feet or more. At Mariveles, where the old submarine tender *Canopus* lay alongside a cliff, the "Rock" could hardly be seen for dust, flying debris, and flames. The destruction was not all one way, however. During that day, Corregidor's batteries shot down thirteen planes.

Admiral Hart was temporarily out of the picture, still en route Java in submarine *Shark*. The whole naval situation was in utter confusion, with no Allied coordination or plans for unified action whatever. If MacArthur was upset, he could scarcely be blamed.

Wind and weather were so favorable that it was still dark when *Lanikai* arrived at the haven planned for the day's hideout, Cabulauan Island. We lay to for half an hour, rolling gently in the long swell, awaiting dawn. It was a monumental piece of luck we did so.

At first light, *Lanikai* built up to about six knots and entered the calm, supposedly safe anchorage. It had no high escarpments close to the water's edge, but did offer concealment from seaward on two sides.

Keith, still moving stiffly from his multiple wounds, stood by on the after deckhouse to relay commands to the helmsman. Adair was at "low level conn," hanging on to the forestay out at the end of the jib boom, like some latter-day figurehead. I started up the fore shrouds to the "crow's nest," a Coca-Cola crate we had lashed just below the masthead. The climb called for full attention, step by step, fifty feet up the sagging ratlines. That far aloft, even with a gentle roll, the ship's motion was so magnified that I was sweeping through a wide, stomach-torturing arc, the sea now on one side below me, now on the other.

Safely up, out of breath, squirming into the box, I took one horrified look ahead and let out a yell: *"Back Full! Emergency!"* All around us, reaching up out of the light green water, coral pinnacles the size of cathedral columns almost broke the surface. By some divine Providence, several lay in our wake that had been missed by bare margins. Any one of them could have ripped a gash even in *Lanikai*'s stout bottom that would have opened her up like a watermelon slashed with a hatchet.

Adair spotted these wicked pylons under the forefoot a few seconds later and added his shouts of alarm. The engine obeyed magnificently. There was no "chug, chug," cough and die as sometimes was the case when trying to restart in reverse. We churned to a stop. From then on in, it was broken field running at very slow speed, conned from my masthead perch, twisting and dodging.

Farther in, an area clear of pinnacles opened up and we gratefully let go the anchor. Or rather more accurately, let go the handy-billy. The latter, to the uninitiated, is a double-action water pump, operated by a couple of men hauling back and forth on a vertical version of the power lever on a railwayman's handcar. This particular handy-billy had seen better, less rusty days. It was expendable, which an anchor was not. In that coral-fouled bottom an anchor could irretrievably hang up.

So much excitement had been caused by the hairy approach that nobody had paid much attention to the distant surroundings. On anchoring, we noted with mixed alarm and curiosity a small sailing vessel a mile away, barely visible against the island's sand and green background. It could hardly be Japanese, and after the reassuring reception of the day before, it seemed unlikely that any Filipino would betray us to the enemy, in the improbable event Japanese turned up in the vicinity.

That the schooner's people lacked any such benign view of us was soon made apparent. Through glasses we could make out a small boat alongside, into which two men tumbled and began rowing like mad for shore. But why take chances? Our launch, with several armed men aboard, overtook them before they made the beach. They were Filipinos all right, and as far as those thoroughly alarmed gentlemen were concerned, we were Japanese. Two-masted schooners as big as *Lanikai* were not common in the Philippines.

It was a poor island, the two men explained. They had plenty of fresh water, but not much food. It might not have been Manila, but as far as our younger Filipino crewmen were concerned, it was a liberty port, their first.

"Keptin! We go get water!" they eagerly volunteered. It was a pretty transparent excuse, but in the dry season we might not have rain to collect in the awning and fill the water barrels on deck for a long time. So fresh water had been rationed for drinking and cooking. Shaving in sea water had its drawbacks. Let them go.

With all available casks and buckets, armed with a little sack of rice for trade goods, the party set out in the launch. If there were any debutantes on the island of Cabulauan, they must have had a ball that day. The men came back with broad smiles and twenty gallons of water they had carried a mile. While ashore, they had sighted seven enemy planes at low altitude north of the island. They were so low, we had missed them, and of more interest, they had missed us. The joss was still holding.

A salt water bath aboard has none of the exotic aspects of a lazy dip on a temperately cool winter beach in the Philippines: "The water is exceptionally clear and a small sand beach furnished excellent swimming . . ." said the journal.

At 6:30 P.M., the unfouled handy-billy broke surface and we gingerly felt our way out of that tricky anchorage. By midnight the wind had picked up, the sky clouded over and although the seas appeared moderate, *Lanikai*, according to the journal, was "rolling considerably." What could a real blow do to her? We would soon find out.

"Destination unknown" could be said to have applied not just to our eventual goal, but to day-by-day progress. Educated guesswork picked out our daily anchorages. It was a matter of correlating several factors: the distance we could run overnight, the sketchy picture presented by the large scale chart, where we thought the enemy might logically have arrived, likely Japanese ship and air movement patterns, what scraps we could reconstruct from "the voice of doom," as we had come to label the gloomy tidings from London—all cranked together with what in Navy lingo is known as "the Jesus factor," something hard to put one's finger on.

There were good anchorages and bad ones along our route. On the morning of the thirtieth, we found we had selected a bad one, Flechas Point, Palawan. Neither from Adair's "low level conn" nor from my Coca-Cola box could we spot the reefs that ringed it; the water was too murky. *Lanikai* rolled and jerked in a heavy ground swell that made life uncomfortable.

Here again, the Stars and Stripes sharing the gaff with the Philippines' colors were not sufficiently reassuring. Through binoculars we could see people ashore—scrambling out of houses, dragging children by the hand, others in arms—a regular panic party. Only after we had wallowed an hour at anchor did several *bancas* gingerly circle, then approach. Once more the schoolmaster was the spokesman. Law and order was represented by the constabularyman in starched uniform. Sure, there had been some Japanese here too. But again that universal misfortune; during the roundup, they had elected to resist.

The traditional chickens, bananas, and coconuts were ferried out. They had no need for rice; it was grown here. But there *was* a small problem. The townspeople had only bird shot for their fowling pieces, poor stuff for winging larger game. Japanese, for example. We turned over several boxes of buck-loaded 12-gauge shotgun shells, and wished them good hunting.

This was a moment of major decision. Should we continue our coast-hugging routine—down Palawan's long, straight length, then the same for Borneo? Both were mare's nests of coral reefs the entire way. Our charts were entirely inadequate for identification of local hazards, which we had so spectacularly discovered several days back at Cabulauan Island. To shoot straight south would mean two days in the wide open, plus two full-moonlit nights. Although Japanese fishermen intimately knew and undoubtedly had minutely charted the local coasts for their Navy, the chances were good they would prefer the open sea. It all depended on the weather. If it were thick and stormy, we might try for a direct shot across the Sulu Sea. We knew the Japanese were in Jolo, which we would pass within a few miles. But they might just as well be in Palawan or Borneo, in which case their location would be wholly a guess on our part. We could at least pinpoint Jolo and stay out of its harbor.

The weather made our decision for us. After the usual dusk departure, we headed east to clear the reefs, then southerly. The decision had to be final. At four to six knots, there was no margin for second thoughts or decisions.

There was only one hazard en route, the Tubbataha Reefs, at or below sea level. But in heavy weather they could probably be avoided. The seas crashing over them would boom like thunder.

During the night, wind and seas built up to near typhoon violence. Rain slashed down, so mixed with salt spray that collecting fresh water was out of the question, even if we had not had to furl the 'midships awning, the catch-water, to save it from being torn to bits. New groans and creaks developed in the straining hull. *Lanikai* was no spring chicken. Would the shrouds pull out and let the masts come crashing down? We set reefed stunsails forward to cut down the hellish roll and wondered what would have happened if *Lanikai* had not had a three-foot keel from stem to stern to help damp the motion. I patted the old girl in gratitude on recalling a ghastly ride just a month before in the keelless gunboat *Oahu,* bucking a similar blow en route Shanghai to Manila, when she rolled over 50 degrees on a side.

One thing was certain; no Japanese planes would be in the air. If this was really a typhoon, which the behavior of the barometer indicated, no Jap skipper in his right mind would be in the open sea. We would chalk up this storm as one to be remembered, for its miserable two days and nights, and for its friendly cloak of concealment.

On the thirty-first, the journal is noncommittal on anything but the weather, which was "squally, wind force three, from northeast. Seas continuing high, ship rolling and pitching heavily."

The gale from the port quarter was on the most favorable possible bearing for filling *Lanikai*'s sails to best advantage, but it was pure hell for developing a corkscrew motion of the ship that made inability to prepare hot food academic. Not many were hungry. Highly partial to fish in any form, the Filipinos had seen to it that we were well stocked with canned salmon, something I had heretofore always classified as fit only for feeding cats. But in this extremity I discovered the stuff was edible. Scooped directly out of the can on the tip of a sheath knife, it settled the stomach and held off hunger pains.

The decks dropped from under, then pushed up again like a rapidly accelerating express elevator in a skyscraper. All were soaked to the skin, with no hope of drying out until the storm slacked off and the tropic sun came out. But tropics or no, it was winter and the combination of cold rain and wind chilled the blood. The wicker chair in which I sat was lashed to the weather rail of the after deckhouse, where an eye could be kept on the double-reefed foresail and storm jibs. The mainsail was unusable because of the wooden "armor" laid over the after deckhouse awning stanchions. The gale sliced flying spray off the wave-tops, thoroughly drenching the steersman on the poop. Bare feet wide apart, he spun the wheel this way and that to minimize the murderous yaw. The brim of his white sailor hat was turned down to shed water, half hiding a grim brown face several shades lighter than normal. As he and some of his young shipmates would often be in the future, he was deathly seasick. But they would never miss a watch, or shirk, or complain—devoted, gutsy, loyal shipmates that they were.

It occurred to me this was New Year's Eve. I planned to think about it in more detail later during my watch below, lashed into the cabin bunk in the darkness. Shortly after noon, dead reckoning put Tubbataha Reefs twenty miles abeam to port, so that we could safely change course from south to southeasterly. This put the wind and seas nearer abeam, which greatly eased the ship's motion. Pitching practically ceased. The sails damped the roll. With *Lanikai* heeled sharply to starboard, waves pounded heavily against the exposed turn of the port bilge, but the ship's list laid me comfortably against the outboard bulkhead to which my narrow bunk was attached. There was no need to "tie in."

New Year's Eve recollections could now be gotten on with seriously and in detail.

On 31 December 1931, the Far East was at peace, if one discounted such minor aberrations as the perennial exchange of shots between Yangtze gunboaters and Chinese "sportsmen." Also, there had been a slight incident in Manchuria in September. Japanese troops, in the South Manchuria Railway Zone by treaty, complained the Chinese had blown up a section of track. But it was well after New Year's that international investigators, the Lytton Commission, turned up with the disclosure a train had passed over these same tracks very shortly after the alleged explosion. The Japanese had an answer for that one. It was an ancient ally we would hear more about later: the *Kamikaze*. The Divine Wind had wafted the train safely over the break. Having thus dumbfounded their League of Nations colleagues, the Japanese walked out of that already moribund body and commenced the war, which thenceforth continued without significant break for a decade.

At peace inwardly and outwardly, the naval fraternity and ladies gathered happily on the Manila Army and Navy Club lawn, New Year's Eve, 1931, to watch the glorious sunset, then brace for a proper job of ushering in 1932. New Year's Eve was the only time during the whole year when ladies were admitted to that holy male sanctum, the bar.

There were very few eligible young ladies in Manila that a young Navy bachelor might escort. I had met several dewy-eyed high school seniors, Army officers' kids, but one had gotten hilarious on a claret lemonade and then there had been hell to pay with Daddy. Those beyond high school age would be "Stateside" at college. A girl who came back after graduation and failed to nail some desperate man's hide to the barn door in three months or less, had to be a boneyard case. Thus, sprightly, unattached girls were scarce. The bachelors could concentrate on looking forward to "up to China in the springtime," and all those luscious White Russian gals in Tsingtao and Chefoo.

So at Manila, the bachelors restricted themselves to making formal calls on seniors and their families ashore, nervously swallowing a couple of decorous drinks. They listened politely to "Missy's" boring monologues of the servants, the children, the shopping and the heat. Then they proceeded to the Club, either to socialize with the younger married set, or retreat to the bar to dine on "free lunch" and roll dice for more drinks than were good for them. On the Club's second floor veranda, "Drunkards' Row," a long file of cots was always available for those who missed the last boat or were in no shape to catch it.

By eleven on this New Year's Eve, the club was jumping. But somehow, I felt left out. I was newly arrived from a Prohibition America. The whole thing was confusing.

"Let's beat it," someone proposed. "In another hour the wives will drop us like hot rocks when hubby arrives for the midnight embrace. Let's go out to Dreamland! Let's pick out a couple of exotic-looking babes and see the New Year come in through Oriental eyes!"

Dreamland was huge, almost as big as a football field, the largest cabaret perhaps in the world. It was a fairyland of lights, swaying balloons, gay Filipina girls in puff-sleeved gowns copied from the Spanish court costumes of centuries before. We pushed our way through the bedlam and found a table.

"Why did you choose me from among all these other girls?" asked Dolores. "I am not so very pretty, or so very young."

It has been my modest experience that most women are seeking reassurance of what they secretly believe but do not necessarily say. From an Oriental point of view, it is possible that Dolores was not pretty. She had a bridge to her nose, though only a small, daintily arched one. The irises of her eyes were so black that they blended with the cornea to make one very large black center in very white eyes. If indeed she had had a mamma who had lost a race with a Spanish soldier in the bad old days, the fact was not apparent; her color was darker than that of the aristocratic Filipina *meztizas,* who carefully shaded themselves from the sun. Her long, slim fingers and strongly upward-tilted eyes suggested a Chinese limb on the family tree. The gold tooth in front would have looked cheap in a Westerner. But framed in Dolores' red lips it became quite something else—a small ornament in an appropriate setting.

It is very possible Dolores really believed she was not pretty. Many pretty women all too often concentrate on this asset, neglecting others, so that they are dull. Dolores was not dull. She was witty and gay and animated. All this blended into a creature of soft warmth of spirit and body that led one to forget the crowd that pressed around.

I had never been in a typical Filipino house before. It was high on stilts, with neat, bamboo lattice steps leading up to its one floor. It was light and airy. The wind could come through the interstices in the bamboo floor and out other openings in the walls. There were no rugs or cupboards to become filled with mold and dampness in the humid, sweltering summers.

Dolores lived there alone. She had said that she was not very young. Perhaps she felt that being twenty-seven was old, and perhaps for the Philippines, this was so. But for myself, I was glad she was twenty-seven, because this had made her wise and kind, and I was very young.

Chapter 12

The New Year dawned auspiciously. As *Lanikai* plowed south on 1 January 1942, there were no sore heads aboard; nobody had been to Dreamland, or the Manila Army and Navy Club, or anywhere else the night before. Far more importantly, the storm held: "Weather thick and squally . . . ship laboring heavily"—ideal for anyone keen on remaining inconspicuous.

"This is a bad stretch," Adair scribbled in his damp pocket notebook. "Nothing sighted so far. Nothing to do but go on. Most of crew seasick. Wind has dropped to about 30 knots. Have lookouts posted fore and aft. If we can't take any opposition with our guns, expect to spread gasoline and burn ship." After a night and day of wild gyrations, blind and deaf to the world beyond our decks, soaked and cold, hanging on for dear life to the stanchions as he stood his watch, even normally ebullient Charlie Adair could be excused a few introspective moments.

With this something less than happy frame of mind prevailing, at 5:00 P.M. that afternoon the shouted word, "General quarters! All hands out!" brought the ship's company tumbling to their stations in a high state of expectancy. There was a good hour of daylight yet to go. One of the Filipino lookouts had seen what appeared to be something more than wind-tossed spume. In the flying salt spray, their naked eyes were better than binoculars. Yes, there it was, a small dark blob materializing on the horizon to port.

We could turn right 90 degrees and run, full-and-by, before the wind, fighting to maintain a lead until darkness swallowed us. With only the fantail showing instead of a broadside, we might even remain undetected. The chances were microscopic that any vessel would be Allied. But if we ran to westward, we would be losing precious southing. With every minute the gates below us were swinging shut. Or, at increased peril we could stay on course a little longer for more positive identification.

The quick decision, as the gambling instincts of our Filipino boys would have had them put it, was "go for broke." We drove on straight ahead. The spook grew alarmingly in length. Then, as though a curtain had been lifted, the haze thinned all at once and there lay an island.

The weather had been too thick for more than a couple of fuzzy sun sights. Charlie Adair, his legs twined around the weather rail to free his hands, handled the sextant. I recorded the time on my wrist watch, then ran below to check it with the chronometer. An error of seconds in time could make our position a mile off. The sights, plus good dead reckoning, had been accurate enough. No doubt about it, this was Pangutaran Island. But who was on it? Japanese?

The chance had to be taken. With the weather rapidly clearing and Japanese known to be at Jolo, this was no piece of ocean to be cruising in broad daylight. In an hour we had anchored a hundred yards from a white sand beach framed with coconut palms and heavy vegetation. Some nipa shacks perched amongst the greenery. Our colors had been hoisted with trepidation, but the few figures that flitted through the grove were more apprehensive than we and no one ventured out.

This was Moro country, peopled by Moslems. Some of them still cherished the belief that shedding Christian blood was an act of merit guaranteeing an increased share of houris in the heavenly hereafter. Each carried a wavy-bladed kris or bolo, hand-forged from old railroad iron or wagon tire, and kept lovingly honed. In the last century they had given the Spaniards a bad time—and the Americans too, after the Spanish-American War, until Black Jack Pershing completed their taming a decade and a half after the U.S. took over the Philippines. Moros still ran *amok*, slashing away at anything in their path until filled with enough bullets to have stopped a dozen normal men. It was for such *juramentados* that my father had bought his long-barreled Colt .45 many years earlier. The Army's issue .38 was not adequate for the job.

Clearly, this was not what our good Catholic Filipino crewmen considered a prime liberty port. None ventured ashore. Just before 10:00 P.M., we got under way and headed south, without the usual quota of news, fresh eggs, squawking chickens, or milk-heavy coconuts straight from the tree.

The unusually late start was dictated by a new element in our cruising. This chain of islands loosely blocked the Sulu Sea to the north so that with the ebb and flow of tides, currents ran fast. With *Lanikai*'s modest ability to make headway, a careful choice of route and time meant making knots toward safety rather than treading water in one spot.

To the east of our course lay Japanese-occupied Jolo. During the night, we would pass it abeam at about 15 miles, less than the range of a 16-inch gun. The wind had died, the weather had completely cleared, and the full moon was obscured all too infrequently by small, slowly moving cotton-fluff clouds. The sea was dead calm. All sail was lowered;

we chugged along on the auxiliary. With that big spread of white canvas down, we felt less conspicuous—but sorely missed those extra knots.

Shortly before 7:00 A.M. on 2 January, in a dawn too bright and clear for comfort, *Lanikai* eased into a magnificent little landlocked cove in Tagao Island. At 50 yards from shore, the ship blended nicely with the greenery, most likely invisible to any but low-flying, extra sharp-eyed observers. Anyway, what Japanese would expect to find an Allied vessel in *that* place? They *had* to be all bottled up either in Manila or Surabaya. Jungle-covered hills rose in echelons behind the shelving beaches that almost encircled the anchorage. The forenoon sun blazed down on sand so white that in another latitude it could have been taken for snow.

We had company. During our approach, *bancas* scurried off in all directions. This was a good sign. As we had so far discovered, the natives on first sight always took us for Japanese. If the locals fled, obviously the enemy was not already here to greet us.

After our flags had gone up to the gaff, one, then two, then a dozen *bancas* headed our way. In no time the ship's side was solidly lined with these gaudy little craft. Their almost black, near-naked, grave-faced occupants peered up at us in polite curiosity, waiting for our initiative in opening the parley.

As the ship swung into the light, early morning breeze, the lovely aroma of breakfast wafted back to the after deckhouse roof, where Alcantara was unlashing the wicker chairs from the railing. Old Gomez, the officers' steward who had been called back from retirement, tottered up the ladder on his game legs, bringing an armload of cushions from below. "Cooky he make plenty good chow this morning!" he said. This would be the first decent meal in three days. The stops were full out: tinned sausages for all hands, dried egg omelette, long corkscrew hunks of bread buttered with pan drippings, wrapped around a stick and baked in the oil drum oven, and sweetened condensed milk for the coffee. In my family, nostalgic tales of old Manila featured that Eagle Brand condensed, heavily sugared milk. As a baby in Cebu, not too many miles from where *Lanikai* then lay, I had been weaned on it.

"These *bancas* are works of art," Adair wrote in his notebook. He sat in yachtsmanlike opulence in one of the deck chairs, digesting the feast and recording the scene for posterity, like any explorer.

> They are carved out of mahogany, smoothly finished, with outriggers on each side extending the length of the boat. What a contrast to the crude dugouts up north! These outriggers are about six inches in diameter, supported by three bamboos extending across the boat. The hull is a mere 12 to 18 inches wide and about eight feet long. Three or four people can crowd on board. Some of the *bancas* are quite a bit larger than this. Many of them have elaborate carvings at bow and stern.

I see one large banca coming in which must be 18 feet long, paddled by five men. There are four outrigger supports. Nearly all of these craft have light canvas sails, usually in some brilliant color. Others are made of alternate strips of white and brown, two to three feet wide. Boards put across the gunwales make a platform on which people can perch themselves. One such boat has what appears to be mama, papa, a boy of about nine, a girl of perhaps seven, and a smaller girl of four or five. The boy is in the bow, paddling, and father in the stern, likewise engaged.

The sails are rectangular, a sort of standing lug rig, with a bamboo strip along the top. High in the water, sharp and narrow, in light airs these little craft shoot along like swallows, at a better speed than we could make.

In dealing with these new friends, our own Filipinos showed a marked restraint, as well they might. Harry Keith had been down this way some time before and had discussed with a Moro headman or *datu* the Filipine government's plan to ease the northern population pressure by settling some Visayans from the central islands down near Tawi Tawi. That was just fine with the *datu*. He would see that their population pressure was relieved. "How we do?" We keel dem!" he said gaily, fingering his bolo.

This rich-appearing island really was poor, explained one of the Moros, many of whom spoke English quite well. Some farming was done on Tagao, but the jungle fought back for every inch of ground tilled. Now, most of them came here only furtively to work from time to time; they were afraid of the Japs, only a couple of dozen miles away. Their planes had been flying over almost daily between Jolo and Borneo. With the usual Japanese passion for routine and good order, they roared over at 6:00 A.M. and 4:00 P.M., like a Tokyo commuter train.

The Moros, with nothing to offer in the way of fresh food, looked none too well fed themselves. They gratefully accepted several cases of our empty Coca-Cola bottles. Along with five-gallon oil tins, bottles were the standard fluid containers in an economy with not much to spare for fancy luxuries such as buckets. One had a sneaking suspicion that with their magnificent little *bancas* and skill at twirling a bolo, these fellows made better fighters than husbandmen.

Our informant told us that just the day before, an American plane had been shot down near Siasa Island, to the north. Four survivors, one badly wounded, had piled into a *banca* and headed for Borneo. With the wind on their tails, it would have been impossible for clumsy old *Lanikai* to have overhauled them, in the unlikely event we had been willing to risk detouring via the Borneo coast.*

* Lieutenant J. B. Dawley, USN, and his Catalina crew reached Borneo, where a steamer took them to Java. Sulfa drugs supplied by a Filipino doctor saved the wounded man.

"Doc" Cossette displays the results of his unique trolling device—a fish breakfast for all hands.

Lieutenant Paul Nygh, RNN, with the Hadji da Epalandoro on his right. Grouped about are the unsmiling, suspicious Celebes natives who sent word ahead that Lanikai appeared to be manned by Germans and Japanese, pretending to be Americans and Filipinos.

At 5:20 P.M., the second, we were under way after windlass trouble delayed hoisting the anchor. Some weeks later this problem would result in near disaster, but for the moment it merely lowered our small stock of irreplaceable spare fuses. During an apprehensive afternoon, our eyes and ears had been sharply tuned for the 4:00 P.M. Borneo-Jolo commuter special; but perhaps this was a Japanese holiday; it failed to show.

The decision to head directly for the Celebes meant casting off our daylight cloak of invisibility—the sheltering island. It would be a second Sulu Sea style gamble—under way one wide-open day, sandwiched between two protective nights. Three elements entered the equation. *Weather:* in January, the possibility of its providing cover was marginal; *an alternate route:* the Borneo coast was longer, peppered with wicked, unmarked coral reefs that could not be spotted in darkness, and there were no offshore islands for daytime concealment; *the Japanese:* obviously they either were already *in* Borneo or about to be, indicated by the almost daily enemy flights. We knew the oil at Tarakan was so pure it could be burned in ships' boilers just as it came out of the ground. The fuel-hungry Japanese certainly would waste no time seizing *that* bonanza, only a fourth of the way down a wholly undefended Borneo coast.

Had there been a chaplain aboard, his supplications might have been credited for favorable—which is to say, bad—weather. Lacking a padre, it could have been only *"Lucky Lanikai"* herself who was responsible for this intervention: "Sea smooth, with moderate ground swells. Overcast and squally. Very poor visibility and heavy clouds." The wind was ideal—on the port quarter, fanning us along at a good clip.

Covering clouds and fair winds do not necessarily make a sailor's day. At 5:00 P.M., with protective dusk already creeping out of the eastern sky, we thought our number at last was up. On the milky sunset horizon, two specks appeared. Wheeling in our direction below the overcast, the specks rapidly grew into a pair of big flying boats. With three engines, they could not possibly be American. What did a Jap seaplane look like? Nobody knew. There were no recognition pamphlets on board.

Bare feet silently padded to battle stations. Ammunition was laid out. Fire hoses were connected and the pumps primed for quick starting.

If the planes were enemy, they would know where their own ships were. But still, they might go through the formality of a challenge. The little searchlight on the forward deckhouse was manned and ready; Radioman McVey, to whom dots and dashes were a second language, stood by at the key to bounce back the Japanese signal instantly. But we knew we could not fool them. They would bomb and strafe.

In the rare possibility they were Allied planes, they could not possibly have heard of our unlikely existence, even less our whereabouts. They would quickly have to be disabused of any notion we were one of the odd conglomeration of craft the thrifty Japanese had been using on the China coast for years.

Civilians may have their little jokes about the "military mind," its lack of originality and sense of humor, and destructive orientation. But when the luxury of procrastination and debate in arriving at a solution cannot be afforded, what has been fed into the data bank of that much maligned mind can generally produce a decision with computer speed and soundness.

The planes would be over us in minutes. If they came straight on, no wing insignia would show until they were almost overhead. That would be too late. We turned away, so that the three-pounder could bear. At their low altitude, this accurate little cannon could elevate enough to get off half a dozen quick shots. Then a turn hard a'port, 90 degrees, so that hopefully not only would the bombs overreach, but our potent 50-caliber machine gun, mounted starboard side forward, firing slugs the size of cocktail sausages, could rake the enemy's naked belly. Every fifth cartridge was an incendiary.

During the many strategy-and-tactics discussions en route, the possibility of Japanese surface interception had been brought up. If we could only get close enough, armament concealed, fishing lines out, we might be able to yank away the gun covers and get off one or two punishing shots. One three-pounder round landed in a destroyer torpedo tube nest might detonate a couple of thousand pounds of high explosive, parting the ship neatly in the middle. One jagged hole punched in a submarine's conning tower would fix its business for war patrol.

Sailing under false colors is a ruse as old as war. The Far East French were "neutral" in favor of Japan. We had no French colors aboard, but the international alphabet flag representing "T" was an excellent tricolor substitute. However, this was no surface encounter involving predictably performing surface sailormen. These were aviators, a notoriously independent breed. Japanese aviators in particular seemed to have trouble recognizing flags anyway, judging from their performance of 12 December 1937, when U.S. flags as big as bedsheets failed to save the Yangtze gunboat, USS *Panay*.*

This clearly was not a time to play flag games. The biggest American ensign in the flag bag went flapping up the topmast halliards to the main peak. If the planes were Allied, we hoped they saw it. If Japanese, they would soon discover it was a battle flag, proudly flying as it had on American warships in many a sea fight over almost two centuries. And by God, the bastards would find out we had a sting! Perhaps even a lucky three-pounder hit. Just one fat enemy bomber was worth at least five *Lanikais*.

Charlie Adair's big frame was jackknifed behind the three-pounder, his shoulder to the yoke, hand grasping the pistol grip and finger on the

* The destroyer USS *Peary*, which left Manila Bay with *Lanikai*, was mistakenly bombed by Australian aircraft.

trigger. Feet wide apart, he braced himself against the gentle roll of the ship. One of the planes sat fixed in the crosshairs of his telescopic sight. On Adair's left, Harry Keith peered at the planes, estimating their range, then cranking it onto the sight bar. On the right, first loader Sparky Walruff had already slammed a round into the chamber and was standing tensely by with a second. On deck, in opened wooden boxes lay six more—shiny eighteen-inch brass cases topped with a dull steel, cucumber-sized shell. In the projectile's base was a delicate fuse that once the shell was in flight, feather-light contact would activate, setting off a high explosive charge, scattering tiny fragments over a wide area. It would kill the largest plane.

On first glance all this might be a scene from the theater of the absurd—a quick-firing boat gun aboard a 28-year-old wooden tub against a war machine that had been undreamed of when the gun came from the factory in 1898. But was it wholly absurd? One fine day in 1938, a Japanese twin-float seaplane was carrying out its daily milk run procedure along a South China waterway—junk busting. For weeks, the junkmen, their ways unchanged in two millenia, had been harried and terrorized by this new scourge. Pirates, warlords, robbers, they had suffered and survived—by courage, tenacity and wits. They were even up to this one. One junk was ready. Its 1842 Opium War muzzle-loading 18-pounder was standing by, charged halfway up the bore with old bolts, horseshoes, chain links and nails. Along came Pilot-san, loafing in at deck level, machine guns blazing through the four-bladed wooden propeller. This was a training ground to blood young pilots in old, expendable aircraft.

A courageous Chinaman stuck it out until the enemy was within spitting distance before applying the slow match to the old cannon's touch hole. When the pall of black powder smoke had cleared away, the plane's disintegrated parts were floating in the water. The cannon had disappeared. Only a large hole in the opposite bulwark remained as testimony. The recoil from its first shot in half a century perhaps, had carried it crashing across the deck and with a mighty splash into the canal's bottomless ooze.

Could not this dainty, slim-barreled little three-pounder cannon do as well?

Up forward, Guns Picking was like a spirited race horse at the starting gate. Up and down and crosswise he swiveled his beloved "fifty," assuring himself that nothing would bind at the crucial moment. A pair of Filipinos stood by him, holding up yards of cartridge belt, like the lace train of a bride, to keep it free of snarls. Between checks of his gun, Picking would squint aft, trying to pick up the low-flying planes. "Come on, you slant-eyed sonsa bitches!" he yelled. Other than the steady chug-chug of the engine and the creak of the rigging, it was the only sound to break the tense stillness.

On the poop, Doc Cossette peered down the barrel of his 30-caliber Lewis machine gun. The cocking lever was back and his feet were braced far apart as though the thing would kick him, in spite of its fixed position on a shoulder-high swivel tripod. With a target changing not a mil in deflection, this was a skeet shooter's dream.

Then, at a critical six or seven hundred yards, with "commence firing!" already framed on my lips, the planes suddenly swung northward, their uptilted wings showing the Netherlands' orange triangle. They were so close we could make out the helmeted, goggled midships gunners, gripping the breeches of their weapons, trained down at us. Would they accept our colors as *bona fide*? Cossette ripped off his undershirt, exposing an ample white belly. We waved our arms in frantic, friendly greeting and yelled to the Filipinos to get out of sight.

The planes wagged their wings in recognition. Reluctantly perhaps, the Dutchmen swiveled their guns inboard, like a disappointed hunter when a forbidden doe crashes into the clearing instead of a sixteen-point buck. In another ten minutes they were gone, swallowed up in the overcast.

As we were to see happen later in Surabaya, there is an almost uncontrollable human itch to shoot, even though the plane is unquestionably friendly. We felt it that day, and presumably so did those Dutchmen above us. I had seen our own gunners shoot down a low-flying American plane over Cavite, and would see Allied planes meet the same fate in Java. The real and lucky miracle in *Lanikai*'s brief encounter was not the completion of a day's crossing; it was that neither side had succumbed to that very itchy urge to pull a trigger.

Lanikai was not the only American to be set awry by those three-engined Dutch Dorniers. The seaplane tender *Childs*, heading south with Patrol Wing 10's commander, Captain Wagner, on board, had sighted three of them. There was mutual recognition and the Dutch planes flew off. The lookouts could have profited by the sharpness which any crow hunter recognizes in those wily birds. If three men go into a copse normally a favorite crow hangout, and only two come out, Mister Crow knows one gunner is still in there, and is alerted. He can count, and turns the ability to his salvation. The chief petty officer standing by Captain Wagner on the bridge undoubtedly could count, but failed to capitalize on it. "Well, here comes one of those four-engined Dutch jobs again," he casually remarked to Wagner. The latter had a quick double take. "Wh-a-a-a-t?" he shouted. "Sound general quarters!" About then, bombs started to break away from the four-engined Japanese plane, fortunately all misses. The Jap must have been out of bombs or more spooky than most, as he left off the attack when *Childs* opened up. With her feeble antiaircraft armament of four 50-caliber machine guns, she would have been very lucky to have connected with any determined attacker.

The light northeast wind held throughout the overcast night. Dawn brought two rewards: water rations were eased by a short, heavy downpour that filled three barrels on deck, and Doc Cossette caught a barracuda big enough to provide breakfast for all hands. This was a good sign; we must be nearing land. With 36 hours of thick weather behind us, our position was guesswork.

Ever-hopeful Doc's trolling device was a practically permanent fantail fixture. A yard-long, inch-wide strip of rubber inner-tubing was attached to the poop deck railing. From the outboard end of this, a heavy fishing line trailed fifty yards astern. In this line, close to the rail, there was a U-shaped loop across the top of which was tied a light string. When a fish hit the bait, the weak string broke, the U straightened out taut, and the rubber took the final shock to prevent the line's breaking. From time to time, the helmsman, stationed abaft the after deckhouse, looked over his shoulder to check the cord. If it was broken, the hook had been hit. Then there would be an excited alarm. "Hey, Doc," Almaden, or Tumbagahan, or Felarca, or Profeta would shout, "come queek! I theenk you gotta feesh!"

What would it be? At slow speeds, possibly a shark. There would be a tussle to get the hard-to-kill critter aboard, then an even tougher job to avoid his snapping jaws and harsh, abrasive, sandpaper hide that could grievously scrape bare legs. There was neither the patience nor the know-how aboard to convert the fins into soup so fancied by Chinese and certain Occidental gourmets. The pressing problem was to retrieve the precious hook, occasionally all the way into the beast's stomach. Then its bloody carcass would be consigned to its cannibal brothers. Perhaps it would distract their attention for awhile from any other fish that might be hooked. All too often at anchor, one beautiful red snapper after another, delectable food fish, helplessly impaled on the hook, would be expertly nipped off just abaft the gills by awaiting sharks.

If, as in the case of the morning's prize, we had a barracuda and it was not detected soon enough, dragging it through the water at seven or eight knots for some time would "drown" it. The gills were unable to function properly under those abnormal conditions.

Doc's yard-long catch was just right—big enough, but not so big as to be poisonous, a nice determination that too many amateur Navy fishermen discovered the hard way after serving up an oversize specimen.

In a sort of shotgun approach, we had hit the north end of the Celebes—exactly where, we didn't know. Following the coast to westward

McVey, Walruff, and LeCompte pose with Balinese dancers.

brought us, by 9:30 A.M., to a small village which Nygh's quick visit ashore developed to be Sabang.

This was our first experience in wholly new territory. In striking comparison with the Philippines, only one man ashore spoke Dutch, the government agent, a Malay. Nygh was embarrassed not only by the language barrier, but by the cold silence of the crowd of fifty or so that surrounded us when the whole group of officers went ashore. "We do not teach them Dutch," he lamely explained. "They make enough trouble as it is." Nevertheless, we were met with protocol appropriate for the distinguished visitors we obviously were taken to be. Not even small coastal steamers ever stopped at such a fly speck of a village.

Senior greeter was the Imam Hadji da Epalandoro. His title and white turban signified he had made the hadj—the holy pilgrimage to Mecca. For a man in his circumstances, what privations he must have undergone to lay away the necessary money, coin by small coin! Then the formalities required by the bureaucratic colonial Dutch, ever watchful of the wards they had sat upon so securely for four centuries. Papers in order, next would be the interminable, sweltering ride stuffed in the hold of some tramp steamer with a hundred or so others, across the Indian Ocean, into the "graveyard of friendship," the ovenlike Red Sea. At last, after a foot-searing trek from the port of Juddah to holy Mecca, he had gazed in rapture on the Kaaba, a small structure housing the Black Stone, a dully shining ruby a foot in diameter given by Gabriel to Abraham. At 76, very old for that insalubrious part of the world, the Imam's gravity and simple dignity reflected an inner peace which escapes most of the more worldly among us.

Backing up the Hadji was village elder Djagoegoe, headman of a poor little cluster of native huts and several tiny Chinese shops behind a magnificent row of coconut palms that fringed the shore. Naked children played in the dirt. A dozen scruffy dogs slunk in the background, uncertain whether to run away or stay and growl from a safe distance at this unfamiliar-smelling group in white shorts and shirts, .45-Colt automatics conveniently slung around in front.

In the center of the village, a small pavilion served as a sort of guest house to put up a government official in the rare event one might visit this little backwater. There, we were served coffee, accompanied by labored conversation via English to Nygh, from him in Dutch to the government agent, and so into Malay for the benefit of the village's elders, seated around the big table on chairs. Lesser citizens squatted on their heels against the walls, uttering not a sound.

The village school, on special holiday to allow the pupils to enjoy this unprecedented occasion, had available several geography books with local maps, which gave some clue as to what our next night's run might bring forth. One of the villagers had been sent off post-haste on a bicycle, twelve miles to the nearest telephone, to alert Donggala, next down the coast, of our expected arrival.

In the afternoon, the Imam, elder Djagoegoe, and the agent-interpreter were brought out to view the wonders of *Lanikai,* down a Coca-Cola in appreciative sips and ceremoniously receive a carefully typed letter each, commemorating the visit. The Hadji had come aboard cradling a large, apparently mesmerized, brilliantly plumaged rooster, which was handed over to me as a parting gift when the group rose to go. The trip around *Lanikai* had made a visible impression—the three-pounder, the "huge" engine, flush toilets and opulent, cushioned wicker chairs on the after deckhouse roof. Clutching a carton of cigarettes as a farewell present, the Imam made a final gesture of beneficence. First he blessed the rooster with a sincerity suggesting he was saying farewell to an old and dear friend. Then he blessed us and the ship with a little ceremony appropriate from one who has viewed the Kaaba. Fringes of the blessing became immediately apparent in the form of a dousing rain that filled all the water barrels on deck. We hoped the ultimate results would prove more favorable to us than to the rooster, whose fate was strongly suggested by the expression on the face of Hilario Velarmino, ship's cook first class, who was taking in the proceedings from the well deck.

The evening should have seen us on our way. But our luck so far, plus the desire to set foot on shore again, plus a minor accident, caused us to declare a day's moratorium in running south. The minor accident had been the near asphyxiation of two-thirds of our engine-room gang—Steve Kret and faithful young Tipay. They had been knocked out by carbon monoxide while repairing the auxiliary generator. Fisherman/gunner/doctor Cossette soon had them mended, the only ill effects a king-sized headache. But they needed a day's rest.

The whole blessed, sunny day we lay at anchor, which allowed a much-needed overhaul of storm-beaten topside gear. In the afternoon, a liberty party went ashore to check out the questionable delights of Sabang and let our Filipinos try making friends with their Malay cousins. They were back in an hour, laden with fresh coconuts in exchange for cigarettes and bits of old rope. The precious cigarettes were immediately cut in two by the villagers and carefully wrapped in cloth for some special occasion. The rope would later be unlaid and reworked into cordage. Driftwood became an important item of commerce, too. The twenty 6-volt automobile storage batteries that made up the battery bank had reached such a state of sulphated insolvency that the electric hot plate was decommissioned. From here on out, we would depend exclusively on Cooky's oil drum stove.

Coasting down the Celebes by seat-of-the-pants navigation, *Lanikai* crossed "the line" somewhere around midnight—119° 30′ east longitude, 0° latitude. This was the world's bellyband, where for centuries its crossing by sailormen has been an occasion for high jinks, initiating the lowly "pollywogs" into the domain of Neptunus Rex, to become "shell-backs." The occasion was not wholly lost on one shipmate. As Adair noted in his little hip pocket journal: "Seriously considered throwing a bucket of cold water on pollywog Captain Tolley, who was sleeping on bridge, but decided with limited bedding it would be too hard to dry him out." Ah! Charlie! You ever-thoughtful friend!

We had crossed the line and were now sliding "down under." But by no means had we shaken the major peril. Earlier, on the western horizon, out in the middle of Makassar Strait, silhouetted against the orange-gold sunset sky, lay the outlines of half a dozen warships. By the looks of them in the dim distance, they were destroyers, operating off oil-rich Tarakan, which was occupied five days after we passed.

About 6:00 A.M. on the seventh, holding near to the coast, we sighted a small steamer four miles off our port quarter, closing fast. In the morning mist there was no making her out. The three-pounder's cover came off, shells were laid out and anxious eyes trained all around. If there was one ship, there might be more. There was little doubt as to the colors flown by those we had sighted the night before. This could be another of the same. We lay to, keeping our stern toward the new-comer. There was not enough wind to lay out our ensign.

In twenty minutes, bone in her teeth, up charged the 1,000-ton Dutch gunboat euphoniously and improbably named *Willibrod Snellius*. In spite of her manned-and-ready 3-inch bow gun, *Willi* might have regretted her impetuosity had we turned out to be a far from stingless enemy. Obviously the skipper had been torn from his early morning slumber to confront the interloper. Hanging on to the bridge railing in flowing pajamas, he bellowed across in fractured English, demanding our business and identity. A lady in negligee, who had been watching from a lower deck, discreetly withdrew.

Nygh, a man of incredibly slow motion in meticulously performing his morning toilette, was finally produced from below, clean shaven and immaculate in white uniform, to carry on the negotiations across fifty yards of intervening water. The conversation shifted to Dutch, as Nygh attempted to clarify things, then the Dutch skipper reverted to English. "Dot Nederlandisch vellow of yourss hass got a zuspicious aggzent!" he shouted. Adair listened with amusement and wrote in his notebook that, "Nygh has been around Americans and British so much in the last few years, we now have him mixing his English with his Dutch."

Suspicions sufficiently allayed, *Snellius* led us into Donggala's little landlocked harbor. This was civilization. Keith and Nygh boated over to *Snellius* to borrow charts, then ashore to check in with the local authorities. The mystery of the Dutch ship's heavy doubts was clarified—we were the subject of that telephone call from Sabang.

"A ship is headed your way," the messenger had warned, breathless from the bike ride and excitement. "They claim to be Americans and

Filipinos, but they really appear to be Germans and Japanese. Take care!"

Keith, Tolley and Nygh all had moustaches. The canny Sabangese knew that Americans didn't wear moustaches. Nygh's accented Dutch fitted in perfectly with this scenario. We were lucky, Assistant Resident* de la Fuente explained in English, that *Snellius* at very least hadn't put a round across our bow.

Outsiders were even more welcome at Donggala than at Sabang. The de la Fuentes had been stuck in this backwash of 4,000 natives for three years, with only three other whites for company. This would be a special occasion—a *riistaffel* (literally, "rice table") lunch.

Their magnificent house stood on a commanding hill, cool and breezy. Tile floors, polished teak and mahogany woodwork, massive furniture covered in brilliant *batik* designs and fifteen-foot-high beamed ceilings made an opulent backdrop for the elaborate meal. Behind each chair at a table that could have seated twenty, a servant stood ready to bring the next dish from the two dozen or more courses that covered every conceivable meat, fish, and vegetable available in those parts. Copious mugs of good Dutch beer helped put out the fire of the curries that laced the meal.

The enormous windows, unscreened, afforded a magnificent view of the sea on one side and the forest-lined harbor on the other. Tucked up in the beams overhead, swallows' nests gave a clue to local mosquito control. During lunch, a half dozen of these graceful birds swooped in and out of the windows, making themselves at home. Malaria was endemic in the country where four hundred years ago, "Jesuits' bark"—quinine—had been taken in quantity to China to cure the rulers of the Celestial Kingdom. Now, the colonial Dutch took their daily quinine prophylactic as religiously as they downed their Bols *schnapps* and had their two-hour afternoon nap. For the natives, there was none of this precious, exportable product of which the Indies enjoyed a near monopoly in the world. In their millions, sick, lazy and indifferent, they scratched at the surface of a huge land bursting with nature's bounty.

The talk at lunch, naturally enough, was of the war. At peace for centuries, the Dutch had forgotten the word. Their Indies forces during four hundred years had been engaged in pacification duties by guerrilla tactics. Warfare against a major power never was a serious consideration. Only the small, partly modern naval forces provided any suggestion that Dutch eyes were in any respect turned beyond their own shorelines. But compared with what the Japanese had available, the Dutch ships had little more than nuisance value.

At that time, none of us at the big table, stuffing ourselves with fiery curry, knew of the real losses at Pearl Harbor. What we did know,

---

* A rank in the Dutch colonial service.

was that the numerical balance of power between the potential "Allies" and the Japanese as of early December was close. Only those who understood the almost total lack of combined purpose on the "Allied" part would have realized how great the imbalance actually was. And high on the list of those who knew were the Japanese themselves.

PACIFIC AND INDIAN OCEAN FORCES
IN EARLY DECEMBER 1941

	BB	CV	CA	CL	DD	SS
British	2	1	1	7	13	
Netherlands				2	7	12
United States	9	3	13	11	80	56
Total Allied	11	4	14	20	100	68
Japanese	10	10	18	18	113	63

BB = battleship; CV = aircraft carrier; CA = heavy cruiser; CL = light cruiser; DD = destroyer; SS = submarine

Perhaps we could be excused for our ignorance. After all, there were some in infinitely higher places with vastly better information whose vital conclusions were no better. A third of a century later, views are still mixed. All sources are unanimous in declaring that Pearl Harbor was a magnificent tactical near-triumph. One can say "near," because the ship repair shops and oil storage tanks were omitted from the target list. As for the strategic impact, there is less agreement. It did unify the American public as nothing else conceivably could have done, and saved Roosevelt from a possible constitutional crisis. But what else?

Had the Japanese *not* hit Pearl, it is within the realm of possibility that the United States would have dragged on as a neutral, Roosevelt and Churchill itching to get the Americans in and Hitler and the U.S. public determined to keep them out. The majority of America's ever-increasing output of war material would have gone to the USSR and Britain, who would have triumphed against Germany without our manpower, although taking longer to do so. Japan, meanwhile, would have taken the Far East, less Australia, and solidified her position to the point she would have balanced the power of a Soviet Union victorious against Germany. With Japan and the USSR squared off, there never would have been such a hugely expensive, hair-raising confrontation with the Soviets such as has faced the West ever since 1945. If one kills all the world's insects, the whole world's ecology is threatened, and if one exterminates all the birds, the insects will take over. Such is nature's balance of power that must be translated into a similar balance in man's sometimes unwise political maneuverings.

As for the Far East, driving out the Japanese failed to save it for the ex-colonial powers. The vacuum resulting from the Japanese defeat affected the United States even more grievously, in bringing about the Vietnam War, most disastrous misadventure in American history.

Perhaps amateur naval strategist Roosevelt and the State Department "military experts" refused to believe it, but most well-informed U.S. naval officers and the Japanese knew that it would have been at least two years before even an undamaged U.S. Fleet could have assembled supply vessels and fully manned and mobilized its ships to the point of presenting any real threat to Japanese power in the Far East. By then, the Japanese hoped they would be well established and heavily protected by shore air bases, well fueled from the Indies and well fed from Burma/Indo-China. The temporary shackling of American offensive power allowed them to use their carrier forces in expediting their occupation of the Far East, while lowering personnel losses. Had there been a U.S. Fleet in being instead of one sitting on the Pearl Harbor mud, the Japanese carriers would have had to stick close by their mandated Pacific islands, about the only enemy territory the short-legged American fleet could then reach.

Had we been clairvoyant, those are the thoughts we might have been thinking and discussing at that delightful round table in Donggala. But the stoic, resigned Dutch, made more so by the generous potions of *schnapps* and beer, and our own sighting of Japanese warships the night before, distant only a few hours steaming, kept our plans within imminent reality. At 7:00 P.M., still groggy with food in spite of a two hour post-feast nap, we hauled ourselves topside and got *Lanikai* under way. "Be out before dark," de la Fuente had warned, "unless you are well charged with quinine. Malaria can immobilize your whole crew."*

The Celebes coast from Donggala on south was studded with islands. Armed with *Snellius'* charts, we could safely hug the shore where Japanese submarines would not venture. By 10:30 A.M. we had reached our target for the day, Korossa. Hills rose six or eight miles back of a flat plain. Only a few thatched huts straggled along one edge of the small bay. "Looks like the depression arrived here some time ago," noted Adair. "Nothing here to hit the beach for."

With small chance of Japanese air or sea contact in these protected waters, we carried on next day until 2:30 P.M., when we reached the minor metropolis of Madjene. Assistant Resident and Mrs. D. F. Uhlen-

* On her way south, the destroyer *Peary* had been harassed by Australian planes and spooked by Japanese reconnaissance craft. For one day, they had stopped at a small island to make jury repairs and give the exhausted crew a full day and night's rest. The ship was brought close to the beach and camouflaged with greenery. Some of the crew slept ashore to escape the heat. Shortly thereafter many were stricken with the virulent tertian malaria, from which a large percentage died.

beck made us welcome with beer and a drive around the teeming town, which looked more like the travel posters. A small pier allowed coastal ships to come alongside to load the locally grown coconuts and pineapples. A good highway led to the big city of Makassar. Along it, for as far as our host drove us, one might have thought it was the prewar Cavite road all over again. Thatched huts stretched in long rows. Dogs, pigs, and children swarmed in the road, dodging the diminutive ponies that trotted briskly in front of two-wheeled carts stacked high with produce. There was a hotel-like guest house available for inspecting officials from "outside" who called from time to time to brighten the lives of the four families who were the only Europeans in town. We would be welcome to stay there, they told us—but it would be a certain sentence to malaria. It was the standard story—get out before nightfall.

Cutting southeasterly across the bay, we lay to at 3:30 A.M., awaiting daylight and clearing of the thin haze. The mainland mountains were in sight but we were unsure of our position on dangerous navigational ground.

The morning sunshine brought the most glorious sight. Ahead lay the Spermonde Archipelago, an area of coral reefs and small islands, some of the latter less than half an acre in size, dotting the sea as far as the eye could reach from the Coca-Cola box crow's nest. All were covered to the narrow sand shoreline with the most brilliant green vegetation, like jade jewels set in the azure blue of the surrounding sea. Everywhere, literally hundreds of small boats lay beached on the islands, or lying off, their crews casting nets. Others were simply drifting, their occupants inactive, perhaps overpowered by the beauty of the scene as were we, but more likely enervated by the lifelong effects of malaria.

Threading our way through this fairyland, we came that afternoon to our first real city—Makassar, *Lanikai*'s dignity having been enhanced by the presence of a pilot who had boarded us on our approach.

The first visit ashore, to make official calls, confirmed that if possible, Makassar was even more beautiful than the sea through which we had just passed. Spotless wide, straight streets ran between impressive, balconied, pastel buildings. Enormous, stately palms lined roads and dotted lawns. A tropic sun in a cloudless sky accentuated the brilliant colors of masses of flowers that filled yards, parks and public squares. It was a piece of Hollywood's "Wizard of Oz" in living color and slow motion.

We apologized for the informality of shorts and open-necked shirts as our only available uniform. The names and titles of the dignitaries who received us rolled from the tongue like those of participants in a royal levee: the Governor of the Eastern Islands, His Excellency G. A. W. Ch. de Haze Winkleman; His Excellency the Resident of the Celebes, Dr. B. Y. Burger; the Colonel Commanding, H. Vooren; the Senior Naval Officer, Commander A. S. de Bats.

It was de Bats who a month earlier had jumped in the open two-seater biplane and scouted out the approaching armada to determine its nationality—Allied or Japanese. If he failed to return it could be deduced they were enemy.

Mme. de Bats was a Javanese princess, very dark and very beautiful. There was wide tolerance for racial intermingling in the Indies. A recent commander in chief of the land forces had been of mixed blood, although outright marriage to a Javanese was not considered good for promotion.

The hospitality ashore was overwhelming; something approaching state dinners at the opulent Societé Harmonie the two nights in port, cocktails, tours of the city, and liberty for the crew ashore to walk the streets and gape at shops in a tropical heaven the like of which none of us had seen before.

Aboard *Lanikai*, in modest return, Velarmino and Gomez conjured up a marvelous lunch with delicacies found ashore. The guest list was limited by available accommodations and from among those we felt such relative juniors as ourselves could appropriately invite: British Consul George Nimmins, KPM Steamship Line's D. W. van Amsdel, British-American Tobacco's McShane, de Bats, and our old Donggala friend, the skipper of *Snellius*. After the near approach of those Japanese destroyers, he had made an agonizing reappraisal of the situation and steamed south.

The talk ashore was almost exclusively of one thing: the war. The day before, Japanese paratroopers had taken Menado, on the Celebes' north tip. The same day they had swarmed ashore at Tarakan, as smoke billowed up from the burning oil wells and storage tanks set afire by the Dutch proprietors. When would they reach Makassar?*

The general attitude was one of total resignation. These friendly, unaggressive, pessimistic people had lost everything at home in Holland, to which most had once hoped to return. Total disaster faced them here. They simply did not think in terms of the crunching Japanese power— its overwhelming air strength, seasoned amphibious forces, and strong parachute detachments. The Dutch forces were scattered in small, help-lessly weak and unsupported units at coastal towns. In many of them, only the commanding officer was European, and he a reserve officer with little military experience. Armed with obsolete rifles, with no artillery or tanks, what little communications equipment they had wholly primitive, the first few enemy shots would send the native troops flying, discarding their uniforms as they ran.

With full bellies and hearts low at the thought of the easily pre-dictable and early fate of good and kind friends, *Lanikai* set sail at 2:15 P.M., running again. *Her* belly was full too, having received 7,080 liters of diesel oil, 185 liters of gasoline, and 200 liters of lubricating oil. There

---

* In a little more than three weeks: 9 February 1942.

were fresh provisions in quantity, and ice to keep them. Our kind luncheon guests who had watched fascinated while Velarmino produced a feast on his oil drum stove, had eased his problems by sending out a quantity of charcoal. There was no bill for anything, which was just as well. There was no money on board other than the few pesos we had in our shirt pockets. "This is on the Queen," they said, "reverse lend-lease."

De Bats warned of enemy submarine activity nearby. Some ships had been torpedoed. To reassure ourselves, we let go a couple of trial 3-pounder rounds. The blind-loaded shells went whistling out too fast to follow with the naked eye, but there was a highly satisfactory series of bright splashes where the solid slug went skipping along toward the horizon.

In spite of this demonstration of potency, wisdom suggested keeping off the steamer tracks. Defending ourselves in a pinch was one thing; aggressively hunting submarines at six knots with a 3-pounder was quite another. We could crank geography into our defense plan. Two island groups, Postilion and Paternoster, lay between the Celebes and Lombok like a broken, scattered string of beads. Between these dots of islands the sea bottom rose to within fifty feet of the glass-smooth surface. This was not likely submarine operating territory. The water was so incredibly clear that the ship seemed to be suspended in air. How far down were the multitudes of fish? Fifty feet? Ten feet? It was difficult to tell in water of such clarity. Tiny fish darted this way and that, dodging the larger ones that cruised fearlessly like so many divisions of battleships. But who cared? There was chicken and red meat and good Dutch sausages lying on the ice in our hold.

At first, what appeared to be black storm clouds appeared on the southern horizon. Picking our way through this maze in a heavy blow would have been a greater hazard than any submarine. But soon the clouds took and held a definite shape. Obviously they were the great mountainous spine of Lombok, sixty or more miles away, rising steeply out of the sea to over 12,000 feet. In a dead calm, on a glassy sea, chugging along at six knots hour after hour on the engine alone, we seemed to bring those mountains no nearer. On the islets we passed, some no larger than a football field, an occasional native hut showed through the mass of vegetation. How did people exist on those flyspeck islands, where tropical gales sometimes reached a hundred miles an hour? Did they live, love and die in this Crusoe-like existence, knowing nothing of a world beyond their microcosm of coral sand?

On the fourteenth, a lone plane passed on opposite course five or six miles away. We went to general quarters with less elevated pulse than had been the case farther north. Japanese aircraft could scarcely be expected here. With no sign of sighting us or of recognition, the plane droned on out of sight. Since our reporting at Makassar, perhaps we had been transferred from the list of those overdue and presumed lost to the list of the quick.

At 6:00 A.M. on the fifteenth, the coastline of Lombok at last rose from the sea, like a frame under the mountain that had seemed almost to loom over our heads for the last day. An hour later, we anchored in a small bay. Beyond the palm-fringed shoreline, rice paddies stretched back to the base of the hills. People plodding behind water buffaloes in the fields continued placidly about their business, apparently paying no attention to the new arrivals.

Walruff and several of the Filipinos putt-putted ashore to a small pier that jutted out from near a group of small buildings. We watched Sparky being led away by several gesticulating natives.

Walruff, we learned later, carried out a touchy mission. He had found nobody ashore with a common language. So by tugs and pantomime, his greeters had got him to a telephone and put his ear to the odd-looking instrument which his new friends urgently indicated stood ready to solve the problem. After several false tries on Walruff's part, what passed for English crackled from the other end. It was a Dutch police official, one "Meneer" Smith. Reports indicated, he said, that a Japanese ship had just put in and was landing men. He had mobilized the local defense forces, in the form of two dozen local militiamen, who were at that very moment highballing it down the road with orders to shoot on sight. Now, having been enlightened on the character of the "Japanese" by Walruff, Smith urged him to intercept these militia gentlemen and explain the situation before they opened up on Lanikai.

In no time at all, there appeared a cloud of dust which soon materialized into a bus that screeched to a halt and immediately commenced disgorging a highly excited lot of uniformed natives armed with long-barreled rifles. Under normal circumstances, the plucky Walruff could scarcely have been taken for a Japanese. But "normal" did not fit the current scenario. Matters had not been improved by the locals, who passed on to these newcomers the chilling news that back at the pier were a couple of characters in the boat who could very well be Nips.

A second cloud of dust then bore down, which turned out to contain a sparkling new Harley-Davidson motorcycle. Out of the sidecar hopped the agitated author of all this furor, "Meneer" Smith himself. He soon got matters properly sorted out. The incident had several amusing angles, he thought, amiably demonstrating a better sense of humor than one usually finds in his normally rather stolid race. Aside from the opéra bouffe proceedings in general, Smith found it quite funny that he, Smith, with an English name, was a Dutchman, whereas Walruff, with a Dutch name, had just come close to being knocked off by his erstwhile kinsmen several times removed. They should swap names, Smith thought. Whatever Walruff might have been thinking at that point, the odds are that it was not in a humorous vein.

The whole contretemps soon crystallized into a friendly Smith-Walruff encounter involving several mugs of Heiniken's beer in the cool shade of an awning on the inevitable Chinese *tienda*, or whatever the local term was for these ubiquitous establishments. Walruff made arrangements to procure some fresh fruit, plus additional dividends in the form of the latest war news and the story of Smith's life. The busload of recently agitated cops had cooled off and they were animatedly socializing with the townsmen, no doubt well pleased at the outcome and the unexpected excursion. Those aboard *Lanikai* were watching developments as best they could through binoculars and to put it simply, wondering what the hell was going on.

Smith was happy for the diversion. Like so many of his colonizing countrymen, he was making more money than he would at home, and doing less to earn it. Retirement came sooner, too. But so many of these fellows were stashed away in some god-forsaken backwash for three or four years without European companionship. Perhaps there would be a native "housekeeper," who would bear them a child or two, but provide little real companionship or intellectual stimulation. Such an existence could pall.

Smith felt his transfer from Bali only a few months before was a retrograde step. In Bali, the ladies all went topless, displaying figures that would have sent any red-blooded sculptor charging off for his mallet and chisel. Here on Lombok, not only were the damsels well covered up, but the population in general was far more truculent than the gentle people of Bali, whose pace was that of the caribao that drew the carts and tilled the rice paddies. The bare breasts of the young women in their smooth, round fullness expressed nature's bounty on this lush isle where all that life required for happiness and sustenance came with little effort.

The foregoing was the idyllic propaganda bit brought back aboard by Walruff, along with a boatload of fresh fruit and vegetables furnished gratis by the genial Meneer Smith as part recompense for the earlier gaffe.

Sorong Djoekoeng, which Walruff had discovered to be the town's name, was no place to dally. The water was very deep—no bottom at 15 fathoms—a mere 200 yards from shore. From there in, it shelved rapidly, like the slope of an underwater mountainside. At Makassar, they had warned that in the current season, it could blow up a storm of hurricane force on the Lombok coast in a matter of hours. With such wretched holding ground on a lee shore, in heavy weather we would be dead ducks. That Bali was one day away may possibly have influenced the decision to hurry on.

It was here that the anchor engine nearly did us in. At 11:00 P.M., in close to pitch darkness, we started heaving in the anchor chain. To enter a traffic funnel like Lombok Strait, we wanted good nighttime cover.

The windlass switch was closed, the chain came in a link or two, then stopped as a flash of blue light illuminated the forecastle. A blown fuse. Then another. And another. By that time, the anchor was "aweigh" but far from being housed. In the heavy current, we drifted to seaward. Soon there was a light thump, as *Lanikai*'s three-foot keel grounded. We were on a pinnacle whose sides dropped almost straight down. As the tide receded, the ship started to heel. The desperately dangerous aspect of it was that with the keel aground and nothing under the turn of the bilge when she rolled farther over with the falling tide, she would not come to a normal rest on keel and turn of bilge, but continue to roll toward the horizontal until the water came in on deck, then down the hatches. There would be a final gurgle and it would be all over. We put on life jackets and cleared the two boats—the punt and motor launch.

A 200-pound kedge anchor slung from the poop deck rail aft for just such emergencies. We carried it out in the launch at the end of a heavy manila hawser to keep the stern from swinging farther up.

By 7:00 A.M., the tide had turned. By then the ship was critically far over, the water lapping the deck edge. We slowly righted. But *still* we stuck. On the after deckhouse was our "armor plate," several tons of sandbags that hopefully shielded the "citadel" below from bomb splinters. "Over they go, boys!" We turned to and tossed sandbags overboard as sandbags seldom have been tossed before. At the same time, the motor launch churned away, a small tug pushing against the side to counteract the current setting us aground. The ship rose, inch by inch. Would she be lightened enough? Could we get off before the current pushed us back again, higher this time—certain to swamp on the next low tide? It was "go for broke" all over again. Then we felt that wonderful sensation that any professional sailor instinctively recognizes—the weight of the sea under us. We were free! It had been a full day of struggle and worry that Meneer Smith might have the company he yearned for. At 11:00 P.M. we headed out, and thirty minutes later turned westward for Lombok Strait. Bali next stop!

Chapter 13

On 1 January 1942, the same day that *Lanikai* was slogging her way southward from Palawan, the submarine *Shark* arrived in Surabaya, Java, where the remnants of the Asiatic Fleet was gathering and where Admiral Hart expected to organize a last ditch stand. The first thing he heard, on arrival, was a rumor of a new Far East Allied command about to be set up, with him as naval chief. He testily informed Admiral Glassford he wanted no part of it.

Even more disconcerting was a message from the Chief of Naval Operations, Admiral Stark, in Washington:

```
    291432: EXTRACTS FROM MACARTHUR'S DESPATCH OF DEC
26 INVOLVING YOUR FLEET FOLLOW: "ENEMY PENETRATION

IN PHILIPPINES RESULTED FROM OUR WEAKNESS ON THE SEA
AND IN THE AIR (GARBLE) SURFACE ELEMENTS OF ASIATIC

FLEET WERE WITHDRAWN AND EFFECT OF SUBMARINES HAS
BEEN NEGLIGIBLE. ENEMY HAS UTTER FREEDOM OF NAVAL AND

AIR MOVEMENT. NETHERLANDS EAST INDIES BASES ARE STILL
AVAILABLE AND MUST BE RETAINED. STRONG NAVAL FORCES

MUST SEEK COMBAT WITH ENEMY. COMMUNICATIONS CAN BE
MAINTAINED. UTMOST RAPIDITY OF ACTION BY AIR, NAVY

AND GROUND FORCES IS ESSENTIAL. WISH TO EMPHASIZE
NECESSITY FOR NAVAL ACTION AND FOR RAPID (GARBLE) BY

LAND, SEA AND AIR." I FEEL THAT I MUST LET YOU KNOW
THAT THIS AND OTHER MACARTHUR DESPATCHES CREATE AND

SUPPORT UNFORTUNATE IMPRESSIONS DESPITE DULY EMPHA-
SIZED REPRESENTATIONS AS TO THE MEANS YOU HAVE TO

WORK WITH. ....I MUST URGE UPON YOU TO CONSIDER UN-
DERTAKING CALCULATED RISKS GREATER THAN WE HERE ARE

NOW AWARE OF. KING* CONCURS
```

* Admiral Ernest J. King, CinC Atlantic Fleet, about to replace Stark as CNO and become additionally "COMINCH," Commander in Chief, U.S. Fleet.

Hart's immediate reaction was to supply a thumbnail picture of the war to date:

```
021120 HART REPLYING TO STARKS 291432. HAVING
SENSED SINCE ABOUT 10 DECEMBER THAT THIS FLEET MIGHT
BE CHARGED WITH THE LOSS OF THE PHILIPPINES I HAVE
KEPT RECORD STRAIGHT TO PROVE OTHERWISE. I REALLY
THINK THAT MY PRECEDING DESPATCHES WITH YOUR GENERAL
KNOWLEDGE OF THE SITUATION SHOULD BE SUFFICIENT TO
COMBAT ERRONEOUS IMPRESSIONS. A DEFEAT IN THE PHILIP-
PINES WILL BE PRIMARILY INCIDENT TO TOTAL LOSS OF
CONTROL OF THE AIR WHICH FOLLOWED CLOSE UPON FIRST
JAPANESE ATTACK MADE NINE HOURS AFTER THAT ON PEARL
HARBOR. IT IS AXIOMATIC THAT FLEETS MUST HAVE BASING
FACILITIES FOR THEIR OPERATIONS AND OUR BASE HAS HAD
NO FIGHTER PROTECTION WHATSOEVER, WHICH AS MADE EF-
FECTIVE BY RADAR SYSTEM I HAVE REPEATEDLY POINTED OUT
AS THE FIRST ESSENTIAL. IN CONSEQUENCE OF ENEMY'S
COMPLETE FREEDOM IN THE AIR, EVEN OUR SUBMARINES HAVE
NOW BEEN FORCED OUT OF MANILA BAY. INCIDENTALLY, I
FEAR THAT THEY HELD ON THERE TOO LONG. WITHDRAWAL OF
SURFACE SHIPS WAS ACCORDING TO YOUR OWN PLAN AND
PLEASE RECALL THAT ON 27 OCTOBER I PROPOSED TO FIGHT
THE CAMPAIGN FROM MANILA BAY WITH THIS ENTIRE FLEET.
YOUR REJECTION OF THAT PROPOSAL WAS CORRECT, AND WE
SHOULD RECEIVE YOUR FULL DEFENSE AGAINST CRITICISM IN
FOLLOWING THE PLAN. AFTER MAKING DUE ALLOWANCE FOR
THE FACT THAT RESULTS WITH SUBMARINES COME SLOWLY, I
CONFESS DISAPPOINTMENT WITH THEIR EFFECT AS THUS FAR
KNOWN, BUT AS YET I AM UNABLE TO JUDGE WHETHER THIS
IS DUE TO THEIR INEFFICIENCY OR TO THE EXCELLENCE OF
ENEMY ANTI-SUBMARINE MEASURES.*
AS REGARDS TAKING GREATER RISKS, I HAVE FOLLOWED YOUR
141535 OF DECEMBER, WHICH MENTIONED THE SACRIFICE OF
BRITISH MAJOR UNITS, AND I FEEL THAT I SHOULD NOT
EXPEND MY SURFACE FORCES EXCEPT ON CHANCES OF LARGE
RESULTS. AT PRESENT, SUCH CHANCES ARE SLIM DUE TO
COVERAGE OF ENEMY SURFACE SHIPS BY AIR AND OUR OWN
LACK OF ANY AIR PROTECTION....I WILL PROJECT MY OP-
ERATIONS AS FAR NORTHWARD AS POSSIBLE. I WAS PER-
SONALLY RELUCTANT TO LEAVE MANILA LARGELY BECAUSE I
EXPECTED UNFOUNDED CRITICISM OF THE STEP....
```

The Admiral might have added, all chances were slim. A month later the Japanese would be bombing Surabaya and on 4 February the Asiatic Fleet ceased to exist, with its last units reassigned to a new Southwest Pacific Force. Hart, already past retirement age, returned to the United States where some time in June 1942, one of the most remarkable and revealing communications of the war caught up with him. It was a registered letter, in the ordinary mail, from Admiral Stark, with a note

---

* It was of course largely due to defective torpedoes, a fault of the Bureau of Ordnance and Gunnery and not the submarines.

attached: "This letter to be delivered with the most possible speed. Send air mail as far as Pearl Harbor—thence via quickest transportation."

Dear Tommy,

. . . As to the substance of our despatch, I agree with it all one hundred percent. Some day I will tell you just how the despatch was written, why it had to be written and of my regret even for sending it. I am not "Boss of the Show" and there are times when we all have to say "Aye, Aye, Sir." I am keeping no copy of the letter and no notes in any stenographer's note book and I would be glad, if after having read it, you would destroy it. . . .

I don't get down on my knees very often, but if I were to do so right now it would be to thank God you didn't stay in Manila too long and that you have done everything just as you have done it.

Again, I was perfectly delighted with . . . your message.

Sincerely,
/s/ Betty

In Hart's sawtooth squiggle on the envelope was: "Not received until about June 1942. Then no reason to destroy."

Hart would have been a fool to do away with this prime piece of evidence that, in the view of the top professional naval man, his Far East strategy had been correct.

Admiral William Standley, the Chief of Naval Operations from 1933 to 1937, had remarked that Roosevelt had an inflated opinion of his knowledge of strategy and tactics. It was a dangerous delusion frequently manifested.

In October 1940, Roosevelt was considering a blockade of Japan's maritime traffic to North and South America by a patrol of American warships in two lines—from Hawaii to the Philippines and from Samoa to the Netherlands Indies. Admiral J. O. Richardson, then the Commander in Chief, U.S. Fleet, at Pearl Harbor was justifiably horrified. Fortunately, this scheme came to nothing.

In April 1941, Roosevelt told Admiral Stark to be prepared to send some cruisers out in the direction of the Far East. "I just want to keep them popping up here and there and keep the Japs guessing." He didn't mind losing one or two cruisers, he said, but wouldn't want to chance losing five or six. That wild scheme too, fortunately was batted down, this time by a jittery State Department.

In July 1941, he proposed sending an aircraft carrier loaded with planes to a Siberian port as a means of delivering Lend-Lease aircraft. CinC Richardson, meanwhile, had been relieved of his fleet command for "hurting the President's feelings" by resisting FDR's determination to keep the Pacific Fleet in its exposed position at Pearl Harbor. Richardson's relief, Admiral Husband Kimmel, wrote Stark that any such aircraft carrier deployment would be tantamount to initiation of a Japanese-American war, adding that, "If for reasons of political expediency, it has been determined to force Japan to fire the first shot, let us choose a method which will be more advantageous to ourselves."

In late December 1941, to Stark's and Hart's chagrin, Roosevelt was at it again, directing the strategy of the Far East war as prompted by MacArthur through his direct communications to Washington.

During 1940 and 1941, various Allied conferences aimed at combined action or command in the Far East had had small success. The Dutch were reluctant to risk offending the Japanese by any sign of cosying up to Japan's *bête noir,* the United States. Britain was ready to cooperate, but the United States was inclined to let the British and Dutch go it alone, feeling that Americans, who were stone cold to fighting for blitzed London or even over torpedoed U.S. destroyers in the Atlantic, were far less ready to die for Singapore, Bandoeng, or for that matter, even Manila.

As the sex of a rhino is of interest only to another rhino, so the diplomatic aspects of setting up ABDACOM (Australian, British, Dutch, American Command) are of interest only to another diplomat. Suffice it to say here that after a month-long Anglo-American wrangle in Washington, it was agreed to give overall command to a British officer, navy command to an American, air command to a Briton, and land command to a Dutchman.

Although Churchill was reluctant to have a British skipper take command of an obviously sinking ship, he assigned General Sir Archibald Percival Wavell as ABDACOM. The latter had been relieved of his command in North Africa after failing to smash Rommel. Air Chief Marshall Sir Richard E. C. Peirse was appointed ABDAIR (air forces) and Dutch Lieutenant General H. ter Poorten, ABDARM (army forces).

Feeling that Vice Admiral C. E. L. Helfrich, the Dutch naval commander on his own home ground in Java, was a more appropriate choice, Admiral Hart accepted the post of ABDAFLOT with reluctance. The cool correctness of Helfrich in his dealings with Hart soon made clear that both shared the same view.

General ter Poorten had been commander of Dutch military forces in the Indies. Helfrich was not only his navy opposite number, but a cabinet officer as well—Minister of Marine of the Dutch exile colonial government. Furthermore, he was *Royal* Navy, whereas ter Poorten was merely *Territorial* Army, a less prestigious designation. Thus, under Hart, as Dutch naval commander, Helfrich was even further galled to find himself a rung below ter Poorten, who was Hart's equal.

On Wavell's arrival in Java on 10 January, Hart went over to the new ABDACOM headquarters at Bandoeng to check in. At Hart's age of 64, the long submarine trip plus the steamy railroad ride from Sura-baya had left some temporary marks on the tough old sailor that he and Wavell jokingly brought up. Wavell then passed on the gist of this chat to Churchill, who suggested to friend Roosevelt that perhaps Hart was not up to the job physically. Admiral King leaked this exchange to Hart, who in his usual straightforward manner, confronted Wavell with it. Hart found him desperately embarrassed, mumbling something unin-telligible in clipped guardsman's English, clearly revealing his implica-tion in the "plot."*

When Admiral Hart assumed command of the Asiatic Fleet on 25 July 1939, he was six weeks over 62 years old. For decades, the "cruise" had averaged two years or less, giving Hart a safe margin to complete a full term before mandatory retirement at 64; but the way the 1941 stream was shaping up, it clearly was not the time to changes horses in the middle of it.

Admiral Stark repeatedly brought up the subject in his monthly letters, in the most glowingly flattering terms telling Hart it was next to impossible to find anybody of his stature and experience. He had seriously considered Rear Admiral Chester Nimitz, then Chief of the Bureau of Navigation, but "that is like losing my right arm," Stark wrote.

For his part, Hart expressed willingness to call it quits. He was a tough, wiry little man, an amateur golfer who carried so little fat he probably could have buttoned himself into his Midshipman full dress jacket.

Rear Admiral Glassford was sufficiently senior and was available locally, but he too had been on the Asiatic station for two years, all of it in the less than salubrious Yangtze Valley. There *must* be a flag officer at or near Shanghai, decreed the State Department. It was only with some degree of independence and "to hell with State" that Hart had come south from China in the autumn of 1940, with the pronouncement that he did not intend to return. Thus, Glassford, already due to go home, stuck at Shanghai exercising his ample diplomatic talents and, damned by faint praise by both Stark and Hart, was passed by, while Hart continued on well beyond retirement age.

How Hart came to be CinC Asiatic makes an interesting vignette of history. In 1939, Admiral William Leahy, then the Chief of Naval Operations, and Rear Admiral J. O. Richardson, the Chief of the Bureau of Navigation, which handled personnel assignments, armed themselves with a list of eligibles and headed for the White House. They expected a tussle over assignment of the top fleet commands, knowing that Roose-velt would have a list of his own.

* Wavell could have spared himself these apprehensions. Hart, hale and sharp to the end, outlived him by 18 years.

Quarterback Leahy's starting lineup was Admiral King for the Atlantic command (then called the Patrol Force, U.S. Fleet), Hart for CinC U.S. Fleet, and Admiral Nimitz for CinC Asiatic Fleet. Would Coach Roosevelt buy it? Leahy, highly respected by the President and soon to become his precedent-shattering White House chief of staff, urged consideration of his good friend and Naval Academy classmate Hart. This highly talented officer's age would make it his last crack at the job, Leahy pointed out. "Take that name off the list!" the President ordered.

Roosevelt had a long memory. After World War I, when he was assistant secretary of the Navy in Wilson's administration, the Navy's top submarine enthusiast and expert probably was Captain Thomas C. Hart. He was fighting for a submarine office in the Navy Department. There, next to the seats of the mighty, it could better further the objectives of that fast-developing weapon which had just come very near to winning the war for the Germans. Roosevelt fought the project. Hart triumphed; the office was established, with Hart heading it, his policies therein continuing to irk the assistant secretary. Hart had won a battle but lost a war, as Roosevelt never forgot or forgave a defeat.

To return to the high command selections, a compromise was reached. The Atlantic command was raised to fleet status with King as Commander in Chief on 1 February 1941. Hart assumed command of the Asiatic Fleet on 25 July 1939. Richardson was assigned to duty as Commander Battle Force, in the Pacific, from 24 June 1939, and on 6 January 1940 was "fleeted up" to become CinC U.S. Fleet, when he relieved Admiral C. C. Bloch. Precisely one year less one day later, Richardson learned Roosevelt was removing him from command.

Roosevelt's festering wound had been imparted by Richardson at a White House lunch on 8 October 1940, where the other guests were presidential alter ego Harry Hopkins, and elder naval statesman Admiral Leahy, then governor of Puerto Rico. When the question of strengthening the Asiatic Fleet came up, the President asked Admiral Leahy his views. "Whatever was sent out would be lost in the event of war," Leahy said. He thought that if anything *were* added, it should be only the least valuable element, perhaps a light cruiser. With a sailor's bluntness, Admiral Richardson said that with such a prospect, he would send nothing at all.*

The President then refuted Richardson's views on keeping the fleet

* Apparently Richardson was not too impressed with Leahy's opinion. The following month, he wrote Hart of his plans to prepare an Asiatic reinforcing detachment of four heavy cruisers, an aircraft carrier, nine destroyers, and four fast minelayers. Stark confirmed the reinforcements plan. Of course, the grandiose scheme came to nothing.

in near mid-Pacific, in effect, saying: "Despite what you believe, I know that the presence of the fleet in the Hawaiian area has had, and is now having, a restraining influence on the actions of Japan."

Richardson's reply was honest but something less than diplomatic: "Mr. President, I still do not believe it, and I know that our fleet is disadvantageously disposed for preparing for or initiating war operations."

The President was adamant, saying that returning the fleet to the west coast would be regarded by Japan and the U.S. public as a "step backward." Additionally, the President enlightened the Commander in Chief, U.S. Fleet, on grand strategy . . . not quite what was agreed with Churchill the following summer at Argentia, which was kept a dark secret even from his top naval commander, Stark.* The President's strategy statement to Richardson included a tantalizing bit on how he might trap the Japanese: He said that America would not enter the war if the Japanese actually attacked Thailand or the Malay peninsula, or the Netherlands East Indies and perhaps not "even if they attacked the Philippines." But as the war went on, *"sooner or later they would make a mistake and we would enter the war."* [Italics supplied.]

As for Hart's being relegated to the Asiatic Fleet, he managed to suppress his disappointment. In a letter to Admiral Stark, he obliquely referred to his having missed the slot he felt himself best fitted for, but was "reconciled to doing my damndest where I am."

On 15 January 1942, ABDACOM was activated. In its high command were seven British, two American, and one Dutch officer, with headquarters at Lembang, Java, ten miles from Bandoeng. From then until the command dissolved in chaos six weeks later, the ships would be operating under the auspices of His Britannic Majesty George VI until 23 February, and under her Nederlandisch Majesty Wilhelmina until 1 March.

Such fascinating developments, of course, included the *Lanikai,* but none of us aboard that inconsequential little ship either knew or cared.

* Questioned by Senator Ferguson, before the 1945–46 JCC, Stark testified that, "In my replies to Joe Richardson as to what we would do if Japan attacked the British or Dutch, I did not know, and I do not think there was anybody on God's green earth that could tell me . . . and I did not know what the Congress would do. . . ."

Chapter 14

Bali! Romanticists knew there was magic in that word. Dutch policeman Smith had done nothing to destroy the idyll as far as we were concerned. Although the 12,000-foot mountains of Lombok seemed to soar into the sky, the single, gracefully tapered peak on Bali, 2,000 feet less, seemed even more impressive, standing alone in one mighty cone.

As we sailed into Padang Bay, only a gentle morning breeze barely ruffled indigo blue Lombok Strait. Bali itself, misty grey in early dawn, changed to emerald green as the sun rose higher. Hundreds of small fishing boats with candy-stripe sails helped dim any dark thoughts that under it all a Japanese submarine might be lurking.

No sooner had our anchor splashed down at 7:00 A.M. near the town of Denpasar, when out came Mijnheer and Mevrouw Lagerway, he a representative of K.P.M. Lines and the pair of them representatives of a people whose hospitality we had come to discover was unparalleled. Our Lombok policeman friend, Smith, had sent notice of our visit. We were invited to lunch, dinner, a trip around the southern end of Bali, night in the hotel and more of the same next day—guests of Her Majesty.

Denpasar was a tiny port where foreign ships were never seen, so the *Lanikai* brought a crowd of happy, laughing natives and their excited children to the dock. The women were dressed in bright prints, with dresses that trailed the ground—legs were not for showing. But from the waist up, the ladies were naked.

"You will soon get used to it," the Lagerways assured us. "Breasts are like faces. No two persons are identical. You unconsciously arrive at the point where you include them in the identification pattern, so that Europeans, baring only their faces, leave you with what you feel is a more restricted mental print of who is who—something like the poor orthodox Moslems having to identify their veiled damsels by a pair of eyes peeping through a slit. Here it is different. Perhaps you don't know a name. 'There goes old drag-bags!' one might say. Or, 'where is Bali-Bali this morning?' with reference to a pair of shapely twin peaks suggesting the island's principal mountain in duplicate."

Our Filipino sailors eyed the colorful crowd with interest.

"Keptin, sor! When can we go ashore?" said a spokesman for the younger group. Our pulling on halliards and fishing side by side together for so long had brought about an informality not usual in a more orthodox warship.

Told they could go ashore immediately, but to be back by noon, the "boys" were almost instantly in carefully scrubbed white uniforms, little round sailor hats squarely amidships. Lessons in neckerchief tying had been given by our American sailormen. Shoes glinted.

The spokesman came shyly up the ladder and saluted. "We hoff no money, sor," he said, a picture of mixed gloom and expectation. They had been whisked into the Navy, put to sea, and in all the furor had so far never made the acquaintance of a paymaster. If, indeed they ever had had any formal pay accounts made out, they must have contributed to the smoke that enveloped Cavite on 10 December.

Actually, the Far East chit system had so wholly supplanted ready cash in pocket that money took on another character. The question was not how much money you had but how good your credit was. One signed for every conceivable thing, including the collection in church, settling at the end of the month. Thus, it was no great financial wrench when war came along. Then even the chits were forgotten. If something was not too tightly screwed down, or too heavy, take it and welcome! Tomorrow it may be bombed. Grab it. Drink it. Eat it. Jump in and drive off in it. Pay? Forget it!

In a slight deviation from this norm, the thought had struck me while outfitting *Lanikai* that perhaps money might bring me home again. It seemed unlikely that *Lanikai* would. So I had dashed off to the paymaster and collected $256 squirreled up since I had been paid in China a month before. The small wad of bills had gone into a slot in my cabin bulkhead, forgotten until this moment. I produced a couple of dollar bills—a quarter for each of them. There was a flash of white teeth. Then they tumbled into the motor dory for old Belarmino to ferry them ashore.

We sat with the Lagerways on the after cabin roof, drinking coffee. "They should have a good time," said Lagerway. "These people are the soul of good humor and hospitality, with a free and easy way of life that matches nature's bounty here. They are all like happy children, and our paternalism encourages it."

We talked about the Filipinos, who are racially close to the Indonesians. "The Filipinos are basically modest," we explained. "A housemaid can bathe herself in the garden with a water hose, fully clothed in

Left to right, *Radio Electrician C. A. Walruff, USN, Lieutenant Commander Harry H. Keith, USN, Lieutenant Commander Charles Adair, USN, and Lieutenant H. Paul Nygh, RNN, ready to go ashore in Bali.*

Hilario Velarmino, ship's cook first class, kneels before his improvised sandbox stove.

a flowing dress, and never show more than an ankle." Somebody suggested that perhaps it was through their long association with Christianity. But along with religion, enough of the warm Spanish blood had by some sort of transmutation flowed into Filipino veins to elevate the pressure in our sailormen at the sight of those naked torsos. We would soon see how these two brands of Malay made out together.

The American crewmen, after excitedly passing the binoculars from hand to hand for some time, finally drifted off below to catch up on sleep after last night's vigil. With the exception of Paul Nygh, we had become largely nocturnal creatures. Under way in a frail cockleshell, with friendly and hostile submarines plying the same water, and with no recognition signals, one felt safer at night wholly awake on the wide open topside.

As for Belarmino the carpenter, seamy-faced Bosun Magtulis, old Cooky, and gimpy messman Gomez, they had hung up their spurs long ago, retired roosters who now preferred to sit around the capstan and silently fish, each thinking his own private thoughts.

In an hour, the liberty party was back on the dock, waving for transportation. "That's funny!" said Harry Keith. "Home so soon!" Back aboard, the spokesman shot up the ladder two steps at a time, out of breath, eyes popping.

"Keptin, sor! Pleece, sor!" he said between gasps. "Could we pleece hoff another quarter? There is steel another hour before twelfe o'clock!"

The lush island of Bali was unique. There were no proper harbors to attract the commerce that brought the world's ships, strife, greed and "civilization" as it did to Sumatra and Borneo for oil; to Java for rice, spice, and quinine; to the Celebes for "Makassar oil for gentlemen's hair," copra, kapok, and rattan; and to Flores for coffee, sandalwood, cinnamon, tobacco, and mother-of-pearl.

To the million Balinese, death was an occasion for gaiety and celebration; to them as Hindu immortals, it meant rebirth on their own beloved isle. Banishment from Bali would have been the ultimate punishment. At their backs rose the two-mile-high Peak of Bali, the Sacred Mount, the Navel of the Earth, Goenoeng Agoeng. On it lived their ever-present friends, the gods, who saw to it that misery was uncommon and famine unknown.

North of Bali Peak, the Lagerways told us, we would see a subtly different landscape, people and culture. That was where the occasional tourist ship moored, in a little basin so unusual they would wait for us to see for ourselves rather than try to describe it. Of course, no cruise ships came now, but before the war they carried cargos of wealthy, world-circling widows, spending the money their late husbands had slaved a lifetime to accumulate. These graying, buxom ladies would go mad over the magnificent Balinese wood carvings, paired male and female heads, batik prints, and fantastic sculpture in the island's soft stone. The few elderly gentlemen in the party were more interested in nature.

The stone sculpture expressed the ever-present sense of humor of the Balinese. There were bas-reliefs of gaily dressed men on bicycles, the wheels represented by huge lotus blooms. One old stone fellow, certainly a foreigner, in top hat and wreathed in smiles, obviously—as would many more who followed him—liked what he saw. Even the representations of Hindu gods looked benign, happy and cooperative. There was none of the tortured, twisted, sex-oriented demonology of the Indian temple sculpture. These Balinese gods obviously were good fellows, to whom sex was such a natural thing that the repression-bred pornography found in so many other lands had no need for manifestation here.

Thus did the Lagerways prepare us for the fascinating sights we would see that afternoon and the next day.

Shortly after noon, our hosts arrived in motor cars to collect the five officers and more than half the crew for our tour. Along the hard-packed, winding gravel roads, the air was heavy with the perfume of a profusion of multicolored flowers. The deeply worn footpaths alongside the road were bright with hundreds of magnificent Balinese women, their proud, erect postures developed through a lifetime of carrying heavy burdens on their heads.

"Where are the men?" we asked. "This is a highly civilized society," chuckled one of our Dutchmen. "The men, of course, are having a mid-afternoon snooze to prepare them for the cockfights or perhaps fishing when the day cools. The women do most of the work."

We remembered the Lagerways' elementary shipboard lecture on bosoms, which was expanded here where case examples were plentiful. Unless the lady clearly was an ancient, gray, wrinkled grandmother, the bland round Malay faces were much the same. But one could accurately assess with a glance the age of each passing female by the tiny buds displayed by the sub-debs, the perfect, pink-tipped cones of the nubile, the large, half-rounded grapefruits of the young matrons, and the heavily sagging equipment of the middle-aged. And as they must have with all newcomers to Bali, our hosts obviously were enjoying our reactions.

The Assistant Resident of Southern Bali and Lombok, Mijnheer K. Boterhoven de Haan, was temporarily in town, which made the lunch a special occasion. Twenty "boys," some of them solemn, gray-haired patriarchs, circled the table in elaborately printed, floor-length batik skirts, topped with white jackets. Each carried a serving dish heaped with some specialty: meat, seafood, vegetables, grated coconut, pineapple, chutney, nuts, and many other less easily identifiable items. Samples of each piled on top of a mound of rice on each diner's plate produced a five-inch miniature mountain of food that would have made any calorie counter blanch. Perhaps "volcano" of food might be more apt than "mountain"; the curries were blistering hot.

Strong Bols schnapps and good Heiniken's beer washed it all down and helped put out the fire. They also helped us forget for one glorious food-and-bosom-filled afternoon the war that hung over everything.

Earlier that week, enemy paratroopers had floated down on Palembang's oil refineries in Sumatra, the westernmost island. But such was the gigantic sweep of the Indies, greater in breadth than the United States, that it was hard even for space-conditioned Americans to realize that when dealing with those fast-moving little men of Nippon, Palembang, 900 miles from Bali, was altogether too close.

In the small Celebes outposts, the local Dutch had warned us to quit the town before darkness, to avoid malaria-bearing mosquitoes. At Bali, remembering this, we anchored well out in the stream, beyond mosquito range, avoiding the little wooden dock. But what appeared to be the greater sophistication of our Bali hosts disarmed us. They *must* know what they were about. As we would learn later, this was our undoing.

That evening, after a mercifully lighter repast, we watched a fantastic display—the Monkey Dance. In the dim light of a few small, flickering oil lanterns, over a hundred richly costumed performers rythmically swayed, clapped, chanted and danced to the beat of a variety of drums. The still night air was heavy with incense and the perfume of flowers—and well populated by buzzing mosquitoes.

That night, at the luxurious Bali Hotel, we enjoyed our first sleep in weeks between sheets, on a real bed, with most of our clothes off. Among us and the crewmen who had watched the dance, there were half a dozen whose blood streams were already filled with the parasites of malaria. Unlike the resident Dutchmen, with their daily prophylactic of quinine, we were wholly defenseless.

Next day, we lunched at the government rest house 4,500 feet up the mountain, looking down on a stupendous view that exactly one month later would be dotted by exploding and burning Dutch supply dumps as the Japanese landed and the defenders withdrew under the enemy's almost unopposed air power.

This was the end of an era and of a way of life that was wholly unique—a fairyland which in those days had been largely a private preserve for a few Dutchmen and the world-cruising wealthy.

By teatime, all hands were back aboard, surfeited with food and beauty. Those of the Filipino crewmen who had been ashore had run through quite a few quarters, to which my depleted store of greenbacks and the general faraway look in the liberty party's eyes gave testimony.

It is a pity that *Lanikai* couldn't have carried a court announcer to roll off the sonorous titles of our Dutch friends: "At 1710," the journal records, "Assistant Resident of Southern Bali, Mijnheer A. J. van Beuge, and the Comptroller of Eloengkoeng, Mijnheer J. C. Smit, called aboard officially." We had no bugle, no boatswain's pipe—not so much as a tin whistle—nothing more than a shouted "attention on deck!" and salutes all around. (The Dutchmen wore white uniforms, gold-trimmed shoulder-boards and military-style caps.) Then there was coffee on the after cabin roof.

Our guests were intrigued by the primitive American method of coffee making: a pot of boiling water, a cup of grounds tossed in, then a few eggshells to clarify the brew. Ashore, our Dutch friends boiled and squeezed a powerful essence of coffee from the crushed beans, then stored it in pop bottles. The coffee drinker poured a finger or two of this syrupy black liquid into a cup and topped it with boiling water. Instant coffee. These fellows should know; they had been doing it for twice as long as the U.S. Navy had existed. Indeed, it was from Java that the old Navy word for this essential seagoing nectar, *jamoke*, took half its derivation, *moke* being the contribution from Arabia—choice Mocha beans to make a blend.

As darkness fell, *Lanikai* stood out to sea and up the coast. Shore-ward, lights twinkled in fishing boats and along a beach that seemed innocent of any thought of war.

The next morning, off the town of Boleleng, it became apparent why the northeast monsoon made the unprotected north Bali coast unapproachable for commercial purposes. Heavy swells lashing into the seawall burst into flying spume, churning up heavy chop around a 100-foot-long pier. To have attempted going alongside would have meant wrecking both the pier and ship.

It is well known that a Dutchman's veins carry a good proportion of salt water, so it was no surprise that after a number of unsuccessful and risky tries at launching, two of that intrepid, seafaring race came bobbing out in a surfboat manned by half a dozen native oarsmen. They were the local police chief and Mijnheer E. Luuring, Assistant Resident of Singaradja, Bali's principal town. We should proceed on to Tjeloekan, they said. A program for the day had been laid out—lunch, calls, tour, native dance, and dinner. It began to dawn on us that we *must* be some-thing special. Yes! That was it! We were the first specimens representing the initial "A," for American, that these Bali-bound Dutchmen had so far seen in this new "ABDACOM" they had been hearing about. When they looked at that handsome, brass-mounted three-pounder stern chaser, it suddenly had been brought home to them that they were no longer fighting a war alone.

"You will like Tjeloekan," they said. "It is something like a large duck pond, with a narrow entrance like a drydock's gate. When a cruise ship moors there, it all but fills it. There are no facilities; just a landing stage, the surrounding jungle and a road to town." Then they asked us if we needed provisions, jumped in their plunging boat and were gone.

By noon, we were anchored in 35 feet of water in one of the most remarkable "harbors" that could be imagined. Wholly protected from the sea by a narrow entrance channel several hundred feet long, this pea-green, grotto-like little spot was another example of the uniqueness of that wholly unique island. Only a troop of those friendly mountain gods could have scooped out such a phenomenon.

Lieutenant Colonel W. P. Roodenburg, Bali's garrison commander, on whom we called first, seemed gloomy and almost hostile. Perhaps his military mind understood more clearly than those of the civilians that *Lanikai*'s sad little three-pounder was not so much a symbol of new, powerful allies as it was an agonizingly accurate caricature of the current military strength of the United States in the Far East—the clay-footed giant who just had been humiliated at Pearl Harbor, and currently was suffering disaster after disaster in the Philippines. Help the Dutch? He desperately needed help himself!

Mijnheer Boterhoven de Haan, our South Bali friend, hosted another prodigious *riistaffel* lunch, followed by Balinese dancers in brilliant costumes, under the shade of enormous trees in the Residency compound. Almost as fascinating as the pirouetting dancers, clashing cymbals and drums was the dense crowd of Balinese spectators, watching every movement as silently and intently as any Metropolitan Opera House audience might follow a prima ballerina on opening night. Yet this audience had seen these ritualistic performances a thousand times since childhood.

From the Residency, we moved to Luurings' for cocktails to whet our appetites for Chinese dinner at the club. "Fat men float better!" our hosts amiably explained, when we groaned at the sight of more and more succulent dishes. Twenty of us—Army, civilian officials, and wives —sat around a huge, square table, gaily unaware that with the exception of the four Americans, all present would be dead or prisoners of war before the next two months were out.

Many of the crewmen had been ashore and similarly treated to lunch, dance, tour and dinner, so that the sight of recent deliveries on board failed to arouse the enthusiasm it might have a few weeks earlier. All of it—25 pounds beef, 148 eggs, 15 pounds cabbage, 10 pounds beans, 30 pounds bread, 20 pounds pork, 5 pounds lettuce, and 700 pounds ice—was charged to the account of Her Gracious Majesty, the Queen.

It had been almost a month since we left Manila Bay. We were in a hurry to get to the end of the line, *some* line where we might stop this damned running away—perhaps even turn and fight. Wonderful as our Dutch friends had been, at Surabaya we would find our own people. We could then reassess the situation and try to sort out our individual

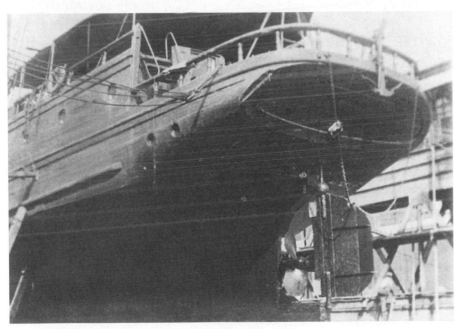

In Surabaya drydock, Lanikai's bottom gets a much-needed scraping, and an extension is welded to the rudder to give better control. Heavily timbered and with a deep keel, Lanikai was well built to withstand the two typhoons which mercifully hid her from the enemy in the Sulu Sea and south of Java.

lives. We were grateful for *Lanikai* and felt we had gotten on wholly familiar terms with her and with each other. But she scarcely was the craft to spearhead a force entering Tokyo Bay, which we optimistically felt should not be too long in the future. So, from the club we went straight to the ship, and by 2:00 A.M. were headed west.

At 4:00 A.M. the alarm "All hands! General Quarters!" brought us groggily to our feet. The black shape dead ahead was so close that loud noises might be carried across, revealing our identity. We rounded up into the wind and lay to, ready to kick ahead with the engine to bring our stern gun to bear on whatever was approaching. Our mental cobwebs spun by the sharks-fin soup and *samshu* wine were swept away in an instant by the tension. The agonizing wait was proof that time is not an absolute measuring stick; some five minutes are longer than others. Was it a submarine? Off the east channel entrance to Surabaya would be a good place for one, and certainly it could not be ours; this was not yet good hunting ground for finding Jap surface ships. Then we dimly made out the lines of a fishing boat, a big one.

Was this still Indian country? What scant information we had picked up in Bali had been, as one says in the Navy, strictly "scuttlebutt." Such, for example, as the recent arrival in Sydney, Australia, of France's huge liner SS *Normandie,* loaded with 1,500 planes and 600 aviators. Or was it 600 planes and 1,500 aviators? They weren't sure which.

With discretion overpowering our desire to hurry on, we anchored at breakfast time near Java's northeastern tip, rolling uncomfortably in the open sea as close to the steeply rising coast as we dared. After those gargantuan Bali feasts, and with 20 pounds of succulent pork on ice, for once, not a single fisherman manned the rail.

A well-timed arrival in Madoera Strait was indicated. Our Bali friends had warned us that mines protected the entrance. We should not arrive before daybreak. The *Lanikai* left the lee shore anchorage at 1:45 A.M. and made a perfect 8:30 A.M. approach to the Dutch patrol boat guarding the minefield entrance. Did we need help? Information? No? Good! Surabaya straight ahead! There had been a few smoke puffs that looked like antiaircraft bursts on the horizon ahead. But other fears had been minimized. For the first time so far, we sailed along in full daylight without qualms that some floating, upright stick might be a submarine periscope. We were inside the fence at last, with the gate shut behind us.

The wind that filled our canvas also saucily pushed along a fleet of heavily manned fishing boats of bizarre design and multicolored sails. They surrounded us on all sides, with no sign of recognition at our friendly waves. Could these be our native allies, the fellows who provided the flesh of General ter Poorten's Indies armies? We wondered apprehensively, remembering the sullen natives of the Celebes.

Months later, as Javanese spat on Allied prisoners passing along the road, or turned in to the Japanese the survivors of sunken Allied ships who had struggled ashore, such apprehensions turned out to be well justified. The actions of the Javanese were in sharp contrast to the powerful loyalty of *Lanikai's* Filipino crewmen, or the Philippine Scouts and Army fighting and starving and dying in the Bataan jungles alongside "Joe," their American opposite number. It would be a burning lesson in what breeds loyalty and what breeds contempt and hate, equally applicable to the British in Malaya and Hongkong and the French in Indo-China.

To avoid arriving at Surabaya in the middle of the night, we anchored near Ketapang Island in the pond-smooth water of Madoera Strait. It was something like a groom's wedding eve, the last night of utter, complete freedom, on our blessed own. Tomorrow would be the big day—a new life, news, a clue on the coming shape of our individual lives, back in a uniform other than tropical shorts and skivvy shirt.

Underway at 5:30 A.M., we spoke the Netherlands naval station ship off Surabaya at 11:30. Their boarding officer checked out this rather unorthodox-looking ship sporting a stern chaser and flying a U.S. Navy commission pennant. Paul Nygh greeted him in Dutch. The boarding officer eyed him up and down, from curlicued shoulderboard stripes to knee-length hose below his white shorts. "Dis vellow iss vrom Nederland? NO! It cannot be!" he exclaimed. Coupled with the fact Paul didn't *look* like a "Nederlander" (he was a tall, dark, hawk-faced Jew), we had utterly contaminated him, so that his intonation in his own language, as well as his mannerisms probably had been well bent out of proper Dutch shape.

By 2:00 P.M., *Lanikai* was snugly alongside the 3,000-foot Holland Pier in Surabaya, "jewel of the Indies," according to the travelogue accounts of that magnificent natural harbor.

The U.S. Naval authorities, naturally enough, were surprised to see us alive, after close to a month in limbo. The tidings of our arrival in the Celebes had never been digested by ABDACOM, assuming it had ever been passed to them, as requested. It soon would become disastrously apparent that this was to be the norm. In the United States' first multinational alliance, things were getting off to a poor start all over.

Surabaya Harbor was filled with Allied merchant ships, just as Manila Bay had been on 5 December. But unlike Manila, these ships either lacked the individual spunk to try a flight to safety, or the Dutch authorities lacked Admiral Hart's foresight and recognition of the inevitable in forcing ships out of Manila while there still was a chance. Nearly all the Surabaya ships would be lost through scuttling and subsequent Japanese salvage because it was impossible to convince the Dutch the place might fall. Fifty thousand tons of fuel oil was lost as well. Fortunately, a floating drydock had been towed to Tjilatjap, south Java, just before the war, where it was later indispensable in patching up the cruisers *Marblehead* and *Boise.*

Things ashore were in far too great a state of flux for anyone to concern himself with *Lanikai.* The passengers all had left. Good former shipmate Harry Keith had become an engineering staffer with the Netherlands Navy Yard, liaison for U.S. ships. He would see to it that something was done about the too-small rudder, the barnacle-encrusted bottom, and the sulphated battery bank.

Meanwhile, it was no longer necessary to await a rainstorm to have a bath; a hose from the dock kept the tanks full. Fruit, chickens, pork, and fresh vegetables of many kinds tested old Cooky's talents well beyond his earlier fish and coconut-sweetened rice routine.

Glassford had come back in triumph from his rear seat at the Makassar Straits battle and shifted his flag from weary old light cruiser *Marblehead* to the heavy cruiser *Houston,* which had already spent most of January convoying merchant ships between Surabaya and Darwin, Australia. I had served a cruise aboard *Houston* eight years earlier, and paid a visit to her partly out of nostalgia, to have dinner with an old friend and classmate, Lieutenant Commander W. J. Galbraith, and partly to pick up some khaki that would replace my threadbare wardrobe.

Everybody was jubilant about the daring Balikpapan raid, our first offensive action of the war. We had learned a lot. Going in so fast and so close to their targets, our destroyers found the bearing of the enemy ships changing more rapidly than they could train the torpedo tubes. This, plus the short run perhaps not allowing the exploders to arm in time, probably accounted for a lower score than might have been expected.

On a ship heeling violently in sharp turns, deck guns with tele-scopic sights weren't much use at night. The gunlayers simply couldn't pick up, much less stay on, the dimly defined targets.

On 1 February, I was to see *Houston* for the last time, as she cleared Surabaya for sea. The one-third of her crew that survived her gallant end on 1 March, including Galbraith, soon were pulling Japanese supply carts along hot asphalt or sharp-stoned roads, bare feet blistered and bleeding. Those who have seen the motion picture, "Bridge on the River Kwai," know in some small way the years of hell endured by *Houston*'s survivors, slaving in the Malayan jungle. The log of *Houston* for February is in capsule form the sea war in the Far East until the final collapse.*

Glassford, Commander Task Force 5, was having command rela-tionship troubles. Newly promoted Rear Admiral Purnell, considerably

* See Appendix.

junior to Glassford as acting CinC Asiatic Fleet, was in the anomalous position of being Glassford's boss. On 27 January matters were partly but not wholly squared away. The new command, Southwest Pacific, was established; with Glassford as commander and promoted to vice admiral, Purnell became his chief of staff. Glassford records the situation with something of the wistful confusion of the song, "I Am My Own Grampaw!":

> Admiral Hart said that although Southwest Pacific comprised all the units of the former Asiatic Fleet, the latter was "simply deactivated," with himself still as nominal CinC. To complicate matters, I was at a later date designated *de facto* CinC Asiatic Fleet by the Chief of Naval Operations, for administrative purposes. I continued to serve Admiral Hart in his now dual capacity of Supreme Naval Commander and nominal CinC of the identical forces commanded by myself, during the short period he was yet to remain in the area.

Ashore in this new capacity, Glassford could look out his office window on the Surabaya Harbor while juggling a very hot potato passed to him all the way down from MacArthur. Theoretically, MacArthur was a part of Wavell's command, but to insure that no shower of sparks would be struck by any chance assay on Wavell's part to assert his authority over MacArthur, Marshall radioed him that, ". . . Because of your present isolation, this will have only nominal effect on your command." Tactfully, an information copy went to Generalissimo Wavell. Quite the contrary, Wavell had enough troubles of his own without bothering MacArthur, particularly when what MacArthur was demanding was resupply. This was somebody else's problem. The Navy's, perhaps? That was precisely MacArthur's opinion. His pressure in both the U.S. press and on Washington to get supplies to him was tremendous. The submarine *Seawolf* had reached Corregidor 26–27 January with 36 tons of 50-caliber and 3-inch ammunition, taking out 25 high-priority passengers. This was not even peanuts—it was scarcely the skin on a peanut—and furthermore, was a wholly negative use of a potentially powerful offensive weapon.

Glassford, puzzling over this stickler, saw *Lanikai*. Perhaps she could help. I was soon called into his waterside aerie. "First, we'll take out those topmasts," he said, after describing briefly his plan. "They can be seen from too far away." This wouldn't matter, as we had no topsails anyway. We discussed *Lanikai*'s fresh water and food endurance: water, 20 rainless days; food, as long as fish swam in the sea. Material readiness was so poor, we wondered how we ever had made Surabaya, but a few days in the Navy Yard would fix that. Cargo capacity? About 40 tons.

Then came the ultimate question: "What do you think, Tolley?"

"The Japanese hold all the interior passages, sir," I told him. "The only conceivable route would be west of Borneo and Palawan. It took us a month to make the shorter passage directly south. In a month, the entrance to Manila Bay will have an airtight Japanese blockade that only a submarine could penetrate. If you can spare me a couple of motor torpedo boat tubes and a "fish" for each, I might manage to take somebody with me before they get us. As for running a cargo through to Corregidor in *Lanikai,* I would say the chances are less than zero." He would let me know later, he said.

Meanwhile, Keith had kept his word. From the twenty-eighth through the thirtieth of January, *Lanikai* lay in drydock, her barnacle-covered, iron-sheathed bottom bared for a scraping and painting. The "boys" would no longer have to fight the helm; that stubby rudder had a 12-inch extension welded on. The battery bank, tired and old beyond rejuvenation, was cycled several times as the only available treatment. The clutch was overhauled so that there might be a fair degree of expectancy she would back down when ordered. The Indonesian yard workmen, loaded with malaria, took two men to lift what one Cavite Filipino would have run away with, but under their Dutch quartermen, they did useful things to the engine-room equipment.

Then we moved out into the Navy Yard, outboard of a Netherlands Navy sloop. The friendly Dutchmen alongside eyed their new neighbor with interest and amusement. "Vot beetledjip iss det?" they would ask. "Kom end haff zom schnapps bevore dinner!" Coffee under the awning on the after cabin roof, or fried chicken as only a Filipino can produce it, returned the favors.

Across the harbor, on a breezy point, the Dutch naval officers' club provided a rallying place for American submariners. I met an old China friend there one afternoon: Lieutenant Commander W. G. ("Moon") Chapple, skipper of the submarine *Permit.* Like all the others, he was depressed over lack of success of the U.S. submarines.

It was not until July 1943 that the torpedo "experts" finally were convinced that it was not the operators at fault. In that month Lieutenant Commander L. R. Daspit, commanding USS *Tinosa,* stopped Japan's biggest tanker, *Tonan Maru No. 3,* with four hits in her stern. Here was a submariner's dream—an unescorted, 20-000-ton ship dead in the water. Daspit took his time, closing to 875 yards on her beam. Over a period of several hours, he methodically fired eight torpedoes, one at a time, with laboratory care and patience. None exploded, although several were seen to climb up the side and splash back. He saved his last one to take home for an autopsy.

In a February 1972 letter, Rear Admiral C. O. Triebel wrote me the sequel: "We cut the weight of the firing pin in half, a ten-minute, fifty-cent job on any lathe. Then *finally,* our torpedoes exploded pretty well."

Triebel should know, having used the modified "fish" to sink 14 ships, 58,837 tons, about 9,000 tons more than the entire Asiatic submarine force of 28 operational boats accounted for in the first critical four months of the war.

While Glassford wrestled with his resupply problem and a decision on *Lanikai,* there was nothing to do but wait. The wait was not long. At 10:00 A.M. on 3 February, the familiar air raid alarm siren wailed. Thirty minutes later, 26 twin-engined Japanese bombers lazed over at about 14,000 feet. Their accompanying fighters tangled with obsolete Dutch Brewsters and a few American P-40s. A thunderous barrage funneled out of the harbor but as usual, the shells burst far below the enemy planes.

Clearly, these were not the experts who knocked out Cavite. Bomb blasts pounded our chests like baseball bat blows, but the damage was beyond the fringes of the port and navy yard. With the feeble Allied fighter opposition driven off, Japanese fighters swooped low over the yard, strafing. Splashes stitched across open water, then walked into ships or buildings. Even *Lanikai*'s 30-calibers joined the chorus. A Netherlands fighter with one wheel down careened crazily across the yard at low altitude and fell victim to that irresistible impulse; it was shot at by all ships present and very shortly crashed in flames nearby, its pilot probably dead even before the fatal flyover.

Close aboard us, the Dutch destroyer leader *Tromp* was spewing automatic weapons fire at the low-swooping enemy fighters. Manning his 30-caliber chaut-chaut on the fantail, Doc Cossette's sharp eye spotted a heavy piece of running rigging falling from aloft. This was Doc's ship. He took the same solicitous interest in her good health and welfare as he did in the ills of the ship's company. Interrupting his firing long enough to shake his fist at the big Dutchman alongside, he shouted over the zap of the guns, "You squarehead bastards! You've cut our halliards with your goddam popguns!" Then he turned back to his beloved Lewis.

This first air raid on Surabaya was the opening page of the final chapter of Allied defeat in Java. From then on, the port slowly died. Each day, as the bombing continued, fewer and fewer native yard workmen showed up to carry on.

On the fourth, there was no raid. But a more localized attack materialized: the delayed side-effects of that Balinese monkey dance sent Profeta to the hospital as our first malaria victim. In a few more days, it would hit Adair, now at work in Fleet headquarters.

The methodical Japs were still being methodical: pre-lunch *schnapps* time, every other day. On the fifth,

> 1120 Air alarm sounded. Got underway and stood out of navy yard . . .
> 1140 Sighted 18 enemy bombers . . . 17 twin-engined landplanes, and one 3-engined landplane, a darker color than the others. Bombs dropped on airfield and fires started. Several pairs of Japanese pur-

suits circling at about 2,000 feet, and lower at intervals. Expended about 150 rounds of 50 caliber on them.

1255 Secured from air raid. Proceeded into harbor. . . .

The sixth was quiet, but by now, half the yard workmen had doffed their dungarees and were no doubt well up in the hills back of town in the ancestral, bombless digs. But on the seventh, the planes were back. This time, *Lanikai* had anticipated things and already was well out in the harbor when the enemy and the wails of the siren came simultaneously at 12:10 P.M.: "A salvo of bombs from high-flying planes dropped on and around godowns on Holland pier."

1225 Three Japanese fighter planes strafed the airfield, followed by two other trios at about 15-minute intervals. Last trio dropped a salvo of small bombs on the seaplanes anchored off the airfield. *Lanikai* and a number of small Netherlands naval speed boats machine-gunned the Japanese fighters as they passed to seaward. One plane was shot down, and fell into the sea at the harbor entrance.

By this time, Surabaya Harbor had lost much of its charm for Admiral Glassford and staff. They moved to a less popular target area, five miles back from the waterfront. On the seventh, ordered to temporary duty with them as a communication watch officer, I shuttled between ship and headquarters as duty demanded. With access to the communication files, the President's message was amplified by conversations with various staff officers which served to pull away the veil I had heretofore seen through only dimly.

I had not yet gone ashore on 8 February when nine enemy planes roared over at about 11,000 feet. By this time, they had improved their accuracy in bombing and knew within a few feet how high the local antiaircraft guns could reach. Four bombs landed close aboard *Lanikai*, astraddle. I lay on deck as the whine of their descent grew higher and higher. "When will the goddam things *hit?*" you think constantly to yourself as the shrill whistle rises in pitch. Then there is a shock felt in the ship like a huge hammer blow. In a few seconds the chest-thumping BOOOOMMM! arrives. Then there is the motion of the ship as waves from the explosion reach out. Are you hurt? You don't know immediately.

This particular straddle had its compensations. Picking ourselves up and looking around, we saw the muddy roil from the blasts. Tipay saw something else. "Queek! Boyss, get the deengy! Thot bombs just keel a lot of feesh!"

Much of the next week I spent at headquarters, cracking cipher messages, watching the Dutch liaison officers come and go, their faces longer each day. Living in the bachelors' mess, I enjoyed the change of fare, the elaborate protocol of a vice admiral's shoreside "cabin," and

J. L. Cossette, pharmacist's mate third class—doctor, gunner, and fisherman—admires the compass he salvaged from a downed American plane.

Seaman Marciano Felarca dries fish on the forward deckhouse, "which provided a powerful stench when sailing close hauled." In such secluded coves, Lanikai concealed herself by day and sailed by night to escape Japanese air observation.

the company of new friends. Adair was still bedridden, alternately shaking with chills and throwing off the blankets when fever struck him.

As the Japanese moved on the East Indies, the Dutch were desperate and somewhat resentful partners in an obviously failing enterprise, and the various Allied air forces could safely be said to have been, in the jargon of the back country, "independent as a hog on ice." Admiral Hart did his best to get on good terms with his opposite air number, ABDAIR, Air Chief Marshal Sir Richard Peirse, hoping for cooperation between ships and planes. He never made any progress. "The new air commander has not been trained for such cooperation," Hart wrote, with typical New England understatement.[16] Peirse disappeared from Lembang, Java, and was found to have established his command post at Bandoeng, some distance away, a move made without troubling to inform either his boss Wavell, or Hart. At least Hart was able to count on the excellent and loyal support of Lieutenant Colonel E. L. Eubank, who commanded the sad remnant of MacArthur's evacuated B-17 bombers. They, plus a few Dutch and American patrol bombers, provided ABDA-FLOAT's only airborne eyes.

On 14 February, Admiral Hart turned over command of ABDA-FLOAT to Admiral Helfrich. The association had been no better than Hart suspected it would, when he clearly detected Helfrich's chagrin in the very beginning. Later, Hart found that, "He was disposed not to be entirely frank as regards the state and readiness of his forces, sometimes moving his ships about without keeping me informed."[17] The lieutenant governor of the Dutch East Indies, Dr. Hubertus van Mook, clarified the Dutch sentiments, telling Cecil Brown that, "It took me a month and a half of argument in Washington to get Admiral Helfrich appointed to succeed Admiral Hart."[18]

Helfrich may not have been nature's nobleman as far as Hart was concerned, nor experienced in handling large units, but the Dutchman had two qualities in abundance: tenacity and guts. He also saw eye to eye with Hart on the use of warships for offensive purposes rather than according to Wavell's desires being squandered piecemeal as convoy escorts. On 7 February, Helfrich wrote Hart that,

> . . . the striking force must be reinforced by British and if possible American seapower; and that is to be done only if we take more risks by weakening convoy escorts. Against air-attacks convoys can not be defended by warships only . . .
>
> I am afraid that the first air-attack [Doorman] got during the *first* operation of the combined fleet has upset him a little and I hope that he will recover soon, especially after you meating [sic] him at Tjilatjap.
>
> As you know, I am entirely at your disposal and if you think that

I should take command at sea of the combined forces *myself*, I will only be too glad to do so.

The "first operation of the combined fleet" that Helfrich refers to was the battle that halved American cruiser strength. On 4 February, Rear Admiral Karel W. F. M. Doorman, RNN, sallied forth from Bunda Roads, northeast Java, with RNNS *De Ruyter* and *Tromp*, USS *Houston* and *Marblehead*, four Dutch and four American destroyers. The target was a Japanese force of three cruisers, several destroyers, and about 20 transports fooling around the south end of Makassar Straits. At 9:49 A.M., 36 twin-engined Japanese Navy bombers appeared at about 17,000 feet. For the next couple of hours, the Allied force desperately circled at high speed, dodging stick after stick of bombs. *Marblehead*'s steering was knocked out and serious fires were started by two hits. *Houston* took one that set a fire in turret three, incinerating all but two of its crew. *De Ruyter* was badly shaken by near misses that knocked out her antiaircraft fire control. The Japanese lost several planes, but their persistence aborted Doorman's project. Again, lack of air support cost the Allies a probable triumph.

This was the engagement that both Helfrich and Hart felt had shaken Doorman's nerve. It was after this, when Doorman had been ordered to Tjilatjap, that Hart met him there for some spine-stiffening and formulation of further plans. In fact, at that very moment, the enemy force they were plotting to tackle had beat them to the punch and occupied Makassar on 9 February, their only loss a destroyer torpedoed by the USS S-37.

Strenuous efforts had been made to get U.S. fighter aircraft into Java. Some of the earliest arrivals in Australia had been held up because the gun-firing solenoids had been thrown way with the crates. There was a shortage of coolant for liquid-cooled engines. Pilots were inexperienced and the accident rate high.

On 16 January, seventeen P-40s, all but four flown by pilots who had come from the Philippines, set out from Brisbane for a 2,000-mile leg to Darwin, thence 540 miles overseas to Koepang, then 500 more miles to Surabaya. Three crashed en route. The remainder had arrived by 25 January. These were the only American planes available when the Japanese attacked Surabaya on 3 February. Even with twenty-five minutes advance warning, by the time the planes had scrambled and climbed to 21,000 feet, it was too late, although two Japanese were shot down at a cost of one P-40.

On 4 February, thirteen P-40s, escorted by one B-24, made it to Koepang, and next day all but one arrived in Bali. They had refueled as fast as possible, but not fast enough. Only seven of them were airborne when twenty Japanese appeared overhead. Three more P-40s hastily took off and in the ensuing scrap, all but three of the ten were shot down, accounting for three enemy planes. Within two days, an additional eight P-40s had slightly better luck, only two crashing on the way.

On 9 February, nine P-40s and three A-24s took off from Darwin, led by an LB-30. Timor was closed in by clouds. The long-legged LB-30 turned back to Darwin, leaving the P-40s to crash in forced landings. The A-24s came off only slightly better. Taken for the enemy at Koepang, they were so badly damaged by AA fire that only one managed to proceed on to Java next day. A second flight of nine P-40s left Darwin on the tenth and all made it safely to Java.

Thus went the reinforcement effort: too little, too late. Once in Java, coordination with the Dutch was plagued by technical difficulties that even the most cordial personal relationships could not overcome. If there were American fighter planes operating over Java in those last days, we at Surabaya never saw them. Nor did the even more hard-pressed Allied ships, bravely staggering to sea, some damaged already, others low on torpedoes, unable to adequately fuel in port because of Japanese attacks almost daily, condensers leaking from near misses, ammunition low, sleep inadequate. These were the real heroes.

On 16 February, Charlie Adair, still weak from his bout with malaria, sent down a powerful hint that there was very little time. "Gas up, chow up, and stand by!" was Charlie's terse and clearly understood alert. To that we added a generous pile of firewood, filled the water tanks and picked up a motorboat discarded by a U.S. submarine as being useless topside baggage in wartime. It was far too heavy to hoist aboard *Lanikai*. We unbolted the engine and stowed it on deck. The boat itself would be towed astern as a final means of escape in case *Lanikai* somehow or other came to the end of her long road, an event which in the face of current developments, did not seem too far-fetched.

Three of our boys were in the hospital, two with malaria and one convalescing from appendicitis. We couldn't abandon them. Felarca and Profeta we managed. "But Alcantara you cannot have," said Lieutenant Commander C. M. Wassell, navy medical officer. "He would break open and die in such a ship as *Lanikai*," which he appeared to consider little more than a rowboat.

This remarkable, heroic man,* who some affectionately called, "Shaky Jake," was affected by a trembling caused by God knows how many fevers and plagues lived through as a medical missionary in China

* Played by Gary Cooper, in Cecil B. deMille's 1944 movie, "The Story of Doctor Wassell," in which is portrayed his feat in evacuating American wounded from Surabaya to the south coast at Tjilitjap, where they were taken aboard ship in a hairbreadth escape from Java, imprisonment and probably death. Wassell was awarded the Navy Cross.

before being commissioned as a naval reserve officer. With Surabaya in chaos, the enemy on its doorstep, Wassell, with superhuman effort, managed to set up a railway train and load it with some three hundred walking and stretchered wounded. Among them was Alcantara.

Charlie, his worldly belongings in a seabag, came aboard before dark. Chief Radioman McVey was back too, with a volunteer. He had sold *Lanikai*'s virtues to Radioman First Class Louis E. Cook.

The entry in *Lanikai*'s journal for 17 February 1942 was wholly in character:

> 0515 got underway and stood out of harbor to eastward, on verbal authority of Commander Southwest Pacific. Destination not specified and unknown, depending upon circumstances.

Chapter 15

By mid-February 1942, the rush of events in the Far East indicated that time was running out for the Allied cause. In one week the Japanese landed in New Britain; bombed Batavia, Surabaya, and Malang, Java; and landed at Singapore and at Palembang in Sumatra. On 14 February, Vice Admiral C. E. L. Helfrich, Royal Netherlands Navy, relieved Admiral Hart as Commander in Chief, Allied Naval Forces, in the Southwest Pacific. The next day Singapore, the impregnable fortress and keystone of the British defense effort in the Far East, surrendered.

It was at about that time that Rear Admiral Purnell met Charlie Adair in headquarters at Surabaya. "Pack a bag. We're going to sea!" he said tersely, then hurried on with the business of closing out his office. His boss, Admiral Glassford, had already left for Bandoeng, to be nearer Admiral Helfrich's headquarters.

On those few words hung the lives of at least three American naval officers in Surabaya.

After Admiral Hart had inspected the cruisers *Houston* and *Marblehead,* damaged in the 4 February battle of Madoera Strait, he had made it clear to Generalissimo Wavell that Allied naval operations could no longer go on in such a one-sided manner. If Hart earlier had thought Admiral Doorman needed bucking up, Wavell evidently now felt the same way toward Hart, as indicated by his letter of 9 February:

> I'm sure you'll realise that I absolutely and entirely appreciate the feelings of your Navy and the ships that suffered such damage and casualties the other day. But a man with any sense of grievance against his own side won't help win a war. . . . Any fellow can fight when things are going well, its the fellows who can keep on fighting without loss of spirit when things are going all wrong that win a war. That's how you beat us a good many years ago and the way

we've beaten other people, and the way we'll surely win through together this time. I'm sure that's the way you're putting it to your sailors, its the way I'm trying to get it over to our troops.

We must hold the NEI and it's going to take some hard fighting and heavy losses.

Yours,

/s/ A. P. Wavell

Hart replied immediately in a handwritten letter, dated 11 February:

Your note of 9 February written after I had told you of certain feelings among American naval personnel which resulted from their experience in Luzon: The cruisers which were damaged east of Java did not have these experiences—they were not in the area. As I thought I had made clear to you, I had just visited these cruisers and found the spirit of the people very good indeed.

Well, it seems that I again failed to make you understand, looking back over these four weeks during which I've been under your command I [must? writing unclear] realize that it is largely my own fault and since I served under British command during the other war, it should not have happened.

My own "war psychology" and, I think, that of the rest of the American fleet is not different than is expressed in your note.

Respectfully yours,

/s/ Thos. C. Hart

Three days later Hart, somewhat embittered, turned over his command to Vice Admiral Helfrich. He sent this message to his former flagship *Isabel:* "May God bless you and keep you during the difficult days to come." The *Isabel's* crew lined up topside to wave farewell. Old seadog Hart, one of the major participants in that great Far East drama, "Divided We Fell," was leaving aboard the venerable cruiser HMS *Durban,* headed for India, then the United States. Hart's final directive to Glassford, who inherited what remained of the former Asiatic Fleet, reflected his belief that Helfrich intended to "go for broke," and the hopelessness of it in view of the already heavy Allied losses without commensurate damage to the enemy:

In Java's defense, the expenditure of all U.S. Naval Forces in the ABDA area will be fully justified, providing such expenditure results in measurable contribution to the success of such defense. We must not, by confusing the necessity for holding Java without the ability to do so, fail in timely action toward the withdrawal of command, administrative, intelligence and other personnel on shore which is essential to further operations.[19]

The day after Hart's departure, the sixteenth, Wavell sent a long report to London, presenting his case for the imminent loss of Java. "To sum up," he said, "Burma and Australia are absolutely vital for war against Japan. Loss of Java, though a severe blow from every point of view, would not be fatal. Efforts should not, therefore, be made to reinforce Java which might compromise the defense of Burma and Australia." Of this, the Dutch knew nothing.

From the very beginning, Wavell was gravely handicapped by the split effort that Hart and Glassford so bitterly complained of: lack of actual, undisputed control of the forces supposedly put at his disposal. Lieutenant General Lewis H. Brereton, MacArthur's air officer, who had left Laguna de Bay on Christmas Day in a Navy PBY, described the situation in his diary on 14 January after his arrival in Batavia via Australia: "Sometimes we didn't know where we stood from one hour to the next."[20] He found he had been appointed deputy to ABDAIR, Air Marshal Peirse. This was entirely against Brereton's wishes, as he felt it would compromise and interfere with his running of the American air force.

Brereton was present at Wavell's formal investiture on 14 February. (He had arrived in Java on the tenth.) Other top Americans on hand were Admirals Hart and Purnell, and Lieutenant General Brett, USA, Wavell's deputy. The Dutch honor guard snapped to, and the band broke into "God Save the King." The Americans waited for the "Star Spangled Banner" to follow, but it did not; Wavell made a lightning inspection of the guard and the supposedly multinational ABDACOM was in business.

One of Wavell's first setbacks was a directive from Washington making Brereton commander not just of all U.S. air forces in the Far East, but of U.S. *ground* forces in ABDACOM and Australia. The U.S. ground forces in Java amounted to only a field artillery battalion, but those in Australia were building up to division strength.

Peirse, under Wavell's urging, had been pressing his deputy Brereton to commit the modest American air effort against Japanese airfields in Malaya, to relieve pressure on sorely beset Singapore and Sumatra. It would have been too late for Singapore, which fell on the fifteenth. But in any case, Brereton felt his other hat—air officer to General MacArthur, was the most important one to wear. His planes must be used to try to keep the lines of communication open to the Philippines. That meant their employment against the Japanese amphibians moving inexorably down Makassar Strait and to the east of the Celebes toward Timor. The latter was an indispensable stepping-stone for air-ferrying fighter reinforcements to Java from Australia. Brereton also was more than fully alive to the Luzon reinforcement effort, having been given prime responsibility in the $10,000,000 project to procure blockade runners.

Peirse's total amounted to less than 50 fighters, about 65 medium bombers, 10 dive bombers and 18 B-17s. Patrol Wing 10's few remaining PBYs remained under Admiral Hart's firm control for essential reconnaissance, and the Dutch kept an equally firm grip on theirs for the same purpose and an occasional surreptitious bombing. Arrayed against this weak, battle-worn little force, the Japanese had up to 500 fighters and 400 bombers, including carrier borne, in the great arc stretching 1,800 miles from Singapore to Timor.

When Admiral Purnell told Charlie Adair to pack a bag and be ready to go to sea, it appeared likely that Purnell would take over the Allied Striking Force; Doorman was believed to be too cautious. The component ships were strung between Sumatra, Tjilatjap and Surabaya. Purnell would have taken *Houston* as his flagship and he and Adair eventually would have gone down with her. But in this desperate battle for survival of the last remnant of Dutch colonial empire, the final decision was that a Dutchman commanding was more appropriate.

Thus, with Java nearly lost, Adair was again left on his own as to how to get out. Looking back on his lucky escape from Manila aboard *Lanikai,* he at once turned again to the little craft that sat almost alone in bomb-ravaged Surabaya Harbor.

As a result of Adair's privileged position not only for access to advance top-level information, but the leverage and connections to secure *Lanikai's* release, the ship would make it out of Surabaya mere *hours* ahead of the Japanese. Admiral Purnell would fly out to Australia on the twenty-fifth.

The *Lanikai* headed east all day through 30-mile-wide Madœra Strait, still swarming with bright-sailed fishing craft, and by dark on 18 February had cleared the minefield south of Madœra Island. If any Japs were on the prowl, they must have been busy elsewhere.

Nineteen February 1942 was a day to circle in heavy black in the history of Far East Allied effort. On that day there occurred a series of moves, disasters and decisions that marked a turning point beyond which lay only total disaster.

At dawn on the nineteenth, 188 Japanese carrier-based fighters and dive bombers joined 54 land-based bombers for a raid on Darwin, in north Australia. By nightfall the harbor and town were in utter shambles, any usefulness as a base ended. The USS *Peary* and a number of merchant ships were sunk.

The preceding day, General Brereton had held a ceremony at Malang, the U.S. bomber base, where 74 DSCs, Silver Stars and DFCs were presented, many of them posthumously. Brigadier General Patrick Hurley, President Hoover's secretary of war and now FDR's expediter for Luzon resupply, was on hand to give one of his rousing speeches. That night, he was entertained at dinner by Brereton and Air Marshal

Peirse, and after Hurley's 3:00 A.M. departure for Australia, Brereton and Peirse continued to make a night of it. During this by-breakfast-time very informal bull session, Brereton learned that Wavell had been instructed by London to give up the fight for the N.E.I.

The two sleepless top airmen followed breakfast with a quick inspection trip out to the Djombang fighter base, then displaying more of that fortitude for which airmen in general are well known, flew on over to Surabaya. They arrived in the middle of a Japanese attack on the harbor and installations, and followed the proceedings from the interceptor control room. The American pilots would have found the Dutch fighter director's "English" unintelligible, in the hubbub of combat upstairs, so as an example of the handicaps under which Allied air power worked, an American was rebroadcasting in accents the U.S. airplane jockeys could understand.

That same day, in Surabaya, 11 U.S. fighters tangled with 22 enemy bombers and 16 Zeros. The score: four Jap bombers and one fighter lost, versus two American planes and no pilots. This was close to being the last substantial American air action on Java. That afternoon, Brereton informed Wavell he intended to withdraw the American planes. Both Brett and Peirse backed him up. The crowning blow of the day had been the destruction at Bandoeng, of two of the last three B-17s coming in from India. Clearly, there was no safe place for an Allied pilot to park his plane, or even hang his hat.

Lanikai was wasting no time. The information gap set in immediately after quitting Surabaya, but we had no illusions about Japanese nearness. We could almost smell the saké and pickled cucumbers. It seemed a waste of valuable time to close down all machinery so that our $25 Echophone could pick up the feeble signal carrying London's BBC news. It gave little or nothing on the Far East; the shock of "impregnable" Singapore's fall three days earlier had been a traumatic silencer.

Harry Keith's efforts had worked wonders. The old Union diesel was running like a fine Swiss watch. *Lanikai*'s corroded and frayed electrical system had been checked out and much of it replaced. New main injection valves let ample engine cooling water flow. The overhaul on our passenger, Adair, had been less complete. "I am still weak from 12 days of malaria," he wrote in his hip pocket log, "and just got up in time to make the ship."

Bali Strait is no place for an underpowered ship on a dark, dark night. Surging tides compressed in the funnels at both ends produce swirling, unpredictable currents of up to six knots, which was about *Lanikai*'s top speed under auxiliary power.

Our joss must have been good; in two hours we were through the narrow bottleneck and at 6:40 A.M., anchored in Pangpang Bay. As a sort of anticlimax, a Dutch customs patrol boat chugged out to check particulars. No little old war was going to stop the tidy routine of a country that had been keeping order here for three and a half centuries. Who knows? We might have been smugglers!

Under way at dusk, we hugged the Java coast, headed southeast. On Bali, fifteen miles away, enormous fires lighted the horizon, particularly in the areas of Boleleng and Denpasar, where only a month before we had so happily joined the select ranks of bosom connoisseurs. Even on the west coast, our side of the island, smaller fires blazed. The Dutch evidently were applying the scorched earth policy to deny the Japanese the supplies which could not be defended.

As of 9 February, Allied intelligence knew that the next Japanese thrust would be at Bali, the eastern arm of the octopus reaching out for Java. Bali's airfields were only 100 miles from Surabaya. But Admiral Kubo beat the Allies to it. In his cruiser flagship *Nagara*, with two transports and half a dozen destroyers, he had put his landing force ashore at Sanur Roads, some 15 miles southwest of Padang, where *Lanikai* had spent two enchanted days exactly one month previously. Then Kubo headed *Nagara* and three destroyers for Makassar, followed by two destroyers escorting one bomb-damaged transport. Another transport, plus two more destroyers remained at Sanur. So when Doorman finally got ready to fight, it was this latter, much attenuated force he would be facing.

With the Allied forces divided, the best plan would be a poor compromise. The first wave, coming from Tjilatjap, would be cruisers *De Ruyter* and *Java*, with destroyers *Piet Hein* and USS *Pope* and *John D. Ford*. The second wave, coming from eastern Sumatra, were U.S. old World War I type destroyers *Stewart*, *Parrott*, *John D. Edwards* and *Pillsbury*, under Commander T. H. Binford. Following them in heavy support, was destroyer leader *Tromp*, from Surabaya. A third wave, Dutch motor torpedo boats, was to follow to pick up any cripples.

The whole plan looked sour to Glassford, who probably was wishing that Purnell was in command. At Balikpapan, we had learned the value of surprise, where the first news the enemy has of trouble is a torpedo exploding under his bottom. With the Dutch cruisers going in first, guns getting in ranging shots, star shells popping off, the surprise, if any, would be largely negated.

Both sides lacked radar, but the Japanese had the advantage of years of rigorous night training that only the Japanese character and indoctrination would have sustained. They enjoyed such technically superior equipment as huge, tripod-mounted binoculars with five-inch objective lenses that had exceptional light-gathering power. By comparison, the standard U.S. Navy 7 × 50 binoculars looked like bargain basement opera glasses.

The Dutch cruisers sailed in, straightaway at a disadvantage in that the enemy was against a mist-shrouded coastline while they were silhouetted against a starlit sky. Little damage was done by and none to the cruisers, *De Ruyter* not even opening fire. By the time *Piet Hein, Pope* and *J. D. Ford* arrived, trailing the cruisers, the hornet's nest had been well agitated. There was a spirited exchange of torpedo and gunfire and radical maneuvering on everybody's part. In the melee, *Piet Hein* took some heavy hits, which Dutch sources strongly suggest was the handiwork of an American destroyer, supported by statements of survivors and the fact that after she burst into flame there was no more gunfire.

Shells had hit *Piet Hein*'s searchlight platform and one cut a main steam line. Dead in the water, blazing merrily, her crew fought the flames and in ten or fifteen minutes had got her under way at six or seven knots. But the wounds were fatal. Very shortly she blew up and disappeared.

The two cruisers headed for Surabaya, the *Piet Hein* was sunk, and *Ford* and *Pope,* torpedoes about gone, were headed southeast as fast as their old boilers would take them. The two Japanese destroyers momentarily started firing at each other in lieu of the disappeared opposition.

Now it was Binford's turn. At about 1:30 A.M., his four old destroyers charging up from the south into Banda Strait at 25 knots sighted what appeared to be enemy ships off Sanur. They fired fifteen torpedoes, all of which missed the two circling Japanese destroyers, *Asasio* and *Osio,** who immediately came boiling out. In the spirited exchange of gunfire which followed, *Stewart* was lightly hit. The American destroyers' total of twelve old unprotected 4-inch guns was no match for the equal number of well-shielded Japanese 5-inch guns. Formation in disarray, they continued headlong northeastward and ran into *Arasio* and *Mitisio*.

Here again the gunfire and torpedo action was warm. There were no torpedo hits, but soon *Mitisio* lay dead in the water, with 96 killed and wounded. The Dutch *Tromp* backed up the U.S. destroyers against the two fresh antagonists and both sides traded more hits. At 3:00 A.M., the Allied ships broke off and headed for Surabaya.

In this inconclusive scrap, the Allies' greatly superior force had traded equal damage to surviving ships and lost one destroyer. As for the third wave, there were no cripples to "finish off." Curiously, the motor torpedo boats reported having sighted nothing at all. *Mitisio*

---

* The torpedoes had been set to run deep, as cruisers and transports were the expected targets. Thus, they probably went under the shallow draft enemy destroyers.

must have limped off, as she lived to fight until the Battle of Surigao Strait two and a half years later.

There could be no excuses here of imbalance of air power. The whole affair did not augur well for any further Allied attempt to meet Japanese naval formations on equal terms, and even less so when air superiority lay in Japanese hands. Stunning confirmation would be furnished by the Battle of the Java Sea, just around the corner, both geographically and time-wise.

As Admiral Binford put it later: "You cannot throw ships of four nations together, with no training, no plans, no common signals, and no air of any kind and expect to have success against an enemy that is well trained, with more modern equipment, has air spot and more ships. . . .[21]

Up "north," on 20 February, another submarine, *Swordfish*, figured in a further crumbling of the Allied front; President of the Philippines, Manuel Quezon and family, plus Vice President Osmena and five high staffers were carried out of Corregidor to Panay. Then *Swordfish* turned right around for a second trip, evacuating the High Commissioner Francis B. Sayre, family and staff to Freemantle. That left only MacArthur and Rockwell on Corregidor.

In late January, Quezon, dying of tuberculosis and in a fine rage over the American Europe-first policy, sat in his wheelchair listening to Roosevelt broadcast how thousands of aircraft would soon be on the way to the front: Europe. Roosevelt was a *sinvergüenza* (scoundrel), he said. He would give himself up to the Japanese and declare the Philippines neutral, then both the warring armies could be gotten off the Philippines' back. MacArthur, equally disgusted with what he, too, considered Washington's abandonment of the Far East, plus the Navy's inability or unwillingness to fight, risked his military career by suggesting to Washington that Quezon's plan might be a good thing, hoping the shock value might cause some rethinking on hemisphere priorities. Roosevelt, who in prewar days had given sincere evidence of wanting to do something about the Far East, wrote Quezon an inspiring message that swung him around 180 degrees, loyally into line, by promising that the Philippines ". . . will be defended by our own men to the death." Roosevelt then gave MacArthur a somewhat sterner pep talk, winding up with what might be classified as an advance obituary: ". . . make your resistance as effective as circumstances will permit and as prolonged as possible." There was no hint of relief.

Aboard the *Lanikai* we had not the slightest clue as to what was going on, including Binford's hot little night action off Bali, only fifty miles away. As we crept toward Tjilatjap, our only reassurance was that through courtesy of the Echophone, we knew that in London Big Ben still bonged the hours.

After the Darwin disaster, Glassford had sent tenders *Holland* and *Blackhawk* from Tjilatjap to Exmouth Gulf, in northwestern Australia, along with two submarines in need of overhaul and two destroyers, *Barker* and *Bulmer,* that had been roughly treated by near-misses just east of Sumatra on 15 February. He further had hoped to have tanker *Pecos* dash into Surabaya, fill up with oil, then dash out again to a rendezvous south of Java to fuel ships at sea, safely away from daily Jap raids. But new ABDAFLOAT Helfrich would have none of it. Oil into warships, *javel!* Into tankers and out of Java? *Nie!* Had we known Tjilatjap was about to be abandoned, we most certainly would have headed *Lanikai* straight south.

With Bali lighted up like a distant Times Square, we beat down the southeast Java panhandle the night of 18/19 February, into a strong chop and half a gale. Then heavy rain squalls and mist set in, making it difficult to follow the land, which flattened out into low plain. About midnight, we gratefully rounded the peninsula's tip and with the wind on our port quarter, scudded along on a westerly course, keeping the dark shadow of the coast in sight.

At 6:47 A.M., 19 February, our anchor chunked down in mile-wide, semi-enclosed Rajeg Wesi Bay. We hugged the southern shore, but there was no concealment. In Surabaya, the Dutch had warned that outside the metropolitan areas, the natives would not recognize the American flag. Many Indonesians had seen the Japanese flag on the ubiquitous Japanese shops before the war, or tiny Rising Suns fluttering in the hands of doll-like Japanese children on their national holidays. With its red-and-white stripes hanging limply at the gaff, the U.S. colors could easily be mistaken for Japan's red-rayed naval flag. But the Dutch tricolor was universally well known. "Be practical," said the Dutchmen. "Fly our flag, and the Indonesian home guardsmen may not fire on you by mistake."

We had no Dutch colors, but by flying the international alphabet flag *T* sideways it did admirably. So in Rajeg Wesi Bay, and thence almost to Tjilatjap, *Lanikai* sailed under false colors, with mixed results, as we would soon learn.

Overhead, the air traffic was heavy. Adair wrote that, "Since arrival 2½ hours ago, we have sighted 3 patrol planes, one four-engined bomber, then four more of same, all headed west. Many more planes seen later, but none apparently saw us." Then he added with typical *Lanikai*-born caution: "Don't trust them."

Heavy explosions heard throughout the day from the direction of Bali suggested those overflying planes were American. The enemy landing at Sanur, of course unknown to us, was in progress. Our pitifully small air force was doing what it could to smash it.

The Lanikai *anchored close to shore for daylight concealment on the south coast of Java, 21 February 1942, only a few miles from desperate sea and land actions at Bali. The Netherlands ensign flies at the gaff, as the Dutch authorities had advised that the native home guards took all else to be enemy.*

Under a canopy of jungle trees in south Java, moored bow and stern in clear blue water, we await nightfall to start the next leg of our trip.

On nothing more than a hunch, we decided to lie over a day and night, the first time en route since the northern Celebes. Unable to identify the high-flying planes, lacking any source of news or means of being directed, perhaps we were rushing toward an "appointment in Samara." Make haste slowly. *Lanikai* was around that tough Java corner and headed away from embattled Bali. Another day might clarify things. We moved well out from shore before nightfall to avoid the mosquitoes and back in again at dawn.

All this was only a minor twist for Dame Fate, who heretofore seemed always to be either darkly shadowing just overhead, or at least lurking in the nearby wings. By midmorning, we discovered why she had bade us stay.

Several types of aircraft had been passing both ways during the morning, high overhead. Then at 9:40, a sharp-eyed crewman shouted, "Plane coming in!" We went to general quarters, commenced heaving in the anchor chain and started the engine. Across the bay, a fighter plane was coming down to masthead level and running parallel to the shoreline. Was he about to strafe something there? His wheels were up, but there were no telltale flashes from his guns. Then down he went, in a belly-landing on the sand beach.

In a few minutes we were under way and soon were within three hundred yards of the surf line. There was no need for Picking's 50-caliber; it was a U.S. P-40.

The dinghy was instantly over the side, with McVey, a Filipino crewman, Picking, and Doc Cossette as oarsmen. The pilot had climbed out and was walking around, waving his arms, apparently unhurt. But one could not be sure; Cossette and his little black bag might be needed anyway. McVey might save the radio. Picking would be useful in case salvage of armament turned out to be on the agenda. I went along to man the steering oar, remembering vaguely those paragraphs studied more than a decade ago in that blue-bound Navy Bible, *Knight's Seamanship,* at the Naval Academy. "In a surf too heavy for landing bows-on," it said in effect, "back in, to avoid being pooped. Go slowly, observing the period of the swells. When the smallest approaches, usually the seventh, back as swiftly as possible, run the boat aground, jump out, seize it by its gunwales and drag it up before succeeding swells broach and swamp it."

A stiff breeze across the wide bay had built up sizable waves that broke on the shelving beach heavily enough to suggest following *Knight's* advice. With a combination of good timing and good luck, we made it ashore. The Filipino's previous small boat experience probably had been confined to riding a caribao through a rice paddy. Cossette, McVey and "Guns" possibly had less. There were several overtaking breakers that all but snatched the boat from our hands and dragged it, half-full of sloshing water, back into the bay. But out of breath in the tropic heat, we finally tugged it high and dry.

Now we could turn our attention to the forlorn figure standing by. For a man who had just collected a dozen or more Zero bullet holes in his plane, then landed it wheels-up on a narrow, sandy beach without flipping it over and smothering himself, Lieutenant Lester J. Johnson was understandably slightly on edge. "Boy! He sure cusses beautiful, don't he, Captain?" said Guns Picking admiringly. Like many a U.S. combat pilot of those days, his hours in the air had been all too few. But his views on Japanese, P-40s, the way the war was being run, Zero airplanes, belly tanks and Java were all luridly laid bare in five minutes of fast talk embellished by adjectives that would have made any out-back Australian sheepman green with envy.

When jumped by those superb Zeros, flown by veteran pilots, Johnson had made the proper preliminary combat move of dropping his auxiliary belly tank. Unfortunately, he had been flying on his main tank, which by this time was close to empty, instead of using the gas in his belly tank, which he dropped full. For him, the fight was hot, but short. His P-40 started down in a long glide that brought him to Rajeg Wesi with only a gallon or two of fuel sloshing around in his tank.

From the beginning, we in *Lanikai*, like the plains Indians, hunted for meat, not sport. And what was another man's junk was *Lanikai's* loot—from deckhouse wicker chairs to machine guns and motor boats. When that plane slid in, our thoughts in succession were: What nationality? Is the pilot OK? What salvage does a downed plane offer?

The first question was soon answered; the forward machine guns and Tommy gunners stood down when we clearly saw the U.S. star. Then the pilot climbed out, apparently unhurt. For eventualities in connection with the question of loot, we took along a heavy three-part tackle, wrenches, chisels and hammers, to part various treasures from their moorings.

The plane was sitting with wings flat on the hard-packed sand. Her guns dropped down from below. With the tackle secured to a tree, we and a dozen or more natives who had meanwhile turned up, heaved and sweated in an attempt to move the plane to higher ground. But she didn't give an inch. Soon the rising tide would engulf it. We worked furiously with hammers and chisels to cut through that incredibly tough aluminum alloy skin to get at the guns, to no avail. From the loading port on top, we managed to haul out 800 rounds of shiny 50-caliber ammunition. Doc Cossette had dismounted a compass in the cockpit and proudly stowed it with the pharmaceuticals in his medicine bag.

The tide was rising. The entrance to the fuselage was on the seaward side. McVey could barely squeeze the upper part of his body inside and could work only between breakers. Remembering it vividly thirty years later, he wrote me:

I'd work feverishly for 12 or 15 seconds, then hold my breath while those tremendous breakers crashed down on my back and drove me jammed into the fuselage, then work for a few seconds and repeat the whole cycle. Those planes were built for the ages and almost defied any dismantling. I don't know how long I worked but I felt as if I'd taken the beating of my life.

The radio also defeated all efforts to wrench it loose. Spume from the ever-closer sea continually tossed over us. At least the Japanese would not get our P-40's carcass intact. Johnson reluctantly gave permission to sprinkle the remaining gasoline over the cockpit and set the plane afire. Flames rose up from the fuselage and engine while Johnson's figure receded in the distance, walking down the beach. He had elected to hike it back to camp rather than take his chances with *Lanikai*.

Now began the fight to get out to the ship. For awhile it appeared we might be joining Johnson. A dozen times we launched that blasted boat into the surf, only to have it dragged back again, half full of water, trying its best to turn broadside, where it would have been swamped and rolled over on its beam ends. Near exhaustion, we finally made it, tumbling into the boat, myself last in over the stern. Seconds later, rowing desperately to keep from being dragged back into the surging surf, rising and falling on the long, smooth swells, which no longer broke around us, we were headed safely home with our modest plunder.

Briefly, Johnson had brought us up to date on the military situation as he saw it. There was nothing to stop the Japs in the east, on Bali, he said. In the west, things looked equally bad. A big, heavily escorted convoy of many transports was approaching Sunda Strait. Only the center might hold, he thought. The Dutch troops had done well at Palembang in wiping out a battalion of enemy paratroopers. Perhaps they could hang on in central Java until more Allied air could be brought in from India and Australia.

Alas! Johnson's superficial knowledge of the enemy came through his sketchy preflight briefings which did not make clear, or perhaps more accurately, *dared* not make clear, that with the fall of Singapore and Timor, his hopes of air reinforcement were more than empty. But in our joint ignorance, we did not know these things then, and after an 8:20 P.M. departure from Rajeg Wesi, we sailed on west, Tjilatjap-bound.

After rolling uncomfortably in a beam sea all night, we discovered our choice of the day's anchorage to be so perfect it would have exceeded any specifications we might have drawn up as being optimum. Sempu Island is separated from the mainland by a canal-like passage seventy-five or so yards wide, half a mile long, with steep, wall-like sides of coral rock. The chart showed no soundings in this passage, so we eased gingerly ahead, casting the lead, believing it too much to expect that such a place could have all this and ample depth as well. But our soundings

While anchored on the south Java coast, February 1942, members of the crew augment our rain-water supply by leading a hose from a fresh water spring to casks in the launch; above, the "water detail" heads shipside.

showed from 50 to 180 feet of clear, limpid, blue water. As the "canal" rounded the island in a gentle arc, the mainland side became higher, rising at a steep slope to several hundred feet. A jungle of enormous trees, taller by far than our masts, came down to the water's edge. Moored bow and stern, deep-green *Lanikai* was a wholly invisible part of the scene from anything beyond a few hundred yards. But when Adair and I boated across to the island's gleaming snow-white beach for a swim and a few buckets of the sand for deck scrubbing, we noted one small shortcoming; the tall, light-colored masts betrayed the otherwise perfect camouflage. Several of the lads were soon aloft in boatswain's chairs with buckets of green paint.

A few natives flitted furtively through the forest, but in spite of the Dutch tricolor at the gaff, none ventured near. It was with the regret of all hands that we left this beautiful place, a paradise for swimming and fishing that allowed us to forget for a few short hours that only a few dozen miles away, men were hunting each other like the animals which must have inhabited that jungle behind us.

The anchorage next morning, Sembreng Bay, seemed, if possible, even more of a paradise than the one we had just left. In fifty feet of water, the bottom was clearly visible in all its detail. Monkeys chattered and parrots screamed in the trees that made a cool umbrella over the ship; whether it was the menagerie's complaint at our intrusion, or their daily social intercourse, we did not know. The ship was so close to the shore, which rose steeply, that in order to avoid swinging into it, a manila hawser was led out astern and made fast to a tree.

In the motor boat, several of us explored the small river that entered the north end of our miniature bay. Its waters ran fresh and clear a quarter of a mile from its mouth. But there was no need to risk pollution in its inviting fresh water; nearer the ship, a wrist-sized stream of cold water gushed from a spring close enough to the water's edge for us to lead a hose from it to water casks in the motor boat.

As we ascended the river, several dozen native troops scurried to man breastworks and a group of fishermen fled for cover. But later in the day, some of these near-naked fellows cautiously approached the ship. Soon there was a lively commerce in vegetables and coconuts traded for a few small coins. Perhaps that Dutch flag had turned the trick.

The night's run brought us to Patjitan Bay, where we lay in another of those small, green pockets, anchor out ahead and stern line to rocks ashore. Again, we were a perfect blend with the shore, but this time the "enemy" who discovered us would be on land and not aloft.

Here, the natives were friendly at once. Half a dozen small balsa-wood dugout canoes soon lay alongside, their bilges full of sardine-size fish, glittering and jumping, still very much alive. These were favorites of our Filipinos, who had no nets to catch them. We bought a quantity for next to nothing and laid them in neat windrows on the forward deckhouse to dry in the sun.

Picking's boyhood memories of canoeing got the better of him and he bought one of the balsa-wood boats for five guilders, about $1.50. One hand could lift the eight-foot little craft. The natives' wide-brimmed, conical grass hats looked practical, too. Round, white sailors' hats—or officers' caps too, for that matter—made ridiculously poor protection against tropic sun and glare. So we bought some hats.

About noon, a native identifiable as some sort of official messenger only by a bedraggled military jacket, arrived with a short note: "Please come across the harbor and be identified," it read, signed by the Assistant Resident. "We will come over at dusk," we replied, wondering why his note was written in English. "We do not care to expose ourselves to discovery by enemy aircraft in daylight."

In several hours the messenger was back. The note this time was more preremptory; failing to come across at once for identification would result in military measures, they warned. We repeated our excuses. Then as the sun dropped low, *Lanikai* headed for the small pier on the opposite side of the bay from where we had spent the day; we originally had avoided the settlement as being too tempting bomb bait. If "military measures" had been contemplated, there was nothing in evidence thereof except half a dozen apathetic-looking native troops with long-barreled rifles of an earlier era, lounging around the dock. Waiting for us in starched white uniforms were the Assistant Resident and the chief of police. From the very beginning, they had suspected us, they said, in heavy accents. Now they were so happy to find they were wrong. A check of Dutch vessels had revealed nothing remotely resembling our mysterious, seclusive, gun-bearing craft. What really had tied it, they explained, was our purchase of those hats and the balsa-wood canoe. "We feared," they said gravely, "that the boat was to effect a military landing and the hats were a disguise."

Patjitan was the last of those magnificent little tropical hideaway heavens the south coast provided. Next, for want of a better place, we anchored on the morning of the twenty-fourth in the wide open sea, as close to shore as safety permitted, off Bata Point. It was a rocky promontory that offered very little protection from enemy air observation, not much more from any passing submarine, and none at all from the long, uncomfortable swells that were so mountainous they must have been rolling along, building up size for a thousand miles.

After the unwitting jolt our false colors had imparted at Patjitan, the rotated *T* flag was retired; on anchoring at Bata Point the Stars and Stripes were run up. Immediately, a dozen or so half-naked children who had collected on the foreshore to gape, dashed back into the bush as though one of their Hindu special super-devils suddenly had materialized under their noses.

Had we only known, as *Lanikai* rolled, creaked and groaned, dishes skidded and people held on, we would have lifted up a prayer of thanks for those confounded swells. They were the characteristic, telltale forerunners of a typhoon which, inside that week, would save us all.

Like Surabaya, Tjilatjap was a point of major decision. Just around the corner, we would discover what really was up. Would it be the start of the long fight back? Would we desert old faithful *Lanikai* to leave her rotting alongside some mossy pier, and go off to man something more orthodox? Everybody was a little tense. Our apprehensions were mixed with expectations. Meanwhile, the fish bought in Patjitan, drying on the forward deckhouse, were providing a powerful stench back aft whenever the wind hauled ahead.

By 8:40 next morning, we were off the Tjilatjap minefield entrance, where a Dutch pilot came aboard to coach us safely through. Along with him, for a boarding call, came fellow former Yangtze sailor and classmate Lieutenant Commander Joseph Berkley, skipper of the old China Coast gunboat, *Tulsa*. "These Dutchmen are a little sore with me," he said, explaining that several nights previously he had gone out to escort a newcomer the last few miles. The newcomer, a Dutch merchantman, had a skipper whose sensitivity to the enemy had been sharpened by several close squeaks. In the dark, *Tulsa* looked very much like a Jap to him. At least the bastards wouldn't get his ship's papers and money, he told himself, as he threw them over the side.

There may have been someone alive somewhere whose masterful grasp of English profanity exceeded that of our pilot, to the almost total exclusion of any other useful words in the language. But the odds are against it. Belarmino, whose English was sketchy anyway, made nothing whatever of his orders, which inspired the pilot to even more picturesque, loud and excited efforts than before. But somehow following the rotund Dutchman's richly embellished instructions—or perhaps in spite of them—*Lanikai* worked her way in through the narrow, tortuous channel, through the harbor crowded with all manner of shipping, to her berth. There, I at least, experienced a strange feeling of *deja vu; Lanikai* was moored alongside, of all unlikely objects, a British Yangtze River merchant steamer.

Trifling, but timeless little truisms pop up over the centuries, such as, "What this country needs is a good five-cent cigar." Or the reply of a British prince when asked for some profound statement which might identify him for posterity. "Never miss a chance to urinate!" he promptly replied, remembering the endless official ceremonies to which he was forever being subjected. If anyone had troubled to elicit a similar nugget from *Lanikai,* it unquestionably would have been never to lose an opportunity to gas up, fill the water tanks, the provision locker and the firewood rack.

At 11:40, the air raid alarm delayed translating the foregoing sentiments into immediate reality, but the "all clear" having been sounded an hour later without sight of enemy planes, *Lanikai* soon was alongside the fuel dock. Here, the shoreside state of crisis, panic and disarray fully supported the bad news Adair and I had picked up earlier at U.S. Navy headquarters. The oil company's native employees had all fled some time ago. The Dutch officials in the front office, if not downright hostile, certainly were not cooperative. If we had given it second thought, we would have realized their predicament. These tortured, hopeless civilians were staring into a very near future that promised an end to all their dreams, all they possessed, including their liberty and perhaps their lives. It was not unreasonable that they might look upon their ABDA allies as rats deserting a sinking ship. But at the time and the urgency of *Lanikai*'s requirements, these round-faced, short-spoken, deeply serious fellows suggested too damned much an affinity for the Nazis. We knew that a camp full of them—Dutch Nazis—had been rounded up in the Indies and put behind barbed wire. I was going to get that oil at the point of the gun I was wearing, if it came to extremes.

Between this disgruntled top brass and the disappeared roustabouts, only the middle layer, the frightened but pliable Eurasian clerks, remained available and willing to do the unfamiliar work of twisting the handwheels that set the oil to flowing. After a touch-and-go half hour of palaver and anxious minutes alongside the fuel dock, momentarily expecting an enemy raid, *Lanikai*'s waterline started to rise. Soon, 295 liters of gasoline and 3,784 liters of "solar oil," a high quality distillate that the old Union diesel demanded for best, smokeless performance, had been pumped aboard.

Next in importance came fresh water; rain was a chancy substitute. With the current hectic situation ashore, purification of local water supplies, if such precautions ever existed, probably had become a casualty. So we went alongside the towering, half-empty hull of tanker *Pecos*, not only for water, but whatever other bounty skipper Lieutenant Commander E. P. Abernethy could offer.

Lanikai had not yet been released to go elsewhere. The Navy headquarters ashore professed to lacking authority; it must come from Bandoeng, shouted above the crackling static of the long distance telephone. But any coolie on the street could see that things were in the last stages of the final roundup. This was the end. Waste no time. Australia next stop. Or perhaps India. *Sauve qui peut.*

All hands in *Lanikai* were in something close to rags, and light-weight ones at that, after two months of scrubbing a very meager wardrobe in salt water as often as fresh. If Australia was next, winter came with it. Coasting south, the temperature would drop as the latitude went higher. By any chance, did *Pecos* have some ordinary blue wool sailor uniforms in small stores? Abernethy sent for his supply officer. Yes, there were twenty or thirty suits, the supply officer said, clutching his Bible, the Bureau of Supply and Accounts manual. "But these *Lanikai* fellows have no records, no pay accounts, the ship has no papers—there is nothing to show she is even a Navy ship!" the young man protested. "The manual says here . . ." commenced the supply officer, opening up his paramount authority as any reverend might his holy book. Abernethy cut him short. "To hell with the goddam manual!" he shouted. "Give 'em the goddam uniforms!" This clearly stated directive superseded the S & A manual; we got our uniforms.*

There was other cause for glee aboard *Lanikai* that day, in addition to the acquisition of warm winter clothes all around. On 10 February, Adair had induced ComSoWesPac to send the Secretary of the Navy a message asking permission to enroll the Filipino crewmen in the U.S. Naval Reserve. The answer was awaiting us on arrival in Tjilatjap:

```
...AUTHORITY GRANTED...BUT TO BE DISCHARGED THERE-
FROM UPON COMPLETION DUTY LANIKAI WITH FLEET X MEN
ENLISTED IN NAVAL RESERVE ENTITLED TO FULL PAY AND
ALLOWANCES OF RATE...
```

Abernethy had somehow found time to see to it that not only was *Lanikai*'s crew warmly clad, but that the pockets of those new blues jingled with some currency of the realm that reflected those proud new rates. If the supply officer's manual failed to cover the technicalities here, it was of small consequence; less than a week later, the *Pecos* was sunk by Japanese bombers.

As for the Secretary's admonition on what to do with the *Lanikai*'s Filipino seamen, here too the rules would be bent ever so slightly. Many years later, long after *Lanikai* had not only "completed duty with the fleet" but lay rotting on the sea bottom, over half of those faithful men were either serving in or were retired from the U.S. Navy, most of them as first class or chief petty officers.

But to return to Tjilatjap on the twenty-fifth—tomorrow would tell the tale. Would that release by Bandoeng come in time? For slow, slow *Lanikai* it had to be very soon or never.

* My "undress blues" served through several more months aboard *Lanikai*, then went with me to the USSR. There, the trousers eventually wound up as material for a winter skirt and the jumper became a pillow cover.

Chapter 16

With *Lanikai* on the anxious seat at Tjilatjap and Java crumbling, events around her were taking place with such an accelerating tempo and of such vital significance that they will be set down day by day, although hour by hour almost would be justified.

Former ComABDAFLOAT Helfrich, now the new CinC Allied Naval Forces, was at Bandoeng, in the elaborate Dutch Army-Navy bomb-proof underground headquarters and communications center. His chief of staff, Rear Admiral Palliser, RN, concurrently controlled the operations of British ships. Doorman was aboard flagship RNNS *De Ruyter*. Commodore Sir John Collins, RAN, remained at Bandoeng, overseeing Australian ship movements. Admiral Glassford, a suave and diplomatic anglophile to the point of sometimes wearing a British model patent-leather chinstrap, in his position as ComSoWesPac soon was on the best of terms with both Helfrich and Palliser.

25 February The Dutch assumed full responsibility for the defense of Java, Wavell having departed that date for India in a Liberator heavy bomber. He and his former air commander Peirse had been driven to the airfield by their Dutch chauffeur in a Lincoln Zephyr, the only suggestion of pomp remaining in the command which had begun with such fanfare only six weeks before. Under Dutch Major General van Oyen, there remained 13 P-40s, some piloted by Dutchmen, 6 F2As, 6 Australian Hurricanes, and 3 A-24s. The U.S. warships were wholly under Dutch control with the exception of the submarines, which were, one might say, under "advisory" control; Helfrich could suggest but not order.

General ter Poorten's widely scattered land forces were predominately native, wholly lacking modern artillery and tanks, and as events disclosed, of something less than steadfast quality. Also under ter Poorten were about 7,000 British Imperial troops, and about 540 American field artillerymen.

26 February Lanikai went alongside *Pecos;* water tanks were topped off and final provisions deliveries made. The limited water capacity suggested the wisdom of stowing some additional drinkables aboard. The west Australian coast was dust dry and Africa one hell of a long distance away in case the Japanese moved toward Ceylon, which they did, or Fremantle, which they could have done, as the west Australian coast was completely defenseless. So what better than good Heiniken's beer? A quick trip ashore netted ten or twelve cases of big, one-liter bottles, under what auspices I cannot recall. But one thing is sure—no money was involved. This was Mariveles all over again. Want it? Take it! No questions asked.

At dawn that same day, Allied reconnaissance 250 miles northwest of western Java sighted big trouble: a convoy of 56 transports, escorted by a carrier, 4 heavy and two light cruisers and about 25 destroyers.

Approaching east Java at the same time, 200 miles distant, were reported 40 transports, escorted by a light cruiser and seven destroyers, a second group of escorted transports, and a covering group of one light and two heavy cruisers and about seven destroyers. The first force was under Rear Admiral T. Kurita, the second under Rear Admiral Takeo Takagi.*

This powerful Japanese thrust poised north of Java was expected to reach its Java objective by the twenty-seventh. Facing it in the west was a small Empire unit released from convoy duty by the fall of Singapore. On the twenty-sixth, this little force, the light cruisers HMAS *Hobart,* HMS *Danaë* and *Dragon,* and two British destroyers bravely headed north. Fortunately for them, contact was never made. The five ships returned to Tanjong Priok, fueled, passed through Sunda Strait on the twenty-eighth and never stopped until they hit Ceylon.

In the east Admiral Doorman was feverishly making plans to hit Takagi's force. *Houston, Paul Jones* and *Alden,* also released from convoy duty by Singapore's fall, joined Doorman's strike group, which sortied from Surabaya at dusk and headed north. Cruisers HMS *Exeter* and HMAS *Perth* arrived too late from Batavia to join.

As soon as *Lanikai's* anchor dropped at Tjilatjap on the twenty-fifth, Adair hurried over to the U.S. Naval Port Office. No, he had no control over the movement of ships, explained Captain Hudson, officer

---

* His brilliant chief of staff, Captain Ko Nagasawa, subsequently became the commander of the Maritime Self-Defense Force, euphemism for "Navy," 1957–59, at which time I was on duty in Japan. He reminisced at length with me on the engagements of that period. Another occasional, informal visitor at my Yokosuka quarters was Admiral Kichisaburo Nomura, Japan's 1941 ambassador to Washington, homesick for his former Imperial Japanese Navy haunts and happy to join in a weak whiskey-and-soda while talking over old times.

Lanikai *lies aground off Onslow, West Australia, caught by the 25-foot rise and fall of tide off that coast. High water soon floated "Lucky Lanikai" off, undamaged.*

Wing and wing, Lanikai *surges along before half a gale, approaching Geraldton, West Australia. Officer of the Deck Charles Adair stands ready to grasp the megaphone and shout orders forward, while Chief Gunner's Mate Merle Picking keeps a wary eye ahead.*

in charge. That was strictly Glassford's affair. So Adair shot off a priority message to Bandoeng, to the effect that as soon as *Lanikai* replenished, she be allowed to proceed from Tjilatjap. Whither, no one knew, so no destination was suggested.

What with fueling, provisioning alongside *Pecos,* trying on the new blue winter uniforms and scooting down the channel to sit out the 8:00 to 9:00 P.M. air alarm, it was the next morning before Adair and I eagerly worked our way through streets thronged by men in Allied uniforms to Hudson's office to find that the answer had arrived: "NEGATIVE."

Clearly, this didn't make sense. *Lanikai*'s military usefulness was nil. If the idea was to hold her for the maximum half dozen last-gasp refugees who could be accommodated, the project was self-defeating; each passing minute saw the chances of a successful escape grow substantially dimmer for the dozen and a half already on board. So off went a second message—urgent—a classification generally reserved for enemy contact reports. In view of the rapidly deteriorating situation, it read, and *Lanikai*'s slow speed, it was essential she depart at once. Then Adair picked up the long distance telephone and soon was in a shouted, barely understandable, oft-repeated dialogue with Lieutenant Commander Alexander McDill, flag secretary and Adair's good friend and classmate. The static-clouded exchange revealed little beyond Mac's sentiments that *Lanikai* might be needed for last-minute evacuation of staff personnel. "I'm sorry, I can't hear a word you say, Mac!" shouted Adair. "I take it you go along with me that *Lanikai* must leave right now. What was that? Say again? I should use my own discretion? What? Mac! I just can't HEAR you. I'm going to assume you said its OK to go!"

"Let's get out of here quick, before they change their minds!" said Adair with a wink. We headed for the waterfront at a dogtrot. There on the pier was a U.S. sailor, Wilbur W. Carter, yeoman first class, whose full story we learned later.

In mid-summer, 1941, Carter had been sent to Medan, Sumatra, as assistant in the U.S. Consular shipping office. Both he and his boss, Lieutenant Commander P. W. Rairdan, a U.S. Naval Reserve intelligence officer, were in civilian clothes. The Dutch were taking meticulous care not to suggest to the ubiquitous Japanese that there was any Dutch collusion with Japan's number one bogey man, the United States, and in 1940 had in fact gone so far as to refuse admittance to eight or ten American military language students for the same reason. Don't bait those Japs, the Dutch thought. Close one's eyes long enough and perhaps they would go away. Or head northward into Yunnan. Or Burma. Or Thailand.

Then war broke. On 6 January, Carter arrived in Tjilatjap, after a remarkable trip from Medan, on Sumatra's northwest end, by cross-country safari on foot and by motor car, thence by bomb-threatened coastal steamer. From Tjilatjap there followed a series of shifts to Batavia, to Lembang, and at last to Bandoeng, whence Glassford had moved after relieving Hart. There Carter, as Glassford's driver, had an excellent view of the mighty in action, and also found a much-needed opportunity to recoup his somewhat shaken equanimity. Matters soon fell into place. With typical Japanese punctuality, every morning aircraft made one or two passes over the airfield, after which everybody climbed out of their foxholes, slit trenches and dugouts and went on about business as usual. Chief Pay Clerk Anderson showed up from parts unknown with a suitcase full of Dutch currency to displace the pleasant chit system of dispensing with financial formalities.

With the Japanese driving southward on several fronts, by 26 February the decisions were shaping up that marked the opening of the final and fatal crack in the Allied wall. In the big Dutch underground headquarters, it was "fight." "SACRIFICE IS NECESSARY FOR THE DEFENSE OF JAVA," Helfrich had messaged HMS *Exeter*, HMAS *Perth*, and the three British destroyers, as they left Batavia on the twenty-fifth for their rendezvous with death in Sunda Strait less than a week later.

In ComSoWesPac headquarters next door, the word was "fold." As a clear indicator of American expectations, Admiral Purnell, Glassford's chief of staff, had flown out to Australia on the twenty-fifth to start setting up the new front. The pragmatic Chinese had a word for this evolution since generations before: "Fight to the last man, then withdraw to prepared positions." The equally face-conscious Japanese called it, "an advance to the rear."

To Admiral Palliser, it was far simpler: "The jig is up!"

About this time, somebody had talked Admiral Helfrich into letting HMAS *Hobart*, HMS *Danaë*, *Dragon* and destroyers HMS *Scout* and *Tenedos* get out of the area. Had he listened more carefully to that omniscient Fate leaning over his shoulder, he would have sent out heavy cruiser *Exeter* and destroyers *Encounter*, *Jupiter* and *Electra* as well, and saved them to fight elsewhere.

Thus, in the rapidly accelerating fade-out of Glassford's Bandoeng establishment, Carter was told off to hunt up his old boss Rairdan, supposedly at Tjilatjap. Before Carter reached there on 26 February, Rairdan prudently had already made himself scarce, headed south.

"I had been in Tjilatjap only an hour, I imagine," Carter recorded on tape in Washington's Naval History Division two years later, "when I was confronted by a gentleman wearing shorts and an undershirt, with a sun helmet, who stated that he understood that I desired transportation out of Java. I agreed. 'Do you care to go with us?' he asked. On inquiring how he was going, he told me that he and his party were going in the '*Lanikai*.' I was fairly familiar with the names of the ships of the Asiatic Fleet, but had never heard of the *Lanikai*, and when I asked him what it was, he pointed to a small, two-masted vessel lying at anchor in the bay.

"The *Lanikai*, at a distance, didn't look very large to me. I therefore asked this gentleman who he was and he advised me that he was Lieutenant Commander Kemp Tolley, and that he was commanding officer of that vessel. It was my idea that if *Lanikai* was good enough for Lieutenant Commander Kemp Tolley, it was good enough for me. Therefore, I was ready to go."

Carter's friend, Storekeeper first class J. H. Gorman, was standing farther up the pier. He had made a lucky escape from Singapore and was once more in the agonizing position of a man atop a burning building: jump or stay? "Come on, Gorman!" yelled Carter. "Grab your stuff!" And another slightly skeptical last-minute passenger was added to the roster.

"We picked up our belongings," Carter's narrative continues, "and proceeded with Commander Tolley to an awaiting boat which took us out on board the *Lanikai*. As soon as we went aboard, sails were hoisted, and we got underway."

This was 3:00 P.M., 26 February. In two hours, we had cleared the minefield and were headed east, as close to the beach as we dared go. Carter was correct about everything but the sails. We were coasting along on the auxiliary, under bare poles, to lessen the possibility of being sighted by the cyclopean eye of some enemy submarine lurking off the harbor entrance. With our low speed, we could not afford the luxury of going fifty miles east or west along the coast before turning south, thus hoping to throw off the enemy. At darkness, a mere dozen miles up the coast, we turned due south, still under engine power alone.

27 February As dawn broke, the seas were moderate, sky clear. Having left Java an estimated seventy miles astern, we felt ourselves clear of submarine water. They could be expected to stick nearer the traffic funnel at the harbor's mouth. The prime consideration now was speed. With a spanking breeze broad on the starboard bow, we hoisted all sail at 7:00 A.M., damping the ship's motion and making life more comfortable. Up forward, one could hear the satisfying hiss of the greatly enhanced bow wave as *Lanikai* plunged along at close to eight knots.

During that first night at sea, Adair and I lolled back in the comfortable big wicker deck chairs atop the after cabin, our thoughts and conversation crowded with what the future held. There was no time nor inclination to reminisce at any length on the marvelous manner in which luck had tipped our way so far. Yes, luck in part, we agreed, but good decisions also had played a very important role. As for the present, unable to send or receive radio messages, we were limited to what degree binoculars extended the view of our naked eyeballs—the near horizon.

At departure, our destination, in customary *Lanikai* fashion, had been "undetermined." Having cleared the coast, we asked ourselves, what next? Put ourselves in Japanese shoes, Adair and I told ourselves. What would *we* do? Logically, they had sufficient force to spread it wide.

Where? Most certainly north of Java to occupy and consolidate that rich land as soon as possible. To insure quick success for this project, no reinforcement must be allowed to sneak in the back door from Australia. The south coast and its only decent harbor, Tjilatjap, must be covered. Nor must Allied ships which had slipped through this block be allowed to escape to their new home base at Exmouth Gulf or Broome. Cover that route.

Christmas Island was a potential stepping stone and "water hole" for us en route India, if we chose that course, but this and the Cocos Islands, 480 miles farther west, had radio stations the Japanese would want to silence. We would probably make a timely rendezvous with their raiding parties. Unbeknownst to us, Christmas Island already was being bombed.

So, "go west" was not the answer. By process of elimination, we arrived at the solution: straight south, as fast as sails and engine would drive us.

We missed the booming voice and hearty good humor of Harry Keith, who was far too busy at Tjilatjap to have joined *Lanikai* even had he so desired.

He had been sent over to Tjilatjap, the last escape from Java, to set up a local headquarters. Life ashore was no picnic. In the burlesque of a hotel assigned him, the waterworks consisted of a rooftop open tank filled up with a handybilly from an open well by a "pump boy," whenever the spirit, or more often, a boot in the rump, moved him. The tank held a sort of mosquito larvae soup. "Never tasted a drop of water during my entire stay," Harry said later. "Even washed my teeth with beer."

A constant stream of fleeing foreigners poured through, staying a day or two until they could be wedged aboard ship with only a few minutes' notice. They were forced to abandon cars, furniture, clothes and other impedimenta —the wrong things one generally grabs in a panic situation—the old house-afire syndrome of throwing the chamber pots out the window and carrying the pillows downstairs. Naturally enough, much of this was turned over to Keith with a tearful plea to "send it on later."

The rump staff at Surabaya added to the pile. Keith warned them there was no room for anything, but with a mixture of ill-placed optimism, confusion, and a natural desire to do *something*, even though obviously useless, they sent over a freight car load of desks, chairs, and filing cabinets.

Then came the final day. A PBY flew in low to take off Keith and the few last-ditchers. His ultimate beneficial act had been to get a ship loaded with P-40s out of the harbor. The Dutch refused assistance because they felt Java still might be saved. Keith boarded the freighter, and by judicious use of the tide, cut her lines to the buoys fore and aft and sent her on her way.

In bringing down the curtain, those office chairs, desks, and filing cabinets at last fulfilled their destiny; sold to a Chinaman, the money was used to pay off the pile of bar chits left by the hurrying throng at the hotel. Some bore the names of the mighty—others displaying the ingenuity for which traveling sailors are well known: M. Maus, W. T. Door, Charles Noble, S. Butt, and others more exotic.*

As the opposing forces were shaping up north of Java, a smaller but equally agonizing encounter was already becoming history south of the island. The seaplane tender *Langley* (once the Navy's first aircraft carrier, converted from an ancient collier) was steaming north from Fremantle at an all-out ten knots. On her bobtailed flight deck were 32 P-40s. She also carried 33 U.S. Army Air Corps pilots, who were to fly the planes as soon as they had been hoisted ashore at Tjilatjap. There, huts already were being torn down along a long, straight street which was to serve as an improvised take-off strip. Most of this work was being done perforce by a mixed lot of Allied military personnel, as many of the native laborers had sought more salubrious surroundings after the air alarms had commenced, and those few who remained manifested less than keen enthusiasm in promoting any Allied projects whatsoever.

Langley and her deckload, in a convoy headed for Bombay, India, from Fremantle, had been diverted by her new boss Helfrich. He felt the need for planes was so urgent that she should leave her convoy early and proceed unescorted in spite of the risk. Antisubmarine escort for the last few miles into Tjilatjap was to be provided by the destroyer USS *Whipple*, her bow patched after a collision with *De Ruyter*, and by *Edsall*, leaky and bent aft from having one of her own depth charges explode too close aboard. Each carried one 3-inch antiaircraft gun.

The day was ideal for bombing—clear, with scattered high clouds and a light breeze. Just before noon, 75 miles from Tjilatjap, nine 2-engined planes attacked the *Langley*. The first two glide bombing runs missed, but the third scored five hits and two nears. Soon, *Langley*'s deckload of aircraft was burning fiercely. The ship took a heavy list. Power failed and the pumps stopped. All but sixteen of the men aboard were rescued by the two destroyers, who then sent the old girl to the bottom with gunfire and torpedoes. There was some talk in Glassford's headquarters that she might have been saved had the situation been better handled, but this is doubtful.

At that grim moment, the *Lanikai was not more than 20 miles away.*

---

* Mickey Mouse; Watertight Door; "Charlie" Noble, the ship's galley smokepipe; Scuttlebutt, the drinking fountain.

At 10:00 A.M. that same day, *Pecos* left Tjilatjap to load a cargo of oil at Colombo, Ceylon. Her normal complement of about 125 had been increased to 342. This included casualties from *Houston* and *Marblehead* and the ship's company of destroyer *Stewart,* which was lying on its side, abandoned, in a Surabaya drydock, supposedly demolished beyond Japanese salvage. *Pecos*'s skipper Abernethy had accepted only ambulatory patients from among Doc "Shaky Jake" Wassell's wounded, feeling his ship's chances of survival were too slim. In appreciation of this, he had deck-loaded a number of large bamboo poles, which could be cast loose from their lashings at the last moment and would float free when the ship sank, providing flotation for the extra personnel.

With destroyer *Parrott* as antisubmarine escort, *Pecos* had made only 30 miles when word came of *Langley*'s sinking, less than 30 miles away. Her escorts, *Whipple* and *Edsall,* had picked up survivors. "Mamma said there would be days like this. She must have known!" *Langley*'s radioman had informally sent out before she was sent to the bottom by her escort's torpedoes.[22]

Parrott was detached and *Pecos* ordered to rendezvous with the two destroyers under the lee of Christmas Island, to take on survivors.

28 February The day broke cloudy and threatening, with a freshening wind. Gradually, the long swells on which the ship had roller-coasted shortened into whitecaps and windblown spray. Sailing closer and closer hauled as the wind shifted more and more southerly, *Lanikai* would soon have to tack, change course toward the empty wastes of the Indian Ocean, or douse sail and go it under engine alone.

At 4:00 P.M., drenched sailors lowered the slatting canvas and made it secure, as well as everything loose about the soaking decks. Without the steadying effect of the sails, we hulled along, pitching horribly, course south, at an estimated three knots made good.

With the exception of Adair, myself, and old Cooky, there were few aboard that day who at the moment would have been likely to opt for a life at sea. In a protected spot abaft the forward deckhouse, Cooky held on to the oil drum stove with one hand, steadying a pot of boiling rice with the other. With a handful of raisins and a dollop of condensed milk added, this was the first course; a can of cold salmon and a bottle of beer the second. Such was the standard ration of those who chose to eat during the next three storm-tormented days.

On 25 February, Admiral Doorman had headed north with *De Ruyter, Java, Houston,* and seven destroyers. The sweep developed nothing, so he returned to Surabaya to fuel and give the men a much needed rest. But the respite was a short one; the faithful, beat-up old Catalinas had brought in some solid news: that big eastern invasion force was already a third of the way across from Borneo to Java, at ten knots. "Hit it tonight!" Helfrich ordered Doorman.

At 5:00 P.M., the fleet's senior officers gathered in the relative tranquility of the new naval headquarters in the city, several miles away from the shooting gallery the port had become. The once-opulent Dutch naval club, the Modderlust, where such a meeting might once have been held, had had its walls smeared with camouflage. Gaping holes replaced bright-colored glass windows. People no longer sat on the broad verandas, drinking schnapps and beer, watching the sun sink in a kaleidoscope of tropical color.

At the conference, on Binford's suggestion, he and Doorman's operations officer drew up some simple formations and signals. An American liaison officer and signalman in *De Ruyter* would get the messages to *Houston* by radio—voice or keyed, thence to Binford's destroyers—or direct to Binford. These untried and optimistic plans soon broke down in battle.

Another note of misplaced optimism was Doorman's suggestion that *this* time, the fleet might have fighter protection, which was greeted with cynical laughter. They had heard that too many times before.

Doorman put on a courageous front, declaring that when they had polished off that eastern force, they would move west and knock out the western one.

At 8:00 P.M., the heterogeneous Allied force sortied. Fearing that perhaps he would miss the Japanese altogether if he sailed straight north this time, Doorman coasted westward to interpose himself between the enemy and the expected landing sites.

27 February At 9:30 A.M., Doorman's squadron, low on fuel, sporadically bombed by enemy planes, turned back toward Surabaya without having contacted the Japanese convoy or its watchdogs. *Houston's* anti-aircraftsmen, by then highly professional, had discomfited the enemy planes to the point they did no damage, but all hands were exhausted and dispirited after these wild goose chases.

Helfrich took a dim view of Doorman's withdrawal, and radioed the reluctant strike force commander that "NOTWITHSTANDING AIR ATTACK YOU ARE TO PROCEED TO EASTWARD TO SEARCH FOR AND ATTACK ENEMY." Doorman paid no attention and continued toward Surabaya—until that afternoon, while Doorman's ships were just about to transit the minefield and enter harbor, patrol planes sent definite word on the Japanese position and composition.

This was the scenario for the biggest Japanese sea battle since Tsushima, and for the Americans, the biggest since Santiago. Contrary to the views of most naval experts of the day, who felt that surface actions would be decided within an hour or less of massive exchange of gunfire and torpedoes, this one would drag on for seven hours. But even without the intrusion of Japanese attack aircraft, the heterogeneous Allied fleet suffered an almost total disaster at the hands of a Japanese force only slightly superior in strength but far better handled, further greatly advantaged by spotter aircraft.

By dawn of the twenty-eighth, of Doorman's brave "fleet," only HMAS *Perth* and crippled USS *Houston* and HMS *Exeter* remained, plus half a dozen torpedoless destroyers. Sunk were two Dutch cruisers, two Dutch and two British destroyers.

With Doorman's little fleet swept from the sea, the Japanese convoy north of central Java made its final turn south. Three Allied submarines and about a dozen assorted Allied fighters and light bombers did their meager best, but by nightfall the Japanese were ready to hit the beach a hundred miles west of Surabaya.

By daybreak on the twenty-eighth, Surabaya obviously would be untenable. *Exeter* had come in during the night of the twenty-seventh. At dusk on the twenty-eighth, repaired to the point of being able to make 23 knots, she nosed out the north channel, escorted by destroyers HMS *Encounter* and USS *Pope*. Admiral Palliser's orders were to head north until close to Borneo, then west, then south through Sunda Strait. None at Bandoeng knew that the Japanese already had plugged Sunda, but *Exter's* draft was too great for her to exit via Madœra Strait, whence she could go via Lombok Strait, which Palliser mistakenly felt was heavily guarded.

Also at dusk, Binford's four destroyers sailed—still with no torpedoes. Sensibly, they went via Madœra and Bali Straits, an inside passage behind the enemy's back.

That same evening *Houston* and HMAS *Perth* departed Tanjong Priok. Their escort, RNNS *Evertsen,* was delayed and would come later. They could have used some of that horrible weather in which *Lanikai* was wallowing at that very moment. As *Houston* and consort *Perth* sped west toward Sunda, the moon was full and the weather clear and calm. Hugging the coast to avoid the heavy enemy concentration, the two Allied cruisers entered Banten Bay, only a dozen miles from the "gate" and possible safety. There in the bay lay transports by the dozen, unloading troops.

At about 11:00 P.M., the two Allied cruisers opened up. Their weary lookouts failed to spot a Japanese destroyer which had been shadowing them for half an hour, sending frantic signals for help. She fired torpedoes which missed the Allied ships, but damaged Japanese transports, causing the expedition's commander, General Imamura, to make an unorthodox landing by swimming.

Emerging from the little, semi-enclosed bay, *Houston* and *Perth* met six heavy cruisers, an aircraft carrier, and a squadron of destroyers.

Houston, with only a few rounds of 8-inch ammunition left, soon had both forward turrets knocked out. The 5-inch guns were down to shooting star shells at surface targets; all else was gone. Below decks, the ship already was a shambles. The heavy firing of the previous days had wrenched furniture from its moorings, dumped the contents of bureaus and bunk drawers helter-skelter on deck, and thrown everything loose adrift. In the admiral's cabin, bulkhead and overhead soundproofing lay open and scattered about the deck. People groping through her passageways picked their way through debris, dimly lit by the blue battle lanterns and individual flashlights.

In this frightful melee, surrounded by heavy and light enemy vessels, some within a few hundred yards, *Perth* was opened up like a sardine can by four torpedo hits, and rolled over and disappeared, taking 353 of her 550 officers and men with her.

About thirty minutes later, around quarter of one in the morning, after at least four torpedo hits, an 8-inch salvo that wiped out one engine room, and innumerable smaller caliber hits, *Houston* also rolled over and sank. Of her 1,084 officers and men, 368 survived to straggle ashore or be picked up by Japanese amphibious craft engaged in the massive landing.

One of these was Lieutenant (junior grade) Harold S. Hamlin. He found the Malay population in west Java, historically hostile to the Dutch, equally unfriendly to the Allied refugees. "They lined up to jeer whenever we were transported by truck from one place to another," Hamlin wrote in a March 1972 letter. "They may have killed a couple of *Perth*'s men," he continued, "but in Batavia, the Javanese were apathetic."

The good friend and classmate with whom I had lunched aboard *Houston* several weeks earlier, Jackson Galbraith, was one of those who swam ashore. There, he soon found himself attached to a cartload of Japanese supplies, painfully tugging it barefoot over blistering hot, sharp-pebbled roads.

Captain Rooks, the gallant, quick-witted skipper who had fought *Houston* with such skill through so many engagements, was killed instantly by a fragment as he was standing near his cabin saying goodbye to officers and men about to abandon ship when it became apparent her end was near and no further resistance was possible.

Appreciation of *Houston*'s magnificent record was reflected in the honors bestowed. Captain Rooks was awarded the Congressional Medal of Honor. The senior surviving officer, Commander Arthur L. Maher, the gunnery officer, received a Navy Cross, Silver Star, Navy and Marine Corps Medal, Bronze Star, and Purple Heart, some of these for his later outstanding performance as a prisoner of war.

In Batavia prison camp, a group made up of all officer survivors present and many chief petty officers and others from different parts of the ship reconstructed from memory a remarkable equivalent of a summary log for the month of February. They knew the official one must have been lost and that by the time of their release, memories would have faded. It bears Hamlin's signature, as senior *Houston* survivor in camp; more senior ones had been taken directly to Japan. "Seven copies were made," Hamlin recalls, "on a typewriter belonging to the 131st U.S. Field Artillery, and by about June 1942 . . . the copies were distributed to various officers. As the group split up, copies were sent with each detachment in hopes that at least one would get through. In 1945, in Calcutta, they began piling up under my hospital bed, as officers and petty officers were pulled out of the jungles and towns of southeast Asia. In the end, *all seven copies* of both the log* and the battle report got out."[23]

The Dutch destroyer *Evertsen,* scheduled to accompany *Houston* and *Perth,* was delayed and never caught up. By some miracle, she managed to elude the enemy until actually through the strait. But there, her luck ran out. Two Japanese destroyers cornered her near dawn and in short order she was aground and sinking on Sabuku Island, alas! so close to freedom in the Indian Ocean.

1 March This was the day that was! In something of an understatement, *Lanikai's* journal records, "Ship pitching and rolling heavily. Majority of Filipino crew deathly seasick." Not recorded was the fact that the remainder of the ship's company was in close to similar shape. The weather was pea-soup thick. Intermittent rain and flying spray gradually was filling up the big motor boat being towed astern. At that rate it would soon swamp, eliminating our last hope of escape. If *Lanikai* lost her masts and they holed the side, she could break up. The boat must be saved; somehow, somebody must get aboard it and bail. We hauled it under the plunging counter as near as we dared. Had it caught under *Lanikai's* overhanging poop, both boat and overhang might have suffered grave damage. Tumbagahan, Famero, Felarca, Profeta, Almadin, Taleon, the seamen (Alcantara had been left to an unknown fate recuperating from appendicitis in Surabaya) "I weel do eet!" said each of the sick, gray-faced little men, each willing to risk his life at a hint of the necessity we faced.

During the next two days, one by one, those courageous, loyal lads jumped aboard that wildly lunging boat, in life jacket, at the end of a carefully tended safety line. Then, holding desperately with one hand, they bailed—until the boat had lost its sluggishness and once more rode corklike.

Next would come the slow hauling in close aboard, and a measured

---

* For *Houston's* summary log, see Appendix.

leap for the ship's taffrail. Tumbled on deck, shivering with the wet chill, an exhausted, brown-skinned little hero, no longer able to restrain himself, would lean overside, retching his guts out into the sea.

By 2:00 A.M. on the first, Binford's four old cans, *John D. Edwards, John D. Ford, Alden,* and *Paul Jones,* had cleared the narrow, current-wracked Bali Strait. Fortune rode with them. To avoid being silhouetted against the setting full moon, they hugged the eastern shore. So when they emerged from the narrows, the Japanese destroyer lying on their port hand failed to spot them for some minutes. Then she fell in on a parallel course, and shortly thereafter, two more destroyers joined her. Fire was exchanged at about 6,000 yards, but the battle-weary old ships, torpedoes gone and ammunition low, were wiser to run than to fight. Under full power, with all boilers cut in, they were able to pull away from the Japanese. Binford headed them west, making smoke, to confuse the Japanese into thinking he was headed for Tjilatjap. After thirty minutes of this, he turned his ships due south. Four days later they reached Fremantle.*

No such luck blessed USS *Pope.* She had missed the Java Sea set-to through mechanical trouble, and thus had some torpedoes left aboard. So she was told off to join HMS *Encounter* in escorting *Exeter* on a dash for safety.

As a clear indication of Allied paucity of information, Admiral Palliser had ordered the two ships to exit the Java Sea via the Sunda Strait, where *Perth* and *Houston* had just been sunk a few hours before by vastly superior forces. They were to head north, halfway to Borneo, then turn west, hoping to outflank the Japanese convoy Doorman's force had been hunting.

Shortly after dawn, 1 March, two Japanese heavy cruisers appeared ahead. They were *Nachi* and *Haguro,* which had been Doorman's nemesis. *Exeter* eased to port to avoid, but cruiser-launched float planes kept her under surveillance. Soon, two more heavies, *Ashigara* and *Myoko,* popped up over the horizon to northwestward.

Making 26 knots, the best she could do after her Java Sea Battle damage, *Exeter* and escorts doubled back to the east, the two destroyers screening her in smoke. But the issue was soon settled; hit by gunfire as the enemy closed the range, all power gone, her guns inoperative as a result, *Exeter* took a torpedo for the coup de grace. Shortly thereafter, *Encounter* also went down under a blizzard of shells.

Pope raced on, delaying the inevitable by hiding in an occasional

---

* For his courage, good sense and first-class fighting ability in his series of actions, Commander Binford was awarded the Navy Cross, Silver Star and Legion of Merit by the United States, and an even higher decoration presented by the Queen herself: the Willemsorder, Dutch equivalent of the U.S. Medal of Honor.

rain squall, but float planes always sniffed her out. Shortly after noon, she was repeatedly bombed by carrier aircraft. Lieutenant Commander W. C. Blinn fought a magnificent fight for survival against hopeless odds, twisting and turning skillfully, hiding in rain and smoke. The 3-inch antiaircraft gun fired until it jammed after the seventy-fifth shot, then there was nothing left against the swarm of bombers but two 50-caliber and three 30-caliber machine guns. Earlier, the ship had fired 345 rounds from her four-inch battery. The concussions, plus near misses by bombs, wrecked her boiler brickwork. Speed dropped and water poured in. There was nothing left to do but throw the code books overboard, set demolition charges and abandon ship. But miraculously, only one man died, killed accidentally in setting off the demolition charges.

Adrift in rafts and one boat, the crew still showed fight, albeit unwisely, one man popping away with a 22-caliber pistol at low-flying enemy planes who rewarded these efforts with prolonged and worrisome, but ineffectual, strafing.

The next three days were a major test of Blinn's ability and the crew's determination. Foodless, waterless, they rotated from the rafts to the boat and back again to give each sun-broiled, watersoaked man a short respite. They sang songs, towed the rafts toward Java until fuel ran out—anything to maintain spirit and the will to live. On the third day of this waterborne hell, a Japanese destroyer dragged them aboard. Not a single man of the 151 was missing.

Pope and her crew had fought in three prior engagements: Balik-papan, Badung Strait, and this last, final one—brave ship, brave men. *Pope* was awarded the Presidential Unit Citation, and her skipper, Lieutenant Commander W. C. Blinn, three Navy Crosses. Later, in prison camp, where 27 of the original 151 succumbed to malnutrition and other abuse, *Pope*'s spirit lived on. Her executive officer, Lieutenant Richard N. Antrim, watched in horror as the Japanese continued to beat one of *Pope*'s men, to the point it was apparent he could not survive further punishment. Antrim demanded of the dumbfounded Japanese that he be allowed to take the remaining punishment in the man's place. His Medal of Honor citation reads in part: ". . . he not only saved the life of a fellow officer and stunned the Japanese into sparing his own life but also brought about a new respect for American officers and men. . . ."

Thus died the last Allied surface ship in the Java sea.

The *Pecos,* having left Tjilatjap at 10:00 A.M. on the twenty-seventh to pick up *Langley*'s survivors, arrived there the morning of the twenty-eighth to rendezvous with rescue ships *Whipple* and *Edsall,* and met three Japanese bombers. They had already dropped their bombs ashore, so were in no position to work on the ships, but they would most assuredly tip off their friends.

This, obviously, was not the place to hang around transferring men, so the three ships headed for Exmouth Gulf, the temporary new Allied base, at their best speed of 13 knots—right into a hornet's nest. The day before, a B-17 en route Australia from Java had sighted a powerful Japanese force 150 miles southeast of Tjilatjap, headed northwest. Nobody on the Allied side knew just what the Japanese were up to, but they would soon find out. The four battleships, five cruisers, four aircraft carriers and escorting destroyers, essentially the same force that had hit Pearl Harbor, and still under Admiral Nagumo,* were about to start a rampage in the Indian Ocean.

The *Pecos* had heard of the presence of the Japanese task force, but plowed on. Early in the morning of 1 March, *Pecos, Whipple,* and *Edsall* lay to, boating all of *Langley*'s survivors to *Pecos.* In heavy seas the job took three hours. *Whipple* then got under way for the Cocos Islands, and *Edsall,* loaded with the 33 U.S. Army aviators rescued from the *Langley,* headed for Tjilatjap.

About noon, nine enemy bombers appeared over *Pecos,* whose meager antiaircraft armament of two 3-inch, two 50-caliber, and four 30-caliber machine guns was small deterrent. Clever maneuvering, magnificent work by repair parties and engineers in shifting ballast, stopping holes, putting out fires, and repairing damaged pumps and boilers kept the tough old ship afloat four hours. Postwar information reveals that each of three carriers sent a wave of bombers, and each in their official war diaries claimed her sinking. Actually, it was the last wave, with five direct hits and six near misses, that finally turned the trick.

Before *Pecos* went down, a distress call and position report was gotten off.[24] The oil-covered men in the water felt that perhaps 24 hours would be about their limit. Many of them were from the *Stewart,* which had been abandoned at Surabaya.† Then the *Langley* had sunk under them. Now *Pecos.* If a cat has nine lives, how many has a sailor? In the old American game, three strikes is out. Alas! For many in that group, this rule prevailed.

Darkness fell over the shivering, discouraged men, some hanging onto those providentially-carried bamboo poles, others in one of the

---

* Without loss of a single one of his ships, or even suffering any damage, this remarkable little admiral, sometimes criticized for his timidity at not punishing Oahu more heavily by remaining longer, established an outstanding record. In four months he had cruised a distance equivalent to nearly halfway around the world, sunk 5 battleships, 1 aircraft carrier, 2 cruisers, 7 destroyers, destroyed hundreds of Allied aircraft, and in the Indian Ocean alone, sunk almost 100,000 tons of merchant shipping.

† The thrifty, ingenious Japanese repaired *Stewart,* and sailed her throughout the war, where several years later, Allied airmen were dumbfounded to see on the horizon what must be the ghost of some old four-piper, returned to her earthly haunts. But she was real, her four stacks reduced to three, and recovered in the home islands after V-J Day.

ship's boats that had floated clear. More lay awash in life rafts that offered no protection from the chilly sea that stung the eyes with its salt and thick scum of oil.

Then a light appeared. Japanese? Whoever it was, there was no choice open. A Very's pistol flare was fired by the survivors and the unknown ship cautiously drew closer. It was their old friend the *Whipple* again! She prudently had timed her arrival for after dark. Over her sides hung knotted ropes. The 220 men dragged aboard represented less than a third of those who had been in *Pecos*. Perhaps there were more afloat, too weak to cry out or too far off to make their positions known. If so, their fate was sealed at 9:30 P.M., when sounds of an enemy submarine were picked up by *Whipple*'s listening gear. There was no choice but to drop depth charges, crushing like dynamited fish any men still afloat nearby. With such a heavy human cargo, this was no time to play blind man's buff with submarines; *Whipple* headed for Fremantle as fast as her old engines would take her.

A new peril soon developed, when a careful check of tanks revealed fuel so low that only by proceeding at slow speed could she hope to reach Fremantle. Crawling southeast, she would be easy prey for scouting Japanese planes or roving submarines.

In an April 1972 letter, Admiral Abernethy described those terrible days. "When the survivors of *Langley* were transferred to *Pecos*," he wrote in part, "they were in generally excellent condition, having been transferred almost wholly by boat. But not so when they were again rescued, this time fished out of the water by *Whipple*. Then they were in bad shape indeed. Fuel oil was the worst culprit. Our throats and eyes burned like fire had struck. Our skins peeled as though we had been heavily sunburned from head to toe."

Abernethy's presentiments about Doctor Wassell's patients were well justified: "Only a third of Doc Wassell's patients in *Pecos* survived," Abernethy continued. Wassell put those unable to care for themselves in a Dutch freighter that took all, including the indefatigable old doctor himself, to safety in Australia.

Aboard *Lanikai*, nothing whatever was even suspected of all these portentious happenings, some scarcely over the horizon, and all more or less crucially affecting the ultimate Far East Allied position. Perhaps ignorance was not bliss, but it enabled us to concentrate more effectively on simply existing.

So small a vessel in such long seas rose and fell with stomach-torturing amplitude. Up one side of the watery mountain and down the other we went, pitching to a greater degree than many ships can safely roll. There was no pounding, such as afflicts long, slim, flat-bottomed hulls like a destroyer or cruiser, whose whole forebody plunges out of the sea, then slams down again, the entire ship's structure vibrating like a wet dog shaking himself. A tiny errant chip, we simply rose and fell, our sharp bow and keel slicing down without shock.

Luck and circumstance again flew protectively over *Lanikai.* If we were blind to the world, so were the Japanese blind to us, just another indistinguishable dot on a storm-tossed sea. Perhaps it was Fate also that brought the wind from dead ahead; miserable as it made us, it also forced us to douse those high-visibility sails.

No angel of luck flew over most of those leaving Tjilatjap at our same time. *Pecos* was gone. The gunboat *Asheville,* veteran of a generation of Chinese typhoons and civil wars, plodding south at not much better speed than our own, got off only one desperate radio message: "RAIDER, RAIDER," and was not heard from again.

Fred Lewis Brown was asleep in *Asheville*'s fire room when the sound of shooting awakened him. There had been no preliminary general quarters alarm. One can only assume that out of the rain and mist, there suddenly arose the great, dark-gray shapes of those huge enemy ships.

Brown dashed topside to find the bridge and forecastle heavily hit, with many dead and wounded scattered on deck. Along with most of the surviving ship's company, he soon found himself in the water.

With *Asheville* gone, three Japanese destroyers drew up; Brown was the only survivor rescued. Those Japanese were in a hurry, headed for the Indian Ocean, and with no time nor inclination to be humanitarian beyond finding out the identity of their victim.

Brown was transferred to a Dutch hospital ship, thence to Makassar, where in the spring of 1945, he died. No other *Asheville* survivors were known of.[25]

There are no details on *Pillsbury,* believed to have been sunk in night action by gunfire, by the same ships which finished off *Asheville.*

As for *Edsall,* she too was swallowed up, her fate a secret at the time. But years later, a blurred amateur motion picture sequence taken by a Japanese officer shows the old destroyer's last agonized moments. Hopelessly outclassed in speed and armament, slowed down by heavy head seas, *Edsall* pounded along like a desperate hare, zigzagging ahead of a pack of enormous, baying hounds. The two cruisers gradually closed on her from astern, big shells dropping closer and closer until the inevitable slowing hit, then the wholly one-sided kill.

One can vividly imagine the utter despair of those weary, spray-drenched destroyer men, watching over the stern of their plunging ship, seeing dimly through the rain and mist the inexorable closing of those two big enemy cruisers—four miles, then three, then two—the enemy zigzagging to avoid risking damage to his own forecastles by firing dead ahead—the lazy salvoes awaiting a correction before firing again—then the end. Into such a nameless grave Australian gunboat *Yarra* also disappeared about the same time and place.

According to the Japanese Naval Liaison Office in 1946, there were few records such as logs or battle reports available on the actions which took place south of Java between the first and fourth of March 1942. Most of the meager information available comes from interrogation of officers who were in the task force.

Of all the Allied ships which brushed against this powerful fleet in its sweep through 120 degrees—a third of the way around the globe, from Hawaii to Ceylon—only the *Lanikai* survived.

The second and third of March were such monstrously rough days that *Lanikai*'s journal remained unwritten for the first time since commissioning. A later insertion merely stated that the two days were "identical with 1 March above," which is to say, ". . . wind force three, seas moderate to heavy. Ship pitching and rolling heavily . . ." Actually, this is not entirely accurate. On one of those unchronicled, near-fatal days, through a fleeting rift in the low-lying clouds, through spray, rain and mist, we saw the tremendous bulk of an ash gray ship of carrier or battleship size. Still under bare poles, we instantly turned away, presenting our gray green, slender stern. Then the weather closed again and we saw the spook no more.

Chapter 17

As *Lanikai* plunged and rolled her way south toward Australia, her people were happily unaware of the great and portentious events which were happening in the seas behind her. Fate, and sometimes instant death, lurked always just a few miles over the horizon, a dim nemesis in the swirling mist.

So it was when *Exeter, Pope,* and *Encounter,* in an act of mixed hope and despair, charged out of Surabaya on 28 February, planning an end run around the approaching Japanese and escape via Sunda Strait. The Dutch destroyer *Witte de With* was scheduled to join the party. But most of her men were ashore and could not be rounded up in time. Consequently, instead of going to destruction at sea, she remained in Surabaya, where she was bombed and sunk the next day, with considerable loss of life.

Up north, in MacArthur's bailiwick, matters were critical. The starved, malaria-ridden, dysentery-wracked Fil-Americans were moving their battered lines ever backward. Tokyo's timetable allowed fifty days to reduce Luzon, which they felt was confirmed by their easy sweep from the several beachheads to the fall of Manila on 2 January. But the Japanese badly underestimated Fil-American numerical strength, sense of purpose, and morale. So when Homma launched his initial attack against the Allied "main battle position," he was in for an unpleasant surprise. The Fil-Americans put up an effective and sometimes desperate resistance in spite of no air support, a shortage of close-in infantry weapons such as mortars and hand grenades and, as had been the case almost universally in the Far East since the beginning, both ashore and afloat, a large percentage of dud shells and fickle fuses.

Heavy, sustained Japanese pressure and penetrations around the "impenetrable" Mt. Natib flanks forced the Allies to withdraw in fairly

226

good order to the "rear battle position," eight miles farther back, the movement taking place between 23 and 26 January. In the Philippines, the First Battle of Bataan had ended. There could be no further retreat. This was the last line. "With its occupation," MacArthur informed Marshall, "all maneuvering possibilities will cease. I intend to fight it out to complete destruction."

About this time it was suggested to General MacArthur that the Yangtze River gunboats and minesweepers be allowed to make a run for it to the south with volunteer crews. The staff prepared a reply that, "these vessels are performing essential duties covering entrances to minefields, on patrols toward Manila and off the coasts of Bataan, the vital North Channel and water adjacent to Corregidor . . . but that if the opportunity arises and their essential usefulness ceases, endeavor will be made to permit these naval units to seek safety to south."

The opportunity never arose. Fighting to the very last, their death sentence was fully understood in the dramatic words of their commander, paraphrasing his message to Marshall: "I intend to fight this army to destruction!" he said. "The gunboats are necessary in the defense!"[26]

There was much in what the General said. It was about this time that the "Battle of the Points" began—the dangerous Japanese infiltration attempts behind the line, on Bataan's western promontories, in some cases only a little over a mile from Mariveles itself. These were the attacks so courageously beaten back partly by Commander Bridget's Naval Battalion ashore and at sea by Lieutenant Commander Goodall's "Mickey Mouse battleships," USS *Quail* and Lieutenant John Bulkeley's motor torpedo boats.

The word "Bataan" suggests to most Americans nothing but grim defeat and the subsequent horrors the Japanese inflicted on prisoners in the "Death March." Actually, until U.S. forces landed on Guadalcanal, in August of 1942, it was on Bataan and *only* on Bataan that Allied troops in the early phase of the Far East War fought the Japanese to a standstill. In Malaya, the British, although they outnumbered the Japanese three to two, were kept on a steady run rearward, leaving hot meals on the mess tables, drums of gasoline, undamaged bridges and airfields— "Churchill aerodromes," the Japanese gratefully termed the latter. At the same time, the Japanese were taking over the Netherlands Indies against only token resistance ashore. Resulting from a combination of Filipino and American guts and good leadership, abetted by Japanese stupidity, it was on Bataan alone that these troops atoned for the debacle of Pearl Harbor.

Ever since the beginning of the campaign the Allies had been cut to two scant meals a day, eating horses, mules, snakes, monkeys and caribao when they were lucky enough to snare one. The men were riddled inside with dysentery and outside with jungle rot, and shaking with uncontrolled malaria; there was no point in throwing them into an offensive. It would have been an empty triumph; the Japanese inevitably would be back with superior forces. Meanwhile, the troops could not even comfortably sit out the interregnum; compounding the other shortages, there was a total lack of toilet paper. "No army could ever put its full spirit into the fight while suffering from chronically sore backsides," reminisced George Pollak, in a postwar letter to me.

The Japanese may have faced temporary stalemate in the Philippines, but events were moving fast in the Dutch East Indies. On 1 March, the Japanese landing force that Admiral Doorman had tried so desperately and fatally to intercept commenced fanning out in central Java. The big invasion force *Perth* and *Houston* had blundered into off west Java was ashore and tramping unimpeded toward Batavia.

The jig indeed was up. Admirals Palliser and Glassford made a final call on Helfrich. Palliser told the stolid Dutchman that he was withdrawing all British ships at once. Helfrich acidly pointed out that having sacrificed Dutch ships in defense of Malaya, not only was a little *quid pro quo* in order, but that Palliser himself was being insubordinate. Glassford agreed with Palliser that further resistance was useless, but said that in the case of U.S. ships, he would do whatever Helfrich directed.

About an hour after this confrontation, Helfrich, having seen the Governor General, told Palliser and Glassford that they were on their own; the Allied command was no more. Helfrich thanked Glassford privately on behalf of himself and the Governor General for the loyal support of the U.S. Navy, and included in his farewell an intimation that if Glassford expected to get off Java ahead of him, he had better get cracking.

Allied air reconnaissance based at Surabaya had ceased. The Allied forces remaining in Java were now blind. Taking Helfrich at his word, Glassford and Palliser left immediately for Tjilatjap, arriving there in the evening. Collaborating in getting the last ships out, the two admirals left at midnight via flying boat for Australia. The end of a 400-year-old era had come.

By 16 February the cruiser *Houston* had lost all her float planes but one, and it was apparent that where she was going that one would not be needed. Lieutenant J. D. Lamade was called to the bridge and told to take his airplane and get going; it didn't matter where, just get going. On his way down to the catapult, Lamade pulled a National Geographic map of the Southwest Pacific off the wardroom bulkhead. It looked as if with a full load of gas and good luck, the plane just might make Broome, Australia. Lamade and his radioman, Tubbs, threw out of the plane everything that looked unnecessary and could be pulled loose, the catapult fired them off, and they were away—the last people to leave the *Houston* before she was sunk in Sunda Strait on 1 March.

Fortunately for Lamade, the old battle-weary SOC carried a little more luck than gas. When they reached Broome the tanks were dry.

Marooned at this barren little outpost of Creation, where he found himself the first incumbent "permanent" wartime military officer, Jack Lamade immediately started exercising his abundant initiative in making himself useful. On a dirt landing strip, the U.S. Army Air Corps had left some 55-gallon drums of aviation gasoline, which Lamade wrangled aboard a mini-train to be hauled out to the end of a mile-long pier, the latter necessary to cope with the 40-foot rise and fall of tide. The drums were then hoisted into luggers for transfer to PBY patrol seaplanes that were evacuating personnel out of Java.

One of Lamade's customers was a lieutenant who already had had several very close brushes with death: "One of the pilots came in with most of his rudder shot up," Lamade wrote me in a September 1970 letter. "The pilot was Tommy Moorer.* We patched him up, fueled the plane and off he went."

There was not much at Broome worth bombing, but the Japanese did their best with what was available. On 3 March, nine Zeros roared in and destroyed three PBYs, three Dutch Dornier, and three British Sunderland flying boats, some of them still loaded with refugees for whom there were no facilities ashore.

As in *Lanikai*, perhaps *L* stood for "luck" all over. At any rate, Lamade did it again. While the Zeros were swooping in, so was that 40-foot tide, which floated Jack's SOC in the nick of time. With a very ill radioman in the rear seat, he scooted out low, headed south. At Exmouth Gulf, they made a rendezvous with the seaplane tender *Childs*, which had led a charmed life even since dodging bombs and bullets at Manila until 14 December and then heading south, loaded with enough aircraft bombs and high test gasoline to make her a potential volcano.

"We refueled from *Childs*," Jack wrote me, "then flew south to a town so small the map forgot it. I taxied in to shallow water, lifted my radioman Tubbs from the rear seat and waded ashore. If there is an Australian town, there is a pub, and that is where they parked us. A local good Samaritan putt-putted out with a drum of gasoline next morning and we were off once more—to Geraldton."

There Lamade met a fellow with a unique qualification: an Australian enlisted man who had been at Broome the day of the Japanese attack and who was a personal witness to Lamade's death. "I saw the

---

* Moorer, Lamade, and John Hyland, later to become Commander in Chief, Pacific Fleet, served for a short time in Perth, Australia, before returning to the United States as part of the neucleus of the Navy's growing air power that would bring full retribution for those earlier galling defeats.

airplane hit and blow up!" the Aussie insisted, accurately describing the SOC, the only such plane in the area. The story eventually reached Washington, where it caused a slight modification of the original condolences the Department had sent Jack's parents: "REGRET TO INFORM YOU YOUR SON WAS NOT MISSING WHEN THE *HOUSTON* WAS SUNK BUT WAS SHOT DOWN AND KILLED AT BROOME, AUSTRALIA. . . ."

As for Glassford, who had saved his skin by a midnight flying boat departure from Tjilatjap, he had considerably less luck with his wardrobe. The day we left Tjilatjap, Adair was chugging out to the ship in a launch when Lieutenant Commander Walter E. Linaweaver, Glassford's communication officer, dashed onto the dock.

"Come back!" he shouted. "I have a suitcase of the Admiral's clothes for *Lanikai* to take to Australia!"

"We may not even be *going* to Australia, Hap! Depends on which way the wind blows," Adair called back. "Put it on something reliable and safe, like the *Pecos!*"

Lanikai had been under way over six days with no sight of blue sky or heavenly body. Where we were was anybody's guess. On the morning of 4 March, the wind was still blowing a gale, seas were heavy, and speed was being made good through the water at about three knots. But which direction and how fast were the ocean currents? Perhaps three knots against us? One had to take a calculated risk. Our beer and water would not last forever and the constant salt spray made rainwater undrinkable. So shortly after noon, course was changed to 120 degrees, almost due southeast. Wildly flapping inner jib and single reefed mainsail were hoisted and braced on the new course. They were strong, new #2 canvas, and held the powerful thrust of the gale with no sign of so much as a pulled grommet. Speed picked up to five knots and the hellish rolling was damped to near nothing.

After these days of wild tossing, the crew had got their sea legs back again. All hands were eating with gusto, making up for lost meals. The gray faces of our Filipinos had regained their healthy mahogany. There was even time to think.

The fourth of March was a very special date, washed indelibly into the fabric of my memory by a flood of tears, two years earlier. Typically manlike, I had forgotten a birthday—or more accurately, had not known of the date at all. Then her tears were dried and plans for the day drastically overhauled. I would cancel my daily trip on the crowded, rattling tram up Avenue Edouard VII to Frenchtown for a lesson in Russian declensions and gossip on what was new in the colony of 10,000 Czarist emigrés. No bouillabaisse, crusty French bread and red wine for solitary bachelor lunch at the French Club, followed perhaps by appointments on the Navy's clandestine business in town.

It was spring in Shanghai. Buds were popping out in palest green. Small, bright flowers were blooming in the carefully tended beds opposite the British consulate general, where the signs said, "NO DOGS ALLOWED." The warning barring Chinese had been removed a decade before in recognition of the new Nationalist equality.

We would go to Jessfield park for a Chinese holiday, eat noodles cooked in the open before our eyes and drink pale, deceptively strong tea out of handleless cups.

The Chinese were out in force, enjoying the bright blue of the sky and the soft warmth of the country air. There was none of the hurly-burly of the city's streets, where wretched coolies jostled and hurried and yei-ho'd in their desperate effort to live out another day against a hostile and wholly selfish world.

Small, grave-faced children in gay red hats and hair ribbons watched in silent wonder at songbirds in small bamboo cages, lovingly carried out for an airing by seamy-faced old gentlemen in long black gowns and skull caps tipped by a colored bead. Boys were sometimes dressed as girls, a clever ruse to fool the jealous, but clearly stupid gods, ever on the alert to snatch a valuable man-child. (Girls were of negligible worth.) The backs of the children's pants were seatless, the pragmatic Chinese answer to the diaper problem. This also served to unmistakably reveal the infant's sex, a wide-open secret one can only presume those child-snatching gods were not a party to.

This was a different, simpler world, without the reek of cocktail party cigarette smoke, din of motor exhausts, or the false intimacy and excitement of the French Club's spring-loaded dance floor. We left it with regret at sunset, the chill evening air suggesting that spring had not yet wholly come.

Would I ever see Shanghai again? Or another March fourth? Would I see even *tomorrow!* Lying curled up in a deck chair lashed to the lee rail of the after cabin roof, these gloomy thoughts raced through my mind. Old Gomez had carried the cushions below to save them from the fine spray that from time to time blew all the way from the weather bow and dried in sticky salt on my face. The chair's bare bamboo slats dug into my skinny backside, no longer so well padded as it had been that unhappy midnight when in gunboat *Oahu* I slid down Shanghai's Whangpoo River almost four action-packed months before. Since then, I had dropped down twenty-six degrees of latitude to Manila. *Lanikai* had coasted me down twenty-two more, to Java. Then, down to Fremantle would be twenty-two *more,* this time all in the open sea or off a wholly barren, inhospitable coast. Always *down*. Always retreating. Seventy degrees of latitude—more than a quadrant of the earth's face. Would we *ever* turn and fight? *Where* was that goddam Pacific Fleet? We felt the enemy was everywhere.

By nightfall on the fifth, seas and wind had moderated to the point of our adding another jib and shaking the reef out of the mainsail. Following Columbus's proven theory, we felt if we continued to sail straight ahead eventually we *must* strike land.

By the morning of the sixth, the wind had dropped to a zephyr so mild that the sails slatted and flapped uselessly, so they were lowered to reduce visibility. Without their damping effect, the ship rolled along like a barrel in the long ground swells in wake of the typhoon. The masts swung through such a huge arc it was too stomach-torturing to go aloft and scan the horizon from the Coca-Cola box crow's nest in the fore shrouds. Charlie had taken advantage of the sparkling weather to shoot a series of sun sights that at last gave a clue to our approximate position after a week of blindly groping under heavy overcast. In late afternoon, there was a welcome cry of laaannnd hoooo! from passengers Gorman and Carter, who had preempted the top of the forward deckhouse as watch-and-watch volunteer lookouts, comfortably ensconced in folding canvas deck chairs lashed to the foremast.

From the general chart of all Australia, only one on board, the landfall must be Montebello Island, a part of the Dampier Archipelago, whose fantastic tides and perilous shoals on a waterless coast had been explored during the period 1708–11 by the almost legendary man whose name it bears, Sir William Dampier.

The land was low and barren. What a remarkable comparison with the lush, teeming jungle so recently left! At 5:00 P.M., a little cloud of rust arose from the hawsepipe as the anchor went down in 30 feet of water in what small lee the island offered. There was no bottom to be seen here; the sea was a murky pea green. Near the shore in such shallow water, there should be fish a'plenty. Snappers are bottom feeders, and the conditions here were ideal. As the motor boat went over one side with a landing party, fishing lines dropped over the other side in keen anticipation of fresh meat for dinner; from sea to pan was hardly more than a twist of the wrist for those experts.

Or was it? The first line had no sooner plopped in and run out to the bottom when there was a bite. The careful hauling-in began. Then the tension on the line uncharacteristically ceased and it came aboard slackly. Yes, there was something on it bigger than the original tidbit of pork rind—a fish head, the red green remnant of what must have been a four or five-pound snapper. It had been nipped off as by a cleaver just abaft the gills. Then another, and another, and yet another. Sometimes the head was lacking; only a frayed end of line came up, the precious hook gone. There was excited palaver in Tagalog. "Eet ees shark!" translated one of the boys. "We go get shark hook."

Next over the side went a stout manila line tipped with a four-foot bite-proof wire leader, then a hand-sized hook generously baited with fat ham skin. The fish heads were tossed back in for chum. In seconds there was a heavy swirl and the line tautened like a fiddlestring. They had hooked no monster of the deep, but to those of us who never had seen a six-foot shark floundering on deck like the malevolent, prehistoric creature he is, the scene was memorable. The shark's jaws, double-rimmed by a horrible-looking bandsaw of one-inch triangular teeth, opened and shut with metallic snaps. The excited boys skipped lightly out of his thrashing way, avoiding the harsh, sandpaper skin that would have rasped their bare legs and feet to bleeding rawness.

Six of these man-sized devils were dragged aboard in quick succession, clubbed, beaten and axed into a bloody mess on deck before the fight and life was out of them. In several, the hook had gone down into their stomachs, requiring a near total disassembly to retrieve it.

The boys took this all as a great lark. No mere shark could dampen their infectious, perennial enthusiasm and good nature. There would be no epicurean red snapper or lapu lapu with the evening rice. "OK! No got *all* feesh, we make feesh-head soup!" said Cooky cheerfully. Some edible parts of the sharks were kept and the rest of the bloody mess was thrown back to their cannibal brothers. That seething, tearing mass was a chilling suggestion to do our swimming elsewhere.

The shore party was soon back from their sight seeing; there wasn't much to see, except the tracks of huge turtles that had dragged themselves ashore and back into the sea again. But neither turtles nor eggs were seen. Indeed, had we found one of these armored amphibians, nobody on board would have been qualified to unlock the meat.

There were no soundings on our general chart, so from now on, it was proceed cautiously, heaving the lead continuously. There was no spotting of shoal water from the crow's nest as there had been in the crystal equatorial seas. This was cruising as Dampier, Blygh, Drake, and Magellan had done centuries before, feeling their explorers' way with the cunning of the seaman wholly on his own. The journal's description gives a bleak picture:

> This area is dotted with low, sandy islands with sparse vegetation. The bottom rarely exceeds six fathoms, gently shelving, mostly sand and coral rock. There are occasional reefs that may or may not break. A current of about a knot runs during the height of ebb and flood, with slack water only at high and low tide.

By 4:00 P.M., we lay off what was indicated on the chart as "P. Weld," with the water shallowing so that we could approach the coast no closer than four miles, scarcely worth a long trip in a small motor boat to a spot with no outward sign of human presence. Disappointedly, we turned south, for a try at another charted spot of possible human habitation, Onslow. At any rate, this was the mainland—the great new, raw country of Australia. We had heard of her generous and light-hearted people many times from those who had visited "down under" in the past. Now we were so near and yet so hopelessly far—not only from the fabled Australians, but far more to the point at the moment, from fresh water.

As a shallow water navigator for many years while a China river gunboat sailor, I was well indoctrinated to handle the next episode: at 4:00 P.M., we felt the ship lurch to a halt. The bottom was ever so gently shelving and our speed low, but it was this so-gently shelving nature of the bottom that allowed us to slide up far enough so that backing full to haul off was to no avail. What we did not know about, of course, was the tremendous rise and fall of the northwest Australian tides. This was why Broome had that mile-long pier, and why ships steamed in at high water, remaining to sit on the bare shingle at low tide, so that wagons could be driven out alongside to transfer cargo. The chart did not tell us these things, or that the land held other wonders, such as animals that laid eggs, birds that couldn't fly, sidewalks that rolled up on Sunday and men who nourished a thirst that would make our old Wild West hombres look like Baptist conventioneers. We would have to find out all these things the hard way as we went along.

Thus, it was with considerable relief that the following was entered in the journal:

> At 1615 stopped in 1½ fathoms of water [the ship drew 1½ fathoms], tide near low. Took advantage of solid bottom of smooth sand and decomposed coral rock to careen ship.

> At 1745 ship careened to about 40°, lying on keel and starboard turn of bilge. Inspected bottom on port side and main injection. Found bottom entirely without trace of growth or fouling of any kind. (Note: those Surabaya dockyard workers had done a good job.)

> At 2330 ship floated freely. Moved 1,000 yards to northward and anchored in 6 fathoms. . . .

There was one thrill accompanying the occasion that stirred every-one except the old Filipino boatswain. As the tide receded, the ship remained level, perched and balanced precariously on her three-foot-deep keel. Then, through some slight movement of weight aboard, or a mild wave, with a mighty SWISH, she suddenly rolled over to rest on the turn of her bilge. There was a rumble of shifting loose gear and crash of crockery in the cabin. Chief engineer Wilcoxen, recuperating from malaria, was tossed out of a groggy reverie, and picked up his bed

Skipper Tolley augments the larder in Shark Bay, West Australia.

Crispin Tipay, assistant engineer, holds up a large stingray in Shark Bay, a desolate, unpopulated wasteland.

and bolted up the hatch like a shot, ready to abandon ship aboard his kapok mattress. "We do thees every year Manila-side. Scrape bottom!" old Bosun Magtulis later explained through one of the boys. He had sat unperturbed on the hatch coaming, awaiting the inevitable lunge over, saying nothing to anybody until the minor crisis had subsided, the wreckage swept up and life jackets taken off. With a troublesome hernia, a soggy pleura, hemorrhoids that would have put Napoleon's to shame, and troubled by other creeping ravages of advancing age, good, grey, uncomplaining old Magtulis had enough to occupy his mind without fretting over so simple an evolution as careening ship.

After this small contretemps, in water where it was obvious we would have to creep along with bamboo sounding pole and lead going constantly, the idea of searching out elusive "Onslow" went by the board. We would head south, away from this trap that might find us a party of bleached bones on some wretched reef out of sight of land and humanity.

After midnight of 9 March, heading due south in the gloom, we groped ahead at reduced speed, feeling for the land off Exmouth Gulf. Perhaps our ships still used it. But daylight revealed only the rusted hulk of a 6,000-ton steamer aground on the west shore, some fogbound or incautious fellow who had come to grief long before our probing visit. As for our own ships, we could only guess that they had either been taken care of by the Japanese or fled south. We had no way of knowing more than our eyes told us.

The tenth and eleventh saw our hopes rising, while changing course slightly this way and that to conform to the coast and bring the wind to bear in the most favorable quarter. It was getting noticeably cooler, time to climb into those new blues and oilskins. People braved the smoke around Cooky's sandbox oven to counter the morning chill, like baby chicks closing in on the incubator heater. My rubber mattress moved from the center of the life raft atop the after cabin skylight to the four by six "master stateroom" below, and the skylight itself was closed to conserve cabin heat for the first time since *Lanikai*'s commission pennant had climbed the mainmast three months earlier.

The twelfth was a banner day in several respects. After lunch, a large flying boat was sighted far out to seaward. She *must* be Allied, but we went to general quarters just the same as she lazed placidly on up the coast unmindful of our presence.

The wind, for some time from the antarctic south, and for us thin-blooded "tropicanos," feeling like it, hauled around to northerly. We bulled along wing-and-wing, the ship strangely silent with the wind aft. The surge of foam piling up under the bows made good music: *Swissshhh! Swissshhh!* The sea gurgled its way past, under the billboards, under the triced-up accommodation ladder, and bubbled past the submarine launch towing astern. For some days there had been no need to bail it out.

We were surging along at nine knots or more, almost as fast as a human runs the mile.

With such a large-scale chart, we had felt none too sure of our exact location other than following Charlie's expert noon sun sights, but the night of the tenth gave unmistakable evidence: we were within reach of our first goal. Far distant, the ever-eager lookouts spotted a powerful beam of light sweeping the horizon that could only be the lighthouse off Geraldton. Its characteristics checked.

Logic suggested it was not wise for an unannounced, unidentified —in fact, unidentifiable—ship to approach a wartime, blacked-out city in darkness. We dropped anchor twelve miles from port. That revolving spot of light, although distant, almost seemed to lay a comfortable, protecting shield over us.

The before-taps, nightly acey-deucey game between skipper Tolley and supercargo Adair was less overlaid with tenseness than at any time in recent memory. On the forward deckhouse, passengers Carter and Gorman were so used to sitting out the night as volunteer lookouts that by habit they were still there, though the requirement for their vigilance had close to disappeared. Then the evening chill drove them below. Tomorrow would be the day!

Chapter 18

Twelve miles away across a purple black, rolling sea, lay the sleeping town of Geraldton. Behind it, the continent of Australia stretched 2,400 miles eastward.

The Aussies, grandly isolated in the past, had undergone a series of traumatic experiences which had taken them into the grim reality of the present. Fighting a war a long way from home, Australia's three divisions in the Middle East had been mauled and battered in Africa and had suffered even heavier losses in the Greek and Cretan disasters. On 19 November 1941, the new light cruiser HMAS *Sydney* had been sunk with all hands by the German armed merchantman *Kormoran,* only a couple of hundred miles from Fremantle.* And so far in 1942, an Australian division of 15,000 men surrendered at Singapore, another 1,100 men were taken on Timor, and 3,000 more on Java. Japanese bombers had all but wiped out Darwin and heavily hit Broome. Their midget submarines had even penetrated Sydney Harbor. Nearly every household in Australia had been directly and tragically touched by a war already two years old.

In Australia there remained only one armored division, woefully short of tanks, seven ill-equipped and inexperienced militia divisions, and a volunteer corps of 50,000. Two of the divisions in the Middle East were hurrying home. Churchill had importuned Australian Prime Minister Curtin to divert one of them to help stem the developing debacle in Burma, and concurrently had headed the ships in that direction in full expectation of agreement. But John Curtin, newly elected, said emphatically no, reflecting not only Australia's fearful concern for her own safety, but the general feeling that Britain was willing to fight to the last Australian. The bad blood, burgeoning independence, and soul-

---

* Thus avenged was the sinking of the Kaiser's commerce raiding cruiser SMS *Emden* by an earlier Australian light cruiser HMAS *Sydney* off the Cocos Islands in 1914.

238

searching realignment were clearly reflected in Curtin's 1942 New Year address, which included the Empire-rocking phrase that, "Without any inhibitions of any kind, I make it quite clear that Australia looks to America, free of any pangs as to our traditional links or kinship with the United Kingdom. . . ."

Of course, all of our knowledge of Australia ⸀..me later. Right then, it was as strange to us as it had been to its first visitor, Abel Tasman, who arrived in 1606.

At a suspenseful 6:00 A.M. dawn, 13 March, we hoisted sail and stood in. The pilot met us offshore, clearly more than surprised by what he found. By 10:00 A.M., we were snugged down alongside the grain dock, where we could see that a war was on. Thousands of tons of grain lay under the open sky for lack of shipping. The few trucks and motor cars that stirred up dust on the bone-dry streets were fueled by bulky gas generators. Nearby, a Dutch submarine lay alongside, one of the few Netherlands East Indies units that still remained above water.

Groups of curious citizens soon gathered on the waterfront to gawk at *Lanikai,* this new, if only flyweight reinforcement to the town's defenses. Vegetables, fruit, fresh bread and meat came aboard. There were no bills. "Yar foightin' far us, aren't ya naow, mite?" one donor said. "There is no price tag to *that!*" Tucked discreetly under the produce there might be a bottle of good Australian wine, or of Tolley's Hospital Brandy, distilled by the descendants of that branch of the family that had gone east, while mine had gone the other way.

"Hyar comes that Limey three-ringer!" said the pilot, who had stayed aboard after our mooring to fill us in on the war, Australia, Geraldton, and gingerly try a cup of coffee in lieu of the tea that was more his dish. "He's a bloody barstid, that's wot!" declared our informant with some heat. "Thinks he's runnin' the bloody show hyar, but that's not the harf of it."

We waited with interest while the meticulously blue-clad Royal Navy commander hopped aboard, nodded curtly to the pilot, introduced himself as the senior naval officer present, and asked if he might have a word in private below. In proper Dartmouth accents, he wasted no time in coming to the point. "I seh! Do me a fevah, will yoh? As soon as you were identified as a Yank, these local fellows fairly hopped up and down. You'll soon see them flocking aboard for help and advice which I am sent hyah to provide. They seem to think Britain's let them down and squandered their chaps in Empah defense. Send them cracking back to me, will yoh?"

The hospitality of the townspeople went far beyond free baskets of delicacies. Crewmen were invited into private homes for dinner. Adair and I were taken out to the nearby RAAF airfield to view the sad little collection of old crates that represented the sole protection for those parts, then to join in an evening at the base mess that was an endless succession of, "Come on now chum, yer've got to have one with *me!*" Outnumbered ten to one, neither Adair nor I could recall next day what had been for dinner, assuming such there was. At the local pub the following evening, we found the type of officer-man comeraderie unique to the Australian civilian-turned-military. Drill over for the day, brigadier and batman stood arm-in-arm at the bar and downed such potables as the war still allowed.

Bending ever so slightly the U.S. Navy's strict rules on alcoholic liquors aboard ship, several bottles of Tolley's Best Whisky surreptitiously found their way into the punch served atop the after deckhouse roof at a return engagement for shoreside friends. Flowers decorated the awning stanchions. The big wicker chairs with bright cushions lent a touch of yachtlike elegance. Old Gomez limped around on his rheumatic legs with delicious bits of meat roasted over the open oil-drum fire amidships. Was it kangaroo, beef, or goat? Who gave a damn? At least it was no longer fish.

Within a few days of *Lanikai's* safe arrival at Geraldton, another equally improbable cruise, General MacArthur's, commenced.

Had MacArthur been consulted when Admiral Rockwell released *Lanikai* to sail south, it is quite probable he would have refused permission. He might have reserved her for a blockade-running trip or two as far as Cebu, where crawling along at five or six knots, she soon would have been sunk. Had she remained at Corregidor, her fate and that of her American personnel would have been equally predictable.

Around MacArthur a desperately difficult question revolved. Go or stay? Die gloriously in a sort of *Götterdämmerung,* or leave and become a symbol of resurrection? If it was opted that he get out, wrote MacArthur's old friend General Patrick Hurley, it must be arranged that "his honor and his record as a soldier would not be compromised."[27]

The issue was soon settled by Roosevelt, who on 22 February not only ordered MacArthur out, but added that he should make it snappy. He was to proceed to Mindanao, delaying there no longer than a week to shape things up, then proceed to Australia to assume command of the Allied land and air forces. The evacuation was to be by submarine to Mindanao, thence to Australia by B-17.

On 1 March, Lieutenant John Bulkeley* received a mysterious directive to take the general for a ride in one of his PT boats. What now?

---

* "Bulkeley was a wild man. Daring, courageous, admirable in many ways, but still a wild man . . . a swashbuckling pirate in modern dress . . . long, unruly beard, two pistols, eyes bloodshot and red-rimmed from staring them out on night missions and from lack of sleep. He walked with a cocksure gait. . . . High strung, temperamental, brave and gallant, John Bulkeley was one of the most colorful figures in the Philippine campaign."[28]

agonized Bulkeley. They had been planning an escape dash to the China coast when they were down to one last load of torpedoes and their Philippines usefulness ended. What the hell did *this* mean? Stay in the islands and rot, ending up in a Jap prison camp?

During MacArthur's excursion, the four remaining pasted-together, ramshackle P-40s buzzed overhead as air cover for the half hour they could reasonably be expected to be effective against chance low-level intruders. The general seemed to enjoy his ride. He handed each crewman a pack of cigarettes, and took advantage of the occasion to formally pin on Bulkeley the Army Distinguished Service Cross he had awarded him some weeks before. It made a good cover for MacArthur's real reason to be aboard. By that time, Bulkeley knew the truth; it was not by submarine that the evacuees would be leaving, but in the four remaining PT boats.

"General MacArthur disliked the idea of going on a submarine," Rockwell told M. de Bausset, in an interview for *Paris Match*, "He wanted a deck to pace, and fresh air, which he thought he would get more of in a PT boat." Holy Mother! If he had only known how much fresh air, mixed with plenty of sea water, he was going to get!

The boats were being moved to Cebu, the skippers told their crews as a cover story. That was why they were strengthening the decks with plywood to support twenty 50-gallon drums each on the topside. There was trouble evading the questions of correspondents. Already the stateside newspapers were clamoring that MacArthur be saved for the comeback, a bit of intelligence that immediately spurred the Japanese to beef up their surveillance. By 9 March, there was a marked increase in enemy surface craft activity. Each day increased the peril. All this had converted Rockwell from favoring the submarine project to a belief that speed was of the essence; they could not afford to await the sub, due on 15 February.

By 9:15 P.M. on the twelfth, the four PT boats had cleared the minefields and were high-tailing it south at more than thirty knots, the best their tired engines could do.

With Bulkeley in PT-41 were General and Mrs. MacArthur, their young son and Chinese nurse, one naval and four army officers. Admiral Rockwell and three army staffers rode with Lieutenant R. G. Kelly in PT-34. Four more army officers were with Ensign A. B. Akers in PT-35, and four generals and a lieutenant colonel in PT-32 with Lieutenant (junior grade) V. S. Schumacker.

The lightly built PTs took a beating in the open sea. Most of the passengers soon reached that stage of seasickness where a fatal encounter with the enemy would have been welcomed. In the moonless darkness, without lights, the boats soon became separated. It was afternoon of the first day before PT-34 and PT-41 found each other in the Cuyo group of small, mostly uninhabited islands. "Palm trees waved lazily over a snowy white beach," recounted Bulkeley, in a later, probably more exotic mood. "The cove had a coral bottom and the water was emerald clear."[29]

This was where the submarine was supposed to rendezvous, but the general was having strong second thoughts about that open deck to pace and the fresh air. "He was very anxious to wait for the submarine to pick us up rather than continue on the PT boat," Rockwell told de Bausset. "He finally agreed to continue in the PT, but he turned to General Sutherland, his chief of staff, and said, 'Dick, I can't do anything to Rockwell, but if this is another bad night, so help me, I'll boil you in oil!' "

There were only two PT boats left now. PT-32 had confused PT-41 astern of her as being a Japanese destroyer and had dumped her deck load of gasoline to escape. PT-35 had broken down earlier.

Thus, with 21 passengers between them the two remaining boats headed south at sunset into the heaviest weather yet. A Japanese cruiser was sighted on the horizon and evaded. It was a shaken and utterly miserable lot that dragged themselves ashore to meet Brigadier General W. F. Sharp, commanding the three Philippine divisions of the Visayas-Mindanao Force.

Nobody on the operational level in the Indies—not even Admiral Glassford—was aware of the super secret of MacArthur's journey. Hence, no particular effort was made in filling the order for four B-17s to proceed to del Monte airfield on Mindanao. One cracked up on takeoff, two more gave up in the Australian desert, and the one which finally lumbered into del Monte was in such marginal condition that MacArthur, in no mood to be further chivvied after that boat ride, sent off a blistering message to General Brett in Australia, and another to Marshall that if Brett couldn't produce, then, "The three best planes in the United States should be made available . . . with completely adequate and experienced crews." He was not about to accept the responsibility of consigning the whole party to death by putting it aboard such a clunker as had been sent, he said in effect in closing.

Shortly after midnight on 16 March, in two B-17s which met the general's specifications, the party took off, and by nine the next morning were safely in Darwin.

The Navy had played a stellar role in this highly marginal operation, which required immense fortitude, ingenuity, and a superior feel for the sea. MacArthur reported to Marshall that it had been a trip unique in military annals . . . "due entirely to their [PT boat personnel] invincible resolution and determination." Congress clearly agreed, awarding Bulkeley the Medal of Honor. The Navy appropriately decorated the other PT boat people.

On 16 March, the *Lanikai*, vastly encouraged by the friendly attitude of our newly met allies, set sail for Fremantle, Western Australia.

This was a dangerous coast for low-powered ships. Furious williwaws sent sailormen scurrying for sea room. Forty miles off Geraldton lay unlighted Houtman Rocks—low, rolling sand dunes set above coral reefs, none much above ten or fifteen feet high. Narrow, sandy beaches dropped off from one fathom on one side of a ship to twenty on the other. Many a windjammer had been lost there, our Geraldton friends warned us. Few marooned sailors survived on these waterless flyspecks the six months or more before chance brought a ship within hail.

By 3:00 P.M. the seas and gale had risen. *Lanikai* was pitching heavily, making good no more than three knots. We heaved the lead anxiously and found no bottom, nor could sharp Filipino eyes see much beyond the bowsprit in flying foam and spray. To have come so far to be dashed to splinters on some west Australian reef, a hundred miles from our goal, would have been a sorry climax. Nobody slept. Everybody was soaked and cold. For once, Cooky's cheerful sandbox fire was out. The ship pounded and creaked and groaned, almost as if the old girl were desperately trying to tell us something.

After a miserable night and forenoon, the low coast of the mainland broke through the clearing overcast about 2:00 P.M., and we turned south to follow it. Shortly after midnight on the eighteenth, Rottnest Light, off Fremantle's entrance, popped over the horizon. The beacon light at the end of a 4,000-mile road was at last in sight.

Some odd fugitives have come Australia's way over the centuries, but on 18 March 1942, there was one close to unique. Eighty-two days out of Manila, all sail set, rigging taut and shipshape, brass gun pedestal glistening in the bright sunshine, a little, weatherbeaten schooner triumphantly entered the port of Fremantle. Flying from her gaff were the flags of the United States and the Philippines, swallow-tailed and tattered. Proudly above them floated a wisp of bunting that curious onlookers aboard the Allied warships present thought looked something like a commission pennant. But no, it *couldn't* be! Adair, the American and Filipino crewmen, and myself, burned to near the same color by months of tropic sun, stood in undress sailor blues on the after cabin roof.

No one was more delighted at our arrival than the harbor pilot, our old friend, benefactor and passenger, Harry Keith, his new "brass hat" and commander's oak leaves glistening in the sun that had burst forth to make the joy of our arrival complete.

Lieutenant Commander Charles Adair, passenger, guest navigator, good friend, and competitor in a thousand acey-deucey games, prepared to disembark. By his timely intervention in the release of the ship at Manila, Surabaya, and Tjilatjap, he had most certainly saved from death or capture all who sailed in her.

Four thousand miles, most of them hazardous, had passed beneath *Lanikai*'s keel. Most of her Filipino crewmen had been without previous military indoctrination of any kind, but they had served with loyalty and devotion, displaying magnificent seamanship. One or all could have faded into the landscape a dozen times in the Philippines, but none had chosen to do so. The unpredictable hand of Fate, plus a little skill and luck, had allowed *Lanikai* and her crew to live while many ships and men had died.

With *Lanikai* moored alongside a friendly Australian naval auxiliary, I headed for U.S. Navy headquarters in Perth. There in a passageway lined with offices and clacking typewriters, I met Rear Admiral Purnell. "My God! What are *you* doing here?" he almost shouted. "You're supposed to be dead!"

For some time, the Navy Department's views had coincided with Admiral Purnell's. After the *Wake* was captured at Shanghai, my family had received a telegram from Washington announcing my new status as missing in action, probably a prisoner of war. From Manila I sent home a reassuring radio that I was safe at my birthplace, which skirted censorship while counting on my parents' recalling I had been the first baby born in the brand new Division Hospital at Manila 33 years earlier. *Lanikai*'s subsequent month-long disappearance into limbo produced another telegram of condolences from Washington that I was overdue and presumed lost. My radio from Surabaya, "SAFE INDIA" reassured those at home. The Department's third message reflected Admiral Purnell's view that anyone who had ventured south of Java and was unheard from three weeks later, clearly was "supposed to be dead." So my third radio home, from Australia, confirmed my parents' suspicions that the Navy Department was inclined to pessimism in my case. Indeed, with the Far East war going as it then was, perhaps such an attitude in Washington was not surprising.

Supposed to be dead though we might be, life went on aboard *Lanikai* with renewed verve. Officers from other ships—Dutch, Australian, American—came over to look and chat. Were we *really* a warship? A "Q" ship, perhaps, some would suggest, with a knowing wink. Others were skeptical that we had any status whatever. The senior medical officer of USS *Blackhawk* preemptorily refused to accept poor old bosun Magtulis, suffering in resigned silence from a multiplicity of ills. "He has no health record!" said the doctor indignantly. I left Magtulis in *Blackhawk*'s sick bay and got a receipt for him from the officer of the deck. "He is now your responsibility, sir!" I told the doctor, an elderly three striper. "If this old Filipino hero dies, he does so on your hands." The doctor and I left *Blackhawk* together, he headed for Perth headquarters to complain of my insolence and lack of administrative talent (no health records!) and I to the familiar, friendly surrounding of *Lanikai*. "You have not heard the last of this!" were the doctor's parting words.

Like a long-lost family member, Alcantara hopped aboard soon after our arrival. He had miraculously escaped from the Surabaya hospital aboard Doc Wassell's "last train," thence via a very lucky Dutch ship from Tjilatjap.

From USS *Isabel*, *Lanikai* received for one day's duty several Insular Force Filipinos, to take advantage of *Lanikai*'s special dispensation from Washington to swear our Filipinos into the Naval Reserve. These, of course, were the token five or six Insular Force seamen rushed aboard *Isabel* in early December 1941 to comply with Roosevelt's "suggestion" that for his "three small vessels . . . Filipino crews may [i.e., 'will'] be employed with minimum number naval ratings."

There was painting to be done aboard the only green ship in the Navy. Sails and running rigging needed overhauling. And we most certainly could use some stores. Rope and paint and provisions and tools came aboard by the truckload. Profeta was sent to the newly established supply depot for a flag. "Draw the smallest set of colors they have," he was told. Our only set, flown since commissioning, was in tatters.

Profeta soon returned aboard. "Sor! I haff beeg trouble!" he reported excitedly. "I say I want American flag. The man he say, 'What size? Haff sizes one to nine.' I theenk size one ees small size, so I say geef me size one, plees. Eet ees thees flag he geef me!" Profeta unrolled a U.S. ensign normally flown by a battleship at anchor on Sunday in calm weather. It was almost as big as *Lanikai*'s foresail.

"I try to geef eet back!" wailed Profeta. "Thees man say paper work all done. Can not geef back! Then an officer come to me and he say, 'What the matter weeth you, crazy keed! Stop bothering storekeeper! Don't you hear there ees war going on?'"

There was at least one other who knew there was a war going on and knew USS *Lanikai* had seen something of it—that grand gentleman, Rear Admiral William Purnell, chief of staff, ComSoWesPac. Through him, just as the doctor had warned, I *would* hear more about the Magtulis affair; in short order *Lanikai* received an information copy of his message to the *Blackhawk* which said:

```
...IMMEDIATELY PREPARE MEDICAL RECORDS FOR LANIKAI
PERSONNEL AND PROVIDE ANY REQUIRED SERVICES
```

There were not only curiosity-motivated lieutenants dropping aboard *Lanikai* for a look-see, but more serious higher-ups. One of them, Captain John Creighton, who had made a last-minute escape from his naval observer post at Singapore, was an intelligence professional, now on ComSoWesPac's staff. In 1937, en route China, I had met him in ONI. "Write to me personally," he told me. "If you send anything via official channels it will be cold turkey before it percolates through the

Asiatic Fleet staff, then spends a month aboard ship transpacific. Put it in the Pan-Am clipper airmail."

And so I had done. But unfortunately, one of my reports was sufficiently interesting to elicit a formal commendation from the Chief of Naval Operations, Admiral Leahy, via CinCAF and my own commanding officer. Over CinCAF Admiral Harry Yarnell's signature appeared a short endorsement that he was ". . . pleased to note this evidence of excellent performance of duty." The mild innuendo as to performance of *what* duty, clearly reflected the annoyance of the obviously bypassed Fleet Intelligence Officer. My skipper handed over the letter and shot me as nasty look. "What the hell is *this* all about, young man?" he wanted to know. Then he pushed his swivel chair out and leaned back in it, the mechanism giving forth a grinding squeak. This was a routine he reserved for serious cases. When the skipper heard my explanation, his face broke into a wide grin. "To hell with the Fleet Intelligence Officer!" he said. "He's too confounded full of himself anyway." And that was the end of it; my letters continued to Creighton as before.

The upshot of all this was that Creighton held me in considerable esteem. "What is an experienced intelligence officer like yourself doing in *this* backwash," he said when he came aboard *Lanikai*. "As one of our very few Russian-speaking officers, you belong in the Soviet Union. I'll send a message to Washington right away."

Another distinguished visitor was Vice Admiral Arthur S. Carpender, who had relieved Glassford as ComSoWesPac. Charlie Adair, prouder of *Lanikai* than any father of his firstborn, had chivvied him aboard, eagerly suggesting we be allowed to sail her via South Africa to the United States, with a couple of torpedo tubes mounted to take care of any of the several blockade runners known to be sneaking rubber back to Germany from Singapore, Japanese submarines, or any other heady prey that might blunder into us.

Carpender took one sweeping look at *Lanikai*. "My God!" he cried. "She's no bigger than a motor launch! Africa? Ha! Ha!" But an idea had been germinated.

Adair's access to headquarters' communication files made it evident to him that both American and Australian forces believed there was a good possibility of a Japanese invasion of northwest Australia. Darwin and Broome had been bombed. Families in the area were evacuating to Perth or Brisbane in expectation of enemy landings, or at least a pasting from the air. Certainly there was nothing to stop them. Basic doctrine for *Lanikai* was that unexpected departures for points unknown were routine. Adair's information suggested an early repeat of the past. Aboard *Lanikai,* we hurried to fit her for a sudden departure.

Our foresight paid off. Shortly after Carpender's Fremantle trip, he called Adair into his office. "I have a job for you," he said. "You have had experience in operating a ship close to shore in coral seas. The west coast of Australia is an empty place even in normal times. It is emptier now, with all these people bailing out. It would be easy for Japanese coastwatchers to infiltrate to report on our ship and aircraft patrols. It's also possible that small ground patrols may be operating in that area. I want you to take *Lanikai* and search the coast to Shark Bay." He concluded with the question, "When can you leave?"

Adair, who had kept in close touch with me, was able to give Carpender a one word reply: "Now!"

"No need to sail today," answered the admiral, clearly pleased by Adair's reaction. "Tomorrow will do. Meanwhile, you may be able to think up some additional equipment that might come in handy. Sorry we can't give you any extra men for a landing force. You'll have to use your crew."

There is an old saying that if two Greeks get together, they start a restaurant; if two British naval officers team up, they establish a tennis club; when two American naval officers meet, they set up a watch list. Thus, if Adair, senior to me, were attached to *Lanikai*, he not only would displace me from command, which he was wholly loath to do, but by Navy regulations, one of us would be required to remain aboard ship at all times. With minds like Carpender's and Adair's at work, the problem was instantly resolved: Adair would go as squadron commander; I would retain command. We both would be free to hit the beach arm-in-arm to scout out the enemy, look for suitable emergency aircraft landing strips, or get intelligence briefings at the inevitable pub in the several tiny settlements to be visited during the two thousand mile cruise.

Chapter 19

Since her commissioning on 5 December 1941, *Lanikai* had received just two written communications: the original sealed orders heading her for a possible rendezvous with immortality off Camranh Bay, and the later order to patrol off Corregidor under sail, looking for submarines. Now, she was about to receive a third, the contents of which Adair was fully familiar with, but in best tradition of "sailing under sealed orders," we were not to open until clear of the harbor.

During our fifteen-day Fremantle stay, we had made many friends ashore and afloat. *Lanikai* had been passed from hand to hand, "bumped," so to speak, as each host in turn had to shift position or go to sea. We moored alongside several Australian naval auxiliaries, plus our own *John D. Ford, Heron,* and *Isabel.* Each had supplied our electricity and fresh water. The crew of each had looked down on our decks with a mixture of amusement, interest, and perhaps a little envy at our totally non-Navy existence in a South Sea Islands schooner with New Bedford whaler overtones. Now, ready to sail, we were alongside *Isabel,* with *Lanikai*'s green hull showing not much bigger than a motor launch outlined against the dainty yacht.

There were suspicions in *Isabel* when we requested a topping off of fresh water and diesel tanks and a full ice chest. Then some discerning fellow had seen Adair scrambling aboard with hand luggage. *Isabel*'s skipper, John Payne, called down casually, "Going somewhere?" "We're always going someplace, John," I answered. "Either across the harbor to moor to another mama-san, or in our dreams to South Africa." Then Payne's eyes, ranging our deck, popped wide open. "Saaaay!" Where the hell did you get those Jap helmets?" he said.

In the waist of the ship, Guns Picking was supervising the opening of some crates. Amongst the contents stacked on deck were a dozen and a half bucket-shaped steel helmets. "They're the new model American tin hats, John," I called up. "They sure beat those damn wash basins we copied from the British in World War I. They just arrived at the depot. We got an advance issue."

In the row of crates were two marked in red: DANGER—EX-PLOSIVES. "Where's your baker flag?" John wanted to know, by now clearly with his teeth into something solid. Navy regulations required certain precautions when handling explosives—hoisting aloft the solid red alphabet flag representing B. Fire hoses were supposed to be unreeled and the "smoking lamp out," meaning that smoking was for the time being prohibited.

"Oh! They're just hand grenades, John," I answered off-handedly. "So *that's* what you guys were up to this morning!" John answered tri-umphantly. "I saw your chief back aft showing the Filipinos how to do straight-arm, overhand throws. 'Boy! Have those birds gone *Aussie!'* I said to myself. In town two weeks and trying out for cricket. *Now* I know. Come on! What the hell are you guys up to?"

"Just let's say thanks for the hospitality alongside, John! See you in Tokyo one way or another. We'll be casting off lines in a couple of hours. Forget you saw anything at all."

Lanikai had armed up and slimmed down. "You don't need all that professional talent—three chief petty officers and a first class radio-man," they said at headquarters. I listened with mixed emotions. After 4,000 miles with my Filipinos, I was ready to continue right on around the earth with them alone. But was there something else? Was it really that we once more were not only expendable but that the probabilities pointed in that direction? The heady aroma of high adventure easily overpowered the lurking smell of death the whole project might other-wise have suggested.

As a result of ComSoWesPac's draft of our men, the "minimum number naval ratings" specified by Roosevelt for the original mission was now reduced to three: Guns Picking as "chief of the boat," Steve Kret, machinist's mate second, to spell Crispin Tipay in the engine room, and Doc Cossette to dispense pills, powders, good humor, and well-aimed 30-caliber machine gun bullets. Backing these up were nine Filipinos—the original ten, minus old Bosun Magtulis. Taleon and Alcantara had received radio training as Insular Force seamen. They could stand watch to pick off any messages addressed to *Lanikai*. Only "blind" transmissions could be sent us; we could not send a receipt or a message.

On 3 April 1942, soon after a hearty breakfast of good Australian ham and eggs, *Lanikai* stood out of the harbor on a northerly course "in accordance with ComSoWesPac's operation plan (S) dash 42." If there were any apprehensions on the part of any crew member, there was no outward manifestation. We had no absentees. If there were any hearts left tender and bleeding by the eager maids of Fremantle, none betrayed it. There was no handkerchief-waving from the fantail and all eyes looked ahead.

This tiny initial offensive foray, *Lanikai* and her brass mounted 3-pounder against the Imperial Japanese Navy, was launched at the very nadir of Allied fortunes. By strange coincidence this same day also marked a major Japanese offensive thrust—the opening barrage of the final attack that crushed all resistance on Bataan.

Lanikai surged along under full sail at close to nine knots. A deep green sea tipped by small white caps chopped off sharply at the horizon, whence the cloudless pale blue bowl of the sky reached up over us. Crewmen puttered topside, securing for sea. On this particular piece of ocean, things could change with dramatic suddenness. In such a small microcosm as *Lanikai,* forehandedness was the watchword. Squadron Commander Adair had gotten out his beloved sextant, shot the noon sun and was down in the closet-sized charthouse working out our latitude.

I sat in solitary splendor on the after cabin roof. A few feet abaft and below me, on the poop, Tumbagahan gazed with undivided concentration at the compass, moving the wheel a spoke or two this way or that as the ship yawed in the following sea. A further result of the quartering breeze was that where I sat there was no whiff of cooking aroma drifting aft to give a hint as to what new surprises old Velarmino might be concocting on his sandbox stove. In Fremantle, we had proposed rehabilitating the propane range in the galley. Since Magtulis was no longer on board, Cooky was the ship's patriarch, streaked with gray, older than any of us. When saturnine old Cooky, more loquacious than usual, replied with, "No want gas stove!" that was the way it would be. With village simplicity, ingenuity and age-old native stubbornness toward innovation, he squatted beside his oil drum range, fanning the glowing charcoal.

This was Good Friday. In Shanghai, the little sidewalk flower sellers would in normal times be doing a brisk business for Easter weekend. I could almost smell the fragrance. Just two years ago, we had walked down Canton Road, stopping to buy flowers from a small girl sheltering her few blossoms in a doorway. This was a part of Shanghai that looked far more European than Oriental. No human beasts of burden with their yo-yo poles staggered through those streets. No heavily laden, man-powered two-wheeled carts rumbled by. The few Chinese visible were largely barefoot rickshaw coolies, their sorry rags flapping as they trotted along the smooth asphalt, towing Panama-hatted *taipans* en route club or big business deal.

A few blocks down, the impressive Gothic towers of the English cathedral rose from a carefully tended and well-fenced little park of lovely trees and shrubs. The Settlement police establishment occupied a whole block. On the opposite corner, the mini-skyscraper Robert Dollar Building housed that highly esteemed facility, "NavPur," the Navy Purchasing Office, dispenser of mail, money, courtesy cards for local clubs, and chits for duty-free liquor. They negotiated contracts, arranged pilots, and on occasion even applied their manifold skills in getting some gay young bachelor officer or bewildered navy wife out of a jam ashore. On another corner rose the Hamilton House, in which my ninth floor apartment overlooked the Whangpoo. The mud-green river stretched as far as the eye could see toward the Yangtze, twelve miles downstream, its surface a constantly changing panorama of darting sampans, ragged-sailed junks, and tugs with strings of barges like ducklings following the old hen. An occasional gray warship scattered the small fry as she made her imperious way to special moorings opposite the Shanghai Club. Half a mile downstream, the dark gray bulk of the big old armored cruiser *Idzumo* lay permanently alongside a Hongkew jetty, a grim reminder that the Japanese had come to stay.

Yes, just two years ago, we had walked down those streets, she with a sprig of tiny white blossoms pinned to her jacket and I with a fragrant bouquet in my hand. "I don't know how you call them in English, chéri à moi," she said. "In Paris we always had them at Easter. It was a tradition. We call them 'muguet.' "

This was a sort of Paris too, I thought—sometimes even called "the Paris of the Orient." It had also become the city closest to my heart, for a number of reasons.

"We call them lily-of-the-valley," I translated. And had I been asked to make a wish, it would have been that all other Easters to come be as happy as this one.

Fremantle had been pleasant in a way, but the impersonality of a big port city and the stunned attitude in the remnant of a fleet that had just come reeling south in headlong retreat and defeat made us glad to be out of it and once more on our own. We were a small, tight family in *Lanikai*. Geraldton was a friendly town, a sort of *Lanikai* magnified. It had been the first hand stretched out to us near the end of a voyage that at times seemed about to end in limbo. We looked forward with considerable pleasure to renewing contact with those hearty people.

Even the weather was kind; we bowled along north with a favorable wind at such a rate that in just thirty-five and a half hours, we were once more alongside our familiar grain dock at Geraldton.

"Goin' after 'em, are yer, mite?" one of the welcoming committee wanted to know. These were a far-ranging people. Many had been up the coast to the sheep stations and dusty small towns—little more than a cluster of drab houses—that had sprung up whenever a drop of water trickled out of the ground. We huddled over our charts with these rough-handed, sunburned old men (the young had gone to war) who could supplement our knowledge of the sea with their intimate understanding of the land. And they hated Japs.

"The blighters will bloody well have to tote their water on their backs," said one. "*And* their tucker," added another. They wanted to know how far the 3-pounder could reach. "Gawd! I'd love to have a go at the little barstids! Give 'em a round fer me!" They were intrigued by the strings of numbers on the charts—soundings—the relatively shallow depths of the estuaries and inner reaches of the bays we were to check for evidence of enemy presence, usefulness as seaplane operating bases, or the proximity of open strips of ground usable for emergency landings. Traveling by air, as they all did, none had realized the difficulties a ship drawing nine feet might have in an area of tremendous tidal range, narrow channels, coral heads, widely shelving land, and poor holding ground for the nightly anchoring.

The local harbor pilot, the only nautically oriented member of the "advisory group," warned us to place no confidence in the navigational markers, such as they were shown on the charts. "They're like a bunch of ruddy kangaroos," he said, "here today, another place tomorrow, or gone entirely years ago."

The mention of kangaroos brought forth a burst of laughter all around. When those privy to the joke had got themselves under control again, they regaled us with what Geraldton felt to be prime humor: One of the local ranchers had managed to catch a man-sized kangaroo, outfitted it in a bright red vest and with a sharp crack across the rump, turned it loose up the road toward his neighbor. Ambling along a short while later, he found the results had been more than satisfactory. His friend was dazed and shaken.

"If yer waren't an aold cobber," he declared, "I wouldn't tell yer this, but I'm prepared to swear on the Holy Book that I just saw a big 'roo charge by here diked out in a red vest."

"A likely story," the joker said reprovingly. "Where is he naow? Gettin' fitted fer striped pants an' a claw-hammer coat?" No, he was gone; disappeared over the horizon.

The joker had a simple explanation for this whole phenomenon. "Yer drunk!" he said shortly.

He was not drunk, the other fellow protested, but felt he could use a drop of something strong after what he had just been through. So the two forthwith repaired to the nearest pub. Reaching for his wallet to stand the treat, the joker's face turned white. "Christ!" he muttered. "Me wallet's in that bloody vest!"

Lanikai was back on her old routine—one night stops. In the special case of Geraldton, this was expanded to two nights, so that a full day could be given to gathering information on what might lie ahead, to taking aboard 1,400 gallons of water, and topping off the provision locker and ice box to stave off as long as possible the return to rice and fish.

We were under way at 10:45 A.M., on 6 April, following the coast several miles offshore, carefully searching for any signs or spots which might suggest landing possibilities for our quarry. Via Hero Passage, we entered a little bay five fathoms deep that protected us against a southerly wind and swell. This was "reefy" country all the way; a cock's comb of rugged, broken rock formed a protected anchorage that could shelter a hundred-foot vessel. Man had been here before and left his works, but like so much of the west Australian coastline, presumably had found it too inhospitable to linger.

A sturdy, ten-foot-wide, thirty-foot-long pier excited our imagination; it stopped ten feet short of the shore. Did these pragmatic Aussies carry away the inboard end to balk free loaders? Building the seaward end of a pier first must be something like constructing the top of the chimney first, then working down.

Another visitor had been here much earlier and also had found the place inhospitable, leaving monumental remains as proof. Gomez, who had been ranging the beach for any edible creatures that might be walking, crawling, swimming or burrowing "twix wind and water," came back bearing a piece of evidence, chuckling to his shipmates that he had caught the biggest fish of the cruise. Over his shoulder was a six-foot whale rib.

And was there an Australian Robinson Crusoe about? Or perhaps some infiltrators? Two rowboats were drawn up on the beach well above high-water mark, but nary a footprint nor goatskin-clad gentleman peering out of the scrubby underbrush was seen.

Here also the Geraldton pilot's word of caution about faulty charts brought proof; the big lagoon represented as lying behind the beach, and which should have been choice hunting ground for wild fowl, was nothing but several scattered puddles.

Gaunthame Bay, our next target up the coast, offered no inducement to cross its treacherous protective reef. We passed by with only a binocular search.

On the eighth, *Lanikai's* roller-coaster pitching in a following sea mercifully smoothed out when we entered South Passage, between Dirk Hartog Island and Edel Land, where judging by names, old Abel Tasman and his Dutchmen had preceded us by several centuries. This was the beginning of the proper role of the expedition, in virgin territory where no man lived and few visited. Anything in these parts that moved might be considered fair game. And this included ourselves being misidentified by our own airmen. Daily, Australian aircraft winged by, well out to sea and a thousand feet or so up. If they sighted us at all, they must have been satisfied with our bona-fides. Perhaps it had been

Profeta's enormous American flag, half as long as *Lanikai*. The pilots would spot this brave display and reassure Fremantle that their silent "small ship" was not for the fourth time "overdue and presumed lost."

Here, we all felt at home—anchored in four fathoms of water a hundred yards from shore in water so clear that our Filipinos were immediately leaning over the rail in fascinated inspection of drifting schools of delicious snapper. They were always good broiled or fried, or for one with Japanese tastes, raw and flavored with shredded radish and hot mustard.

The snappers were also good for testing the hand grenades. Unlike those wretched antiques that plagued our beleaguered countrymen on Bataan, these were no duds. They worked. Five seconds after dropping there was a dull thud followed by a geyser of bubbles. Soon, the boys were overside in the skiff, scooping up basketsful of stunned fish. Even the most ardent angler aboard agreed that the instant snapper method beat hook, line and bacon rind routine hands down when wholesale results were the object.

A large, horizontal ice chest on deck was filled with sea water and hooked to a small electric circulating pump. Into this improvised aquarium went the spare fish, where in due course they recovered their equilibrium, equanimity, and their potentiality as fresh protein when we might find ourselves in less fishy surroundings.

Whatever opposition might turn up inside the bay, we determined to be ready for it. Ashore, on a rare flat spot, a range was set up. Colt pistol bullets splapped into man-sized targets painted on boulder faces. With a sound like ripping cloth, Thompson sub-machine guns spat out bursts, making tin cans hop in the sand like alive tortured things. "Not so damn fast! You're walkin' off the target!" Guns Picking shouted. "Just a few at a time, dammit! You wanna try scarin' the enemy to death by shootin' over his head? Hit him! goddammit! Five, six shots at a time!" But that ripping sound was too fascinating. The gun muzzles would climb up as a long burst went out.

This, like many other spots we reconnoitered, was poor holding ground. A thin layer of sand deceptively covered solid rock. With the wind building up and a length of chain ten times the depth of water out to our heaviest anchor—the one normally reserved for typhoons—we could feel the telltale shudder and trembling of the ship's hull that told us she was dragging. At a hundred yards from that sharp-toothed coral shore, it was time to move.

We were now faced with a delicate decision: retrace our track to the open sea, go north, then re-enter Shark Bay from its upper end— or try the extremely tricky South Passage. "Yer takin' yerself a bloody great chance of grounding and nobody to pull yer off an' no great rise and fall of tide to *lift* yer off," the Geraldton pilot had said.

So after leaving the firing range and its poor holding ground we

USS Isabel, *designated specifically by President Roosevelt as one of the "three small vessels" which might be used in carrying out his unprecedented directive, "but not other naval vessels."*

The author in 1973, in Australian Army jacket and beige "horse pants," the uniform he wore to Moscow in 1942, the only thing available in Southwest Australia, which had been swept clean of blue cloth by the survivors of the remnants of the Asiatic Fleet who had arrived earlier.

moved up opposite Cape Ransonnet, Dirk Hartog Island, for two days, awaiting prime conditions and to look things over. This was a bleak land. According to the journal, "The surrounding country is rolling and sandy with a sparse vegetation of shrubs and weeds, mostly dry and brown. There is no water and rain appears to be a rare occurrence. The only signs of human contact are occasional sheep pens where the animals are sheared or kept for shipment during the season for such." Indeed, we thought, if there were any Japanese about they were certainly having no picnic of it.

By midmorning of the eleventh, the wind being weak for the first time in several days, we decided to chance it. Adair climbed out on the bowsprit, like some latter-day figurehead, and as in old times in the Philippines, I shinnied up into the Coca-Cola box crow's nest at the forepeak. We crept forward at half speed under engine alone. The entrance to the channel was four hundred yards wide and five fathoms deep. But as we proceeded, the depth ominously started decreasing. With a glass-smooth sea and the sun astern, I could see the greenish coral bottom and sides, the latter closing in to four hundred yards, then less, then still less. The charted beacons did not in fact exist. Two dark sticks, visible only at close range, that may have been some sort of marker set up by local fishermen, we certainly could not trust. Then, as we passed the inner bar, our ace card was lost; the heretofore transparent water changed to pea soup. At over nine feet, the sounding pole's brightly painted marks dimmed out. And nine feet was *Lanikai*'s draft. Astern, a muddy wake churned up by the propeller told us the bottom was very close underfoot. Then the sounding commenced to drop down: twelve feet, fifteen feet, the end of the pole's reach. Then with the sounding lead—three fathoms, four, five. We were clear. And *Lanikai* was no longer the hunted, but the hunter.

Back in the Philippines, the scale was tipped in quite another way. On 8 April, with the Fil-American forces close to being a rabble, a wholesale scorched earth destruction of military supplies and facilities commenced behind the lines. That night, gallant, fire-blackened, bomb-scarred old *Canopus* backed out into deep water, under her own power to the last, and was scuttled. Throughout the seige, her contributions had been manifold and heavy—repairing vehicles and boats, manufacturing gun mounts, providing a few moments of cleanliness and a ration of ice cream to many a dust-caked, red-eyed Army nurse and itinerant fighter. The drydock *Dewey*, which had faithfully docked the Asiatic Fleet's ships for near two generations, had lain all but submerged for months in a far corner of Mariveles Bay. Perhaps the sharp Japanese eyes had missed her. Or perhaps they were hoping to save her for themselves. If so, it didn't work; half a dozen 155-mm. shells wired as bombs took out her bottom. Tug *Napa* and immobile minesweeper *Bittern*, her vitals left at Cavite, were sent down too. As background, the entire southern end of Bataan took on the appearance of some gigantic Fourth of July celebration. Rumbling, earthquakelike explosions shook the peninsula as ammunition and fuel dumps rocketed skyward in super-colossal, rocketing sheets of orange flame.

On 9 April, without authorization—in fact, against the express orders of General Wainwright, Major General Edward P. King, senior Bataan commander on the ground, came to the agonizing decision that he had wrestled with for the previous twenty-four hours as he saw his front dissolving in chaos. With the greatest personal courage and sense of responsibility, he literally fought his way forward through the streams of retreating Fil-Americans, onto no man's land, where he was strafed by Japanese planes and threatened by blood-lusting enemy troops, disappointed that the white flag he carried thwarted their inclination to run him through on the spot. At 12:30 P.M., General King laid his pistol on the conference table before Colonel Nakayama, 14th Army operations officer, as a symbol of the unconditional surrender of the 78,000 Allied troops on Bataan.

George Pollak, who had considerable time to philosophize on these events while a prisoner of war of the Japanese for three and a half years, furnished some basic thoughts on the matter in an October 1971 letter to me:

> January and February at Mariveles were still relatively civilized. We had Army cots to sleep on in the open, the dry season was on and the mosquitoes weren't too bad. There was enough food, and all sorts of amenities still to be found. We thought things were rough, but we were far from realizing what was in store for us.
>
> The concept of being encircled, of no retreat, engenders a special state of mind. It brings things down to stark reality, and, as a doctor later told me, probably was the reason for the low level of psychological breakdowns that occurred. Subconsciously, one realizes that there is no escape via this route.
>
> I have often pondered the question how one tries to get the entire atmosphere of such a situation as Bataan across to someone in words. The experience itself included so many people, so many events, sights, sounds, and sensations. One can describe a great many of them, but the problem is to get across the *aggregate* impression. In this case—as well as the latter phases of our experience—it is something entirely remote from normal frames of reference. It is like nothing the average person has ever seen or heard. It was, in fact, such a distorted life that when one tries to describe it, the results frequently sound like imaginative fabrications or ludicrous lies. People simply won't believe that such things can happen, or that human beings can behave that way.

On 9 April 1942, the mood aboard *Lanikai* was neither surrender nor even pessimism. We were no longer retreating, praise God, but were beginning the long march back—we were heading north! And what's more, we were the first U.S. Navy surface ship to do so. The journal reflected this belligerent mood: "The crew has been exercised in the use of the Thompson sub-machine gun and automatic pistol, a good range having been available ashore." Even nature was kind: "Large quantities of fish have been caught by the ship's company, much more than can be eaten at once, and measures are being taken to dry a supply for future use." We had plenty of food, and we were learning how to shoot. We would show those Japanese bastards a thing or two, even if nobody else seemed to be trying.

We continued to work our way northward, up the middle of the bay. Brown's Station, on Dirk Hartog Island, harbored neither friend nor enemy. Its staring windows, in rough brown board shacks, looked empty and ghostly, like lidless eyes. We inched on, sounding and probing in water so laden with windblown silt that it was opaque at anything over a few feet.

In the Yangtze, there was a constant peril of silt piling up on a dropped anchor, so that when the inexperienced skipper decided to up anchor and get under way once more, he would discover the river bottom had so built up that his windlass could not break out the deeply buried hook. Here, we had a sort of mirror image; accumulated scale on the windlass shaft had so built up that it prevented free running of the wildcat and we couldn't get the damned anchor *down*. Thus, we were robbed of the pleasure of a personal visit to Brown's something less than attractive Station. By the time we got the wildcat running freely again, we were in Herald Bay, off Quoin Bluff, a good place to spend the night.

Here again, the bottom was so gradually shelving as it approached the shore that we gave up the idea of exploring the brilliant, deep red, 50-foot-high bluffs. The food and water situation must have been more than desperate ashore, as we were surprised to discover that large numbers of flies had managed to find their way out to the ship, anchored at least 600 yards offshore. They must have ridden out on the beam provided by the aroma wafting shoreward from Cooky's steaming goodies.

After rounding Cape Peron, we turned northeasterly into a most aptly named "Hopeless Reach" to Faure Island. So shelving was the approach that we anchored half a mile off, and Adair and I with a small party had to tie the skiff to an awash mangrove bush several hundred yards from land. We waded carefully ashore through water churning with life. Four-foot sharks cruised about in dozens in the shallows. One picked one's way with care; lying flat as boards, almost invisible on the bottom, big skates were basking. Probing ahead with oar or boat hook stirred these nasty creatures into a sluggish wiggling off, lessening the danger of our stepping on or being slashed by the four-inch venomous spike that protruded upward midway along their tails.

We had no sooner weathered this Scylla when Charybdis hit us; as we pushed our way through the scrub, we were assailed by such myriads of flies that only the experience could make one believe that such a thing could be possible. With ravenous avidity they crawled into ears, nostrils, and eyes, and any open mouth. Bare skin was literally black with flies, as others swarmed around, fighting for landing rights.

We beat a hasty retreat, the flies following, as we ran splashing out to the skiff, sharks and skates forgotten. "The damn things will follow us out to the ship!" someone shouted. We stopped short of the boat and beat the water with our oars and boathooks to wash each other free of our tormentors. Even so, it was a week before the last of them that swarmed out with us had been hunted down. This was a phenomenon the like of which none of us had ever seen before. God help any landing party here, friend or foe!

There was no point in further exploration of this insectiverous hell where no man or beast could survive such assailants. We turned north toward what we had been told was the metropolis of Shark Bay.

The little town of Carnarvon might have been transplanted from the scene of a typical "horse opera" of our American nineteenth century wild west, the variation being Carnarvon's close proximity to an arm of the sea. But the sea came here reluctantly—its approach was so shelving that it required a 500-yard-long jetty to reach 18 feet of open, wholly unprotected water.

Any small boy would have been enthralled by the Lilliputian steam locomotive with its string of equally diminutive cars that traveled the jetty on tiny rails. There was enough small boy in all of us to hugely enjoy the breezy, swaying ride "ashore" aboard the rattling, gas-driven scooter.

Carnarvon was down to iron rations, there being scarcely enough provisions to spare for a day or two's fresh food for our fourteen, over and above the requirements of the six hundred townspeople. There were several hardware and grocery stores, but not so much as a filling station, auto repairman or itinerant tinker. And as elsewhere in Australia, these generous people were happy to share with their new allies what poor facilities the war and isolation had left them. "You can call Perth on the telephone," they told us proudly, as if Alexander Bell had just invented the device and installed the first instrument here.

In the social gathering place, the inevitable pub, it was clear that the agents of my remote relatives, the Australian Tolleys, had penetrated these parts. Beans and spinach and catsup and flour might be in short supply, but no bloody fear about the products of Tolley, Scott & Tolley, Distillers, of Adelaide. The bleached deserts of northwest Australia produced many a parched throat, and the Tolleys were not the kind to let them down. That this solicitude was appreciated clearly showed in the interest that spilled over on the American cousin. "Step up an hahve one! A Tolley's Best for Skipper Tolley," they boomed around the bar. "Nah!

yer's money's no good hyar, lad! Yair Carnarvon's honored guest. Fancy! A bloody warship at Carnarvon!" And as to what we could do to our new common enemy, Japan and the Japanese, the language was picturesque, unprintable and highly descriptive.

During the first night, the surge of the swell where we lay alongside the pier almost in the open sea was most trying on mooring gear, fenders, and those hoping to catch some sleep. A heavy ringbolt tore out of the port quarter bulwark, the first damage of any kind the old girl had suffered at our hands in thousands of miles of often hazardous navigating.

The pipe that ran out to the end of the pier filled our almost empty water tanks and once more we were on the move, hunting for suitable seaplane basing areas, Japanese, will-o'-the-wisps, or whatever else the vast, empty bay might offer. We anchored that night, 19 April, halfway between Wedge Point and Koks Island, in a wholly unpromising and unprotected spot. Our apprehensions were justified: "About 0100, indications of dragging anchor. A shift of the wind to southeast causing considerable chop and swell. The breakers to westward sounding closer by the minute and very ominous. Got underway and stood to southward along coast of Bernier Island."

With a stiff wind approaching gale force, in poorly charted territory devoid of any navigational lights, studded with reefs and shallows, the low coastline without easily identifiable characteristics, nighttime cruising was not exactly something to be relished. We watched the dawn break with more than usual relief.

Our friendly old pirate-adventurer-explorer of the past two centuries was recalled again—by sunrise, Dampier Reef lay close aboard on the port hand; over it the seas were ". . . breaking heavily at intervals of about two minutes." It was a good one to have missed in the dark.

We might be forgiven for anchoring early, shortly after lunch. It had been a hard night. In any case, we had come to Turtle Bay. In view of the accurately described features on the chart so far: Hopeless Reach, Dead End, etcetera, perhaps this one meant that turtles actually were about. Ever since our first Australian landfall over a month before at Montebello Island, we had remembered those turtle tracks in the sand. What did a turtle egg taste like? How about some turtle soup, the fare of gourmets? My epicurean grandfather used to regale me with tales of Maryland diamondbacks, and that every kind of meat is represented in these primeval monsters: beef, chicken, pork, and so forth. In Turtle Bay, perhaps we would be able to check the old gentleman's theory.

There were other items of interest besides potential turtles. From where we lay, 600 yards off the beach, we could make out another of those half-ruined establishments that rimmed this desolate bay. On a ramp, a narrow gauge railway toiled up the slope from a dilapidated pier. Where did it go? Why? We approached the beach with interest, but from the ship the surf had looked far less treacherous than we found it close aboard.

Alas! Turtle Bay was a sad disappointment. We could not land through the surf. There were no Japanese on whom to at last test our much rehearsed technique. Worse yet, "No turtles have put in an appearance and the fishing is poor." After lunch, and a profitless overnight stay, we headed southeast in smooth seas and light airs, and by 6:35, were anchored once more in Herald Bay.

On the twenty-first, we again steered southeast, checked our position with Bay Flats Outer Light, the first navigational buoy so far sighted, and entered Denham channel. "Outer Flats" was an accurate suggestion of what might lie farther in—naturally enough, Inner Flats—an area of tidal marshes, shallows, and bars over which ran currents that beset *Lanikai* this way and that in our effort to keep her clear of the treacherous bottom. Was it worth it to visit the little settlement of Denham? *Lanikai's* journal describes it:

> The inhabitants are almost wholly engaged in either pearling or fishing. There is a small cold storage plant, ice plant and a large grocery store. A small hotel and a pub take care of visiting fishermen, pearl buyers and stockmen from the sheep ranches inland. Ships anchor at the buoy offshore and lighter goods out and back. A telephone connects with the south and there is a post office and bank. No supplies available other than ice, fish and mutton.

We were fascinated by this life well over the edge of nowhere. The oysters from which the pearls came were huge rough things the size of a luncheon plate. Inside, the lustrous, pearly-pink nacre glowed softly with iridescent, translucent beauty. From it would come the real profit in pearling: material for button-making. In stinking, upended open barrels the oyster meat sat in the warm sun, while the pearls contained therein sank to the bottom of the liquid in which the rotting mass floated. Cultured pearls from Japan had killed the former high profits in the business, where latter-day pirates had flourished and pearl beds were guarded against poachers by no-nonsense riflemen. Another sad blow had been the demise of the Russian Empire and, as the twentieth century wore on, the decline in fortunes of the Indian princes. It once was that the occasional monster pearl recovered from the barrels could be sold for a fabulous sum—perhaps a quarter of a million dollars. Now, no market existed for such rarities that formerly would have been snatched up to grace the throat of a Russian grand duchess, or an Indian maharajah's turban.

As for ourselves, we had stumbled on riches of a sort which one might say were a dividend of the pearl industry: "Pearling and fishing luggers from Denham range the entire bay, and their store of knowledge covers every aspect of the region." From these horny-handed, rough, profane, kindly fountains of bay lore, we filled our dossiers for the edification of ComSoWesPac, or more accurately, Commander U.S. Naval Forces Southwest Australia, which had become the slightly more appropriate title for the boss of a no longer existent fleet.

This was the beginning of the end of the *Cruise of the Lanikai*. We started retracing our track from Denham's rough and ready, romantic atmosphere of another age, a strange mix of pearls, fish, and sheep, with a smoky, crude, back country pub crowded with roistering, sometimes bawdy, always kind Australian cobbers. We had found no infiltrating enemy. There was none. He was busy elsewhere, consolidating his new empire of 300,000,000 unwilling subjects who once had been American, British, and Dutch. Perhaps our negative search had not been without value. We had gathered some useful information. In miniature, we had carried out our first amphibious operation of World War II—in actual fact, the first *offensive* move made by any Far East American surface warship since the disastrous rout of the Asiatic fleet from the seas.[30]

Captain Creighton had been true to his word; on 24 April, *Lanikai's* radio watch on Perth's broadcast schedule intercepted a transmission that for me would bring the *Lanikai* idyll to a close:

LANIKAI PROCEED IMMEDIATELY TO GERALDTON X LIEUT COMDR KEMP TOLLEY RELIEVED COMMA ORDERED AMEMBASSY

MOSCOW USSR AS ASSISTANT NAVAL ATTACHE AND ASSISTANT NAVAL ATTACHE FOR AIR X LIEUT COMDR CHARLES ADAIR

ASSUME COMMAND X PLANE WILL ARRIVE GERALDTON 27 APRIL TRANSPORT TOLLEY TO FREMANTLE

With a powerful thrust from a northeaster, *Lanikai* pressed southward toward Geraldton at close to eleven knots, the highest so far logged. Shortly after noon on the twenty-seventh, she once more came alongside the grain pier.

"A Navy plane is waiting at the airfield for your skipper!" someone called from the dock as we sent our mooring lines ashore. "They want to take off as soon as possible. We have a car ready to take him out."

There were no speeches, commission pennant presentations or stirring marches by the band. A handshake with Adair and a farewell wave to our little family lining the rail marked the turnover of command. I dared not look back. The memories and associations were far too poignant for an ordinary man to have sustained except by facing ahead, shutting out any last lingering sight of what would be one of the great romantic attachments of a lifetime.

Chapter 20

By the time the *Lanikai* reached Australia early in 1942, a swarm of refugees had arrived ahead of us. Like us, they had seen their proper uniforms go up in smoke or down with a ship, and so were generally reduced to a pair of ragged pants. And by the time the tailors in Western Australia had fitted everyone out in new blues, there was no more blue cloth left for the latecomers. Admiral Glassford ended up with a dress uniform of RAAF sky blue. What I got, on short notice, was an Australian Army jacket of dark khaki, beige "horse pants" with suede-lined knees, and a pair of brown kangaroo riding boots, topped off with a new-style helmet liner.

So attired, I sailed from Albany aboard the old tanker *Trinity*, en route to Basra, Iraq, and after a 30-day journey, arrived in the provisional Soviet capital of Knibyshev to take up my new duties. There I was met by the naval attaché, Captain Jack H. Duncan, who took one look at my outfit and gasped, "*What* the *hell* are *you?*" That was hardly the time for me to reply, "Captain, it's a long story."

It *was* a long story. The cruise of the *Lanikai* lasted not quite five months, but I have spent nearly thirty years following her uncharted path through dusty documents in the archives, trying to find out what happened, and why.

Curiosity was aroused soon after my arrival in Russia, where for a year I was a messmate of the U.S. ambassador, Admiral William H. Standley. Shortly following Pearl Harbor, he had been in Washington as a member of the Roberts Commission, trying to determine who bore the blame for the disaster.

His subtle questioning and suggestions soon reinforced suspicions on my part that had originated some months before—at the final meeting in Manila with Commander Slocum, when he turned the command of

Lanikai over to me. When I had mentioned *Lanikai's* limited water supply, he had replied, "You have a set of international signal flags, don't you? If you run short, ask a passing Japanese warship for some."

Naïve though I might then have been, there was a note of cynicism in Slocum's remark that since has been reinforced by the record. Years later, Slocum wrote:

> I feel sure you realize that by the time you were ready to sail that almost all of us understood that time had run out and that whatever "FDR had in mind" could in all probability never be realized. I suspect my briefing reflected that.[31]

The briefing had been based on a message that could have aroused wonder in any professional naval officer, as it had in Admiral Hart himself. Concerning that message, Admiral Hart wrote Director of Naval History Rear Admiral John Heffernan:

> It was a definite and flat order, so worded as to bear the highest priority. We received it with consternation. Carrying out the order consumed effort we could ill spare from more valuable objectives. As a war measure the project was very ill-advised. Pickets in such locations could not be useful because the Japanese were bound to have them marked down—the order was to place them close to the Indo-China coast—which would mean no chance to let them see anything of value. Therefore, to no commensurate end, we were to risk ships and valuable personnel.[32]

Had I known the contents of the message at that time, the one-way character of my impending cruise would have struck me as doubly likely.

Hart was dumbfounded at presidential intervention in what on the surface qualified only as a very minor tactical matter. Admiral Harold R. Stark, Chief of Naval Operations, was unable to enlighten Hart on the discussion which had brought the move about. But he made clear in the message ". . . report measures taken to carry out President's views. At same time inform me . . ." that he was purely a middleman.

By late 1941, Hart knew there was no dearth of information in Washington on the Japanese movements; it was such information that had brought Roosevelt hurrying back to Washington on 1 December 1941. Thirty years later, describing his efforts to obtain information on the Japanese, Admiral Hart wrote:

> During the latter part of November 1941, I received a rumor from Hongkong . . . to the effect that a large number of Japanese ships was in Camranh Bay. I decided that it was up to me to investigate and that I should assume all responsibility for measures taken, *personally*, and not ask Washington anything. I went ahead thus, on my own as much as possible and not involving even my own staff.
>
> The situation most clearly required air observation because high land makes examination from ships both difficult and slow. My command included "Catalinas", planes well suited for the job and

NAVAL MESSAGE OP-38-R—   NAVY DEPARTMENT

PHONE EXTENSION NUMBER 2042	ADDRESSEES	MESSAGE PRECEDENCE

FROM   OPNAV

RELEASED BY

DATE   1 December 1941

CINCAF

	PRIORITY X
	ROUTINE
	DEFERRED

TOR CODEROOM

DECODED BY

PARAPHRASED BY

	PRIORITY
	ROUTINE
	DEFERRED

INDICATE BY ASTERISK ADDRESSEES FOR WHICH MAIL DELIVERY IS SATISFACTORY

012356   CR0313

UNLESS OTHERWISE DESIGNATED THIS DISPATCH WILL BE TRANSMITTED WITH DEFERRED PRECEDENCE.
ORIGINATOR FILL IN DATE AND TIME FOR DEFERRED AND MAIL DELIVERY

VKBGX   DATE   TIME   GCT

TEXT

     PRESIDENT DIRECTS THAT THE FOLLOWING BE DONE AS SOON AS POSSIBLE AND WITHIN TWO DAYS IF POSSIBLE AFTER RECEIPT THIS DESPATCH X CHARTER THREE SMALL VESSELS

TO FORM A QUOTE DEFENSIVE INFORMATION PATROL UNQUOTE X MINIMUM REQUIREMENTS TO ESTABLISH IDENTITY AS UNITED STATES MEN-OF-WAR ARE COMMAND BY A NAVAL OFFICER

AND TO MOUNT A SMALL GUN AND ONE MACHINE GUN WOULD SUFFICE X FILIPINO CREWS MAY BE EMPLOYED WITH MINIMUM NAVAL RATINGS TO ACCOMPLISH PURPOSE WHICH IS TO OBSERVE

AND REPORT BY RADIO JAPANESE MOVEMENTS IN WEST CHINA SEA AND GULF OF SIAM X ONE VESSEL TO BE STATIONED BETWEEN HAINAN AND HUE ONE VESSEL OFF THE INDO-CHINA COAST

BETWEEN CAMRANH BAY AND CAPE ST.JAQUES AND ONE VESSEL OFF POINTE DE CAMAU X USE OF ISABEL AUTHORIZED BY PRESIDENT AS ONE OF THE THREE BUT NOT OTHER NAVAL VESSELS X

REPORT MEASURES TAKEN TO CARRY OUT PRESIDENTS VIEWS X AT SAME TIME INFORM ME AS TO WHAT RECONNAISSANCE MEASURES ARE BEING REGULARLY PERFORMED AT SEA BY BOTH ARMY

AND NAVY WHETHER BY AIR SURFACE VESSELS OR SUBMARINES AND YOUR OPINION AS TO THE EFFECTIVENESS OF THESE LATTER MEASURES X

TOP SECRET

SECRET

SEE ART 76(4)
NAV REGS

MAKE ORIGINAL ONLY, DELIVER TO COMMUNICATION WATCH OFFICER IN PERSON

President Roosevelt's "three small vessels" message.

they were very well officered. I orally ordered Wagner, my air commander, to set aside some planes for my personal orders, choosing his best, and particularly his wisest pilots.

I briefed the first one of them that evening, only the two of us together, and told him not to talk, then or after he returned; he was to report to me personally. His orders were to take off before day-break the following morning, proceed toward Camranh and see what was in that Bay. BUT—that it was important that he not be seen. To that end he was to use the cloud cover which at that time in the year was fairly plentiful. The pilot was told that if luck was bad and that if he could not see into the Bay without considerable risk of being seen, he was to give it up. Such, more or less, were the briefings of my pilots on all the flights made in the venture; all the pilots used—about four—did very well indeed.

The observations made by the first two flights, added together, gave me a very good summary of the ships in the Bay. I think 25 November was the date of my first report made to the Navy Department. I wrote it myself. It gave the number of ships in Camranh, with their classifications and also said that planes were in the air over the Bay for at least a part of the time. The first report was followed by supplemental ones as additional flights gained more information—but not much of it. I continued the flights often enough to keep a fairly good watch on that Japanese expedition. My despatches giving Washington the information gained did not report how I had obtained it.

The pilots reported to me their belief that they had occasionally been seen by the Japanese. Certainly on one flight two or more of the planes over the harbor headed toward our Catalina. The pilot at once headed eastward, got into good cloud cover, and nothing happened.[33]

Not only was Hart keeping Washington informed on Japanese movements; Stark and Roosevelt both well knew that Hart was conducting such reconnaissance and it was effective, because *Stark had ordered it and the reports were coming in.*

On 30 November 1941, Assistant CNO Rear Admiral Royal Ingersoll prepared in his own hand* a message to Hart to do precisely what he already had been doing surreptitiously on his own. At the top of the paper was scrawled, "Read to the President and he approved." It also carried the endorsement, "OK, HR Stark."

> INDICATIONS THAT JAPAN ABOUT TO ATTACK POINTS ON KRA ISTHMUS BY OVERSEAS EXPEDITION. IN ORDER TO AS-
> CERTAIN DESTINATION THIS EXPEDITION AND FOR SE-CURITY OUR POSITION IN THE PHILIPPINES DESIRE YOU
> COVER BY AIR THE LINE MANILA CAMRANH BAY ON THREE DAYS COMMENCING UPON RECEIPT THIS DESPATCH. INSTRUCT
> PLANES TO OBSERVE ONLY. THEY MUST NOT APPROACH SO AS TO APPEAR TO BE ATTACKING BUT MUST DEFEND THEMSELVES
> IF ATTACKED. UNDERSTAND BRITISH AIR FORCES WILL SEARCH ARC 180 MILES FROM TEDTA BHARU AND WILL MOVE
> TROOPS TO LINE ACROSS KRA ISTHMUS NEAR SINGORA IF EXPEDITION APPROACHES THAILAND. INFORM MACARTHUR....

At least three reports from Hart, made as a result of the foregoing directive, are in the Naval Archives. Two, dated 2 December 1941, report

* See Appendix.

Wartime enmities long forgotten, Admiral Tolley plants trees at Yokosuka, Japan, in a ceremony in honor of Secretary of the Navy John B. Connally, Fleet Admiral C. W. Nimitz, and Admiral Arleigh Burke, Chief of Naval Operations.

nine submarines about 50 miles off the Indo-China coast just north of Camranh Bay, headed south, and three more 180 miles east of Saigon. Additionally, 21 transports were reported anchored in Camranh Bay, with six planes patrolling overhead.

On 1 December, Rear Admiral Leigh Noyes, Director of Naval Communications, drawing on information obtained by breaking Japanese codes, reported to Hart and Kimmel, with information copies to the 14th Naval District (Hawaii) and 16th Naval District (Philippines) that a Japanese-Thai conference was in progress at Bangkok, planning a Japanese attack on Kota Bharu, as well as joint military action with Japan. On 3 December, Noyes sent another, reporting that Tokyo had ordered Japanese diplomatic establishments to destroy their code machines. *But the Japanese Embassy in Washington was to retain one machine.* Did that mean that the United States was not to be immediately attacked?

On 6 December, the information from Noyes on the Japanese-Thai action was confirmed by another intelligence report from Hart—the British had sighted two large groups of ships south of Cambodia Point (Pointe de Camau) headed straight west for Malaya. At the same time, Asiatic Fleet air scouts had spotted 30 ships and one large cruiser in Camranh Bay.

These reports from the Americans and British, and other reports from Indo-China and Shanghai, plus the "Purple" intercepts gave Roosevelt the almost exact composition of Japanese task forces that with absolute certainty would attack British Malaya. But what about their plans for an attack on the United States and the Philippines? Slightly delayed? Much delayed? A simultaneous one? *Or was the U.S. already at war?* On that same day, 6 December, the President had told Budget Director Harold Smith that "We might be at war with Japan, although no one knew."[34] Could he have been anticipating that the next batch of messages would bring the word that a United States warship (the *Isabel?* the *Lanikai?*) had been treacherously and wantonly sunk?

A fascinating speculative point in FDR's message is the reason for his: USE OF ISABEL AUTHORIZED BY PRESIDENT AS ONE OF THE THREE *BUT NOT OTHER NAVAL VESSELS.* [Emphasis supplied.] Was he counting on a sinking and thus unwilling to risk a more valuable ship? Or did he want the "bait" to *look unlike a warship* and so more apt to wantonly be ridden over by the truculent Japanese?

Isabel was the Commander in Chief's "holiday" flagship, a trim little 900-ton vessel converted during World War I from private yacht to miniature destroyer by mounting two torpedo tubes and four small 3-inch guns. The tubes were long since gone. Age had reduced her once 26-knot top speed to about fifteen. With her inconspicuous battery, white hull, and buff deckhouse and twin stacks, she looked to all but the experts to be a typical small merchantman such as used the China coast, as Navy buff Roosevelt could plainly see in the copy of *Jane's Fighting Ships* he kept handy.

Isabel was in such poor materiel condition through advanced age and long tropic use and was of such low military value in general that although rating a lieutenant commander skipper, officers of that rank did not consider her a command worth seeking. One nominee had confirmed this view by taking a preliminary inspection walk, then proceeding to his cabin, where he shot himself. Consequently, at the moment, she was commanded by a junior lieutenant, John Walker Payne, Jr.

Commanding the CinC's yacht, Payne was of course on far closer terms with Admiral Hart than was I, a total stranger. Thus, it was he who briefed Payne, who later wrote:

> On 3 December, I was called to the office of Admiral Hart in Manila and told by him that the *Isabel* was ordered to proceed on a special reconnaissance mission off the coast of Indo-China. A large concentration of Japanese transports was known to be anchored in Camranh Bay. Utmost secrecy was to be observed, actual orders were to be given verbally, memorized and recited to the Admiral. No one was to know the actual mission of the *Isabel* except the Admiral and myself until we were at sea, then the executive officer was to be taken into confidence. A fake operational despatch, CINCAF 030526, was transmitted, ordering *Isabel* to search from Manila, west to the vicinity of the Indo-China coast for a lost Navy PBY plane. The ship was provisioned and fueled to capacity at Cavite. All removable topside weights including motor boats and gangway were cleared from the ship. All confidential material was turned in to the Navy Yard, Cavite, except one prearranged cipher. One additional pulling whaleboat and additional life rafts were taken on board. Additional orders from the Admiral were to fight the ship as necessary and to destroy it rather than let it fall into enemy hands. The ship was to remain white. At night running lights were to be dimmed to give the appearance of a fishing craft. The Indo-China coast was to be approached only under cover of darkness; all movements of Japanese ships to be reported several hours after sighting in the code we held.[35]

Isabel left Manila on 3 December, en route the point close to the entrance of Camranh Bay specified by the President. On that date, Admiral Hart's efficient patrol plane reconnaissance had revealed fifty ships, including destroyers and cruisers, anchored in the bay.

Isabel's cruise was short. At 7:00 A.M. on the fifth, a Japanese Navy plane was sighted. "It circled at an altitude of 1,000 feet, range 2,000 yards, and took pictures," wrote Payne. "We took pictures of him, too. This plane continued to reappear throughout the day. At 1900 [7:00 P.M.] sighted Indo-China coast 22 miles distant. 1910 received message from CINCAF directing us to return to Manila immediately."[36] *Isabel* reversed course and headed home.

The next day, just before noon, a twin-motored Japanese bomber hung on their quarter on a parallel course for some time. At 5:35 A.M. 8 December, the little ship entered Manila Bay, just a few hours after the bombs had started to flail down on Pearl Harbor. It had been a narrow squeak, affirmed by Admiral Hart when next he met Payne: "Well! I didn't expect to see *you* again!"

The Japanese had sniffed around, but cagily refused to take the bait, not being about to tip the hand that held the imperial flush momentarily to be laid on the table at Pearl Harbor. As far as *Isabel* was concerned, Roosevelt's dramatic bid for a *casus belli* had failed.

Perhaps *Lanikai* could still turn the trick! It was unlikely that news of her five-minute christening ceremony had reached Tokyo's ears. She looked about as much like a warship as the *Mayflower* looked like the *Queen Mary*. But she *was* a warship. She had the "minimum requirements . . . commanded by a naval officer . . . a small gun and one machine gun . . ." Unable to transmit, she would be there today, gone tomorrow in the eyes of our patrol seaplanes. One could almost see the shrieking black headlines: "JAPS MAKE DASTARDLY UNPROVOKED ATTACK ON US WARSHIP. ALL HANDS LOST. ANOTHER USS *PANAY!!!*" Public apathy after the Atlantic destroyer incidents, including the *Reuben James* sinking, suggested that perhaps there would be no angry crowds swarming in Times Square demanding war. *But it would give Roosevelt ample justification for immediately entering the Far East war in aid of the British and Dutch!*

And what about the Philippines? Roosevelt was deeply worried about what their attitude would be if Japan attacked the United States without a concurrent attack on them, or if the United States went to Britain's aid, as Roosevelt was morally bound to do by supersecret Rainbow 5, *even though Britain fired the first shot.*

Active, enthusiastic Philippine participation was vital, to provide a base on Japan's lengthy flank. So on 26 November, the President sent a message to U.S. High Commissioner Francis B. Sayre to consult President Quezon "in great confidence" to try to determine if the Philippines would support the United States in the obviously impending war. In the President's message setting up the "three small vessels," there was a clause which just might help Quezon and his possibly reluctant countrymen make up their minds: "FILIPINO CREWS MAY [i.e., will] BE EMPLOYED WITH MINIMUM NUMBER NAVAL RATINGS [i.e., *some* Filipinos but not all]." *Isabel* had no Filipinos aboard; her stewards were Chinese. So before her hurried departure she had been ordered to take a token number, about five, Filipinos from the Insular Force, even though she already had her normal and adequate complement. Yes, there might be big black headlines in the *Manila Herald* too: "FILIPINO SAILORS DIE IN HEROIC FIGHT AGAINST GREAT ODDS. TREACHEROUS JAPANESE ATTACK." Hopefully, crowds would swarm in front of Malacañang Palace demanding war on Japan.

On the distant horizon floated the ghosts of the USS *Maine* and the USS *Panay*.* Would they soon have company in the form of *Lanikai?*

In reply to Stark's postscript to the President's message as to how he was getting his information, Hart replied thirteen and a half hours later with an evaluation:

```
     URDIS 012356; MY VIEWS ARE AS FOLLOWS: THE JAP
MOVEMENT DOWN THE INDO-CHINESE COAST IS ALREADY DE-
FINED BUT IT REMAINS TO BE SEEN WHETHER AIMED AGAINST
THE MALAY PENINSULA, BORNEO, OR BOTH. THAT THE BRIT-
ISH CAN MEET THEIR COMMITMENTS TO GUARD AS FAR AS
CAPE PADARAN AND WE SHOULD USE WHAT WE HAVE LEFT
AFTER GUARDING AGAINST DESCENT ON LUZON IN WATCHING
FOR ONE ON BORNEO. AM RECALLING ISABEL FROM CURRENT
MISSION AND SENDING TOWARD PADARAN. SHE IS TOO SHORT
RADIUS TO ACCOMPLISH MUCH AND SINCE WE HAVE FEW FAST
SHIPS HER LOSS WOULD BE SERIOUS. THEREFORE HAVE TO
RECOMMEND AGAINST CARRYING OUT ISABEL'S MOVEMENT
THOUGH IT IS IMPROBABLE THAT CAN START ANY CHARTERED
CRAFT WITHIN TWO DAYS. AM SEARCHING FOR VESSELS FOR
CHARTER THAT ARE SUITABLE BUT CANNOT YET ESTIMATE
TIME REQUIRED TO OBTAIN AND EQUIP WITH RADIO. ARMY
PLANES ARE RECONNOITERING SECTOR NORTHERLY FROM
LUZON AND EASTWARD FROM SAN BERNARDINO. NAVY PLANES
NORTHWESTERLY FROM LUZON. ALSO COVERING BALABAC
STRAIT AND JOINING UP WITH DUTCH TO COVER MINDANAO-
HALMAHERA LINE. EFFECTIVENESS IS PROBLEMATICAL BUT AS
GREAT EFFORT AS AVAILABLE FORCES CAN SUSTAIN CONTINU-
OUSLY. TWO CRUISERS TWO DESDIVS ARE DEPLOYED WELL
SOUTH, REMAINDER SURFACE FORCES ON LOCAL MISSIONS OR
REPAIRING. HAVE FIVE SUBMARINES OUT NOW, REMAINDER
EITHER PLACED IN READINESS FOR DEFENSIVE MISSIONS OR
HELD HERE PREPARED FOR OFFENSIVE TASKS. WHEN IT IS
CONSIDERED CALLED FOR WILL INCREASE AIR PATROLS AND
SEND OUT MORE SUBS.
```

With the Pearl Harbor attack just ten hours away, Hart sent Washington a secret† priority amplification:

```
     HAVE OBTAINED TWO VESSELS. ONE NOW ENROUTE INDO-
CHINA COAST. SECOND ONE SAILING SOON AS READY. AM
CERTAIN SHOULD NOT OPERATE THEM SOUTH OF PADARAN.
ISABEL RETURNING WAS SPOTTED AND IDENTIFIED WELL OFF
COAST HENCE POTENTIAL UTILITY OF HER MISSION PROBLE-
MATICAL. HAVE NOT YET FOUND THIRD VESSEL FOR CHARTER.
```

* *Maine,* blown up in Havana harbor in 1898, precipitated the Spanish-American War. The *Panay,* sunk by Japanese aircraft in the Yangtze River, 12 December 1937, with three lives lost, had a highly inflammatory effect on American public opinion. In a preview of the excellent newsreel of the sinking, taken by ace cameraman Norman Alley, FDR ordered parts deleted to avoid making evident the deliberate nature of the attack, which might push the public too fast toward a war for which we were not yet prepared.

† "Top secret" was not instituted until 1944.

The "one now en route" was *Lanikai,* awaiting daybreak to transit the Corregidor minefields. The "second one" was the schooner *Molly Moore,* half *Lanikai*'s size, never commissioned. Pearl Harbor had made the mission superfluous. As for *Isabel,* clearly Hart was using his exceedingly sharp intellect to read between the lines of the President's message. He was saying, in effect, "I understand what you are up to, and now that the Japanese know *Isabel* to be a U.S. warship, they are not going to sink her."

Some historians have seized on Roosevelt's proclivity for dabbling in naval affairs as an explanation of his "three small ships" directive. Samuel Eliot Morison, generally quoted by the layman as the U.S. authority on World War II naval history, takes this tack. Using as an example Roosevelt's proposal that U.S. cruisers "pop up unexpectedly" here and there in the Pacific to "keep the Japs guessing," Morison wrote:

> The President's later proposal to Admiral Hart to operate river gunboats as picket boats in the South China Sea did not stem from the same idea, but from a desire to supplement the work of our patrol planes in reporting Japanese ship movements. A suggestion was made at the Pearl Harbor Inquiry that this was an intentional provocation; but naturally the United States has a right to send its ships anywhere on the high seas.[37]

After World War II, in reviewing Morison's work, Admiral Hart suggested many changes. The "three small ships" episode, he stated

> . . . should be rewritten to accord with facts or be entirely omitted; it is not a piece of history of which to be proud.

As of 1959, with the eleventh reprinting, no correction had been made, including the fact that *Isabel, Lanikai,* and *Molly Moore* were not "river gunboats."

Concerning Morison's grotesquely understated line that "A suggestion was made at the Pearl Harbor Inquiry that this was an intentional provocation," the record shows that the matter received far more than a "suggestion." George Morgenstern prefaces some of the congressional testimony on the subject with:

> If Japan was not going to force a war, the President was quite willing to do so.[38]

He then followed with the statement of Representative Keefe, a member of the Republican minority group whose efforts to clarify the record were systematically sabotaged by the Administration:

> The President's directions were that the commander-in-chief of the Asiatic Fleet was to charter three small vessels to form a 'defensive information patrol.' The minimum requirements to establish these ships as United States men of war would suffice in manning

them. These requirements were: command by a naval officer and mounting of a small gun and one machine gun. The employment of Filipino crews with the minimum number of ratings was authorized. The ships were to observe and report by radio Japanese movement in the West China Sea and the Gulf of Siam. The President prescribed the point at which each vessel was to be stationed. One vessel was to be stationed between Hainan and Hue; one between Camranh Bay and Cape St. Jaques; one off Pointe de Camau. All these points were clearly in the path of the Japanese advance down the coast of Indo-China, and towards the Gulf of Siam. The Navy Department did not originate this plan. The Navy Department would not have directed it to be done unless the President had specifically ordered it. Adm. Hart was already conducting reconnaissance off the coast by planes from Manila. So far as the Navy Department was concerned, sufficient information was being received from this air reconnaissance. *Had the Japanese fired upon any one of these three small vessels, it would have constituted an overt act on the part of Japan.* [Emphasis supplied.][39]

In addition to Keefe's "suggestion," there were many hours of questioning and testimony of Admirals Hart, Stark, and Ingersoll on and beating around the "three small ships." As Hart described it in a letter dated July 1966:

> . . . I was a full day on the witness stand before that committee [JCC]. In a long afternoon of it, Ferguson, Brewster and Keefe took a lot of time shooting questions at me. All were pretty clumsy, not having much in their minds to go on . . . Had [Keefe] possessed any knowledge of the picket ship incident it would have been another matter.

Alas, Keefe had some strong suspicions. But he and the other inquisitors were truly "pretty clumsy" against razor-sharp witness Hart, who confined his answers to a simple reply to the question, without amplification.

Hart himself, who had retired in June 1942 but remained on active duty, had in early February 1944 commenced a one-man, four-month investigation of Pearl Harbor. He was intimately familiar with all the other investigations that were conducted—including the infamous 1941–42 Roberts Commission whitewash, the 1944 Naval Court of Inquiry, and the 1945 Hewitt Inquiry. He had acted as Stark's counsel before the Naval Court of Inquiry. Probably no man alive knew more about the facts of Pearl Harbor and of the eventful week preceding 7 December 1941 than Admiral Thomas C. Hart.

As for Roosevelt's readiness to promote an incident to force the United States into a war its people and Congress did not want, incontrovertible proof has been revealed by the late December 1971 release of some 950 volumes of formerly top secret British government papers.

Among them were minutes of a 19 August 1941 British cabinet meeting in which Prime Minister Winston Churchill reported on his conversations with Roosevelt earlier that month at the Argentia conference.

The minutes, quoting Churchill indirectly, said:

> He [Roosevelt] obviously was determined that they should come in.
>
> If he were to put the issue of peace and war to Congress, they would debate it for months.
>
> The President had said he would wage war but not declare it and that he would become more provocative. If the Germans did not like it, they could attack American forces.

In connection with the President's "shoot on sight" order of 8 October 1941, which *de facto* opened hostilities against the European Axis powers, the President's thinking was revealed at Argentia, as recounted by Churchill at the same cabinet meeting:

> The President's orders to these [convoy] escorts were to attack any German U-boat which showed itself even if it were 200 to 300 miles away from the convoy. Everything was to be done to force an incident.

On 1 December 1941, when Roosevelt concluded his White House conference with Hull, Stark, and later Hopkins, Stark hurried back to his office where he handed the specifics of Roosevelt's "three small vessels" directive to Rear Admiral Royal E. Ingersoll, Assistant Chief of Naval Operations. The message was ready for the code room before 6:00 P.M.

The full details of that critical White House session seem destined to go to the grave with the participants. But ten years later, in his book, *Design for War,* Justice Frederic R. Sanborn, author and historian, made an educated guess:

> It can almost surely be conjectured that the problem discussed at the White House that noon was how to get America to enter the war if only Thailand, or only Singapore, should be attacked by Japan . . . to devise an "incident" in which Japan would commit the first overt act by firing on the American flag and simultaneously sinking one or more American warships.[40]

Admiral Ingersoll's testimony before the Joint Congressional Committee for the Investigation of Pearl Harbor is almost as revealing as if one had been seated in Roosevelt's office during that 1 December conference:

Having established that Admiral Ingersoll was familiar with the "three small vessels" message, Senator Ferguson (R) continued the questioning:

F. You released that message, did you not?

I. I am not sure whether I released it or not, but I had a very large part in preparing the message.

F. What was the purpose of that message? It was three small vessels to form a defensive information patrol. They were to go over to Camranh Bay, Cape St. Jacques, and one off the Point of Camau. Now I have marked in here, and they are many miles away from the Philippines, in fact they are way over so they can watch the movement into the Malay Peninsula, are they not?

I. That is correct.

F. Will you tell us why you wanted to have these small men-of-war out in the Gulf of Siam watching for a movement on the British possessions?

I. The reason we wanted them there is because it says in the beginning of the despatch the "President directs that the following be done as soon as possible." That was our reason for doing it. Admiral Stark was told by the President to do it.

F. Was there any reason given by the President to do it?

I. Not that he told me. I do not know what he told Admiral Stark except to do this. I do not know whether he told Admiral Stark his reasons or not.

F. You had no reason but you prepared this despatch?

I. Admiral Hart was already conducting reconnaissance of that coast by planes from Manila.

F. Do you know the reason for the statement, "FILIPINO CREWS MAY BE EMPLOYED WITH MINIMUM NUMBER OF NAVAL RATINGS TO ACCOMPLISH PURPOSE WHICH IS TO OBSERVE AND REPORT BY RADIO JAPANESE MOVEMENTS IN WEST CHINA SEA AND GULF OF SIAM." Why did they want to use Filipino crews?

I. The only reason I can ascribe is that possibly Admiral Hart did not have sufficient men to do it, and he could simply take a ship which was already manned by Filipinos, put a naval officer on it, put a gun on it, hoist an American flag on it, and it would then be a man-of-war.

F. That is what you were trying to do at that time?

I. That is what we were told to do, sir.

F. You took it rather as an order?

I. That is the reason it starts off the "President directs that the following be done."

F. This was not something being done by the Navy as the Navy; it was the Commander in Chief doing it?

I. I am sure that Admiral Stark would not have done this unless he had been told.

F. Did you see any useful purpose that would be accomplished by these three small men-of-war as lookouts there?

I. We did not initiate the movement, sir, and we were getting, I think, so far as Admiral Stark was concerned, sufficient information from Admiral Hart by the searches which his planes were making.

F. Now that brings up the certain matter of planes. Could you tell us whether or not these were really men-of-war, so that if they had been fired on it would have been an overt act against the United States?

I. May I read this again more carefully?

F. Yes, it was to have a cannon and a machine gun.

I. It says at the beginning: "MINIMUM REQUIREMENTS TO ESTABLISH IDENTITY AS U.S. MAN-OF-WAR ARE COMMANDED BY A NAVAL OFFICER AND TO MOUNT A SMALL GUN AND 1 MACHINE GUN WOULD SUFFICE."

F. Yes. Would that have been an overt act if one of these small boats had been fired upon?

I. It would have been.

After Stark had hurried off from the White House on 1 December with the "three small ships" message, Hopkins remained for a visit by British Ambassador Halifax, for the umpteenth time during the course of the year hoping to get some commitment to the British on the question of U.S. armed support in the Far East in case of Japanese attack. But Roosevelt heretofore had been carefully noncommittal, as had Hopkins in London, explaining the constitutional curbs on any such promises. But perhaps after having got the "three small ships" message off, things looked different. He told Halifax that in case of any direct attack on the British or Dutch, "we should obviously be in all together," adding later that the British could certainly count on American support, *though it might take a few days before it was given.* (*Isabel* would not arrive on her Camranh Bay station until the fourth, Washington time.)

On the evening of the third, Roosevelt was willing to go a bit farther; he assured Halifax that by "support" he meant "armed support."[41]

The diary entry on 3 December by Treasury Secretary and Roosevelt's good friend Henry Morgenthau corroborates the President's cockier feeling: "The most important thing is that the President said he is talking with the English about war plans as to when and where the USA and Great Britain should strike, and that is what he is waiting for."[42] To the "war party," Stimson, Interior Secretary Harold Ickes, Morgenthau, and certain elements of the State Department, things were looking up. An 18 October 1941 entry in Ickes' diary suggests why: "For a long time I have believed that our best entrance into the war would be by

276

way of Japan. Undoubtedly we are nearer this eventuality than ever before. Japan has no friends in this country, but China has. And of course, if we go to war against Japan, it will inevitably lead us into war against Germany."[43]

Two highly qualified witnesses have clarified beyond doubt that any expectation of *Lanikai*'s fulfilling a reconnaissance mission was pure fantasy: she could not communicate with anyone by radio, and the staff of the Commander in Chief Asiatic Fleet knew it, as probably Admiral Hart did himself.

In April 1971, Commander A. B. Ward, USN, Retired, wrote me:

> I was then a Warrant Radio Electrician, and installed a radio receiver (not a very good one) in *Lanikai* in the Cavite Navy Yard. Because we had no transmitters, none was installed. . . .

Actually, *Lanikai* had a transmitter, but of such questionable merit that it is reasonable for Ward to have discounted it, as he added in his letter that, "We salved our consciences on the basis she would be operating in radio silence anyway." In a May 1972 letter, Commander J. W. LeCompte, USN, Retired, describes the set he remembers as a chief radioman and passenger in *Lanikai* from Manila to Java:

> I went through the complete radio installation of the *Lanikai* several times. The transmitter was a home-made rig, probably made by a radio shop in Manila or by some ham. It was originally a ¼ KW quenched gap spark set, but had been rebuilt into a tube set, using a UV204A tube. The power supply was a motor generator driven by the ship's DC system and giving about 115 volts AC in the output to the plate transformers. Evidently one of the windings of the plate transformer was open, as I could never obtain any high voltage.

In December 1941 Commander John McCrea was serving as Admiral Stark's aide. When there was something too hot even for coded messages, scrambler telephone or written word, McCrea hopped on an airplane and carried it, personally, to Hawaii or Manila. Invariably, after each of Stark's frequent visits to the White House, he called McCrea in and briefed him on what had transpired. But not on 1 December 1941. McCrea didn't even know the message existed. Later, however, as presidential aide, McCrea did have the opportunity to appreciate the President's elephantine memory. He would have to look up items of interest to the President that had happened twenty years before, when he was assistant secretary of the Navy. Roosevelt—and everyone else around him—certainly remembered the *Panay*.

The Yangtze River gunboat USS *Panay* had been bombed and sunk by the Japanese almost exactly four years earlier. The incident had been discussed at the 28 November War Council Conference in connection with the President's sending a personal message to Hirohito. Certainly those hectic December 1937 weeks were still bright in the President's memory. The American people had been so wrought up that Roosevelt had felt safe in exploring a bellicose line. Five days after the sinking, he proposed to Britain that Japan be jointly blockaded, and Captain Royal Ingersoll, who later as an admiral was to set up Roosevelt's "three small vessels" message, was sent to London to explore the possibilities. A joint code book was one of his projects. It was quickly compiled and limited distribution made in the fleet. But Prime Minister Neville Chamberlain lost his nerve and rejected the proposal that could have meant war in Asia then instead of in Europe a year later, with ultimate results beyond the wildest guesses.

Another who vividly recalled those edgy December 1937 weeks was Ambassador Joseph Grew in Tokyo. In December 1940, he wrote "Dear Frank" an assessment of Far Eastern affairs, warning that, "A progressively firm policy on our part will entail inevitable risks—especially risks of sudden uncalculated strokes, such as the sinking of the *Panay* which might inflame the American people . . ."

The attack on Pearl Harbor magnificently confirmed the validity of Grew's and the President's equations that *incident = popular indignation; popular indignation = declaration of war.*

On the JCC witness stand, Stark successfully withstood efforts to unearth what the White House discussion had been about. In a 1962 interview of Stark, historian Percy Greaves broached the subject of the "three small vessels" and what might have been behind them. Admiral Ben Moreell, who accompanied Greaves, interrupted with illustrations of how FDR had obsessions on things one day and forgot them the next. The question was never answered; Admiral Stark sat mute.

Eight years later, Stark's silence was echoed by Admiral Hart:[44]

> I brought out of the war my notes containing those [*Lanikai*] facts and also some of my thoughts and personal opinions surrounding them. Only Admiral Stark could have *known* anything more of the inception—the whys and wherefores—of the picket ship idea. My relationships with him were close and I did expect that he would someday begin to talk about it. He never did. I feel that I should take the same attitude for, as far as I know, Stark has not given out to anyone, by word or in print. I destroyed my record on the subject some time back.[45]

As for Admiral Hart's own JCC testimony, for history's sake, one regrets either the questioners' inexpertness or the JCC counsel's dedication to protecting the Administration. In describing that experience,

278

Admiral Hart said: "About the incident of *Isabel* and your little ship; the counsel of the Joint Congressional Inquiry, Richardson, as I later ascertained, knew about it but did not bring it out. I was afraid they would ask me about it. Then the fat *would* have been ignited, for Senators Brewster and Ferguson were mainly bent on discrediting FDR."

Hart had told me earlier that although Roosevelt had been inimical to his later career, he did not feel justified in fighting a dead man. But almost thirty years after I took command of the *Lanikai*, he had softened slightly. At a small luncheon, he mentioned to Admiral Harry Hill: "I once had the unpleasant requirement to send this young man on what looked like a one way mission," he said. Then he told about *Lanikai*'s narrow escape because war broke out before she had reached her assigned station. "Would you tell Admiral Hill if you think we were set up to bait an incident, a *casus belli?*" I asked. "Yes! I think you were bait!" said Admiral Hart. "And I could prove it. But I won't. And don't *you* try it, either!"

I *am* trying, Admiral Hart, and in remembrance of your wisdom and near clairvoyance in masterfully managing for three years a command with vast responsibilities, small resources and little support, I can only hope that in looking down from an old sailor's snug retreat, you will approve setting the record straight.*

There are many theories to explain why things were or were not done. Some are based on ineptness of or lack of communication between high level personnel. Others, on the wide gulf separating the Army and Navy at almost all levels; still others on the overpowering requirement for close to total secrecy to guard a vital advantage, the Japanese cryptosystem breakthrough, which if compromised might be an irretrievable loss.

The honesty and honor of a good many military officers and government officials have been opened to serious question, not excluding the President himself. To Admiral Kimmel, the issue seemed stark and clear:

> I had of course heard of the three small ships sent in 1941 to the Indo-China coast in the hope of creating an incident. When that and other moves failed to involve us, the betrayal of the fleet at Pearl Harbor was decided upon.[46]

Would the Japanese have taken the bait? Of course they passed up *Isabel*, once identified. But several days later the situation had

* Admiral Hart died 4 July 1971, at age 94.

changed. The Japanese task force moving on Malaya had only one conceivable objective. But of course, Roosevelt's "small vessel"—*Lanikai*—was not on station off Pointe de Camau. There had been insufficient time. Had she been, it is not impossible that the course of history might have been slightly altered.

About midday 7 December (Manila time) an Australian reconnaissance Hudson observing the convoy 70 miles south of Pointe de Camau escaped a pursuing Japanese plane. A British Catalina on patrol before daylight in the same area failed to report contact or to return to base. On the same day, a merchant vessel and a cruiser were sighted by another British Hudson at about 5:50 P.M. about 112 miles north of Kota Bharu, and the cruiser fired on it.

Clearly, at this stage, the Japanese could be expected to be less than friendly to snoopers, whoever they might be. Had *Isabel, Lanikai,* or *Molly Moore* been in their path, the story might have been different. If the *Lanikai* had made U.S. headlines—US WARSHIP WANTONLY SUNK—that Sunday morning in Hawaii might have been different. At Pearl Harbor, the ready ammunition boxes would have been unlocked, watertight doors closed, and planes dispersed with guns loaded and pilots ready. And a little more attention might have been paid to that "large unidentified group of aircraft" which radar spotted approaching Oahu before breakfast on that fateful morning, 7 December 1941.

Epilogue

Following my detachment of 28 April, Adair skippered *Lanikai* until 22 August 1942, when the old ship hoisted her fourth flag, the Australian naval ensign.

Exhibiting her usual talent for tight and unknown places, *Lanikai* poked around exhaustively in the several groups of coral islets that made up Houtman Rocks. They visited gray fishermen on Rat Island, noted tidal currents to which a low-powered ship is most sensitive, and checked for the rare possibility of a Japanese lookout station. A good deal of time was spent in Geraldton, using it as a base for shipkeeping and minor overhaul until the final return to Fremantle on 19 May. Thereafter, the log shows many temporary transfers of various crewmen to the hospital. That late, late show on Bali months before was still getting in its deadly licks—recurrences of malaria. Painting ship, airing sails, and overhauling the machinery kept all hands busy.

During July, it became obvious something was in the wind. Days were spent running the ship over the degaussing range, checking her magnetic signature. Where in the world—or locally—could she be going where mines were a menace? Even Admirals Lockwood and Carpender came aboard for a look, and serious, low-toned chat.

With the arrival of appraisers on board 7 August, all doubts vanished. Shortly thereafter the ghouls commenced their work; some of the guns, spare manila rope, and Charlie Adair's well-worn sextant went to the USS *Childs*. *Isabel* got the chronometer, Thompson sub-machine guns, and the remaining 49 hand grenades. The Navy Board of Appraisers decreed that *Lanikai* was worth $32,280—hull, masts, rigging, engine, and steering gear—plus another $3,402 for loose items, which may or may not have included several of those bottles of Tolley's Hospital Brandy in the medicine chest.

Through the good offices of Commodore B. H. Loxton, Australian naval attaché in Washington, the Australian Navy Department picked up the trail from 22 August 1942 until her final disappearance from the

Australian scene, almost exactly four years after first touching those shores.

Lanikai operated as a United States Navy Unit based on Fremantle until August 1942. Operations included a reconnaissance of the West and North West Australian coast departing Fremantle on 3rd April 1942.

On 13th March 1942, it was decided to transfer five of the twenty long range US submarines based at Fremantle to Albany. Consequently, on the 15th March 1942 the submarine tender Holland and five submarines proceeded to Albany. The Seaplane Tender Childs was also transferred to Albany to provide facilities for patrol aircraft.

In June 1942, it was decided to construct Boom defenses at Albany and to transfer Lanikai to Australian control for conversion to a Boom Gate Vessel; on 22nd August 1942, the US Navy Commission Pennant was hauled down and Lanikai taken over by the Royal Australian Navy.

Following the transfer Lanikai was taken in hand by the West Australian State Engineering Works. Conversion included provision to accommodate a crew of twenty-five. Masts were removed and replaced by a single signal mast and a 10 ton diesel powered winch other Boom Defense equipment was installed. Conversion was completed in December and on 9th December she was commissioned HMAS Lanikai.

Lanikai with the Lugger Boyd in tow departed Fremantle on 20th January 1943, but was forced to return to repair storm damage. She sailed again on the 10th March and arrived at Albany on the 15th March 1943.

The Boom Defenses which consisted of an Anti-Torpedo Net laid across the entrance to Princess Royal Harbour were completed in August 1943. Lanikai assumed duty as the Gate Vessel on 2nd September 1943 when the defense became fully operational.

In May 1945, it was decided to remove the Albany Boom Defenses and return Lanikai to Fremantle. Dismantling of the defenses commenced on the 20th July and was completed on the 7th August 1945.

On the 16th August 1945, HMAS Karangi (Boom Defense Vessel) departed Albany towing Lanikai and the Lugger Boyd. En route, storm conditions were encountered rounding Cape Leeuwin. Boyd was cast adrift and subsequently sunk by shelling from HMAS Gladstone. Karangi and Lanikai arrived Fremantle on 21st August 1945.

Lanikai paid off on 22nd August 1945 for reconversion to schooner rig. This work was completed in January 1946, and on 21st January the Naval Officer-in-Charge, Fremantle, returning the ship to the United States Navy. She departed Fremantle for Manila on the

23rd January. Subsequent recorded movements are: arrived Geraldton 25th January; departed Geraldton 3rd February; arrived Koepang 25th February; departed Koepang 26th February for Manila.

In the Royal Australian Navy *Lanikai* was commissioned a Tender
to *HMAS Leeuwin* under the command of Temporary Boatswain
Ernest F. Denning.

After Koepang, ambiguities creep in. The net resolution of these,
as best they can be sorted out, suggest that at Ambon, in a moment of
exuberant celebration, a fire that was built topside got out of hand and
penetrated the engine room. At any rate, when *Lanikai* finally put in
her appearance at Manila, she was in something less than top shape.
Luzon Stevedoring Company, acting for Colonel Grimm, her actual
owner, refused to accept her in this condition and submitted a claim for
$87,000 as their estimate of cost of her replacement.

Lanikai was then towed to Manikani Island, Samar, where a con-
tractor was operating Navy facilities in a surplus ship repair program.
En route, bad weather hit, and the vessel partially swamped, further
aggravating her already poor condition. By this time the ante had been
upped to $125,000 to put her in acceptable condition, so back to Subic
she went for another, hopefully more realistic price from the naval repair
facilities.

At Subic, waterlogged, forlorn and abandoned, Fate at last caught
up with the old ship after a third of a century. *Lanikai*, ex-*Hermes*, went
down ingloriously in a violent typhoon.

Where are those stout souls who stood the watches through those
long tropic nights thirty years ago—who manned the guns, fished, scanned
the skies for enemy planes, painted, hauled on halliards and pulled oars,
awaited with impatience the safety of the night, and cheerfully took
what came? Many have prospered. Others have lost touch. Some are dead.

The first to go was Dutch Lieutenant Paul Nygh, believed to have
been killed in an infiltration attempt on Flores in 1943. His bereaved
parents in Holland carried on a correspondence with Adair after the
war, seeking to know more of Paul's last days.

Next casualty was cheerful, indispensable "Doc," James Lee Cossette, whose death in June 1947 left us with no details, but fond
memories.

Belarmino, better known as "Chips," who was man-of-all-trades,
barber, carpenter, and senior helmsman, was discharged in October 1944
as a carpenter's mate first class, probably for ill health, and died in
October 1944.

Charles A. Walruff, our cocky, no-nonsense "Sparky," retired as
a commander in 1955, after 30 years' service. He died of an apparent

heart attack in September 1962, while employed as a senior flight engineer by General Dynamics. A whiz at electronics, he had been decorated by King George VI with the Order of the British Empire for his contributions to development of airborne radar techniques.

Rear Admiral Harry Keith retired at Annapolis, and passed away after a heart attack in March 1969, while on a Pacific cruise. The yacht *Lanikai II,* owned by his son, Harry H. Keith, Jr., is a living remembrance of a good ship.

No address is available for Armando Alcantara, who was, when last reported, working as a radioman in a Philippine government ship.

Crispin Almadin, address unknown, received a bachelor of education degree and commenced a teaching career in Manila.

Simplicio Gomez was dicharged in January 1961, and according to Taleon, who saw him since in the Cavite area, "just takes life easy."

Old Bosun Vincente Magtulis and Prudencio Tumbagahan were last known to be in Manila in 1947.

Mario Famero retired as a machinist's mate first; his last known address was Dale City, California.

Ray H. Wilcoxen, the chief engineer, has disappeared: his address and retirement rate or rank are unknown.

Charlie C. Kinsey, the boatswain, retired as a warrant officer, and was last known to be in San Diego.

About the others, there is more detailed news:

Rear Admiral Charles Adair, after leaving *Lanikai,* served on the staff of "MacArthur's Amphibious Navy," described in the book of the same name, by Vice Admiral Daniel Barbey, U.S. Naval Institute Press, 1969. Adair helped plan and execute some fifteen assault operations that brought fulfillment of MacArthur's promise, "I shall return!"

For seven years following retirement in 1956, Charlie worked for General Electric, and the next seven—apparently a lucky number, judging from his success—with Ling, Temco, Vought. Now, still basing at Annapolis, he is on his own, assisting in setting up a consulting group in Washington and taking an occasional acey-deucey lesson from me on my frequent visits to Annapolis.

Lieutenant Commander Wilbur W. Carter finished his 30 in 1961, having served almost exclusively in communications, communication security, and NSA—in Washington, California, Alaska, and the Pacific Northwest. He has even better reason than most of us to remember Australia with affection—in Sydney he met Elizabeth, who became his bride. Carter now operates the Foreign Exchange and Collection department of the Berkeley branch of Crocker National Bank.

Electronics Technician's Mate First Class Marciano Felarca retired in Norfolk, and writes that he has "five girls and a boy. It is really a problem to send them all to college. Since they are all "A" students, my wife and I are determined to do it. . . . With God's help and my savings

284

in the service, I was able to establish my own business. I bought old houses and repaired them to rent to service men. As of now I have 17 houses renting. My wife does all the bookkeeping, and also has a part-time job as piano teacher. I do all the repair work. It is a great struggle and I believe it could be done."

The name of our ship lives on; Miss Lanikai F. Felarca graduated from the University of Virginia in June 1972, having stood second in her high school class, as had her younger sister Ramona, who entered the University of Virginia in the autumn of 1972. Glory be to God! What faith and hard work can accomplish!

Lieutenant Commander John H. Gorman has been an expatriate for some years, "where the cost of living is low, and there is virtually no terrorism or vandalism. We have not locked our front door for eight years, and there is no drug abuse because the penalties are so stiff." This happy spot is on the beach, a mile from the U.S. Naval base at Rota, Spain. Retired in 1959, Gorman has enjoyed a career that well justifies the Navy's slogan about seeing the world—from Singapore, to Australia, then Ceylon, India, New Jersey, Norfolk, Guam, Spain, with side offers to Peru and Moscow that were not taken up. In India, he met his bride, daughter of a British Army captain. She and the three children join Carter in his love for Spain, where for some years between retirements, he worked with several U.S. government agencies.

Warrant Officer First Class Stephen J. Kret left *Lanikai* for the submarine tender *Otus*, fighting the war in the Pacific aboard her, step by step, island by island, until the end at Okinawa. Steve's 30 years were up in 1967, and ever since 1958 he has been "in and out of California, still dreaming of settling down in Texas some day." Since Navy retirement, he has been with the Navy Exchange System, headed for a second retirement in 1977, "and I'm sure I'll be ready for it," he adds.

Commander J. W. LeCompte, always the competent technician, remembered in detail the peculiarities of *Lanikai*'s "moss encrusted radio," but was short on describing his own career other than his return to the States in 1945. With 35 years active duty, "Frenchy" retired in 1958, and now owns and operates a commercial photo company in Santa Barbara, California.

Charles T. McVey went to the staff in Perth until October, then served in the seaplane tender *Preston* as she worked her way northward toward her one-time home port of Manila. In 1943 he went to the USS *California* until that veteran battlewagon decommissioned in 1946. Following this, came tours as communication officer at Port Hueneme, boss of the San Juan Navy radio station, communication officer on the staff of the Chief, Naval Air Reserve Training, and so to retirement as a lieutenant commander in 1953.

There was no submarine lookout duty in retirement, but excitement just the same with the Los Angeles Fire Department, until a second retirement in 1971. Mac is active in church, civic and community work, and the family carries on the military tradition, their son being a ten-year veteran, a captain in the U.S. Air Force.

Merle Picking was advanced to warrant officer soon after *Lanikai's* transfer, and shortly thereafter headed for the Naval Mine Depot, York-town, Virginia, for a refresher course. About to be assigned as instructor after finishing, Guns requested return to the Southwest Pacific instead. "The skipper at Yorktown must have thought I was 'Asiatic,' " Picking wrote me in 1972, "but he arranged it, and I was ordered to the USS *Preble* as mining officer with promotion to ensign. We made most of the major invasions, including sweeping Leyte Gulf three days before MacArthur came up with the invasion force."

After a tour at Yokosuka, Japan, as officer-in-charge of the big ex-Japanese ordnance depot, Guns retired in 1954 as a lieutenant, to go "mercantile" in California, where he has been employed by several large corporations in selling and management. The Orient rubbed off heavily on the Pickings. "We have a hobby of collecting old Chinese art," he writes, "and now are constantly on the go to antique shows, auctions and flea markets. Our collection may not be as valuable as Brundage's, but I think we enjoy it more."

Santiago Profeta I last saw in Yokosuka, Japan, in 1959. He had got out of the Navy, then came back in with a new serial number which I do not have, and thus cannot trace him through the Navy Department.

As "the ship's kid," the wayward, high jinks scamp of *Lanikai,* always full of jokes and laughter, it was not easy to recognize the balding, mature second class machinist's mate aboard a fleet tug at Yokosuka. "I never knew anything about Profeta's part in any such remarkable exploit," said his skipper, when over a cup of coffee in his little cabin I unfolded *Lanikai's* story. Profeta desperately wanted leave to fly to Manila and play the part of groom in a second, hopefully more success-ful wedding. "Sure, he can have leave!" said the skipper, a bluff, tough ex-enlisted man himself who admired small ship sailors.

Taleon, who on naturalization changed his name to "Denie D.," retired as a chief radioman, and since has been riding the world's travel as well as its radio circuits. In his civilian career he worked for two commercial companies before returning to Uncle Sam's bosom in U.S. Civil Service as a teletype technician, which has taken him to Washing-ton, D.C., Alaska, and now Greece, where he is installing Navy com-munications equipment. "Why not stick around in San Diego, instead of always *going* places?" his wife, like Navy wives over the millennia, naturally enough, complains.

A June 1972 postcard picturing gorgeous Greek island scenes bears sentiments many a traveling sailor has expressed: "Having just a wonder-ful time. Sight-seeing is exciting on this foreign soil. Will be home Christmas. Regards, Taleon."

All this is a long, long way from 8 December 1941, when, as Taleon recalls thirty-one years later, during a starry, peaceful night, lights twinkling cheerfully on nearby Corregidor, "I stood my first watch on the Fox schedule, where I partially copied the message that said Japan attacked Pearl Harbor . . ."

Bouncy, able Crispin Tipay, the engineer who came in a package with *Lanikai*, spent the war in Australia in lines where his expertise was valuable—operation of construction machinery, carpentry, erecting quonset huts, barges, and mess halls. In a recent letter he recalls some of his lasting impressions of those days. When we fueled in Fremantle on first arrival, the depot failed to appreciate *Lanikai*'s dainty appetite. It was not ordinary diesel her old Union engine demanded, but a higher grade, sometimes called "solar oil." Tipay recalls the dire results, as we cut in that tank and smoked so heavily off Carnarvon those ashore thought we were afire.

"You might remember," he wrote, "after we refueled at Fremantle, after we set sail again, I found out that 'my' engine was putting out a lot of strange smoke, so that I decided on my own to get rid of some of the new fuel oil we took aboard. But because I could not properly explain the situation to Kret, he came up and told you about it, and when you came down to ask for my explanation, I could not utter a reasonable word, but in my mind I felt what I had done was right."

Later, Tipay could have made himself lucid, as he tells in his letter that after being transferred ashore at Fremantle, "I worked very hard although my morale was low. It was a good thing I met a girl friend in Fremantle, who taught me much about the English language, both spoken and written."

"The Navy has been good to me," Tipay writes in closing. "After joining the fleet reserve [as a machinist's mate first class], in 1962, after 21 years service, I was able to attend full time schooling in the University of Araneta, Quezon City, for three years, where I enjoyed my studies." When last heard from, in mid-1971, Tipay was visiting his only daughter, married to a chief petty officer stationed in Washington, D.C.

In a May 1972 letter, Hilario Velarmino, "Cooky," whose ingenuity will stick in the memories of his shipmates for a long time to come, suggests he yet harbors those virtues of rugged simplicity that he demonstrated half a lifetime ago:

"I was surprised but glad to hear from you! So you are still alive and kicking! So am I.

"Our home is still in Cavite City, but I'm always staying in Olongapo, a five-hour drive. Right now I'm leading a simple life, gardening, taking care of grandchildren.

"Last January my wife and I celebrated our fiftieth wedding anniversary. Thank you for writing me."

Included with the neatly printed letter was a picture of a bespectacled patriarch in a handsome *barong Tagalog*, the Filipino male's dress-up costume, an openwork shirt. On his right was a serene lady in lace, his wife. Between them stood a beautiful little girl of perhaps five, the youngest grandchild.

So have our good shipmates of *Lanikai* lived, prospered, and died, carrying on in honor and faith, well justifying the judgment of an omniscient Fate who spared us in those black days of the war's early months.

Source Notes

Admiral Robert L. Dennison, who wrote the Foreword for this book, knew the Far East well, first as a destroyer commanding officer, then as Admiral Hart's liaison officer with U.S. Army Forces Far East and its sometimes controversial commander, Douglas MacArthur.

On Hart's departure for Java, Dennison, then a lieutenant commander, was on Corregidor with Rear Admiral F. W. Rockwell before leaving on Hart's order via a 40-day submarine war patrol to Java. There, he served as chief of staff to Admiral Hart's successor, Vice Admiral W. A. Glassford.

Leaving Java at the last minute, again via submarine, Commander Dennison became chief of staff to Commander Allied Forces, East Australia, Admiral Rockwell.

With four stars, Admiral Dennison commanded U.S. Naval Forces, Europe, then assumed CinC Atlantic Command, and CinC U.S. Atlantic Fleet, and Supreme Allied Commander Atlantic.

1. From an unpublished manuscript by Malcolm McGregor Champlin, "One Man's Story."
2. Admiral F. W. Rockwell, USN (Ret.). "Mon Odyssee Avec MacArthur," *Paris Match*, 7 August 1965.
3. Major General Charles A. Willoughby and John Chamberlain. *MacArthur, 1941–1951* (New York: McGraw-Hill Book Co., Inc., 1954), pp. 22, 23.
4. A. A. Hoehling. *The Week Before Pearl Harbor* (New York: W. W. Norton & Co., Inc., 1963).
5. *National Review*, 13 December 1966, p. 1261; Vice Admiral Frank E. Beatty, who was present at the meeting as Secretary of the Navy Frank Knox's aide.
6. *Foreign Relations of the United States, 1941*, Department of State, Vol. IV, pp. 613–14.
7. In a March 1973 letter to the author.

8. Frances Perkins. *The Roosevelt I Knew* (New York: Harper & Row, 1946).
9. From a letter dated 1 October 1971, when he was Captain Richard K. Anderson, USN (Ret.).
10. In a letter to Commander C. C. Hiles, USN (Ret.).
11. "From Dover Straits to Corregidor Deep," U.S. Naval Institute *Proceedings* (February, 1952).
12. "The Strange Assignment of USS *Lanikai*," U.S. Naval Institute *Proceedings* (September 1962).
13. *Paradise Holiday* (Honolulu, Hawaii, 1935).
14. Record Group 80, File 28694-65:26, the National Archives.
15. In a tape recording to the author.
16. Admiral Hart's 1942 narrative, in the Naval Archives.
17. Hart's 1942 narrative.
18. Cecil Brown. *Suez to Singapore* (New York: Random House, 1942), p. 508.
19. Enclosure (A) to CSWP Secret Serial SA-24 of 27 March 1942, file A12, the Naval Archives.
20. Lieutenant General Lewis H. Brereton. *The Brereton Diaries* (New York: William Morrow and Co., 1946), p. 77.
21. In an April 1972 letter to the author.
22. Samuel Eliot Morison. *The Rising Sun in the Pacific* (Boston: Little, Brown & Co., 1950), p. 363.
23. For the complete story of Hamlin's desperately cruel years in Japanese captivity, see "The Last Battle of the *Houston*," *Shipmate* Magazine, May 1946, faithfully reflected in the motion picture, "Bridge on the River Kwai."
24. Rear Admiral E. P. Abernethy. "The Pecos Died Hard," United States Naval Institute *Proceedings* (December 1969).
25. From a postwar statement by Joe Sam Sisk, storekeeper second class, a *Houston* survivor, made to the Casualty Section, Bureau of Naval Personnel.
26. In a 19 November 1962 letter, General MacArthur authorized me to use this quote.
27. Brigadier General Patrick Hurley, in a letter to General George Marshall, 21 February 1942.
28. Champlin. *One Man's Story.*
29. W. L. White. *They Were Expendable* (New York: Harcourt, Brace and Company, 1942).
30. Rear Admiral Charles Adair, USN (Ret.). "Search the Coast to Shark Bay," *Shipmate* (September 1972).
31. Letter from Slocum to the author, 18 November 1970.
32. Letter from Admiral Hart to Rear Admiral John Heffernan, 5 May 1952.
33. Letter from Admiral Hart to the author, 1 October 1970.
34. Hoehling. *The Week Before Pearl Harbor.*
35. Report of John Walker Payne, Jr., in the U.S. Naval Archives, Washington Navy Yard.
36. Ibid.

37. Morison. *Rising Sun,* p. 57, n. 20.
38. George Morgenstern. *Pearl Harbor, the Story of the Secret War* (New York: Devin-Adair Company, 1947), pp. 301–302.
39. Ibid.
40. Frederic R. Sanborn. *Design for War* (New York: Devin-Adair, 1951).
41. Sir Llewellyn Woodward. *British Foreign Policy in the Second World War,* Vol. II (London: Her Majesty's Stationery Office, 1971), pp. 170–73.
42. John Morton Blum. *Years of Urgency, 1938–1941* (Boston: Houghton Mifflin Co., 1965), p. 392.
43. Harold L. Ickes. *Secret Diary of Harold L. Ickes,* Vol. III (New York: Simon & Schuster, 1954).
44. Letter from Admiral Hart to the author, 6 October 1970.
45. Admiral Hart's voluminous remaining papers are now in the U.S. Naval Archives.
46. Letter from Admiral Kimmel to the author, 10 April 1965.

Bibliography

OFFICIAL PUBLICATIONS

Reports of General MacArthur; Japanese Operations in the Southwest Pacific Area, Vol. II, Part I, Government Printing Office, Washington, D.C., 1966.
U.S. Army in World War II; Strategic Planning For Coalition Warfare 1941–1942. Matloff and Snell, Office of the Chief of Military History, Department of the Army, 1953.
U.S. Army in World War II; The War In The Pacific—The Fall of the Philippines. Louis Morton, Office of the Chief of Military History, Department of the Army, 1953.

BOOKS

Barnes, Harry Elmer. *Perpetual War for Perpetual Peace.* Caldwell, Idaho: The Caxton Printers, Ltd., 1953.
Beard, Charles W. *President Roosevelt and the Coming of the War.* New Haven: Yale University Press, 1948.
Burtness, Paul S. and Ober, Warren U., eds. *The Puzzle of Pearl Harbor.* Evanston, Illinois: Row, Peterson and Company, 1962.
Brereton, Lewis H. *The Brereton Diaries.* New York: William Morrow & Co., 1946.
Brown, Cecil. *Suez to Singapore.* New York: Random House, 1942.
Burns, James MacGregor. *Roosevelt, the Soldier of Freedom.* New York: Harcourt Brace Jovanovich, 1970.
Edmonds, Walter D. *They Fought with What They Had.* Boston: Little, Brown & Co., 1951.
Farago, Ladislas. *The Broken Seal.* New York: Random House, 1967.
Grew, Joseph C. *Ten Years In Japan.* New York: Simon and Schuster, 1944.
Hart, Liddel. *History of the Second World War.* New York: G. P. Putnam's Sons, 1971.

Hoehling, A. A. *The Week Before Pearl Harbor*. New York: W. W. Norton & Co., 1963.

Hull, Cordell. *The Memoirs of Cordell Hull*. (Two volumes.) London: Hodder & Stoughton, 1948.

Karig, Commander Walter, USNR, and Kelly, Lieutenant Welbourn, USNR. Battle Report—*Pearl Harbor to Coral Sea*. New York: Rinehart & Co., 1944.

Kahn, David. *The Codebreakers*. New York: The Macmillan Co., 1967.

Morgenstern, George. *The Story of the Secret War*. New York: Devin-Adair Co., 1947.

Morin, Relman. *East Wind Rising*. New York: Alfred A. Knopf, 1960.

Morrill, Lieutenant Commander John, USN, and Pete Partin. *South from Corregidor*. New York: Simon & Schuster, 1943.

Morison, Samuel Eliot. *The Rising Sun in the Pacific*. Boston: Little, Brown & Co., 1950.

Perkins, Frances. *The Roosevelt I Knew*. New York: Harper & Row, 1946.

Robinson, Edgar Eugene. *The Roosevelt Leadership*. New York: J. B. Lippincott Co., 1955.

Robson, R. W. *The Pacific Island Handbook*. New York: The Macmillan Co., 1946.

Rutherford, Ward. *Fall of the Philippines*. New York: Ballantine Books, Inc., 1971.

Sanborn, Frederic R. *Design for War*. New York: Devin-Adair Co., 1951.

Sherwood, Robert E. *Roosevelt and Hopkins*. New York: Harper & Row, 1950.

Stimson, Henry L. *On Active Duty in Peace and War*. New York: Harper & Bros., 1948. Reprinted New York: Octagon Books, 1971.

Tansill, Charles Callan. *Back Door to War, The Roosevelt Foreign Policy*. Chicago: Henry Regnery Co., 1952.

Thorpe, Brigadier General Elliott R. *East Wind Rain*. Boston: Gambit, Inc., 1969.

Toland, John. *But Not In Shame*. New York: Random House, 1961.

———. *The Rising Sun*. New York: Random House, 1970.

Tolley, Rear Admiral Kemp. *Yangtze Patrol*. Annapolis: U.S. Naval Institute Press, 1971.

Tsuji, Colonel Masanobu. *Singapore: The Japanese Version*. New York: St. Martin's, 1960.

Underbrink, Robert L. *Destination Corregidor*. Annapolis: U.S. Naval Institute Press, 1971.

Ward, Russel. *Australia*. Englewood Cliffs, New Jersey: Prentice-Hall, Inc., 1965.

Welles, Sumner. *Seven Decisions That Shaped History*. New York: Harper & Bros., 1950.

White, W. L. *They Were Expendable*. New York: Harcourt Brace & Co., 1942.

Wigmore, Lionel. *The Japanese Thrust*. Adelaide, Australia: The Griffin Press, 1957.

Willoughby, Major General Charles A., and Chamberlin, John. *MacArthur, 1941–1951*. New York: McGraw-Hill Co., Inc., 1954.

Wise, William. *Secret Mission to the Philippines*. New York: E. P. Dutton & Co., 1968.

Wohlstetter, Roberta. *Pearl Harbor, Warning and Decision*. Stanford, California: Stanford University Press, 1962.

PRINCIPAL DOCUMENTS

From the Operational Archives, Naval History Division, Navy Department, Washington, D.C.:

Command File; World War II:

Personal and official papers of Admiral Thomas C. Hart.

Story written by Rear Admiral Welford C. Blinn, USN (Retired), for Navy Cross television series.

Action Reports, World War II:

Reports of actions off Balikpapan, Badung Strait, and in the Java Sea.

Pearl Harbor Attack File:

High command message traffic pertaining to period just before and just after attack.

BOOKLETS

Peckworth, Lieutenant Commander Dana, USN, *The Cruise of the "Lucky" Lanikai*. Privately printed, 1964.

Winslow, Captain Walter G., USN (Retired). *USS HOUSTON, Ghost of the Java Coast*. Bethesda, Maryland: Winslow Books, 1971. (History of the USS *Houston*, with final crew list.)

The Hawaiian Annual, 1918, Thos. G. Thrum, Publishers, Honolulu, T.H.

PERIODICALS

Articles from U.S. Naval Institute *Proceedings:*

Abernethy, E. P. "The *Pecos* Died Hard." Vol. 95, December 1969.

Davison, T. W. "The Second Battle of Manila Bay." Vol. 69, May 1943.

Ferriter, C. A. "Captain of the Whip." Vol. 68, November 1942.

Mack, William P. "Macassar Merry-go-Round." Vol. 68, November 1942.

———. "The Battle of the Java Sea." Vol. 69, August 1943.

Tolley, Kemp. "The Strange Assignment of USS *Lanikai*." Vol. 88, September 1962.

———. "Yangpat—Shanghai to Chungking." Vol. 89, June 1963.

———. "Divided We Fell." Vol. 92, October 1966.

Articles from *Shipmate* Magazine:

Adair, Charles. "Search the Coast to Shark Bay." Vol. 35, July–August 1972.

Champlin, Malcolm. "December, 1941." Vol. 34, December 1971.

————. "Bataan, February 1942." Vol. 35, February 1972.

————. "Escape From Corregidor." Vol. 35, March 1972.

Hamlin, H. S. "The *Houston*'s Last Battles." Vol. 9, May 1946.

Tolley, Kemp. "Cruise of the *Lanikai*." Vol. 30, January 1967.

————. "ABDACOM, Our First Multinational Alliance." Vol. 31, November 1968.

Winslow, Walter G. "They Could Have Been Killed." Vol. 34, March 1971.

Miscellaneous:

Walruff, Charles A. "The Lucky 'Lanikai,' a Dangerous Voyage Through Jap-Infested Waters." *Yachting*, September 1943.

Appendix

PRE-PEARL HARBOR
CRYPTANALYTIC NET, LATE 1941

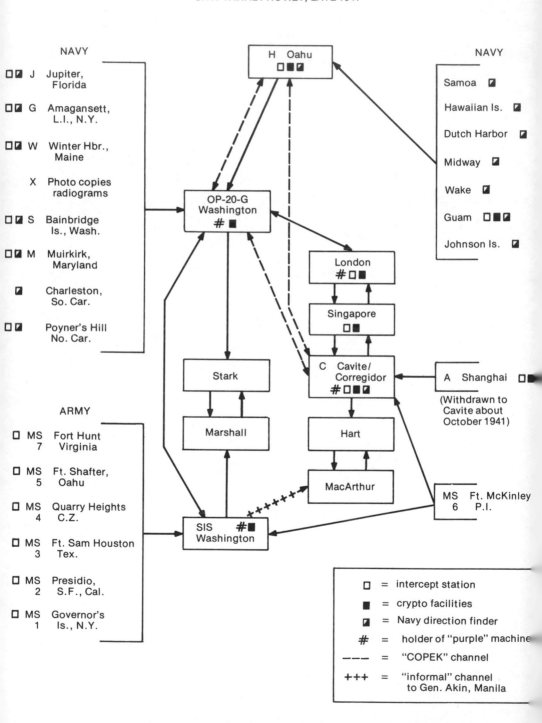

Final War Warnings

On 29 November 1941, the Chief of Naval Operations quoted the U.S. Army's 27 November "war warning" which paralleled the Navy's, and sent it to the Commander in Chief, Pacific Fleet, for information, plus several lesser naval commands.

> Negotiations with Japan appear to be terminated to all practical purposes with only the barest possibilities that the Japanese Government might come back and offer to continue. If hostilities cannot repeat cannot be avoided the United States desires that Japan commit the first overt act. This policy should not repeat should not be construed as restricting you to a course of action that might jeopardize your defense. Prior to hostile Japanese action you are directed to undertake such reconnaissance and other measures as you deem necessary but these measures should be carried out so as not repeat not to alarm civil population or disclose intent. Report measures taken. A separate message is being sent to G-two Ninth Corps area re subversive activities in the United States. Should hostilities occur you will carry out the tasks assigned in Rainbow Five so far as they pertain to Japan. Limit dissemination of this highly secret information to minimum essential officers.

The Chief of Naval Operations then added his own postscript for naval compliance:

> Undertake no offensive action until Japan has committed an overt act. Be prepared to carry out tasks assigned in WPL46 so far as they apply to Japan in case hostilities occur.

Author's note: The admonition to await a Japanese overt act was on the direct order of the President to Stimson that it be included. Japanese sinking of one of the "three small vessels" would have qualified admirably if not spectacularly.

SEALED SECRET

NAVAL MESSAGE NAVY DEPARTMENT

PHONE EXTENSION NUMBER	Op-12 Ext. 2992		ADDRESSEES	MESSAGE PRECEDENCE
FROM Chief of Naval Operations	FOR ACTION		CINCAF CINCPAC	PRIORITY X ROUTINE DEFERRED
RELEASED BY DATE November 27, 1941.				
TOR CODEROOM DECODED BY PARAPHRASED BY	INFORMATION		CINCLANT SPENAVO	PRIORITY ROUTINE DEFERRED

INDICATE BY ASTERISK ADDRESSEES FOR WHICH MAIL DELIVERY IS SATISFACTORY

GKVJL BVKLW 272337 0971

UNLESS OTHERWISE DESIGNATED THIS DISPATCH WILL BE TRANSMITTED WITH DEFERRED PRECEDENCE.
ORIGINATOR FILL IN DATE AND TIME FOR DEFERRED AND MAIL DELIVERY

	DATE	TIME	GCT

HELLS

MM THIS DESPATCH IS TO BE CONSIDERED A WAR WARNING X NEGOTIATIONS
WITH JAPAN LOOKING TOWARD STABILIZATION OF CONDITIONS IN THE
PACIFIC HAVE CEASED AND AN AGGRESSIVE MOVE BY JAPAN IS EXPECTED
WITHIN THE NEXT FEW DAYS X THE NUMBER AND EQUIPMENT OF JAPANESE
TROOPS AND THE ORGANIZATION OF NAVAL TASK FORCES INDICATES AN
AMPHIBIOUS EXPEDITION ~~PROBABLY~~ AGAINST EITHER THE PHILIPPINES *THAI*
OR KRA PENINSULA OR POSSIBLY BORNEO X EXECUTE AN APPROPRIATE
DEFENSIVE DEPLOYMENT PREPARATORY TO CARRYING OUT THE TASKS ASSIGNED
IN WPL46X INFORM DISTRICT AND ARMY AUTHORITIES X A SIMILAR WARNING
IS BEING SENT BY WAR DEPARTMENT X SPENAVO INFORM BRITISH X
CONTINENTAL DISTRICTS GUAM SAMOA directed
take appropriate measures against sabotage MM
COPY TO WPD [WAR DEPT]

Enciphered, Calls
BYRAB
ELM-35
GUNEC
ELM-142
SEE ART 76(3)
To Spenavo
NAV RADM

SECRET DECLASSIFIED

MAKE ORIGINAL ONLY, DELIVER TO COMMUNICATION WATCH OFFICER IN PERSON

45425

The Navy's last warning, Chief of Naval Operations message 272337 of 27 November 1941, and the subject of so much acrimonious debate, was drafted by Rear Admiral R. K. Turner, Director of Navy War Plans. The handwritten additions were by Rear Admiral Royal Ingersoll, Assistant Chief of Naval Operations, and releaser of the message. Unquestionably his boss Admiral Stark gave a final OK, and perhaps even the President. Clearly, the accent is on a Far East attack, with no hint of Pearl Harbor.

There is some persistent rumor to the effect that commencing 4 December, all war warnings of any sort had to be cleared through Army Chief of Staff, General George Marshall. This is corroborated by Admiral Stark's actions on the morning of 7 December. Pressed by his advisors to warn Kimmel urgently as a result of the 14-part Japanese message just intercepted which clearly meant a break in relations, Stark deferred to Marshall's sending the only final warning. Delaying until almost noon, Marshall got it off by commercial telegraph, routine precedence, instead of instantly by Stark's direct scrambler telephone, or in 15 minutes by the Navy's high power radio. Marshall's warning arrived by bicycle messenger about eight hours after the Japanese planes. Inspired by these same Japanese intercepts, Secretary of the Navy Knox dispatched a warning message to Kimmel the evening of the sixth. It never arrived, its being misplaced not likely, and the authority to kill a cabinet officer's message not widely held.

Supporting the above is an interesting tale that if someday corroborated by release of British wartime documents might modestly alter the face of history.

Under the circumstances, one cannot name particulars. At any rate, let us say that during a postwar Caribbean cruise aboard a British-manned vessel, a young merchant officer was entertaining a distinguished American guest with a story of his father's long employment by the Chinese government in a top intelligence capacity. In early December 1941, Dad's agents in Japan had picked up the details of the Pearl Harbor attack plan. Postwar investigation has revealed that some 75 high level Japanese were aware of it. As well demonstrated in the Sorge case, Japan's deepest secrets were not inviolate. The Pearl information was at once transmitted to London, thence to Roosevelt. The latter then is assumed to have taken Marshall into his exclusive confidence, as Roosevelt felt that Marshall was intensely loyal to him and that he dominated affable but weak Admiral Harold ("Betty") Stark.

The "plot" was to insure that nothing developed to cause the Japanese to call off the attack and rob the President of that desperately needed *casus belli* that the "three small ships" so far had failed to provide.

General Marshall made himself unavailable on the evening of 6 December, and, allegedly on a horseback ride, during most of the forenoon of the seventh, while a large Japanese amphibious force was known in Washington to be poised a few hours steaming off Malaya. The fourteen part intercept that caused Roosevelt to exclaim to Hopkins on the evening of the sixth that, "This means war!" thus allegedly was first seen by Marshall late that fatal Sunday morning—when after considerable delay he finally reserved for himself the exclusive right to send off a warning—by routine precedence and commercial facilities. Was all this simply a lapse of good judgment on the part of the second most influential man in the U.S. government? Or was it, in football parlance, a desire to "eat up the clock"?

In any case, did the President really expect such a magnificent Japanese show? Perhaps a nuisance raid which would give him that "first overt act," but not the gory loss of over 2,000 men. Just a few days over twenty years after the event, Admiral Ben Moreell wrote to historian Dr. Harry Elmer Barnes:

"I frequently made long airplane trips with Secretary Knox. After we got tired of working and reading we used to talk about many things. One day we were discussing F.D.R., and I remarked that I thought his most unusual characteristic was his complete confidence in himself, that I had never seen him indicate any doubt about the correctness of his position on any issue. I then asked Mr. Knox whether he had ever seen such doubts. He replied, 'Yes, on the afternoon of Pearl Harbor. I went to the White House and he was in the Oval Office. When I went in he was seated at his desk and was as white as a sheet. He was visibly shaken. You know, I think he expected to get hit; but he did not expect to get hurt.' "

Read to President & be approved
Operad

To CinC AF
Info CinC Pac.

Indications that Japan is about
to attack points on KRA Isthmus
by oversea expeditions. In
order to ascertain destination
this expedition and low securing
our position in the Philippines
desire you cover by air the
line Manila CAMRANH
BAY on three days commencing
upon receipt this dispatch. Instruct planes
to observe only & They must not
approach so as to appear to be
attacking but must defend
themselves if attacked. Understand British air forces
will search arc 180 miles from
TEDTA BHARU and will move
troops to line across KRA isthmus
near SINGORA if expedition is approved. THAILAND
Inform MacArthur
British mission here informed.

On 5 and 6 December 1941, Admiral Hart and Vice Admiral Tom Phillips, RN, Commander in Chief, British Naval Forces Far East, conferred at Manila. The results are contained in the following message:

From Commander in Chief, Asiatic Fleet
To: Chief of Naval Operations
Information: Commander in Chief, Pacific Fleet

(1) We have met and discussed the problems with which we are faced in the Far Eastern Area.

(2) In the early stages of a war with Japan occurring at the present time, the initiative must inevitably rest with the Japanese.

(3) It is consequently not possible for us to draw up definite plans to be carried out by all our forces at the outbreak of war, and the most we can do is to decide upon the initial dispositions that appear to us best suited to meet the probable Japanese actions. Plans for submarines and naval aircraft are definite and ready.

(4) We are agreed that it is of great importance to prevent any Japanese movement through the Malay Barrier.

(5) We are agreed on the following initial dispositions:

(A) British battle fleet to be based on Singapore and operate as required from there as a striking force in connection with any Japanese movement in the China Seas, Dutch East Indies and through Malay Barrier.

(B) Cruiser striking force to be based on East Borneo—"Surabaya—Darwin" to act as a striking force in connection with air reconnaissance. This force can provide cover, and when necessary, escort, for convoys within the Dutch East Indies and Philippine area or for an occasional important convoy from Australia to Singapore.

(C) The minimum cruiser force should be maintained in the Australia—New Zealand area to deal with a moderate scale of raider attack or escort important convoys.

(D) The minimum cruiser force to be maintained in the Indian Ocean to escort important trade.

(6) The actual dispositions of forces to give effect to "5" are contained in Appendix 1.

(7) We consider it very important that action in the Far East area should be co-ordinated with the movements of the U.S. Pacific Fleet, and we hope we may be informed of the time table visualized for the movement of this fleet to Truk in accordance with Plan "Rainbow V". The release of cruisers from Australia and New Zealand is intimately connected with the movements of this fleet.

(8) All operations of U.S. Army aircraft which touch the operation of any naval forces to be co-ordinated through CINCAF.

(9) The setting up and use of a joint headquarters is found impracticable at this time.

(10) Strategic control: Strategic control as between H.M. and U.S.

forces for the present to remain under respective commanders in chief and their operation to be co-ordinated under the principle of mutual co-operation.

(11) Tactical command. The policy in force in the North Atlantic will be followed.

(12) We consider that liaison officers should now be exchanged between the United States Asiatic and British Eastern Fleets, and are taking the necessary action.

(13) We consider that if the above is agreed to in principle by Dutch, Australian and New Zealand authorities in consultation with British Commander in Chief Eastern Fleet, next week, then all that remains to do in way of conference is the perfection of details by our respective staffs.

Signed/   Thos. C. Hart and
            Tom S. V. Phillips

An addendum to the message then follows:

1. With the growth of our forces in the Far East, it will be important to be in a position to undertake more offensive operations. Such operations are not practicable from Singapore, and we consider that it is necessary to have, in due course, a base further north from which to operate.

2. Manila is the only suitable base available, and we consequently consider that the necessary measures should be put in hand to enable Manila to be used by the British battle fleet. The question of just what action is necessary for this purpose will be discussed by our staffs.

3. We consider that we should aim at having Manila available as a base by the first of April 1942, if this can be done.

   Appendix 1. Singapore; battleships: *Prince of Wales, Repulse, Revenge, Royal Sovereign;* cruisers: *Mauritus, Achilles, Tromp, deRuyter, (Australia?)* (and later, *Hobart?*) Destroyers: Ten British, 6 Dutch, 4 U.S. (see note). Sourabaya—Darwin—East Borneo: *Houston, Marblehead, Cornwall, Java,* 4 destroyers (U.S. See note). Australasia: *Australia* or *Canberra, Perth, Leander,* 3 AMC. Indian Ocean: *Exeter, Glasgow* (20 knots) two "E" class, 3 "D" class, 4 "C" class, 5 AMC.

   Footnote: Hart's understanding is that we build up destroyer force to operate with the British battleships as they increase in number. At present, the two destroyer divisions are deployed with his cruisers, one division being in full readiness at Balik Papan to proceed to Singapore upon declaration of war. (CinC Eastern Fleet requests above be forwarded First Sea Lord as personal message from him.)

Author's comment:

The anomalies in the above message are near dumbfounding. It *had* to be perfectly apparent to all that any reference to use of Manila as a base in April 1942, or the placement of capital ships, only two of which were present in the Far East, was an exercise in fantasy. Every sign pointed to war within days, if not hours. One can only assume a gross underestimate of Japanese capabilities.

Most shocking is the belated nature of the conference, an *in extremis* gesture, with no provision for the most vital feature of all: immediate unification of command, including the not inconsequential Dutch naval forces. Too little and too late would be a more than charitable epitaph. But one must remember that Admiral Stark had enjoined Admiral Hart months before to avoid United States involvement.

Commander in Chief
United States Fleet
U.S.S. PENNSYLVANIA
Flagship

26 February 1940

Dear Betty,*

The remarks in your letter of 18 January about the situation in the Far East, the possibility of something breaking without warning and my need to be mentally prepared are somewhat disquieting.

When the China incident started and on every opportunity until I left the job as Assistant C.N.O. I used to say to Bill Leahy,† be sure to impress the boss that we do not want to be drawn into this unless we have allies so bound to us that they cannot leave us in the lurch.

There is a possibility that this constant repetition has something to do with the trip of Ingersoll [to London].

When this understanding was reached it had some value but under present conditions it has little value as it affords us the use of a base in exchange for an obligation to protect about two and a half continents.

I strongly feel that you should impress on the boss that an Orange war would probably last some years and cost much money, my guess is 5 to 10 years, 35 to 70 billion dollars. . . .

I have always thought that our Orange plan was chiefly useful as an exercise in war planning, to train officers . . . and to serve as a basis for asking for appropriations and as a guide to strengthening

* Admiral Harold Stark, Chief of Naval Operations.
† Admiral William D. Leahy, USN, Retired, then governor of Puerto Rico; previously Chief of Naval Operations.

our Navy and its shore facilities. As to actually executing the O-1 plain I hope we will never be called upon to do that unless the Administration fully realizes the probable cost and duration of such a war and unless our people are prepared to support an expensive war of long duration.

Even if we could take Truk what would we have? A secure anchorage, nothing else, several thousand miles from our nearest drydock and adequate repair facilities and still hundreds of miles from the enemy country. Of course it could not be taken without some underwater damage. To actually put on real pressure we would have to have a real base that would take many years and much money. . . .

I hesitate to write you because the written word is so easily misunderstood. Also I do not know what your ideas are, what is the meaning of our diplomatic moves, or our Senators' talks, or our neutrality patrol. But you are the principal and only Naval Adviser to the boss and he should know that our fleet can not just sail away, lick Orange and be back at home in a year or so. Also the probable cost of any war should be compared with the probable value of winning the war. . . .

All of this letter may be needless but I know that if you do not tell the boss what you really know and feel about the probable cost and duration of an Orange war, *NOBODY WILL.*

I would hate to see our leaders make a move from which they could not gracefully withdraw and which would eventually force us into a war, half-heartedly supported by our country. In other words before this nation takes a step I hope we will carefully examine the direction we are heading, where we will eventually go and be prepared to realistically pursue the course whatever the cost. . . .

Hastily,
/s/　J. O. Richardson
[Commander in Chief, U.S. Fleet]

NOTE: On 6 January 1940, Admiral Richardson became CinC U.S. Fleet, and almost exactly a year later was summarily relieved of command by Roosevelt. Such sentiments as expressed above obviously did not please the "boss." A facsimile of this letter in its entirety in Richardson's handwriting appears in Vol. 14, pp. 924–27, PHA series.

Important Messages

FROM: CINCAF   Secret 231525 (23 June 1941)
TO: CNO

THE FOLLOWING IS MY ANALYSIS OF AVAILABLE INFORMATION
(MAINLY DIPLOMATIC INTERCEPTS): IF JAPAN STARTS NEW

WAR IN IMMEDIATE FUTURE IT WILL BE AGAINST RUSSIA.
SUCCESS IN THE ADVANCE AGAINST RUSSIA WILL BE

NECESSARY BEFORE JAPAN MAKES ADVANCE TO THE SOUTH.
HOWEVER I CONTINUE ON THE ASSUMPTION THAT NEXT

JAPANESE MOVE WILL BE IN THIS DIRECTION. DOES YOUR
ANALYSIS AGREE WITH MINE?

(Note that Admiral Hart, CINCAF, is not squeamish
about revealing his use of the Purple Machine
gleanings, a source Admiral Kimmel and General Short
were deprived of through General Marshall's and
Admiral Turner's horror of compromise.)

FROM: CNO   Secret 031939 (3 July 1941)
TO: CINCAF, CINCPAC, CINCLANT, COM 15 (Panama),
        SPENAVO (Singapore)

(in part) ...WHILE AN ADVANCE AGAINST THE BRITISH AND
DUTCH CANNOT YET BE DEFINITELY RULED OUT CNO IS OF

THE OPINION JAPANESE ACTIVITY IN THE SOUTH WILL FOR
THE PRESENT BE CONFINED TO SEIZURE AND DEVELOPMENT OF

NAVAL ARMY AND AIR BASES IN INDO-CHINA. RUSSIAN
NEUTRALITY PACT WILL BE ABROGATED AND MAJOR MILITARY

EFFORT WILL BE AGAINST RUSSIAN MARITIME PROVINCES
PROBABLY TOWARD END OF JULY THOUGH ATTACK MIGHT BE

DEFERRED UNTIL AFTER COLLAPSE OF EUROPEAN RUSSIA.... .

FROM: COM 14 (Pearl Harbor)
       Confidential 150055(15 October 1941)
To: CNO

MY CONSIDERED OPINION IS THAT THE HAWAIIAN DEPART-
MENT IS LACKING IN ADEQUATE NUMBERS OF PILOTS AND

BOMBING AND PURSUIT PLANES. ALSO THAT THE ANTIAIR-
CRAFT PROTECTION IS LACKING IN NUMBERS AND RANGES

OF GUNS.

(Admiral Bloch, Commandant 14th Naval district, was
jointly responsible with General Short for the
security of the Pearl Harbor naval base and the
Hawaiian Islands.)

FROM: CNO   Secret priority 091812 (9 December 1941)
TO: CINCPAC
INFO COM 12 (San Francisco); COM 13 (Seattle), COM
      HAWAIIAN COASTAL FRONTIER (Admiral Bloch),
      COM 11 (San Diego)

MY 090139 PLACES COMMANDER HAWAIIAN NAVAL COASTAL
FRONTIER FULLY UNDER YOUR COMMAND FOR ALL PURPOSES.

YOUR 090253 WAR AND NAVY DEPARTMENTS ARE BENDING
EVERY EFFORT TO REINFORCE THE PACIFIC FLEET AND THE

ARMY HAWAIIAN DEPARTMENT WITH SHIPS AIRPLANES TROOPS
AND ANTIAIRCRAFT WEAPONS. YOU WILL BE PROMPTLY IN-

FORMED AS TO PLANS. IN VIEW OF RAID ON WEST COAST
IT IS NECESSARY ALSO TO PROVIDE ADDITIONAL FORCES

FOR THAT REGION ALASKA AND THE CANAL ZONE. FOR THIS
SAME REASON YOUR COVERING OPERATIONS ASSUME ESPECIAL

IMPORTANCE AND IT WILL BE NECESSARY TO PROVIDE ADE-
QUATE ESCORTS FOR CONVOYING BETWEEN HAWAII AND WEST

COAST. WHEN CARRIERS ARE USED FOR TRANSPORTING PLANES
TO OAHU THEIR OWN COMPLEMENT MAY REINFORCE ARMY AIR

DEFENSES OAHU BUT SHOULD BE WELL DISPERSED AMONG
DIFFERENT FIELDS AND EFFECTIVELY CAMOUFLAGED. BECAUSE

OF THE GREAT SUCCESS OF THE JAPANESE RAID ON THE
SEVENTH IT IS EXPECTED TO BE PROMPTLY FOLLOWED BY

ADDITIONAL ATTACKS IN ORDER RENDER HAWAII UNTENABLE
AS NAVAL AND AIR BASE IN WHICH EVENTUALITY IT IS

BELIEVED JAPANESE HAVE FORCES SUITABLE FOR INITIAL
OCCUPATION OF ISLANDS OTHER THAN OAHU INCLUDING

MIDWAY MAUI AND HAWAII. UNDER PRESENT CIRCUMSTANCES
IT SEEMS QUESTIONABLE THAT MIDWAY CAN BE RETAINED BUT

IT IS HOPED THAT JOHNSON PALMYRA AND SAMOA MAY BE.
IN EXPECTATION OF FURTHER AIR RAIDS AND INADEQUACY

OF DEFENSES OAHU CNO CONSIDERS IT ESSENTIAL THAT
WOUNDED VESSELS ABLE TO PROCEED UNDER OWN POWER

SHOULD BE SENT TO WEST COAST AS SOON AS POSSIBLE WITH
DUE REGARD FOR SAFETY FROM CURRENT RAIDING FORCES AND

VERY GREAT IMPORTANCE OF EFFECTIVE COUNTER ATTACKS
ON THESE RAIDERS BY YOU. UNTIL DEFENSES ARE INCREASED

IT IS DOUBTFUL IF PEARL SHOULD BE USED AS A BASE FOR
ANY EXCEPT PATROL CRAFT NAVAL AIRCRAFT SUBMARINES FOR

SHORT PERIODS WHEN IT IS REASONABLY CERTAIN JAPANESE
ATTACKS WILL NOT BE MADE. CONSIDER IT ESPECIALLY

IMPORTANT THAT SUBMARINES AND TENDERS NOT SUFFER
LOSSES. SUGGEST WIDE DISPERSAL THROUGH VARIOUS LOCHS

AND PROMPT AND EFFECTIVE CAMOUFLAGE MEASURES.

(This message, reported to have been set up principally by General Gerow and Admiral Turner, reflects
Secretary Stimson's fears that the American line of
defense might well turn out to be the Rocky Mountains.)

310

FROM: OPNAV (Chief of Naval Operations)
                                    10 December 1941
INFO: Naval Attache, Melbourne, Australia
                                    URGENT

THIS IS 101958 OF OPNAV FOR ACTION CINCAF FOR INFO
CINCPAC SPENAVO LONDON AND ALUSNA MELBOURNE YOUR

101330 WHEN IN YOUR JUDGEMENT IT BECOMES NECESSARY
TO RETIRE FROM THE PHILIPPINE AREA DO SO IN THE

DIRECTION OF NORTHWEST AUSTRALIA RATHER THAN SINGA-
PORE X AT PRESENT IT IS THE CHIEF OF NAVAL OPERATIONS

IDEA THAT YOUR TASK WOULD THEN BECOME TO SUPPORT THE
DEFENSE OF THE NEI AND AUSTRALIA AND RAID ENEMY

FORCES AND SHIPPING X REQUEST YOUR COMMENT WHEN
CONVENIENT TO KEEP ARMY DUTCH AND BRITISH INFORMED

INCLUDING THE NAVAL BOARD OF AUSTRALIA

(SPENAVO = special naval observer; ALUSNA = U.S.
Naval Attache)

(Note: It is interesting to observe that even after
the outbreak of hostilities, there is no suggestion
of United States naval forces acting in collaboration
with either Dutch or British forces afloat. Clearly,
any proposals born of the Phillips—Hart conference at
Manila 5—6 November fell on barren ground in
Washington. The thirty—day delay in activating
ABDACOM would cost the Allies dearly.)

FROM: CNO   Secret priority 170115 (17 December 1941)
TO: CINCPAC

CNO IS NOT YET SATISFIED THAT HAWAIIAN ISLANDS ARE
SAFE FROM CAPTURE. CNO CONSIDERS IT POSSIBLE FOR

JAPANESE CARRIERS AGAIN TO DESTROY A LARGE PART OF
THE SHORE BASED AIRCRAFT AND IF THIS OCCURS A SECOND

TIME THEY CANNOT BE REPLACED EXCEPT AFTER A LONG
PERIOD. JAPANESE CARRIER STRENGTH IS SUCH THAT YOU

CANNOT GUARANTEE THAT LANDINGS BY JAPANESE TROOPS
WILL NOT BE MADE ON UNDEFENDED ISLANDS OF THE

HAWAIIAN GROUP. . . .

(Prepared and released by Admiral Turner)

FROM: CNO   Secret priority 170105 (17 December 1941)
TO: CINCAF

. . . WHEN IN YOUR JUDGMENT YOU CAN FROM ELSEWHERE
MORE EFFECTIVELY DIRECT THE OPERATIONS OF YOUR FLEET

CNO APPROVES YOUR DEPARTURE FROM MANILA AND THE PRIOR
TRANSFER SOUTHWARD OF ADVANCE BASE PERSONNEL AND

MATERIEL. ASSURE MACARTHUR YOU WILL CONTINUE YOUR
FULL SUPPORT OF THE DEFENSE OF THE PHILIPPINES AND

UPON YOUR DEPARTURE PLACE ALL REMAINING NAVAL AND
MARINE PERSONNEL UNDER MACARTHURS COMMAND AND MAKE

AVAILABLE TO HIM NAVAL MUNITIONS AND STORES AND
EQUIPMENT

(Prepared and released by Admiral Turner. Admiral
Hart remained in Manila until 25 December, as of
which date it was declared an open city, which made
the Navy's position on Luzon anomalous.)

Crew List of USS *LANIKAI*

On departing Manila Bay, 26 December 1941:

Tolley, Kemp, Lieutenant, USN, Commanding

Kinsey, Charlie Capers, Chief Boatswain's Mate, USN

Picking, Merle Lamont, Chief Gunner's Mate, USN

Wilcoxen, Ray Hilland, Chief Machinist's Mate, USN

Durant, Gerald Dale, Radioman First Class, USN

Kret, Stephen Joseph, Machinist's Mate Second Class, USN

Cossette, James Lee, Pharmacist's Mate Third Class, USN

Velarmino, Hilario, Ship's Cook First Class, US Fleet Reserve

Gomez, Simplicio, Mess Attendant First Class, US Fleet Reserve

Tipay, Crispin Malto, Insular Force Machinist's Mate Second Class

Magtulis, Vincente, Insular Force Coxwain

Belarmino, Baldomero, Insular Force Seaman First Class

Alcantara, Armando, Insular Force Seaman Second Class

Almadin, Crispin Guzman, Insular Force Seaman Second Class

Famero, Mario, Insular Force Seaman Second Class

Felarca, Marciano Matos, Insular Force Seaman Second Class

Profeta, Santiago Reyes, Insular Force Seaman Second Class

Taleon, Demetrio "D", Insular Force Seaman Second Class

Tumbagahan, Prudencio, Insular Force Seaman Second Class

USS *LANIKAI* Passengers

From Manila to Surabaya:

Keith, Harry H., Lieutenant Commander, USN

Adair, Charles, Lieutenant Commander, USN

Nygh, H. Paul, Lieutenant, Royal Netherlands Naval Reserve

Wahruff, Charles A., Radio Electrician, USN

LeCompte, James W., Chief Radioman, USN

McVey, Charles T., Chief Radioman, USN

From Surabaya to Tjilatjap:

Adair, Charles

From Tjilatjap to Fremantle:

Adair, Charles

Carter, Wilbur Wesley, Yeoman First Class, USN

Gorman, John Harry, Storekeeper First Class, USN

Reconstruction Summary
of the Log of USS *HOUSTON*
February 1942

1—Departed Surabaya about 1100 in company with *Paul Jones* and *Whipple* enroute Makassar Straits to act as covering party for *Marblehead* and destroyers due to attack enemy south of Balikpapan about midnight 2 February.

2—Underway all day without event. Approximately midnight, message received from *Marblehead* saying "Risk too great." *Houston* turned about and proceeded toward Madoera Strait.

3—Arrived Madoera Strait about 0800. Already at anchor there were HNMS *Tromp, de Ruyter, van Ghent, Piet Hein,* and *Banckert,* and US destroyers *Bulmer, John D. Edwards, Pope, Ford, Pillsbury, Paul Jones* and *Whipple* and tanker *Pecos. Marblehead* arrived shortly afterward. Admiral Purnell arrived via PBY for conference with Admiral Doorman (ComStrikeFor). Planes returning from first air raid on Surabaya came overhead, looked us over and continued on. Air defense stations manned.

4—Underway about 0300, in column—*de Ruyter, Houston, Marblehead* and *Tromp.* Air defense about 1020 while enroute Makassar Strait. About 54 planes, Mitsubishi 97's, participated. Struck by bomb about 1230 while going to assistance of *Marblehead,* which had been hit by a bomb which disabled her steering mechanism. Our hit burned out number three turret. *Houston* proceeded south toward Alas Strait at 30 knots. Secured from air defense about 1300. Entered Alas Strait just as darkness was falling.

5—Arrived Tjilajap about 1630. While enroute from Alas Strait, air defense sounded for one plane, later identified as Dutch PBY. Moved wounded ashore. Began fueling from dock.

6—Funeral services held for 46 *Houston* dead. *Marblehead arrived.*

7—Funeral services held for *Marblehead* dead. Inspection by Admiral Hart and Commander Bruner.

8—*Marblehead* into drydock. *de Ruyter* moored forward of *Houston*. Admiral Glassford on board.

9—*De Ruyter* departed for Bali Strait with *Tromp, Piet Hein, Evertsen,* and American destroyers *Stewart, Parrott, Bulmer,* and *Barker.*

10—*Holland* and *Blackhawk* enter Tjilatjap harbor. *Houston* underway for Darwin, Australia, about 1500. Met *Otus* in narrows. *Trinity* in bay.

11—Enroute Darwin.

12—Enroute Darwin.

13—Enroute Darwin.

14—Arrived Darwin. Fueled from dock.

15—Departed Darwin about 0300 in company with *Peary, Swan, Warrego, Mauna Loa, Meigs, Tulagi* and *Port Mar,* enroute Koepang. Tailed by one four-engined flying boat. Requested air support. One P-40 showed up. Antiaircraft bursts fired to indicate location and presence of enemy flying boat. Run made by flying boat at about 10,000 feet. No bombs dropped. P-40 departed. Smoke seen on horizon, source unknown.

16—About 0845, exchanged signals with Lockheed Hudson to southward. About 0900 picked up again by flying boat. Air defense at 1100. Thirty-six twin-engined Mitsubishi 97's, 9 four-engined flying boats, took part in attack. Catapulted Lieutenant Lamade in SOC. Principal target *Houston.* Only on last run were bombs dropped on convoy. One near-miss on transport *Mauna Loa,* with two wounded transferred to *Houston* about 1700. Convoy ordered to return to Darwin. Koepang had been taken by enemy.

17—Enroute Darwin.

18—Arrived Darwin. Fueled from barge. Departed about 1730 for sea, headed in direction of Broome, Australia, for rendezvous with Lieutenant Lamade and recovery of plane.

19—Cruised in vicinity of Broome until 1800. ComSoWesPac ordered *Houston* to Tjilatjap.

20—Arrived Tjilatjap at dusk. Submarine alarm on approach; U.S. submarine. Fueled from dock.

22—Departed Tjilatjap about 0800, course 180°, then west.

23—Steered northerly course. Entered Sunda Strait at dusk. Passed through during the night.

24—Arrived Surabaya roads about 1530. Air defense sounded as fighter planes were seen overhead. No attack; identity unknown. Tied up to Rotterdam pier. Shifted berth to Navy Yard dock about 2330. Fueled. HNMS *Java* passed, leaving Surabaya.

25—Moored alongside dock outboard of *de Ruyter*. Bombed. No hits. Shortly after sunset, underway with *de Ruyter* and *Java*. Course approximately 090°.

26—Underway, course changed to 270°. Returned to Surabaya 0900. Anchored in stream. Bombed, no hits. About 1600 *Exeter, Perth, Encounter, Electra,* and *Jupiter* entered. 1730 *Houston, Electra* and *Jupiter* fueled from Dutch tanker. Departed Surabaya at about 1930 in company with *Java, de Ruyter, Paul Jones, Edsall, John D. Ford, John D. Edwards, Witte de With, Kortenaer, Electra,* and *Jupiter.* Course 090°, *de Ruyter, Exeter, Houston, Perth,* and *Java* in column. Dutch destroyers leading, American destroyers bringing up the rear.

27—Underway, course changed to 270° about 0100, search for enemy force continued. Air defense about 1330, one plane resembling Lockheed began dive bombing approach. Fired on by *Houston,* turned and went off. Return to Surabaya. Submarine discovered in entrance minefields. Identified herself as American. Ordered to turn back to sea at 1430. Air defense sounded. Three enemy "SOC's" overhead about 1615. Enemy force sighted by planes making for Bowiean Island. Striking Force to intercept. First salvo fired from *Exeter* 1630 at enemy battle line. Battle continued all day and night and early morning.

28—*Houston* in company of *Perth,* only survivors of Allied battle line, enroute Batavia. Arrived Batavia about 1430, fueled. Departed Batavia for unknown destination via Sunda Strait about 2000. 2300 general quarters. *Houston* and *Perth* engaged by enemy surface craft in or near Sunda Strait. *Perth* sunk about 2345.

MARCH 1, 1942

On or about 0040 while engaging with numerically superior enemy naval force the USS *Houston* was sunk by gunfire approximately 8 miles northeast of Saint Nicholas Point light.

The President of the United States takes pleasure in presenting the BRONZE STAR MEDAL to

CAPTAIN KEMP TOLLEY

For service as set forth in the following CITATION:

"For meritorious service as Commanding Officer of the U.S.S. LANIKAI from 8 December 1941 to 27 April 1942. Commanding an auxiliary schooner converted to a camouflaged radio picket vessel, Captain (then Lieutenant) Tolley participated in the early phases of the defense of the Philippines, carrying out courier, patrol, and intelligence duties. Later, he volunteered to run the Japanese air and surface blockade to join the Allied Forces in the Netherlands East Indies where he served with distinction with the American-Dutch-British-Australian Forces until waters in that area became untenable. Refusing passage on a larger vessel, he again ran the Japanese blockade, sailing his small ship to Fremantle, Australia. By his outstanding professional skill and cool courage in the face of extreme difficulties and dangers, Captain Tolley upheld the highest traditions of the United States Naval Service."

The Combat Distinguishing Device is authorized.

For the President,

/s/William B. Franke
Secretary of the Navy

Asiatic Fleet

Commander in Chief: ADM Thomas C. Hart, DSM
Commander Task Force 5: RADM William A. Glassford, DSM

CRUISERS
Houston (F)
 CAPT A. H. Rooks, CMH, MW,
 BL, KIA
Marblehead
 CAPT A. G. Robinson, NC
Boise
 CAPT S. E. Robinson; 29 January,
 CAPT E. J. Moran

TANKERS
Pecos
 LCDR E. P. Abernethy, NC
Trinity
 CDR W. Hibbs

Destroyer Squadron 29
CAPT H. V. Wiley

Blackhawk, tender
 CDR G. L. Harris

DESTROYER DIVISION 57
 CDR E. M. Crouch
Whipple
 LCDR E. S. Karpe
Alden
 LCDR L. E. Coley, NC
John D. Edwards (F), PUC
 LCDR H. E. Eccles, NC, SS, BK
Edsall
 LCDR J. J. Nix, LOM, KIA

Paul Jones (F)
 LCDR J. J. Hourihan, NC, SS

DESTROYER DIVISION 58
 CDR T. H. Binford, 2 NC, LOM,
 SS, MW
Stewart (F)
 LCDR H. P. Smith, NC, BK
Parrott
 LCDR E. N. Parker, 2 NC, SS,
 MW; 28
January, LT J. N. Hughes, NC

Paul Jones generally operated as a unit of Division 59, without Captain Wiley embarked.

Notes:

BK	Dutch Bronzen Kruis (cross)	MW	Dutch Militaire Willemsorder equivalent to CMH
BL	Dutch Bronzen Leeuw (lion)	NC	Navy Cross
BS	Bronze Star	POW	Prisoner of war
CMH	Congressional Medal of Honor	PUC	Presidential Unit Citation (Navy)
DPOW	Died as a prisoner of war	SS	Silver Star
DSC	Distinguished Service Cross	WIA	Wounded in Action
DSM	Distinguished Service Medal	*	Ships lost prior to 1 May 1942
DU	Distinguished Unit (Army)		
(F)	Unit flagship	#	Later served with Inshore Patrol
KIA	Killed in action		
LOM	Legion of Merit		

Bulmer
LCDR L. J. Manees, 28 January
LT D. A. Harris
Barker
LCDR L. G. McGlone

DESTROYER DIVISION 59
CDR P. H. Talbot, NC; 28
January, LCDR E. N. Parker,
2 NC, SS, MW

Peary
LCDR H. H. Keith, LOM, WIA;
10 December, LT J. M. Berming-
ham, NC, KIA
Pope, PUC
LCDR W. C. Blinn, 3 NC, BK,
POW
John D. Ford, (F), PUC
LCDR J. E. Cooper, 2 NC, SS, BK
Pillsbury, PUC
LCDR H. C. Pound, NC, BK, KIA

Submarine Squadron 20
CDR John Wilkes, DSM

Canopus, tender
CDR E. L. Sackett, NC, BS
Holland, tender
CAPT J. W. Gregory, LOM

SUBMARINE DIVISION 201
LCDR R. B. Vanzant, BS
S-36
LT J. R. McKnight
S-37
LT J. C. Dempsey, NC; 1 March,
LT J. R. Z. Reynolds
S-38
LT W. G. Chapple, NC
S-39
LT J. W. Coe, NC;
LT F. E. Brown
S-40
LT N. Lucker
S-41
LT G. M. Holley

SUBMARINE DIVISION 202
CDR W. E. Percifield
Seadragon
LCDR W. E. Ferrall, NC
Sealion
LCDR R. G. Voge, NC, BS
Searaven
LCDR T. C. Aylward, NC;
LCDR H. Cassedy

Otus, tender
CDR J. Newsom
Pigeon, rescue vessel, 2 PUC, DU
LT R. E. Hawes, NC; LCDR
F. A. Davis, USNR, NC

Seawolf
LCDR F. B. Warder, NC;
18 January, LT R. L. Gross

SUBMARINE DIVISION 22
CDR J. A. Connelly
Snapper
LCDR H. L. Stone
Stingray
LCDR R. S. Lamb;
LT R. L. Moore
Sturgeon, DU
LCDR W. L. Wright, NC
Sculpin, DU
LCDR L. H. Chappell, NC
Sailfish
LCDR M. C. Mumma, Jr., NC;
LCDR R. G. Voge, NC, BS
Swordfish
LCDR C. C. Smith, 2 NC

SUBMARINE DIVISION 203
CDR E. H. Bryant, DSM
Pickerel (F)
LCDR B. E. Bacon, NC

Porpoise
  LCDR J. A. Callaghan;
  LT J. R. McKnight
Pike
  LCDR W. A. New
Shark
  LCDR L. Shane, KIA
Tarpon
  LCDR L. Wallace
Perch
  LCDR D. A. Hurt, POW
Permit
  LCDR A. M. Hurst; 13 February,
  LT W. G. Chapple, NC

SUBMARINE DIVISION 21
  CDR S. S. Murray
Salmon
  LCDR E. B. McKinney, NC
Seal
  LCDR K. C. Hurd, NC
Skipjack
  LCDR C. L. Freeman;
  LCDR J. W. Coe
Sargo
  LCDR T. D. Jacobs
Saury
  LCDR J. L. Burnside
Spearfish
  LCDR R. F. Pryce; 7 March,
  LCDR J. C. Dempsey, NC

Aircraft, Asiatic Fleet
CAPT F. D. Wagner, DSM

Langley
  CDR R. P. McConnell
Childs
  LCDR J. L. Pratt, LOM, BS
William B. Preston
  LCDR E. Grant, LOM
Heron
  LT W. L. Kabler, NC
PATROL WING 10
  CAPT D. F. Wagner, DSM

PATROL SQUADRON 101
  LCDR J. V. Peterson, DFC
PATROL SQUADRON 102, DU,
  PUC
  LCDR E. T. Neale, 2 SS
UTILITY UNIT
  LT J. C. Renard

Inshore Patrol, DU
CAPT K. M. Hoeffel, NC, DSM, SS, POW

Mindanao, DU
  LCDR A. R. McCracken, NC,
  POW
Luzon, DU
  LCDR G. M. Brooke, NC, DPOW
Napa, DU
  LT N. M. Dial, NC, DPOW

Oahu, DU
  LCDR D. E. Smith, NC, DPOW
Lanikai, DU
  LT K. Tolley, BS

Minecraft

MINE DIVISION 8
  LT T. W. Davison, NC
#*Finch,* DU
  LT T. W. Davison, NC

Bittern
  LT T. G. Warfield, SS

MINE DIVISION 9
  LCDR J. H. Morrill, NC, SS
#*Quail DU, PUC
  LCDR J. H. Morrill, NC, SS
#*Tanager, DU
  LT E. A. Roth, NC, DPOW

Lark
  LCDR H. P. Thomson, BS, BK
Whippoorwill
  LCDR C. A. Ferriter, NC, BS, BK

Motor Torpedo Boat Squadron 3, DU
LT(JG) J. D. Bulkeley, CMH, 2 DSC, 2 SS, WIA

Coastal Gunboats

*Asheville
  LT J. W. Britt, KIA

Tulsa
  LCDR T. S. Daniel;
  LT J. B. Berkley

Note: Most of those listed above who are still living, or their survivors when available, were contacted to verify decorations, which are those awarded between 8 December 1941 and 1 April 1942. It has been impossible to check the personal records of the remainder, so that there may be some omissions. Ranks and fleet organizations are as of December 1941.

Index

Hawaii: Stark attempts to get Fleet brought back from, 52; British suggests no U.S. battleships at, 55

Hawaiian Sea Products Co.: buys *Lanikai*, 108

Hawes, Lieut R. E.: heroic action at Cavite, 82, 117

Heffernan, Rear Adm John B.: as Director of Naval History, 264

Heffron, Paul T.: xii

Heiniken's Beer, 172, 208

Helfrich, Vice Adm C. E. L., RNN: position in ABDA, 163; takes over as ABDAFLOAT, 184; relieves Hart, 188, 189; forbids oil to leave Java, 196; new Allied Navy commander, 207; urges sacrifice, 211; diverts USS *Langley*, 214; orders Doorman to attack, 216; dissolves ABDA, 228; 184, 185

Henry, Lieut (jg): heroic work at Cavite, 117

Hepner, Francis J.: xii

Hermes, schooner: building, internment, taking into U.S. Navy, war history, 99–107 *passim*; her end, 283

Heron, USS: prewar placement, 74; commanding officer, 118; at Java, 124; at Fremantle, 248

Hewitt, Adm H. K.: Pearl Harbor inquiry of, 273

Hiles, Lieut Comdr Charles C.: views on Kimmel, 90, 91; xii

Hindu: religion on Bali, 170, 171; 203

Hirohito, Emperor: in favor of moderation, 46; President's message to, 44, 278

Hitler, Adolph: attacks USSR, 24; avoids war, 152

Hizen, HIJMS: blockades Honolulu, 1914, 100, 101

Hobart, HMAS: narrow escape, leaves Java area, 208

Hoeffel, Capt K. M.: commands Inshore Patrol, 69

Hoehling, A. A.: author, 32

Holland, USS: at Manila, 53; heads south, 54; in Task Force 1, 74; in Surabaya, 124; to Exmouth Gulf, 196

Holland Pier, Surabaya: 177

Hollin, Ens (Deck) Edward, USNRF: captains USS *Hermes*, 105

Homma, Lieut Gen Masaharu: underestimates Americans, 226

Hongkong, BCC: Hart and MacArthur dispute control of troops passing through, 25, 26; tailors at, 116; falls, 124; rumors from concerning Japanese movements, 264; ix, 177

Honolulu: Japanese espionage at, 26; *Hermes* at, 107–109 *passim*; Japanese blockade of, 1914, 100, 101

Honolulu Advertiser: stories of 1914 Japanese blockade in, 100, 101

Hooper, Vice Adm Edwin B., Director of Naval History: xii

Hopkins, Harry: presidential adviser, 23; Richardson antagonizes, 165; "three small ships" conference with FDR, 274, 276; xi, 47

Hornbeck, Dr. Stanley: strong proponent of keeping Fleet in Hawaii, 23; gives odds on war, 42

Houston, USS: in Task Force 5, 75; in action, 185; survives Java Sea battle, 217; Hart inspects damage to, 188; destroyed, 217–19 *passim*; Lamade's escape from, 228, 229, 230; ix, 54, 58, 118(n), 124, 178, 191, 208, 215, 219, 219(n), 220, 228; appendix

Houtman Rocks, Southwest Australia: emperil *Lanikai*, 243; *Lanikai* explores, 281

Hudson, Capt L. J., former Commander South China Patrol: activities at Tjilatjap, 208, 210

Hue, Indo-China: one "small ship" to be stationed near, 273

Hull, Cordell: recalls FDR to Washington as Japanese approach Malaya, 47; opposes Richardson, 23; confers with Kurusu, 38, 39;

Osmeña, Sergio: Philippine vice
president, evacuated, 195
Otus, USS: at Manila, converted
from SS Fred Morris, 53, 53(n),
54; in Task Force 1, 74; hit at
Cavite, 82; at Surabaya, 124; 58, 74
Ott, Gen Eugene, German Army:
ambassador at Tokyo, 35

PA–K2: Japanese crypto system, 34,
35
P–40: fighter aircraft, into Java, 185,
186; crashed on beach, 198, 199;
census of on Java, 207; Keith
saves shipload of, 213, 214; four
remain on Bataan, 241
Padang Bay, Bali: 167
Pandakan, Manila: oil storage area,
8
Palawan, Philippines: Lanikai's
prewar visits to, 110; alternate
route for Lanikai, 132; 179
Palembang, Sumatra: Japanese
paratroops land at, 172, 188
Palliser, Rear Adm A. F. E., RN:
controlled British ships, 207; "the
jig is up," 211; orders to fleeing
ships, 217, 220; withdraws British
ships, 228
Pan American Airways: 117
Panay, USS: Japanese sink in 1937,
44, 44(n); large identification
marks failed to save, 143; model
incident for Lanikai to follow,
270, 271; FDR remembered, 277,
278
Paranaque, Manila: tough district, 7
Paris Match: Rockwell interviews
on MacArthur in, 241
Parker, Vice Adm E. N.: xi
Parker, E. O.: xii
Paternoster Islands: shield Lanikai,
156
Parrott, USS: in Task Force 5, 54;
at Badung Strait battle, 193; picks
up survivors, 215
Parsons, Comdr Charles, USNR: xii,
112

Patjitan Bay, Java: Lanikai's sojourn
in 202–204 passim
Patrol Force, U.S. Fleet: 165:
Admiral King to command, 165
Patrol Wing 10: dispersion of, 74;
evacuates Philippines, 114
Paul Jones, USS: in Task Force 5,
54; in Battle of Java Sea, 208,
215–17 passim; heads for Australia,
220
Payne, Lieut junior grade J. W., Jr.:
checks on Lanika's doings, 248;
commands USS Isabel, takes her
to Indo-China coast as one of the
"three small ships," 269, 270
PBY: evacuate VIPs, 9; attack Jolo,
123, 124; evacuates Brereton, 190;
few remain on Java, 190, 191;
evacuates Keith, 213; scout
Camranh Bay, 264–68
Peary, USS: at Cavite, 53; hit on 10
December, 82; skipper killed,
118(n); departs Manila, 120;
bombed by Australians, 143(n);
hit by malaria, 153(n); sunk, 191
Pearl Harbor: Ambassador Grew
warns of possible surprise attack
on, 24; Japanese intentions
revealed, 26; Japanese spy on,
31; Far East news of, 55;
Washington panic after, 91;
Hermes at, 104; losses concealed,
151; triumph? 152; humiliation of,
174; Hart investigates, 273;
conjecture on, 280
Pearl Harbor Attack Force:
assembles, 39; subject to recall, 46
Pecos, USS: at Manila, 53, 54; in
Task Force 1, 74; refused Java oil,
196; supplies Lanikai, 205, 206,
208, 210; heads for Colombo,
ordered pick up survivors of
Langley, 215; sunk, 221–23
Peirse, Air Chief Marshal Sir Richard
E. C., RAF: commanding air
component of ABDA, 163;
uncooperative, 184; Brereton
deputy to, aircraft available to,

Tojo, Gen Hideki: replaces Konoye, 36, 45, 46

Tonan Maru No. 3: American torpedoes fail to sink, 180

Tolley, Scott & Tolley: distillers, Adelaide, 259

Torpedoes: air flasks explode at Cavite, 82; near worthless, 54, 54(n), 161, 180; Japanese high level drops of, 77; Japanese and American—compared, 78;—at Badung Strait, 194; 178

Triebel, Rear Adm C. O.: 180, 181

Trinity, USS: at Manila, 53; in Task Force 5, 54, 75; in Task Force 1, 74; Tolley to Iraq via, 263

Triton, schooner: in South Seas trade prior World War I, 99

Tromp, RNNS: cuts *Lanikai's* rigging, 181; in aborted task force mission, 185; at Badung Strait battle, 193, 194

Tsingtao: 135

Tubbatha Reefs: 133, 134

Tubbs, Radioman: from USS *Houston,* 228, 229

Tulsa, USS: in Manila Bay, 53; heads south, 54; at Surabaya, Christmas, 124; spooks Dutch merchantman off Tjilatjap, 204; 74, 118(n)

Tumbagahan, Prudencio: Filipino crewman, 146, 219, 250, 284

Turner, Rear Adm Richmond K.: "capsizes" ONI, 29, 30, 30(n); in Savo Island disaster, 32(n); expects Japanese to attack USSR, 45; balks effort to warn Kimmel, 48; explains Rainbow 5, 61, 62; prewar predictions, and post-Pearl Harbor panic, 91; 24, 31, 32, 34, 49, 60

Tutuila, USS: bombed at Chungking, 24

Twenty-one Demands: by Japan on China, 102

University Club, Manila: 8

Utter, Lieut Harmon C.: 9

van Amsdel, D. W.: 155

van Mook, Dr. Hubertus: 184

van Oyen, Dutch air commander in Java: 207

Vandenberg, Sen. Arthur: discloses FDR's promise to Churchill, 41

Vargo, Electrician's Mate 1st Class Joseph: sees Cavite destroyed, 80

Velarmino, Ship's Cook 1st Class Hilario: 155, 156, 287–88

Vigan, Philippine Islands: Japanese land at, 114

von Luckner, Count Felix: 104

Vooren, Col H., Dutch Army: commanding officer, Celebes, 154

Wagner, Capt Frank D.: 57, 145, 265

Wainwright, Brig Gen Jonathan M.: opposes surrender, 257; 116

Wake, USS: left at Shanghai, 14; captured, 244

Wallace, Henry: 47

Walruff, Radio Electrician C. A.: 9, 120, 121, 157, 158, 283, 284

War Cabinet: 44

War Council: 39

War warnings: sent out, 41; discussion of 58, 60; Kimmel's instructions via Stark's—, 63; Hart's interpretation of, 89

Ward, Comdr A. B.: on *Lanikai's* radio, 277; 9

Warfield, Lieut Thomas G.: takes SS *Mareschal Joffre* to safety, 88

Warm Springs, Georgia: FDR hurriedly recalled from—on 1 December, 264; 46

Washington, USS: 73

Wassell, Lieut Comdr C. M., USNR: heroic evacuation of wounded, 186, 186(n), 215, 223, 245

Wavell, General Sir Archibald, British Army: commands ABDA, 163; contretemps with Hart, 164; MacArthur's superior, 179; chides Hart, 188; warns London Java falling, 189; investiture as ABDACOM, 190; leaves Java, 207

The Naval Institute Press is the book-publishing arm of the U.S. Naval Institute, a private, nonprofit, membership society for sea service professionals and others who share an interest in naval and maritime affairs. Established in 1873 at the U.S. Naval Academy in Annapolis, Maryland, where its offices remain today, the Naval Institute has members worldwide.

Members of the Naval Institute support the education programs of the society and receive the influential monthly magazine *Proceedings* and discounts on fine nautical prints and on ship and aircraft photos. They also have access to the transcripts of the Institute's Oral History Program and get discounted admission to any of the Institute-sponsored seminars offered around the country.

The Naval Institute also publishes *Naval History* magazine. This colorful bimonthly is filled with entertaining and thought-provoking articles, first-person reminiscences, and dramatic art and photography. Members receive a discount on *Naval History* subscriptions.

The Naval Institute's book-publishing program, begun in 1898 with basic guides to naval practices, has broadened its scope to include books of more general interest. Now the Naval Institute Press publishes about one hundred titles each year, ranging from how-to books on boating and navigation to battle histories, biographies, ship and aircraft guides, and novels. Institute members receive significant discounts on the Press's more than eight hundred books in print.

Full-time students are eligible for special half-price membership rates. Life memberships are also available.

For a free catalog describing Naval Institute Press books currently available, and for further information about subscribing to *Naval History* magazine or about joining the U.S. Naval Institute, please write to:

Membership Department
U.S. Naval Institute
291 Wood Road
Annapolis, MD 21402-5034
Telephone: (800) 233-8764
Fax: (410) 269-7940
Web address: www.navalinstitute.org